THE
NORTH
AMERICAN
MUSLIM
RESOURCE
GUIDE

THE NORTH AMERICAN MUSLIM RESOURCE GUIDE

MUSLIM COMMUNITY LIFE IN THE UNITED STATES AND CANADA

MOHAMED NIMER

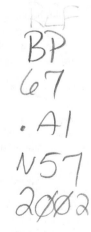

Routledge
Taylor & Francis Group

NEW YORK AND LONDON

Published in 2002 by
Routledge
29 West 35th Street
New York, NY 10001
www.routledge-ny.com

Published in Great Britain by
Routledge
11 New Fetter Lane
London EC4P 4EE
www.routledge.co.uk

Library of Congress Cataloging-in-Publishing Data

Nimer, Mohamed, 1960–
    The North American Muslim resource guide : Muslim community life in the United States and
Canada / Mohamed Nimer.
        p. cm.
Includes bibliographical references and index.
    ISBN 0–415–93728–0
    1. Muslims—North America—Directories. 2. Islam—North America—Societies, etc.—
Directories. I. Title.
    BP67 .A1 N57 2002
    297' .025'73—dc21   2002003793

For my parents, wife, and children.

CONTENTS

GLOSSARY OF ORGANIZATIONS

AAI	Arab American Institute
AAUG	Arab American University Graduates
ACCESS	Arab Community Center for Economic and Social Services
ACJ	American Committee on Jerusalem
ADC	American-Arab Anti-Discrimination Committee
AMA	American Muslim Alliance
AMC	American Muslim Council
AMJ	American Muslims for Jerusalem
AMPCC	American Muslim Political Coordination Council
CAIR	Council on American-Islamic Relations
CAIRCAN	Council on American-Islamic Relations-Canada
CIC	Canadian Islamic Congress
CPAAO	Council of Presidents of Arab American Organizations
CPAP	Center for Policy Analysis on Palestine
ICNA	Islamic Circle of North America
IIIT	International Institue of Islamic Thought
ISNA	Islamic Society of North America
KAC	Kashmiri American Council

KCC	Kashmiri Canadian Council
MAS	Muslim American Society
MAS-W. Deen Mohammed	Muslim American Society led by Imam Warith Deen Mohammed
MPAC	Muslim Public Affairs Council
NASIMCO	North American Shia Ithna-Asheri Muslim Communities

FOREWORD

American Muslims have grown tremendously over the past thirty years. Their community organizations have increased rapidly, but until now there have been few sources of reliable information about the community and its structure. This literature gap has narrowed, thanks to *The North American Muslim Resource Guide*.

Congratulations to Dr. Mohamed Nimer. This volume is a culmination of his research on Muslim communities in the United States and Canada for the past four years. He had the foresight to recognize that this work is essential for a factual understanding of where the Muslims of North America stand in today's societies.

The book answers frequent public inquiries about who represents Muslims. It provides ample evidence that Muslims are diverse in the ways they think and act. The book's extensive coverage of the various types of community groups—how they relate to one another and how they have defined and addressed their concerns is indeed enlightening. *The North American Muslim Resource Guide* shows that Muslims are not only immigrants and African Americans, mosques and Islamic schools, local and national organizations, or religious and ethnic associations. As effectively illustrated in this volume, the Muslim experience in the United States and Canada includes diverse types of individuals and organizations. They share a determination to maintain their communal identities while contributing to making America, Canada, and the world a better place for all humanity.

Omar Ahmad
Chairman, Board of Directors
Council on American-Islamic Relations
Washington, D.C.

PREFACE

Americans—and Canadians—who never invested in outreach to their Muslim neighbors were violently awakened on September 11, 2001, to the fact that they share a common destiny with millions of fellow citizens who belong to the Islamic faith. American Muslims, too, were shaken by the horrific nature of the terrorist attacks on New York and Washington, D.C. As will be demonstrated throughout this book, Muslims and others in churches, synagogues, mosques, ethnic community centers, and other civic groups have begun to build stronger communications channels. Still, some national political commentators have continued to pose this question: Who speaks for Muslims?

This question is not new, and it has naturally arisen because Muslims have paid little attention to presenting the institutional make-up of their communities to Americans and Canadians. To fill the information gap, I began in 1997, as part of my work with the Council on American Islamic Relations (CAIR), to develop the American Muslim Databank Project, which aimed to account for the collective expressions of Muslims in North America. This work generated a wealth of data, which led to the writing of this book. Of course CAIR is one of the subjects under examination; its contribution to the development of the American Muslim community is acknowledged in its rightful place—that is, in the domain of public affairs.

This volume, therefore, is an introduction to the structural development of Muslim organizations in North America. It is an attempt to offer a road map of the Muslim groups in the United States and Canada and to explore their place in the North American context. Not only does this work identify the players in the various domains of Muslim life, it also attempts to examine how they have conceived of and addressed the concerns of their communities. While the first draft of this manuscript was being completed, the attacks of September 11 took place. Thus I attempted to augment the book with the unfolding Muslim responses to the tragedy and its aftermath.

Nearly half the organizations mentioned in this volume are Islamic centers and schools. Past scholarly attention to Muslim life in North America has focused on these primary institutions. But the rapid growth of the Muslim population also has been accompanied by an increasing involvement of Muslims nationally and locally in education and outreach activism, mass communication, public advocacy, social service delivery, and international relief work. Although this book does not propose to offer a detailed account of every aspect of Muslim institutional life in North America, it does provide a synthesis of the Muslim collective experiences.

Readers will become acquainted with various Muslim worldviews, which are based primarily on faith and ethnicity. Readers will also appreciate the challenges Muslims have faced in building their communities, in identifying with and seeking the protection of the constitutional frameworks of the United States and Canada, and in forging alliances with other nongovernmental entities. All this notwithstanding, this book has two more unique advantages: it offers ethnic population data and a listing of Muslim organizations. I hope that the wealth of information will offer a guiding light to future research.

Admittedly, I may not have examined ethnic Muslims as thoroughly as I have faith-based groups. But I know of no other work with a more extensive coverage of ethnic Muslim groups. Indeed, some leaders in the faith-based side of the ideological spectrum may point out that the examination of ethnic clusters has awarded credit to very small entities. The sheer number of these groups and their collective impact, however, should not escape any serious observer. Among the detractors to this work may be members of the Muslim community, including some intellectuals (both religious and secular), *imams* (prayer leaders), and *alims* (religious scholars). These individuals may think that I have narrowed the scope of their relevance to the collective experience of Muslims in North America. Upon serious examination of the contents of this book, however, I believe they may realize that the world of Islam in North America has changed tremendously since the days in which one thinker or religious figure was capable of representing the full spectrum of Muslim thought and action.

Outside of the Muslim community, open-minded analysts will at the very least find this work informative. Pundits who choose to interpret Muslim activism through the eyes of such extremists as Osama bin Laden and his cohorts may be disappointed. Some may even become resentful when they realize that this work does not seek to gloss over September 11 and its aftermath, but attempts to shed light on what it has meant in the lives of North American Muslims.

Many people have made this work possible. Omar Ahmad, Nihad Awad, and Ibrahim Hooper, founders of CAIR, first suggested that I develop the research into a book about the American Muslim community. My research was aided enormously by former and current staff of CAIR, particularly Tannaz Haddadi, Farkhunda Ali, Suad Haddad, and Mathew Dent, for helping to track down key bits of information. Many interns have also helped in sorting information and data entry. I also owe deep gratitude to my good friends who have watched the Muslim community development over the years, traded ideas with me, encouraged me when I was right, and corrected me when I was wrong. In particular, I am grateful to Professors John Esposito and Yvonne Haddad of Georgetown University for their insight and encouragement.

Many other people contributed to this book by sharing their expertise. I am especially grateful for the patience, kindness, and feedback of Hussein Ibish and Khalil Jahshan of the American-Arab Anti-Discrimination Committee; James Zogby and Helen Samhan of the Arab American Institute; Jamal Barzanji of the International Institute of Islamic Thought; Naim Baig and Zaheer al-Din of the Islamic Circle of North America; Imam Mustafa al-Qazwini of the Islamic Education Center of Orange County, California; Imam Mohammad Ilahi of the Islamic House of Wisdom in Detroit, Michigan; Sayyid Syeed of the Islamic Society of North America; Imam Yusuf Saleem of Masjid Mohammed in Washington, D.C.; Omar al-Qadi of Mercey International; Shakir El-Sayyid and Suheil Ghanouchi of Muslim American Society; Ayesha Mustafa of the *Muslim Journal*; Salam al-Marayati of the Muslim Public Affairs Council; and Riad Salooji of CAIR–Canada.

A number of individuals also made the fine production of this volume possible. Mary Kay Linge read an earlier version of the entire manuscript with a searching eye for detail and provided substantive editorial comments. Thanks also to Routledge staff: Kevin Ohe was the original sponsoring editor; Terry Fischer copyedited the book; Mark O'Malley and Jeanne Shu exhibited high professional standards throughout the production process.

—Mohamed Nimer
Washington, D.C.
June 2002

INTRODUCTON

History will record that as the second millennium drew to a close, Muslims in North America were coming of age—their numbers had grown enough to allow them to establish a local presence in every major city and town, and they had shown all the signs of determination to carve a space for themselves in the continent's pluralistic mosaic. Even the worst terrorist act in U.S. history, the September 11 attacks on New York and Washington, D.C., by Muslim extremists, failed to stem this tide.

But who are American Muslims? Who are Canadian Muslims? How are they similar or different from other Muslims in the world? How do Muslims view the laws and practices of Americans and Canadians? How do many Muslims live in North America, anyway? What do they want? How do they organize themselves? How do they become visible in public life? Where do they stand on public policy issues? What does that visibility mean for America, Canada, and the Muslim world? How did Muslims react to the terrorist attacks of September 11, 2001? What does it all mean for the future of American Muslim relations?

In an attempt to answer these questions, this book offers a guide to North American Muslim populations—their organizations, concerns, and involvement in America's religious, civic, and political life. In this sense, this book is something of a departure from a most recent literature that has fixated on the debates between the ideologues of the Muslim world. Important as this inquiry is, it focuses too much on the works of particular writers, actions of certain groups, or decisions of selected leaders.

It is not an easy task to offer a holistic understanding for the human experience of Muslims. Compounding the challenge is the fact that inquiries about Muslims anywhere in the press and in academia have been loaded with stereotypes and segmented narratives of Muslim life. There is little publicly available information in the North American context about Muslims and their communities. So one cannot claim to make sense of the collective efforts of Muslims without the benefit of an exhaustive investigation into who is doing what. That is exactly how the research for this book proceeded after the launching of the American Muslim Databank Project.

Relevant government sources were also gathered, especially with regard to population and immigration statistics. Unfortunately, the detailed ancestral data of the 2000 U.S. Census has not yet been released, so the census information in this book is more than ten years old. But the 1990 Census data has never been adequately analyzed with a focus on the ethnic populations that make up a large proportion of the American Muslim community. So the examination of this data set remains worthwhile. For information on Muslim communities in Canada, the latest available data was released in 1996. To account for the substantial African American Muslim population, College Board data, which provide ethnic and religious profiles of students taking the Standardized Achievement Test (SAT), was used as a basis for estimation. An updated estimate of the population information was made by extrapolation.

In addition, mailing lists from Muslim community organizations were collected. Helpful sources in the initial stages of gathering this information included the Muslim Student Association, the Islamic Society of North America, the *Muslim Journal*, and the Arab American Directory in the United States. In Canada two particular sources have been very useful: *Muslim Guide to Canada* and the mailing lists of the Moslem Group and the North American Shia Ithna-Asheri Muslim Communities Organization. Internet searches also yielded several regional lists, as well as hundreds of local ethnic associations and community centers. Moreover, public records available through Lexis-Nexis were obtained.

The lists were then consolidated into one database and duplicate entries were identified. Survey forms have been regularly mailed to all organizations since 1999. This allowed for database updates and the collection of further information about the organizations and their activities. Telephone calls were made to augment the mailing effort. Also, site visitations were made and in-person interviews were conducted with key leaders and executives of national, regional, and some local organizations. Moreover, literature and communication material produced by the organizations have been obtained.

After data collection, the next step was to classify the information into coherent functional categories. The classification of each group into organizational types was based on an analysis of their primary activities. As events unfolded, so did the data collection effort. This included the frequent checking of websites of American and Canadian Muslim groups. The process resulted in a wealth of information on the internal dynamics of community organizations and their interactions with their larger North American surroundings.

Chapter 1 offers a synthesis of the major influences shaping the ethnic and religious worldviews of Muslims, giving a sense of purpose to the mushrooming organizational structure of North American Islamic groups. The impact of such influences on the meaning of citizenship in Canada and the United States and the membership in global communal life, along with the repercussions of September 11, is outlined. Chapter 2 traces the Muslim population in number, ethnic diversity, and social profile.

Chapters 3 and 4 describe the process and progress of building the primary community organizations—mosques and Islamic schools. Chapter 3 traces changes in the evolution of mosque communities since the early decades of the twentieth century, but focuses on the institutional elements of mosque life and what it means to the community as a whole. Chapter 4 outlines the variety of educational options for Muslims in North America and focuses on the movement to build private religious schools. Chapter 5 examines the contributions of major national groups that have worked to organize and shape the character of local religious communities.

Chapter 6 outlines the various ethnic associations that have been organized (largely outside the mosque communities) on the basis of affinity to ethnic and national origin attachments. This information reveals that sometimes ethnicity and faith converged and produced ethno-religious organizations. It also shows how ethnic bonds sometimes mix with the occupational interests of professionals who have grown to see the entire world as a job market.

Chapter 7 sheds light on the efforts of Muslims to build organizations that offer charitable assistance to the needy worldwide. This chapter also traces the increasing attention paid to North American Muslims needing social assistance. Efforts to establish service programs targeting refugees, uninsured patients, and women are highlighted.

Chapter 8 examines ethnic and religious community media. Press and telecommunication ventures are described along with the types of targeted consumers and the effects of marketing realities on the quality and content of information products.

Chapter 9 discusses public affairs agencies that work to represent their members in the public square. Here the main players advocating Muslim concerns are introduced and their efforts are put in the larger context of the political systems of the United States and Canada, including interactions between Muslims and others over public policy matters. Also, close attention is paid to the transformative impact of Muslim claims to rights under the constitutions of the two countries. Relations between Muslims and others are examined, as interest groups play a prominent role in the political systems of the United States and Canada.

Chapter 10 sheds light on Muslim community think tanks—the efforts they make to analyze Muslim issues, and the guidance they have offered in rationalizing grassroots approaches to interfaith dialogue and public advocacy. In the conclusion, the findings are revisited in an attempt to summarize the major trends defining the current state of affairs of Muslims in North America.

Following the Conclusion, there is a Directory of Organizations that includes contact information on various Muslim organizations. The directory lists Islamic schools, mosques and Islamic centers, and other Muslim organization located throughout the United States and Canada. It provides resources for further research concerning Muslim life in North America and is intended to be as complete as possible.

ONE

UNDERSTANDING THE
MUSLIM MAINSTREAM

Demographers believe Islam is the fastest growing religion in North America. With scant presence at the turn of the twentieth century, the continent's Muslims now number in the millions—almost all living in the United States and Canada. The presence of Muslims in Mexico is negligible, despite the growing number of Muslim converts. The history of Islam in the continent, however, is centuries old and can be traced to the days of slavery, when Muslims were among the slaves brought from Africa. Slaves could never openly practice Islam, although historical accounts suggest that many slaves resisted the religious persecution of their masters and privately kept elements of the faith.

Islam was later reintroduced to North America by Muslim immigrants, who began arriving after the end of the nineteenth century and whose number increased rapidly after the mid-1960s. Today a growing portion of this multi-ethnic population group includes a generation of U.S.- and Canadian-born citizens. A parallel movement in the United States, the Nation of Islam (NOI), contributed to the increased awareness of Islam among African Americans since the 1930s. A large segment of the group has converted to mainline Islam since the early 1960s. The NOI adopted several Muslim beliefs and practices—albeit mixed with elements from Christianity and subjected to racial ideas of community identity. But the conversion to mainline Islam among North America's indigenous populations has grown and now includes not only African Americans, but also tens of thousands of whites, Latinos, and Native-Americans.

Some previous studies have examined the pressures of assimilation on Muslim immigrants and its impact on their religious and ethnic identities. Other studies have illuminated the history of African-American Muslims. Other works have focused on the formation of selected Muslim groups. But little attention has been given to the social and political conditions of Muslims in North America and the institutional responses of Muslims to these conditions. This information gap colors the knowledge available on the human experience of North American Muslims.

The religious and ethnic diversity among Muslims has prompted a growing tendency to express Islam in its simple and essential forms—away from the dogmatic discourse that characterized the postcolonial experience of the Muslim world in the twentieth century. Muslims living in North America are closer to seeing the big picture of the world's increasingly global communications and economic systems. While individually they have invested their energies and wealth for their own pursuit of happiness, Muslims also have established a web of organizations to meet the spiritual, educational, social, and political concerns.

Despite the ancestral and institutional diversity, today American and Canadian Muslims strive to be treated as loyal citizens and equal partners in the building of their countries. Because of the Islamic belief that Muslims make a unique *ummah* (a community of believers), religious bonds connect North American Muslims to their coreligionists around the world through religious discourse and community-centered religious practices. But faith is hardly the sole force shaping the experiences of Muslims (or, for that matter, the experiences of all other faith groups): ethnicity remains a strong factor. The constraints of the law, the demands of the economic structure, and the cultural and intellectual influences of the surrounding society are equally important in framing the development of Muslim communities. Any synthesis of the development of Muslim communities in North America must account for these overarching factors.

FAITH

To understand the Muslim commitment to faith, one must appreciate the agreement among Muslims that the scripture they read today, the Qur'an, is the same text that Muhammad, the Prophet of Islam, passed on to his companions in the seventh century. Many early Muslims not only committed the Qur'an to memory, they also recorded it during a twenty-three-year experience of revelation. Muslims believe that God has revealed his intent to humans through chosen messengers and that Muhammad was the last of God's messengers and received the last of all divine scriptures.

Other main themes that run through the Qur'an include the Muslim belief in God's angels, including Gabriel, who transmitted God's revelations to his messengers; God's scriptures, which are believed to communicate the same message, even though they contain different details; God's messengers, who exemplify what God wanted from man and thus deserve to be the human agents who communicate God's commands to people; and the Day of Judgment, a time when people will receive the reward (Heaven) or punishment (Hell) for their deeds on earth.

The Qur'an repeatedly makes the point that all the prophets preached the same message: the belief in the One God who created people from Adam and Eve, made them with different colors, tongues, and nations and sent them guidance to follow. God also created people with the inclination to do right, but freed their minds to choose between right and wrong. Individuals, therefore, bear the consequences of their actions. The Qur'an states that even nonbelievers are rewarded during their lifetime for their good deeds.

A good portion of the Qur'an narrates stories of the struggles of the prophets and the believers before Muhammad's message, especially during the time of Abraham, Noah, Moses, and Jesus. Twenty other messengers of God are also mentioned, though less frequently. Many more prophets are said to have existed, but God chose not to mention them by name in the Qur'an. Unlike the Bible, however, the Qur'an is not chronologically ordered. It contains 6,000 ve.ses in 114 *surahs* (chapters). As comparative religion scholar Ismail al-Faruqi points out, God's oneness serves as the central theme of the scripture. Essentially, the Qur'an emphasizes ethical conduct in people's personal lives and in relations among them. A good Muslim must be God-conscious and must seek knowledge, earn a living, work hard, treat his or her family well, as well as treat people with fairness. Murder, theft, and adultery are considered to be grave sins.

The Qur'an, however, does not prescribe each aspect of a believer's obligations, and so commands believers to obey the teachings of God's messenger. Thus Muslims consider Hadith to be an essential source of religious guidance. Hadith collections consist of documented sayings, deeds, and approvals of the Prophet Muhammad. Hadith, however, is only secondary to Qur'an as a source of Islamic knowledge, as most of the reports attributed to the Prophet were written down after he had passed away. Muslim scholars throughout history have developed elaborate criteria to determine the validity of Hadith. Only a small portion of the collection—about fifteen thousand reports—has been deemed authentic.

Mainline Muslims understand passages of the Qur'an and Hadith within textual and historical contexts. Interpreting the texts, Muslim jurists developed a body of literature that became called *Shari'ah*, or Islamic law. The development of this legal tradition, also called *fiqh* (jurisprudence), manifests much diversity; it includes Hanafi, Shafi'i, Maliki, Hanbali, and Ja'fari—schools of jurisprudence named after the jurists who founded them. At some point, so many different views existed that scholars began exploring the common threads in the works. Muslim religious scholars came to a conclusion that the objective of Islamic law was to secure and develop life, mind, faith, family, and property. As life became more complex, jurists widely accepted a distinction between *Ibadat* (matters of worship), which are less subject to change and reinterpretation, and *mu'amalat* (human dealings), which are ever-changing and require continuous testing against the goals of Islamic law.

This formulation has many contemporary advocates and has influenced the development of legal systems in many Muslim countries. Still, it is presumed to be based on human reasoning—also called *ijtihad*—about the meaning of religious texts and their relevance to the questions under examination. Yet only the Qur'an and Hadith are revered texts. While the works of scholars are highly respected and studied in the major centers of religious learning, they are considered human efforts that are subject to error.

Historically, Muslim jurists who developed Islamic law were among the best legal and scholarly minds that Muslims had. Some of the scholars excelled not only in religious knowledge but in philosophy, math, algebra, science, and medicine. Ibn Khaldun is accredited in Western literature as being among the early social scientists of the world. In contemporary North America, aside from being a religious minority, Muslims find themselves in a country with a highly developed secular legal tradition. Thus the very development of the Muslim community in relation to the public sphere differs drastically from the process that transpired in Muslim-majority countries. For the common practicing Muslim, the essentials of the faith remain the most important issues in their religious life.

THE FIVE PILLARS OF PRACTICE

Informed by the Qur'an and authentic Hadith, Muslims worldwide heed five pillars of practice. The Qur'an teaches that rituals are meant to serve as a reminder for the faithful to stay on the straight path of moral conduct. The first of the religious pillars is witness (*shahadah*), affirming that there is only one God and that Muhammad is his messenger. In the broadest sense, any person who professes these main articles of faith is a Muslim. Muslims may manifest different views on religious interpretation and variance may be found in the practice of their faith, but the belief in God and the Prophet Muhammad has remained central to Muslim religious life throughout history.

Prayer (*salat*), which is a formal worship, is the second pillar of Islam. Observant Muslim men and women offer prayer five times each day—in the morning, at noon, in the afternoon, after sunset, and after dusk. After cleansing themselves, worshippers face toward Mecca to pray, kneeling down and touching their foreheads to the ground at various times as a sign of their submission to God.

Many Muslims may not strictly observe the daily prayer obligation, but most affirm their religious duty before their Creator and may communicate such conviction to their children. Many attend the weekly congregational prayer on Friday, which includes an address from an *imam* (prayer leader) and takes place in the mosque. Although Friday is not considered a sabbath day, the Qur'an instructs Muslims to leave work and business and go to the mosque at noon. Women are encouraged, although not required, to take part in the weekly prayer. This exemption is seen as an accommodation of mothers who may be caring for infants and young children. The prayer experience of Muslims also includes verbal supplications, called *dua'*, and attendance of communal prayers on major holy days.

The annual fast (*sawm*) during the Muslim month of Ramadan is the third pillar of the faith. The month of Ramadan is the ninth month of the Islamic lunar calendar. During the fast, Muslims must refrain from eating, drinking, and sexual pleasure from break-of-dawn to sunset each day. Ramadan is a period of personal restraint and renewed focus on moral conduct. It is also a time to empathize with those who are less fortunate and to appreciate what one has. Children, women who are pregnant or nursing, travelers, and sick and frail persons are exempted from the fast.

Hard data are not available to quantify the percentage of the Muslim community that adheres to the fast obligation. However, it is widely believed that religiosity increases during Ramadan. Mosques worldwide usually swell during the holy month—and those in the United States and Canada are no exception. In North America, however, observation of the month can be a distinct challenge for many. While workplaces and schools in Muslim countries schedule their days around the demands of Ramadan, most Muslim employees in the West must juggle the time requirements of their jobs and those of their faith. Of course those Muslims who own businesses enjoy much more latitude than those who work for others to earn a living.

Interestingly, many Muslims believe that the observance of Ramadan in North America, where the faithful must maintain regular work schedules, is a purer form of Islamic practice than current custom in many Muslim countries. Here, Muslims must carry on with normal daily activities in addition to their religious obligations. While the religious intent of Ramadan is to allow each person time to examine his or her own habits and practice self-control, it has been turned into a month of celebration and work slowdown in some Muslim countries. In these countries, there is more leniency granted during this month and the focus becomes more on the ritual elements of the fast rather than the spiritual aspects. For example, businesses may close down during the day to make things easier for those who are fasting. There is also a greater indulgence in food comsumption, and late-night entertainment during the month's evenings has become the norm.

The giving of alms (*zakat*) among the poor is the fourth important pillar of Islam. Muslims are instructed to commit 2.5 percent of their wealth, apart from outstanding debts, to the needy every year. Individuals who possess liquid (or semi-liquid), assets such as cash, shares, and stocks worth more than three ounces of pure gold ($750 in current value) are bound by this obligation. In addition Islam prescribes that once a year each household must donate the equivalent of one day's sustenance for a poor household of equal size. This giving is called Break-the-Fast Alms (*Zakat al-Fitr*), and it is considered to be the least amount of what well-off Muslims owe the poor. Moreover, Islam encourages charity (*sadaqah*) in general. Chapter 7 examines community organizations collecting and distributing alms and charity contributions. However, local Islamic centers remain the primary collectors and distributors of the alms.

The fifth pillar of Islam is the pilgrimage (*hajj*) to Mecca. Pilgrimage plays a significant role in many faiths. In Islam, physically and financially capable adults are required to go on a pilgrimage to the city of Mecca, in the southwestern part of today's Saudi Arabia, at least once in their lifetime. Muslims believe that this is where Abraham and his son Ishmael built the first house of worship on earth, the Ka'bah—Mecca's centerpiece. Pilgrimage starts in the beginning of Thul-Hijjah, the twelfth Muslim month, and lasts for about a week.

While the pilgrimage is an annual gathering of members of the Muslim *ummah*, it is essentially a spiritual experience. Before setting out, a pilgrim must redress all wrongs, pay all debts, and arrange to have enough funds for his or her own journey and for the maintenance of family members who remain behind while the pilgrim is underway. Pilgrims wear special clothing—simple garments that strip away distinctions of class and culture, so that all stand equal before God. The rites include circling the Ka'bah, and going between the hilltops of Safa and Marwa as Hagar, the wife of Abraham, did during her search for water. Then the pilgrims stand together on the wide plain of Arafa and join in prayers for God's forgiveness, in what is often seen as a preview of the Day of Judgment. Pilgrims close the rites by sacrificing animals (*Qurbani*), whose meat is usually packed up and shipped to poor communities around the world.

At least two million people, including thousands from the United States and Canada, gather in Mecca each year from every corner of the globe, providing a unique opportunity for Muslims of different nations to meet one another. Muslims who do not take part in the pilgrimage usually fast the last day of the season and offer a cash donation. The other holy places that the Qur'an and Hadith recommend for religious visitation include the Prophet's mosque in Medina, which is also in Arabia, and the third holiest place for Muslims: the Aqsa Mosque in Jerusalem.

In addition to the main pillars of practice, Muslims who follow the Qur'an avoid alcohol and pork. Many practicing Muslims only eat *zabihah* (properly slaughtered) meat and poultry. This generally means that Muslims shun bars and are selective in buying food. Because of the growing demand for *halal* (permissible) foods, shops have opened in many American cities and neighborhoods offering products prepared in accordance with Islamic specifications. But since the Qur'an stipulates that food prepared by the "People of the Book," namely Jews and Christians, is permissible (granted the avoidance of alcohol and pork), Muslims also shop in supermarkets and eat in restaurants offering choices that accommodate their dietary requirements.

Islamic religious texts also instruct men and women to behave and dress modestly. Muslims believe men and women should be valued and judged by their intelligence, skills, and contributions to the community, not by their physical attributes. There are a number of ways in which Muslim men and women express such teachings. Some devout Muslim men wear beards and may also wear a small head covering, called *kufi*. Muslim women, when in public, wear attire known as *hijab*. While varying in style, *hijab* usually cover the hair, neck, and body, except for the face and hands. Many Muslim women do not follow this traditional interpretation of the Qur'anic requirement of modesty in clothing, but many do avoid skimpy or flamboyant outfits. Due to the growing Muslim population in North America, these faith-based modes of dress can be seen more frequently and in more varied contexts. While their use has caused controversy—usually in uniformed occupations—the issue is increasingly regarded as a freedom of religion matter in the workplace and at school.

FAMILY LIFE

The Qur'an and Hadith are emphatic in stressing the role of the individual in relations to others and to God. Each adult is responsible for his or her own actions and decisions in life. Before reaching adulthood, an individual's upbringing is the responsibility of the parents (or guardians for orphans). The Qur'an and Hadith emphasize the role of the family in the various stages of life, so much so that an individual's social life is assumed to center around the family. The Prophet Muhammad told his companions, "The best amongst you is the best to his family." Chapter 8 will demonstrate that Muslim communications networks in North America have become increasingly family-oriented in programming and information products.

The building of a family starts with the selection of a partner. Premarital and extramarital relationships are considered adulterous in the teaching of the Qur'an. Muslims generally frown upon the dating lifestyle so prevalent in the West; many do not accept dating even as a means to marriage. Still, young men and women do meet in schools, the workplace, and community centers. Nonconsensual marriage, such as the tribal custom of arranged marriages found in some countries, is frowned upon by much of the Muslim world today, especially among educated individuals within the various populations. In North American Muslim communities nonconsensual marriage is rare. The Qur'an and Hadith make consent a condition for a valid marriage, which is religiously defined as a contractual relationship between an adult male and an adult female. The emphasis on choice in American Muslim marriages does not preclude a role for parents, siblings, and friends. Ultimately, though, marriage decisions remain in the hands of young couples.

Islamic religious texts delineate rights and obligations that should be observed by family members, but clearly state that marriage should be based on mutual understanding, love, and assistance. Husband and wife should make themselves available to satisfy each other's needs. The Qur'an and Hadith place a default responsibility on husbands to provide for their families, but wives are allowed to work and keep their earnings. In reality, couples make their own arrangements in distributing the responsibilities of the household, which is in line with the spirit of the Qur'an and the practice of the Prophet, who worked for his wealthy wife. North American Muslim women are more likely to find jobs and develop careers outside the home than are their counterparts in Muslim countries. Some Muslim women maintain separate bank accounts, but help in household expenditures when the husband's income is not sufficient. Others prefer joint accounts, keeping personal gifts separate.

The Qur'an and Hadith neither prohibit nor establish polygamy. Nor does the Islamic faith regard it as virtuous. Polygamy was practiced widely in the pre-Islamic Mecca before the Qur'an restricted it, which made monogamy the rule in Muslim life. The verse allowing polygamy reads, "And if you fear that you cannot act equitably towards orphans, marry such women as seem good to you, two and three and four; but if you fear that you will not do justice between them, then marry only one . . ." The Qur'an translator and interpreter Abdullah Yusuf Ali explains that the verse comes after a battle in which the Muslim community had lost many men. This circumstance would be a compelling reason for a man to seek more than one wife.

Today polygamy is legal in many Muslim-majority societies; in other countries (like Tunisia and Turkey) it is illegal. In countries that allow polygamy, marriage contracts may proscribe the possibility of a second wife. Studies about the practice have seldom examined the men and women in polygamous relationships. Most concerns about polygamy have revolved around its abuse, especially in cases of well-to-do men marrying women of less affluent backgrounds. In North America, where polygamy is illegal, the practice is rare among Muslims.

The Qur'an acknowledges the possibility of discord between husband and wife and sanctions a role for other family members to reconcile differences, so long as there is love between the spouses. Although the Qur'an allows divorce, it clearly stipulates that marriage should be seen as a lifelong commitment. Anecdotes circulate in the community suggesting that Muslims in the United States and Canada are more likely to divorce than Muslims overseas, but less likely to do so than other citizens. A pattern of serial marriage and divorce has been noted among Muslims in North America, but since this practice is generally frowned upon in the community, the dominant commitment to a stable marriage life prevails.

Muslim couples in North America usually lack the extended family support system that is strong in Muslim-majority countries. *Imams* attempt to fill the vacuum and social workers are often called to help couples in marital distress. As a result, social service agencies geared specifically to the needs of Muslims, including women's shelters, marriage counseling services, and domestic relations tribunals are emerging in various cities across the continent.

Muslims generally disfavor abortion; children are seen as the most precious gift from God. The Qur'an prohibits female infanticide, which was widely practiced in pre-Islamic Mecca. The Qur'an also scolds men who express discontent when their wives give birth to female babies. The Qur'an instructs these men to be mindful that "male is the same as female." Rearing children is the responsibility of both parents, who must provide for them and never favor one over another. Muslim parents teach children to be proud of their heritage that stresses the values of honesty, integrity, love for parents, and respect for members of the other gender and kindness to neighbors, the elderly, and the disadvantaged. These values offer an added reinforcement for Muslims who choose a profession in social work when they graduate or volunteer time to charitable organizations.

Just like in the society as a whole, a cultural gap exists between Muslim parents and their teenage children, which is only more pronounced in North American-raised teenagers and their immigrant families. Although no data measures the impact of such a gap in the lives of young Muslims and their various responses to it, some patterns can be discerned from conversations at community centers. Many Muslim teens brought up by parents with minimal attachment to the faith are drawn to pop culture. Some are hooked on MTV and keep up with the latest film and music releases. Facing an identity crisis as they transform to adulthood, and noticing a discrepancy between the rules and values espoused by adults and adult behaviors, some teens may even leave home to live on their own.

There is also a countervailing trend among Muslim teens, especially those raised in homes with nurturing and supportive parents. In such an environment, teenagers in a stage of constructing a sense of selfhood, yet inexperienced and emotionally and financially dependent on their parents, may even grow into a stronger sense of Muslim identity than their parents had wished for them. Such young Muslims may become fans of rap music featuring socially responsible themes consistent with Muslim values, but still are able to connect with seemingly clashing emotions in the teen's world. These boys and girls often join Muslim youth groups or local sports clubs, allowing them to meet friends outside family circles. As such, they often grow into a coherent, confident sense of self-identity and of belonging to family and to a Muslim community. Indeed, Chapter 4 will show that the core purpose of the growing Muslim school movement is to promote such values.

COMMUNITY

One main influence in the formation of Muslim community organizations has been the split between the Sunnis and Shias. This is true everywhere in the contemporary Muslim world. Shia Muslims, who make up about 10 to 15 percent of the estimated 1.2 billion worldwide Muslim population, live as a majority population group in Iran, Azerbaijan, and Bahrain and as an influential minority group in most Muslim societies, especially in Iraq, Lebanon, and Kuwait. Sunni Muslims, who account for the rest of the world's Muslim population, come from various ethnic backgrounds and live all over the globe, but are concentrated in four dozen Muslim-majority states. The numerical representation of Sunni and Shia Muslims in North America is generally not different from that of the world as a whole, although many converts do not attach themselves to any sectarian labels. Examining the roots of such division is worthwhile because it has continued to impact Muslim life (even prior to the Iranian revolution).

From the Sunni (which means follower of the path of the Prophet) perspective, the genesis of the Shia (which means supporter of the House of the Prophet) community was political in nature. After the death of the Prophet Muhammad, Shias believed that the leadership of the community should remain within the family of the Prophet—namely in the hands of Ali, the cousin of the Prophet and husband of his daughter. Shias also believed the Prophet himself named Ali as his successor, an assertion contested by Sunnis, who believed the leadership of the Muslims was a matter for people to decide. The Sunnis supported the Prophet's closest companion, Abu Bakr, to become the leader (also called Caliph), while the Shia remained in the opposition. Ali—highly respected among all early Muslims—became the third Caliph.

Subsequently, Shia scholars developed the concept of *imamate* (leadership) based on the lineage of the Prophet. Shia scholars argue that kinship to the Prophet allowed the *imams* a greater degree of exposure to his traditions and thus the *imams* were in a position to attain more knowledge and wisdom. Most Shias, perhaps 95 percent, are called *Ithna-Asheri* (twelvers) who believe in twelve

Grand Imams—all descendants of the Prophet—who were divinely protected against sin. The last of these Grand Imams, al-Mahdi, is believed to be living out of the public view since the tenth century until his re-emergence in the latter days. The Sunni tradition does not accept the idea that a human being has been living in absentia somewhere for hundreds of years, although it maintains that God has saved Jesus from crucifixion and will return him in the latter days to re-establish virtue and justice on earth.

Shia and Sunni Muslims agree that the Qur'an and Hadith are the main sources of the Islamic faith and both traditions recognize the Qur'an as the final uncorrupted and divine revelation of God. Scholars of the two traditions are split, however, on Hadith verification. Shia scholars, for example, do not accept narratives transmitted by the three Caliphs who succeeded the Prophet Muhammad in the leadership of the community. Nor do they accept narratives from other companions of the Prophet who were seen to have taken the wrong side in the conflict between Ali, the first of the Shia twelve Grand Imams, and the Umayyad Ruler Mua'wiyah.

The Sunni tradition developed by way of four major schools of classical jurisprudence. The works of these schools continue to influence the training of religious scholars today. Contemporary Sunnis, however, recognize *alims* who are respected for the depth of their knowledge of the Qur'an and Hadith and the scholarly works of jurisprudence. Another group of religious leaders consist of *imams*, whose main function is to lead prayers at mosques. In most Muslim countries in which ruling parties control mosque functions, *imams* do little beyond leading prayers. In North America *imams* assume a much greater role in the daily life of Muslims. In addition to leading prayers, *imams* counsel worshippers and perform community leadership roles. In North American mosques, *imams* are increasingly chosen among those with a degree of expertise in the scholarly traditions of the faith and required to possess adequate communications skills.

As for the Shia, in the absence of al-Mahdi, common folks follow the guidance of religious authorities called *marji's* on the interpretation of the Qur'an and Hadith. There are about half a dozen *marji's* today living in Iran, Iraq, and Lebanon. But there are many more *mujtahids* (less-expert religious scholars) around the world, including some in North America. Shia *mujtahids* usually lead prayers in some mosques—thus by definition they are *imams* too. This duality in the role of scholars is sometimes present in Sunni community as well, but no hierarchy exists in Sunni for the *alims*.

For many these Shia–Sunni differences seem like matters of the past; Shia and Sunni traditions agree on all the basic elements of Muslim faith and religious practice. The Shia tradition, however, includes additional requirements of charitable giving. A devout Shia is expected to give *khums* (one-fifth) offerings—that is, 20 percent of his or her earnings over basic living expenses—in support of the community's *imams*. Also, Shia Muslims celebrate Ashura, the tenth day of Muharram—the first month of the Muslim calendar. It marks the martyrdom of Hussein, grandson of the Prophet Muhammad, third *imam*, and one of the most revered figures in Shia history. For Sunni Muslims, Ashura coincided with the day God saved Moses and his followers from Pharoah and his soldiers. The faithful usually commemorate this day by fasting and reading the Qur'an.

Also, the Shia tradition has allowed the practice of *muta'* (temporary marital relationship), undertaken before potential spouses decide to break the relationship or make it permanent. During this temporary marriage the couple may choose to become intimate, or may agree to limits on their physical contacts. Shia scholars believe *muta'* is legitimate, so long as it is practiced between consenting adults with the approval of their parents. However, young people are warned against its liberal use. As Mustafa al-Qazwini, Imam of Islamic Educational Center of Orange County, California, writes in *Inquiries about Shi'a Islam*, "temporary marriage is the exception and last resort when permanent marriage cannot be afforded or becomes extremely difficult."

Many Muslims in North America do not identify with a particular mosque community or even mode of interpretation, nor do they commit themselves to follow any particular *alim, marji'*, or *mujtahid* (often called *ayatullah* by Shias). In local mosque communities around the continent, the role of the local *imam* is becoming very prominent, albeit circumscribed. While *imams* and other scholars offer guidance, many believers take this advice simply as a religiously informed viewpoint, not as a representation of the will of God. However, because of the *Khums* practice in Shia Islam and the rise of the *ayatullah* class in the aftermath of the Iranian Revolution, Shia clergy wield more authority than Sunni *imams* do. Still, the role of most *imams, alims*, and *ayatollahs* in the lives of Muslims in North America is mainly felt in the domain of worship, religious education, and family counseling, and less so in other aspects of daily life.

As will be demonstrated in chapter 3, *imams* are often employees of mosques, which administer to many communal needs besides worship. Whether Shia or Sunni, Muslims in North America face similar sets of problems as they devise educational programs in mosques or pursue the establishment of Islamic schools. The daily life challenges faced by the continent's Muslims seem much more important than the historical splits between Shiism and Sunnism. Thus, despite the differences in some aspects of devotion and the authority of religious figures, the patterns of activity that define local Muslim community life are not tremendously divergent. Because of a growing recognition of a shared destiny in North America, it is no longer uncommon to find Shia and Sunni Muslims worshipping together and attending the same school. Chapter 5 discusses how national and regional community development organizations tackled these issues.

Aside from the two branches of the mainline Muslim community, a number of offshoot groups are usually lumped with Muslims in American popular thought. Many Muslims attribute this fact to misunderstanding generated by inaccurate or biased coverage on television or in school textbooks. For example, while most Sufis (mystics) in the world are considered members of mainstream Islam, some Sufi orders in North America advocate a different creed that focuses on spiritual healing. Some of the largest Sufi groups (such as the Sufi Order in the West) do not claim affiliation with Islam. Many Sufi orders have representatives and teachers in the United States and Canada, but there are only a handful of established Muslim Sufi mosques.

Several other groups have also been misconstrued as part of mainline Islam. One is the NOI under Minister Louis Farrakhan, which is usually referred to as the Black Muslims. Contrary to Muslim beliefs, the movement maintains that Fard Muhammad, an immigrant from India who taught NOI founder Elijah Muhammad, was God walking on earth. Also, the Qadyani sect (sometimes called Ahmadi) recognizes Mirza Gulam Ahmad as the resurrection of Jesus and a prophet who came after Muhammad. There are also Baha'is, who believe that men named Bab and Baha'u'llah were prophets after Muhammad and that the Baha'i scripture, *Tue Kitabi Aqdas*, supersedes the Qur'an. Another faith group is the Druze community, which maintains a belief in reincarnation and divides people into a lay uninitiated class and a holy initiated clergy. Such beliefs set these groups apart from the Muslim community.

Despite these differences of belief, members of these sects share ethnicity and national origin with most Muslims. Ahmadis are mainly of Pakistani and Indian origins; the NOI is African American; the Druze community is Arab; the Baha'is are mainly Iranian. Muslim members of each group celebrate the same ethnic days and favor similar ethnic foods. The Druze and the NOI have had better relations with Muslim community groups than have the Baha'is and Ahmadis. Druze activists, including entertainer Casey Kasem, publicly advocate Arab-American issues. The NOI has recently resumed contacts with the mainline African-American Muslim community.

ETHNICITY

As will be detailed in chapter 2, the Muslim population in the United States and Canada consist of a diverse ethnic makeup. Although many have Middle Eastern, South Asian, and African roots, Muslims descend from all corners of the world. While North American Muslims generally identify themselves as part of the worldwide Islamic faith community, most maintain attachments to their ethnic bonds. In the lives of Muslims, as is true of members of many other groups, ethnicity has meant native tongue, physical attributes, and special foods, folklore, and occasions. In the increasingly global system of communication and economic production, ethnic ties have also meant jobs, business, and kinship for Muslim immigrants. This is especially the case in the United States because the sponsorship of immigrants beyond the nuclear family has been discouraged. According to the U.S. Immigration and Naturalization Service, the waiting period for bringing a brother or a sister to the United States on an immigrant visa may exceed twelve years. Thus for many recent immigrants, family is here and abroad. The Internet has made some of these interactions among people in distant parts of the world more affordable and fast.

Some ethnic Muslim immigrants bring practices with them—including such controversial practices as cousin marriage. This practice, however, is more frequent in certain ethnic communities, such as descendants from Egypt, where marriage between cousins is common. This anecdotal information, however, has not been quantified by studies. The religious teachings of Islam discourage such practices; the Prophet Muhammad urges Muslims to marry nonrelatives. The Qur'an also allows Muslim men to marry Jewish and Christian women, a factor that may have facilitated interfaith marriages. It does not, however, permit Muslim women to marry outside of the faith, lest they be placed under pressure to renounce their religion. Generally Muslim women in the United States and Canada continue to observe this injunction; few do not.

Some Muslim immigrants who arrived in the United States and Canada as singles have married outside their ethnic and religious community. The shared faith and emphasis on family, along with a shared sense of destiny, has contributed to an increasing number of intercultural marriages. Nonetheless, most Muslims still marry within their own ethnic group. Thus the institution of marriage often reinforces ethnic ties at the same time that it causes the Muslim community in North America to become further enmeshed with the surrounding culture, in both interracial and interfaith terms.

Many ethnic Muslims do not practice Islam fully, but they give their children Muslim names and celebrate Islamic holidays. The main Muslim holiday is called *Eid* (Festive Day). It occurs twice per year—on *Eid al-Fitr* (Breaking the Fast Day) and *Eid al-Adha* (Day of Sacrifice). For both occasions Muslims take a day off work and school to attend communal prayer and community celebration activities. *Eid* occasions are the most joyous days in Muslim community life. Many community centers plan carnivals for children featuring amusement rides and entertainment.

Milad al-Nabi (Birth of the Prophet), which occurs on the twelfth day of Rabi' al-Awwal (the third month of the Islamic lunar calendar) commemorates the Prophet Muhammad's birthday. It is more emphasized in the Shia and Sufi traditions, even though it has no roots in religious texts. Some Sunni Muslims observe *Milad al-Nabi* as a form of veneration of the Prophet, perhaps through organized lectures and prayer at mosques, homes, or other facilities. Some Muslims in the United States and Canada find *Milad al-Nabi* equivalent to Christmas and thus emphasize it in the lives of their children.

As will be shown in chapter 6, hundreds of groups and centers have been established along ethnicity and homeland attachments. One goal is shared by all ethnic groups: self-preservation and mutual assistance in a universe that is much larger and ever changing. The spiritual and ethical values of Islam challenge these ethnic groups to recognize all they have in common and require that ethnic and social interests are pursued within the parameters of moral standards. The Qur'an states,

> Oh people, We created you from a single pair of a male and female and made you into nations and tribes, so that you may know each other; verily the most honored among you in the sight of God is the most righteous of you; and God has full knowledge and is well-acquainted.

Faith-based groups fear that organizations formed on the basis of race, language, and history may appreciate religious values only when they serve limited ethnic interests. On the other hand, ethnic Muslims fear that religiously oriented leaders may succumb to narrowly defined concepts of the community, hence alienate ethnic or nonpracticing Muslims. Despite the differences between religious and ethnic communities, Muslim groups have forged political alliances that often include groups outside the faith. As for leadership, many Muslims believe any portion of the community receives recognition by organizing and serving its members. Ethnic and religious Muslims may often part company, but they all function under the same body of laws and civic culture.

CITIZENSHIP IN A GLOBAL WORLD

The U.S. Constitution establishes a system of government intended to provide for domestic security and national defense, to regulate commerce and industry, and to promote the general welfare of the people. Citizens are obligated to pay taxes and serve in the military when drafted. In return, citizens have the right to vote, speak and practice religion freely, bear arms, and be secure in their private property. Under current law, citizens who commit certain crimes lose their right to vote. In times of war citizens who fight or aid an enemy can be tried for treason. In Canada the constitution refers to all laws, rules, and practices that structure the function of the Canadian political system. Canadian citizens have rights and duties similar to those of their American counterparts.

From a legal perspective, loyalty to country means obeying the law. While the Constitution is the ultimate frame of reference that defines how people can live together, what makes America's system of government work is the voluntary involvement of people in their government and their community. American society is organized along lines of many types of interests including ethnicity, religion, gender, occupation, business, region, residence, and ideology. The organizations that embody these interests have extensions and relations all over the globe—and wherever they go, money and ideas follow. The Canadian government and civil society are largely similar to their American counterparts. Many churches, businesses, and other interest groups in the United States have sister organizations in Canada.

Muslims, too, maintain ties across borders. But some Muslims maintain an isolationist attitude toward U.S. and Canadian societies. Some proclaim pride that Muslims suffer much less than the rest of people in the continent from the social consequences of contemporary life: alcoholism, drug addiction, AIDS, crime, suicide, divorce, out-of-wedlock children, and abortion. Some even believe that Western societies are largely hedonistic and morally corrupt. They believe Muslims ought to stay away from contacts with the organized society. Instead, they propose to focus only on *da'wa* (call to Islam) to American and Canadian citizens.

Most Muslims disagree with the view that American society is decadent. They point out that all communities suffer from social maladies, Muslim societies included. They also say that painting Western societies with such a broad brush is not much different from stereotyping Muslims as fanatics. Moreover, these Muslims count many values in North America that are consistent with Islamic moral teachings and are present more vividly in North America than in most Muslim countries. These cultural values include hard work, entrepreneurship, and individual responsibility, to mention a few.

Many Muslims believe the civic cultures in the United States and Canada value an information-based discourse and stress negotiations between the various parties as a means to make public decisions. In contrast, most Muslim societies in the world lack functioning processes to avoid violence in the settlement of political differences. Thus while community is saved in most Muslim countries from a total collapse by kinship ties, ethnic bonds, and religious norms that abhor crime, a political mainstream is lacking because of the absence of a secure public space outside of governmental structures.

In the early 1980s American Muslims began to debate a role in the public arena. Although most Muslims favor contacts with civil society groups and members of the general public, some question whether they should take part in the formal structures of government in predominantly non-Muslim societies. Most skeptics argue that large numbers of Americans and Canadians are disenfranchised and shun the political process, which tends to benefit the rich and powerful. Yet such voices have never studied American society to reach such a conclusion.

The overwhelming majority of ethnic and religious Muslims support active participation in state and society institutions. The majority view reasons that Muslims stand only to lose if they do not become involved, and to gain if they do. They also reason that the laws of America and Canada guarantee religious freedom. The 1980s and 1990s have witnessed the growth of local and national public affairs groups that promote political activism and give a public voice to Muslims.

Regardless of participation, people cannot avoid meeting their obligation to defend the nation. The number of Muslims in the Canadian military is unavailable, but in the various branches of the U.S. military, an estimated ten thousand Muslims serve. While in the past some Muslim servicemen have claimed conscientious objection—like former boxing champion Muhammad Ali during the Vietnam War—others participated in the war effort against Iraq, a Muslim country, in the 1990–1991 Gulf War. Some of these servicemen participated simply to fulfill their jobs; the issue of fighting against other Muslims apparently was not a main concern for them. Others sought to limit their participation to non-combat duties. Others were stationed in Muslim-majority Gulf countries, where they worked with other Muslims in the U.S.-led coalition. Some of these Muslim servicemen believed the war was justified because it aimed at punishing an aggressor—an Iraqi army that invaded its neighbor Kuwait.

While Muslims attempt to reconcile the demands of faith, ethnicity, and country, many promote the ideal of universal brotherhood as a basis for harmonious coexistence between people. Some intellectually inclined Muslims make sure their children do not confuse nation, ethnicity, or religion with nationalism. They argue that nationalism anywhere in the world is an ideology that can and has lent itself to aggressive designs based on an us-versus-them attitude. Instead, American Muslim parents often teach that being good to one's nation lies in commitment to the rule of law and to the values of freedom, equality, liberty, justice, and tolerance.

Being part of a nation also implies the emotional identification with the country when it is threatened and the joy it experiences for being free. Thus many Muslims join others in the annual fireworks on Independence Day. Muslims in North America have also come to appreciate Thanksgiving, whose theme of gratitude is similar to the Islamic teaching that encourages Muslims to thank God for all the good things one has. The Prophet Muhammad said "In the Name of God" before eating and drinking and "Thanks to God" once he finished. For many ethnic Muslims, Thanksgiving is similar to harvest day, still celebrated in their countries of origin. While some Muslims eat their preferred ethnic food on Thanksgiving, others serve the traditional American turkey and pumpkin pie. Still, some cling to the notion that the concepts of holiday and thankfulness are religious matters covered by Islamic practices. Consequently, these Muslims express appreciation to those who celebrate Thanksgiving, but ask to be tolerated if they choose otherwise.

Muslims generally view Christmas and Easter as religious holidays exclusively for Christians, just as *Eid* is for Muslims. Some Muslims may exchange season greetings with their neighbors, coworkers, and classmates on religious and secular occasions. Others are reluctant to participate in social gatherings that celebrate the religious holidays of other faiths. To them, nonparticipation is a matter of religious freedom, which is protected under the U.S. Bill of Rights and Canadian Charter of Rights. As discussed in chapter 9 Muslims have engaged in public relations battles to establish such an understanding with fellow Americans and Canadians.

As a result Muslims have become increasingly acquainted with the players and process of political discourse. Muslims' political affiliations, however, are far from uniform. While many African-American Muslims identify with the Democratic Party in the United States, some immigrant Muslims associate with the Republican Party. A majority of Muslims, however, are independent voters, preferring to support candidates based on their records and their sympathies toward Muslim community concerns. Because there are no firm records of Muslim participation in Canadian politics, Canadian Muslim views are not as well known, although immigrants generally have favored the inclusive policies of the Liberal Party.

THE UMMAH AND THE SEPTEMBER 11 ATTACKS ON THE UNITED STATES

Muslims in North America are more aware than the general public about events in the Muslim world, which is ravaged by political and economic turmoil. Muslims make up a disproportionate number of the world's refugees—displaced and stateless persons. Many Muslims—including Palestinians, Kashmiris, Kurds, and Chechens—live under extremely repressive conditions. In many countries Muslim minorities are denied equal treatment across Europe, Asia, and Africa; sometimes they are even subjected to genocide and massive destruction of life and property (such as in Burma, Bosnia, and Kosovo). In strife-stricken, Muslim-majority countries, non-Muslim minorities have also been abused (such as in Indonesia and Sudan).

The harsh conditions experienced by many Muslims in other countries are due to complex historical, political, and economic factors, which usually include decisions made by local leaders. In many Muslim-majority states, the political and military elites who took over after colonial troops departed in the 1950s and 1960s have focused on maintaining political power and have given little attention to building polities that are capable of reconciling the ethnic, religious, and economic cleavages in their societies. As a result, millions of people live in misery and discontent. In the early 1990s some states like Somalia and Afghanistan degenerated into chaotic civil wars. Meanwhile, the peace process between the Palestinians and Israel broke down, as Israel continued to build settlements in the occupied territories.

The United States has not been involved directly in most of the Muslim societies in turmoil and maintains good relations with most Muslim states. Many of these states joined the U.S. coalition against Iraq in the 1990–1991 Gulf War and participated with the United States in peacekeeping operations around the world. The United States does not have a single policy toward the whole of the Muslim world. Muslims live in many countries, with each country maintaining its own bilateral relationship with the United States. But the United States also provides economic and military aid to Israel and oppressive regimes, policies that cause anger against America in many Muslim countries—particularly in the Middle East.

In the 1990s a number of anti-American bombings were carried out by radicals with suspected membership in the Egyptian Islamic Jihad and its affiliate al-Qaedah organization. But terrorist attacks have not been carried out exclusively by foreigners. In 1995 Timothy McVeigh, a white Christian, was charged and later executed for the bombing of the Murrah Federal Building in Oklahoma City, the worst act of terrorism on U.S. soil until the September 11, 2001 attacks on New York and Washington. Leaders of al-Qaedah, including Osama bin Laden, praised the attacks and those who carried them out, in defiance of a worldwide Muslim condemnation.

Ruling factions and opposition groups of all stripes in Muslim countries publicly condemned the September 11 attacks. *Alims* and *imams* here and across the globe, representing official institutions among the Sunni and Shia branches of Islam as well as scholars affiliated with Islamic grassroots movements, issued statements emphasizing that the acts of hijacking commercial aircrafts and using them as weapons violated Islamic law, which prohibits the targeting of noncombatants. The tragic event impelled Muslims to become increasingly public about reasserting the original meaning of *jihad*.

Muslims have argued that *jihad* has been mistakenly translated as "holy war."

Literally, *jihad* means to strive, to exert effort. It is a broad Islamic concept that includes struggle against evil inclinations within oneself, struggle to improve the quality of life in society, struggle in the battlefield in legitimate warfare, or fighting against tyranny or oppression. The Prophet Muhammad said that taming one's rebellious nature into complete submission to God is the greater *Jihad*. The verses of the Qur'an that allow war (*qital* or *harb*) came after the early Muslims were persecuted and attacked by the pagans of Mecca. But these verses do not permit random violence against nonbelievers and noncombatants.

War is permitted only on the condition that the enemies initiate hostilities. There is no justification in the Qur'an or Hadith for fighting to subjugate others and control their wealth and possessions. Compelling people to covert to Islam is contrary to the Qur'anic clear instruction that "there should be no compulsion in religion." Legitimate war is one that is conducted in a manner that avoids noncombatants—that is, those nonfighting personnel and property, including women, children, worshipers, places of worship, trees, and crops. In justified acts of war, the Qur'an allows justice-based retribution. Acts of retaliation, however, must be proportionate. Even when hostilities are initiated, an openness to respond to peace initiatives should be considered. For individuals, the Qur'an and Hadith condems those who fight for personal gain or to satisfy anger.

Muslim scholars working in official and nonofficial capacities reached a unanimous conclusion that the attacks of September 11 involved a well-planned plot against noncombatants and as such they represented an unquestionable violation of Islamic teachings. Furthermore, the North American Council of Fiqh issued a religious opinion in conjunction with Muslim world respected *alims*, stating that it is religiously permissible for enlisted American Muslims to take part in the fight against terrorism. Justifying the opinion, the council stated that Muslims are part of American society and must assume their share in its defense, and that the campaign to apprehend those responsible for the attacks and to stop future attacks on innocent people meets the criteria of a just war under Islamic law. Issuance of this opinion marked the first time in U.S. history that a reputable body of Muslim scholars sanctioned Muslim participation in an American war effort.

Other North American Muslim leaders and various community organizations stepped up the public effort, identifying with the victims of the attack and calling for a swift justice against the perpetrators. As Muslims expressed revulsion at the methods of the terrorists, they refused to lay the blame on the United States for all the turmoil faced by Muslims. At the same time, they have maintained criticism of the U.S. Middle East policy, which many believe has failed to achieve stability or peace.

Still, American Muslims have only begun to take an active role in the foreign policy debate. Chapter 10 will show that groups dedicated to researching American policies toward Muslim countries began to emerge after the 1980s. Their general tendency is to look for improved relations between the United States and Muslim countries. In doing so they are moving away from the ideology-based discourse on foreign policy in favor of understanding policy as a dynamic political process. Also, Muslim groups have increasingly expressed sympathy for the world's oppressed peoples, regardless of their faith and ethnicity. Most important, they have vehemently opposed notions developed after the end of the Cold War that suggest a pending clash of civilizations between Islam and the West. Instead, Muslims wish for the U.S. government to take an active role in ending conditions of extreme injustice against the Palestinians, Kashmiris, Chechens, and Kurds. As will be shown later, due to the heavy-handed U.S. policy in the Middle East, its tilt toward Israel and the breakdown of the peace process, the plight of the Palestinians have recently taken center stage in the foreign policy agenda of Muslim organizations. Also, the question of Jerusalem has received special attention because of its importance to the Islamic faith.

Whether indigenous or foreign-born, Muslims who have built their lives in America are growing appreciative of several factors of the quality of life they enjoy: that many aspects of American life are quite consistent with the Muslim belief system; that interactions among people are becoming increasingly global; that, while Muslim countries may show signs of degeneration in religious, economic, and political life, Muslims in the United States and Canada strive to practice their faith in a purer form. But even though North America has been the land of freedom and opportunity for Muslims, a contentious relationship still exists between the United States and much of the Muslim world. Many American Muslims believe they are caught in the middle of this contention and seek to help reformulate the relationship on the basis of dialogue and cooperation. Faith-based Muslim public affairs groups have addressed the issues in broad terms. Ethnic Muslims have addressed foreign policy concerns more intensely and followed events more closely. Yet Muslims in North America are generally preoccupied with the challenges facing the development of their community organizations.

Clearly Muslim views in North America span a continuum between the poles of faith and ethnicity, with many shades in between. As later chapters of this book will show, these hues have colored the organizational structure of Muslim communities. Although the term American Muslim has gained increasing popularity, it has somewhat masked the community's pluralism. Muslims practice their faith in various ways: some heed all religious practices, others do not. Still, other Muslims are strictly secular and see religion only as a foundation for personal moral conduct. Faith-based worldviews stress an identity centered on a commitment to a set of shared religious values. Ethnicity-centered worldviews emphasize the shared experiences of ancestral groups. Religious community organizations are multiracial, while ethnic groups are multireligious. Muslim population dynamics are discussed further in the next chapter.

TWO

POPULATION GROUPS

MUSLIM POPULATION NUMBERS

There is no definitive count of the number of Muslims in North America. But the government of Canada, unlike that of the United States, tracks its population by religious affiliation. According to Statistics Canada, there were more than 96,000 Muslims in Canada in 1981, about 0.4 percent of the total population. The 1991 census counted 253,000 Muslims, or about 1 percent of the population. These numbers reflected an increase of 263 percent in just one decade—much of the growth due to immigration. If this pattern of growth remained constant throughout the 1990s, Muslims could have reached more than 665,000 by 2002—or two percent of Canada's 31 million-strong nation.

By law, the U.S. Bureau of the Census is not allowed to compile religious data on the nation's people, but it has traced their ethnic ancestry. In addition, the Immigration and Naturalization Service (INS) has kept information on the origin of U.S. immigrants. These data provide a basis for a statistical exploration of the U.S. population groups coming from parts of the Muslim world. Such an examination is worthwhile, even though the information offers little solid ground for the estimation of U.S.-born Muslims.

Therefore, estimates of the U.S. Muslim population remain sketchy. In the March 1981 *Annals of American Academy of Political Science*, Arif Ghayur wrote that U.S. Muslims numbered 1.2 million. However, he offered no specific INS sources for the figures on immigrants in his citations. He also added an arbitrary number of 75,000 African-American Muslims, leaving in doubt the reliability of his overall figure. Carol Stone wrote in "Estimate of Muslims Living in America" that in 1980 there were three million U.S. Muslims of immigrant extraction, but she too offered little documentation of that number. She also cited from a newspaper source an unsubstantiated figure of one million African-American Muslims in the United States.

Based on Ghayur's and Stone's studies, in 1998 Ilyas Ba-Yunus and Moin Siddiqui wrote *A Report on the Muslim Population in the United States*, which projected that the Muslim population would rise to seven million by 2000. Their report, however, did not validate the previous estimates. Despite all the questionable numbers, these works do offer a workable approach to enumerating the Muslim population. These studies break Muslims into their constituent ancestry groups and attempt to use available statistics about each to construct a total number. Below, this methodology is cautiously replicated and anchored in verifiable data.

On immigrants, the schema suggests first multiplying the percentage of Muslims in their countries of origin by the total number of persons from those countries admitted to the United States, then adjusting the resulting figures to account for natural growth. The underlying assumption here is that the religious profile of immigrants resembles that of their countries of origin. This, in some cases, should be qualified because many non-Muslims have come to the United States from Muslim-populated states.

U.S. government records show that prior to 1965 the number of people migrating from regions heavily populated with Muslims was relatively small. As table 2.1 shows, the INS admitted 517,367 people between 1820 and 1965 from the Balkans, India, the Arab world, Africa, and Turkey (which prior to 1924 was the Ottoman Empire, called Turkey in Asia and Turkey in Europe by the INS). Most people arriving during this period were not Muslim, even those coming from the Middle East.

The number of immigrants increased rapidly after 1965, when Congress abandoned racial and national origin restrictions in immigration laws. Numerous factors caused many Muslims to flee their homelands. Several regions with large Muslim populations continued to suffer under conditions of war and foreign occupation, although most Muslim states have since gained independence. Moreover, in the postcommunist era, Muslims fell victim to genocidal wars, especially in the Balkans. In addition, the faltering economies of post-independence states and high unemployment rates among college graduates added more reason for many to seek new lives in the labor-demanding societies of North America.

INS figures show that from 1966 to 1980 emigration from Muslim world regions jumped to 865,472. The number of arrivals grew to 997,000 from 1981 to 1990, and then to 921,100 in the seven-year period from 1991 to 1997. These waves of immigrants originated mainly in the Middle East, South Asia, and Africa. Throughout the years the number of immigrants from these areas has risen steadily. In the first 145 years prior to the 1965 immigration liberalization, an average of 531 people arrived per year. From 1966 to 1980, the average of yearly arrivals increased to 57,698; in the following ten years, it rose again to 99,700; and in the past seven years it peaked at 131,586.

Determining the number of Muslims among these immigrants is a matter of guesswork. To reach a conservative estimate, one can reverse the religious distribution of communities in the various countries of origin whenever there is a reason to believe that non-Muslims had more motive to migrate. Hence the following assumptions can form a basis for the calculation:

- U.S. immigrants from lands under the Ottoman Empire and colonial powers prior to 1965 were only 10 percent Muslim—the rest being mainly Christian. Most of these immigrants were classified by the INS as Turkey in Asia and Turkey in Europe. Anecdotes about early Arab immigrants in that era suggest that many were Syrian and Lebanese Christians. But Muslims, too, had reason to migrate: nationalistic fervor in the late 1800s and early 1900 pitted Arabs of all faiths against the Turks.

- Muslims made up only 10 percent of Egyptian immigrants from 1966 to 1980. Coptic Christians are assumed to make up the rest. Many Copts fled the nationalization measures of the Nasser government and the stagnant Egyptian economy after 1965.

- Muslims accounted for only 30 percent of the Lebanese who came to the United States between 1980 and 1990 after that country's 1975 civil war. Most of the arrivals were Christian, although many Shia Muslims from southern Lebanon also migrated.

- Muslims make up only 11 percent of the immigrants coming from Israel and the Palestinian territories under its control. This proportion represents only the Muslim citizens of Israel, although the total number of Muslim subjects under Israel and the Palestinian National Authority accounts for more than 40 percent of that region's inhabitants. Credible reports suggest that Christians, especially Jerusalemites, left in much larger numbers than Muslims after Israel occupied the West Bank and Gaza in 1967.

- Muslims made up about a third of the Indian subcontinent's population between 1820 to 1960. In much of this period, the whole region was under British colonial rule; Pakistan and Bangladesh were still part of India.

- Muslims constituted only 1 percent of the Iranian immigrants arriving from 1980 to 1990, following the 1979 Iranian revolution. Most of those who left Iran are assumed to be Jews, Zoroastrians, Christians, and Baha'is, although many Muslims who disagreed with the philosophy and politics of the revolution left as well.

- The percentage of Muslim immigrants from the former Yugoslavia is not adjusted upward, although they had more reason to migrate from both the communist government and its nationalist successor. Likewise, no adjustments are warranted for other countries, where political and economic hardships impacted people irrespective of their religious affiliation. This holds especially true for the newcomers from South Asia, Africa, and the Caribbean.

As calculated in table 2.1, about 3.3. million people arrived to America from regions of the world populated heavily by Muslims between 1820 and 1997. They represented only 5 percent of the total of 64 million immigrants in this

TABLE 2.1

IMMIGRANTS FROM REGIONS WITH MUSLIM POPULATIONS, AND ESTIMATED NUMBER OF MUSLIM ARRIVALS: 1820 TO 1997

Region/Country	Immigrants 1820–1965	Muslim Factor	Estimated Muslims	Immigrants 1966–1980	Muslim Factor	Estimated Muslims	Immigrants 1981–1990
Balkan	**74,125**		**15,222**	**82,905**		**15,752**	**19,200**
Yugoslavia	71,893	0.19	13,660	82,905	0.19	15,752	19,200
Albania	2,232	0.7	1,562	1,562			
South Asia	**16,209**		**5,349**	**241,498**		**61,719**	**338,400**
India	16,209	0.33	5,349	205,398	0.13	26,702	261,900
Pakistan				36,100	0.97	35,017	61,300
Bangladesh							15,200
Other Asian							**26,600**
Afghanistan							26,600
Azerbaijan							
Uzbekistan							
Arab Origins	**208,050**		**20,805**	**196,900**		**106,267**	**182,100**
Egypt				42,700	0.1	4,270	31,400
Palestine (Israel)				39,500	0.11	4,345	36,300
Iraq				29,800	0.96	28,608	19,600
Jordan				43,600	0.925	40,134	32,600
Syria							20,600
Lebanon				41,300	0.7	28,910	41,600
Turkey in Asia (Ottoman)	208,050	0.1	20,805				
Iran				**56,600**	**0.99**	**55,751**	**154,800**
Turkey	**161,833**		**16,183**	**25,400**		**25,146**	**20,900**
Contemporary Turkey				25,400	0.99	25,146	20,900
Turkey in Europe (Ottoman)	161,833	0.1	16,183				
Subsaharan Africa	**57,150**		**19,431**	**121,169**		**41,197**	**120,100**
Ethiopia							27,200
Nigeria							35,300
South Africa							15,700
Other African countries	57,150	0.33	19,431	121,169	0.33	41,197	41,900
Caribbean/South America				**141,000**		**10,098**	**134,900**
Trinidad and Tobago				86,400	0.06	5,184	39,500
Guyana				54,600	0.09	4,914	95,400
Total	**517,367**		**76,990**	**865,472**		**315,930**	**997,000**

Sources:
U.S. Bureau of the Census, Statistical Abstract of the United States (1966) Immigrants by Country of Last Permanent Residence: 1820–1965.
U.S. Bureau of the Census, Statistical Abstract of the United States (1987) Immigrants by Country of Birth: 1961 to 1985.
U.S. Bureau of the Census, Statistical Abstract of the United States (1997) Immigrants by Country of Birth: 1981 to 1995.
U.S. Bureau of the Census, Statistical Abstract of the United States (1999) Immigrants by Country of Birth: 1981 to 1997.
Cental Intelligence Agency, *The World Factbook.*
Richard Weekes, *Muslim Peoples: A World Ethnographic Survey.*

Muslim Factor	Estimated Muslims	Subtotal of Immigrants 1820–1990	Subtotal of Muslims Estimated	Immigrants 1991–1997	Muslim Factor	Estimated Muslims 1991–1997	Total Immigrants 1820–1997	Total Estimated Muslim 1820–1997	% of Total Estimated Muslim Immigrants
	3,648	**173,998**	**34,622**	**31,700**		**6,023**	**205,698**	**40,645**	**3**
0.19	3,648	173,998	33,060	31,700	0.19	6,023	205,698	39,083	3
			1,562					1,562	0
	106,778	**596,107**	**173,846**	**393,500**		**147,597**	**989,607**	**321,443**	**27**
0.13	34,047	483,507	66,098	274,600	0.13	35,698	758,107	101,796	9
0.97	59,461	94,400	94,478	83,500	0.97	80,995	180,900	175,473	15
0.873	13,270	15,200	13,270	35,400	0.873	30,904	50,600	44,174	4
	26,334	**26,600**	**26,334**	**42,100**		**39,208**	**68,700**	**65,542**	**6**
0.99	26,334	26,600	26,334	13,600	0.99	13,464	40,200	39,798	3
				12,300	0.934	11,488	12,300	11,488	1
				16,200	0.88	14,256	16,200	14,256	1
	110,287	**587,050**	**237,359**	**149,200**		**110,947**	**736,250**	**348,306**	**29**
0.9	28,260	74,100	32,530	28,000	0.9	25,200	102,100	57,730	5
0.11	3,993	75,800	8,338	22,800	0.11	2,508	98,600	10,846	1
0.96	18,816	49,400	47,424	26,800	0.96	25,728	76,200	73,152	6
0.925	30,155	76,200	70,289	25,100	0.925	23,218	101,300	93,507	8
0.805	16,583	20,600	16,583	16,600	0.805	13,363	37,200	29,946	3
0.3	12,480	82,900	41,390	29,900	0.7	20,930	112,800	62,320	5
		208,050	20,805				208,050	20,805	2
0.1	**15,480**	**211,400**	**71,231**	**89,000**	**0.99**	**88,110**	**300,400**	**159,341**	**13**
	20,691	**208,133**	**62,020**	**15,700**		**15,543**	**223,833**	**77,563**	**7**
0.99	20,691	46,300	45,837	15,700	0.99	15,543	62,000	61,380	5
		161,833	16,183				161,833	16,183	1
	43,031	**298,419**	**103,659**	**105,300**		**43,973**	**403,719**	**147,632**	**12**
0.435	11,832	27,200	11,832	31,900	0.435	13,877	59,100	25,709	2
0.485	17,121	35,300	17,121	37,900	0.485	18,382	73,200	35,502	3
0.016	251	15,700	251				15,700	251	0
0.33	13,827	220,219	74,455	35,500	0.33	11,715	255,719	86,170	7
		275,900	**21,054**	**94,600**		**7,284**	**370,500**	**28,338**	**2**
0.06	2,370	125,900	7,554	41,000	0.06	2,460	166,900	10,014	1
0.09	8,586	150,000	13,500	53,600	0.09	4,824	203,600	18,324	2
	326,248	**2,377,607**	**730,125**	**921,100**		**458,684**	**3,298,707**	**1,188,810**	**100**

Notes:
The Muslim Factor is the average of Muslim population percentages in *The World Factbook* and *Muslim Peoples*.
*Data in the 1966–1980 column for Turkey cover the period from 1960 to 1980.

period. The total number of estimated Muslim immigrants was 1,188,810. Now the task is to determine the extent to which these waves of immigrant populations have multiplied. Studies show that the natural growth rate of the American Muslim population is much higher than that of the rest of the nation. John Weeks's study of the Muslim population in San Diego, *Counting the Number of Muslims in the United States: Estimates for the U.S. and Results from a Pilot Project in San Diego*, concludes that the growth rate of the Muslim population in that city is capable of doubling the number of Muslims every six years. Ilyas Ba-Yunus conducted a more meticulous sample of Illinois Muslims in *Muslims of Illinois: A Demographic Report*, which suggests that the Muslim population of Illinois is capable of doubling itself every seventeen years.

Assuming that the Ba-Yunus finding is true, one can extrapolate that the population of those who came between 1820 and 1965 may have doubled at least three to four times, growing from around 75,000 to a range of 600,000 to 1.3 million. The wave of immigrants who arrived from 1966 to 1980 may have doubled once or twice, growing from a population about 316,000 to a range of 600,000 to 1.2 million. Those arriving between 1981 and 1990 may have added half their number or nearly doubled it, from about 326,000 to a range of 489,000 to 652,000. Therefore, by 1990 the Muslim population hailing from immigrant origins could have ranged from 1,689,000 to 3,152,000. One has to add the number of fresh arrivals who may not have multiplied. From 1990 to 1997 about 459,000 Muslims may have arrived in the United States. In all, by 2002 the number of Muslim immigrants and their descendants may have reached a minimum range of 2.1 million to 3.6 million.

Estimating the number of indigenous Muslims in the United States, especially African-American Muslims, is even more difficult. Sources that can shed some light on the number of these Muslims are scarce. The College Board, which develops placement tests for American high school students, has maintained data on the ethnic and religious profile of students who take the SAT test every year. Students are asked to indicate their religious preference and ethnic background on their tests. Table 2 represents the ethnic makeup of students who chose Islam as their religious preference in 1995 and 2000. Of all responding students, Muslims represented 0.8 percent and 1 percent in these two years, respectively. (This suggests that the population of Muslim high school students grew by 25 percent in five years, which is not far from the Ba-Yunus finding that the Muslim population can double in seventeen years). If one assumes that the proportion of Muslim high school students represents their weight in the general population, then by 2000 Muslims numbered 2.8 million of America's 281 million people. The College Board data, however, may represent an underestimation because (1) more than 17 percent of the students did not indicate any religious preference; and (2) the sensitivity of the question may have led many minority students, Muslims included, not to disclose their faith.

This figure—2.8 million—is almost a middle point in the range of estimates of Muslims from the new immigrant groups. The College Board data, however, shows that Hispanics, Native Americans, and African Americans made up 20.4

TABLE 2.2

ETHNICITY AND RELIGIOUS PREFERENCE OF
STUDENTS TAKING THE SAT TEST

Student Profiles	1995		2000	
	Number	Percent	Number	Percent
Ethnicity of students listing Islam as religious preference				
American Indian	20	2.4	51	0.4
Black or African American	1,428	17.0	1,349	11.1
Hispanic	86	1.0	118	1.0
White	1,498	17.8	2,005	16.6
Asian, Asian American, Pacific Islander	3,103	37.0	4,701	38.9
Other	2,176	25.9	3,625	30.0
No Response	83	1.0	222	1.8
Subtotal	8,394	0.8	12,071	1.0
All students taking SAT	1,067,993	100.0	1,260,278	100.0

Source: The College Board

percent of Muslims in 1995 and 16.5 percent in 2000. This does not include Anglo-American converts, whose numbers are in the "White" category. The number of Anglo-American Muslims is hard to come by.

On the basis of the College Board data, one can assume that Muslims from the major American population groups represent roughly 18 percent of the total Muslim population. Their number, then, could be somewhere from 460,000 to 790,000, which raises the minimum Muslim total to a range of 2,560,000 to 4,390,000—or an average of 3.5 million, representing less than 2 percent of the United States population. The North American population, therefore, may range from 3,225,390 to 5,055,390, with an average of 4.1 million. Again, it must be pointed out that this estimate of Muslim numbers is conservative and rudimentary. It does not include small communities of immigrant Muslims, such as the Chinese, Indonesians, Malaysians, Filipinos, Vietnamese, and Cambodians. Clues to speculate about their numbers are almost nonexistent. Therefore, more rigorous research must be conducted before one can claim any scientific basis for the Muslim population in the United States.

CONVENTIONAL POPULATION GROUPS

The College Board data is not an accurate representation of the ethnic distribution of Muslims in the United States; it collapses the ethnic categories that would describe most Muslims into "Asian," "White," and "Other." However, the information does show that Muslims are found among some of America's largest population segments. African Americans accounted for 17 percent and 11 percent of

Muslim students in 1995 and 2000, respectively. Computing the number of African Americans based on their percentage among those with Islamic preference in the College Board data, an average of 14 percent, yields a population of 359,100.

Looking at the profiles of students broken down to religious preference by ethnicity yields different results. A total of 119,591 students identified themselves as "Black or African American" in 2000. Of these, 1,349, or 1.1 percent, chose Islam as their religious preference. African Americans in the 1995 data totaled 103,872, including 1,428, or 1.4 percent, who said they were Muslim. If a middle percentage of 1.2 is applied to the 36.4 million African Americans counted in the 2000 Census, the number of Muslims in this community can be estimated at 436,800. Thus, on average, African-American Muslims may number 398,000.

Major cities where African-American Muslims have established mosques and community organizations include Chicago, New York, Los Angeles, and Atlanta. It is widely believed that most members of this group are converts, but now there is a generation of African Americans who were born and raised in Muslim house-holds. While African-Americans Muslims are usually thought of as blue-collar workers, a growing number are white-collar professionals. Most Anglo-American converts are believed to be women, although men make up a substantial number of this population. Many occupy vital positions in community organizations. No organizations exist for Anglo-American Muslims; they are dispersed throughout the continent and tend to emphasize faith over ethnicity.

There are fewer Latino Muslims than Anglo-American Muslims. The largest gatherings of Latino Muslims are found in New York City, Southern California, and Chicago—places that historically have had large Hispanic and Muslim populations. In the Washington, D.C., region, the population of Latino Muslims is largely from Mexico and Central America, as it is in the western states. In eastern cities, including Miami, there are significant numbers of con-verts from Puerto Rico and Cuba. According to the College Board data, Latinos who chose Islam as their religion accounted for 1 percent in both 1995 and 2000, which means their number in the Muslim community is not far behind that of their Anglo-American counterparts. The College Board data also suggest that among American Indians, 2.4 percent in 1995 and 0.4 percent in 2000 were Muslim. Both figures seem too high. It is possible that some students from the country of India identified themselves as American Indian.

NEW POPULATION GROUPS

Most Muslims in North America originate in Muslim countries. According to Statistics Canada, the Canadian population in 1996 included 188,435 Arabs, 590,145 South Asians, and 137,315 Africans (of course, these groups include many Christians, Hindus, and Sikhs). To a certain extent, this distribution resembles the ethnic makeup of Muslims in the United States, except that there is a negligible number of African Americans in Canada.

The U.S. Bureau of the Census conducts a count every ten years. The ethnic ancestry information for the 2000 Census is not available yet. The 1990 Census reveals that 2,441,273 Americans traced their origins to countries and regions of the world with substantial Muslim populations (see table 2.3). This seems a severe undercount of immigrants from the Muslim world and their descendants, however. For one thing, it is only 64,000 more than the total number of immigrants, from 1820 to 1990; it should have accounted not only for the newcomers but also for generations of their offspring.

MIDDLE EASTERNERS

Many events in the Middle East throughout the twentieth century resulted in the flight of refugees to North America. World War I was fought, in part, in the region and was followed by the breakup of the Ottoman Empire and the expansion of European colonial rule in the area. Moreover, the Arab–Israeli conflict, military coups in several major countries in the 1950s, the civil war in Lebanon and the Iranian revolution all sparked waves of immigration. The Iraq–Iran war from 1980 to 1989 effected tremendous damage to both countries, exhausted the economies of the Gulf region and caused many people to seek life elsewhere. The devastation of Kuwait and Iraq in the second Gulf War of 1990–1991 and its subsequent turmoil created tens of thousands of Arab and Kurdish refugees. The violence following the cancellation of elections in Algeria in the 1992 and the suppression of hijab in Turkey at the end of the decade added new reasons for people to flee.

There are three major ethnic groups with roots in the Middle East: Arabs, Turks, and Iranians. Compared to the other ethnic groups described in this chapter, the Arabs are the most numerous in the United States, although they are not the largest ethnic group in the Muslim world as a whole. The INS admitted 587,050 Arab immigrants to the United States between 1820 and 1990. Of these, an estimated 237,359—or a minimum of 40 percent—were Muslim. The proportion changed in favor of Muslims, however, between 1991 and 1997, when an additional 149,200 immigrants were admitted. Thus of the total 736,250 Arab immigrants, an estimated 348,306—or 47 percent—are Muslim. This comparison, of course, does not account for population growth, which would make the percentage of Arab-American Christians much higher, simply because they arrived much earlier. Arabs make up about 29 percent of the total number of Muslim immigrants that have come to the United States.

Interestingly, the U.S. Bureau of the Census counted 852,412 persons of Arab ancestry in 1990, which means that this population group increased by a meager 45 percent in the 170 years since its members began arriving in the United States. These Arabs live in all states, but are concentrated in California, Michigan, New York, Illinois, and Florida. In all, 127,364 people identified their heritage as Arab. Another 725,048 people identified their ancestry by country of origin. These included Egypt, Lebanon, Syria, Palestine, Jordan, Iraq, Saudi Arabia, Yemen, Morocco, and Algeria.

Of all the Arab subgroups, the earliest U.S. immigrants came from Lebanon and Syria. Many of these people, especially Christians, came in the late 1800s

TABLE 2.3

U.S. POPULATION BY SELECTED ANCESTRIES IN THE 1990 CENSUS

Ancestry/Country of Origin	Number
Arab	127,364
Algerian	3,215
Egyptian	78,574
Iraqi	23,212
Jordanian	20,656
Lebanese	394,180
Middle Eastern	7,656
Moroccan	19,089
Palestinian	48,019
Saudi Arabian	4,486
Syrian	129,606
Yemeni	4,011
Other North African and Southwest Asian	10,670
Iranian	235,521
Turkish	83,850
Pakistani	99,974
Asian Indian	570,322
Bangladeshi	12,486
Afghan	31,301
African	245,845
Eritrean	4,270
Ethiopian	30,581
Ghanian	20,066
Kenyan	4,639
Liberian	8,797
Nigerian	91,688
Sierra Leonean	4,627
South African	17,992
Sudanese	3,623
Ugandan	2,681
Other Sub-Saharan African	20,607
Guyanese	81,665
Total	**2,441,273**

Source: U.S. Bureau of the Census, *1990 Census of Population: Ancestry of the Population in the United States*

and early 1900s and were labeled by the INS as Turks in Asia. Immigrants continued to come after the civil war in the mid-1970s and the Israeli invasion and bombardment of Lebanon since 1978. Syrian migrants also began arriving as early as 1880 and represent the second largest group of Arab Americans. Many physicians of Syrian descent live in Flint and Lansing, Michigan. More recently, Syrians fled the Ba'athist rule that took hold in the late 1960s.

Syrian and Lebanese communities are found in Dearborn, Michigan; Ross, North Dakota; and Cedar Rapids, Iowa, home of the oldest surviving mosque structures in America. Syrian Americans are found in even larger numbers in New York, California, New Jersey, and Florida. In all, Lebanese and Syrian immigrants represent the largest of all Arab subgroups, although they may not be the largest subgroup among Muslims. Most of the Syrian and Lebanese Americans are Orthodox Christian and Roman Catholic.

Another sizable Arab group is that of the Palestinian emigrants, whose home region has experienced tremendous turmoil over the past fifty years. In 1948 about 750,000 Palestinians were forced out of their homeland by Israel; in 1967 another 300,000 were displaced. Palestinian refugees who lived in Southern Lebanon were again displaced by Israel's frequent raids in that area after 1978. In addition, the 1990–1991 Gulf War ended with the departure of about 400,000 Palestinians from Kuwait. The United States and Canada, however, have not taken in Palestinian refugees; most Palestinian immigrants to North America have been students and shop owners. And anecdotal evidence suggests that most Palestinian immigrants to the United States may be Christian, even though more than 80 percent of Palestinians are Sunni Muslims.

Muslims of Palestinian ancestry have also come to the United States from Jordan. The 1990 Census recorded more Palestinians (48,019) than Jordanians (20,656) in the Arab-ancestry category. But the INS has admitted 76,200 Jordanians—and has no record of admitting any Palestinians. Because Palestine has not been recognized as a state, many Palestinian and Jordanian Americans are small-business owners, but a growing segment is composed of middle-class professionals. Today they live in pocket communities in Chicago, Illinois, Paterson and Jersey City, New Jersey, and Cleveland, Ohio.

Other substantial Arab subgroups within the U.S. population include the Egyptians, the Iraqis, and the Yemenis. Egyptian Americans are mainly Sunni Muslims, but there is a large Coptic Christian population. Most live in California, New Jersey, and New York. The Iraqis are the most diverse of all the subgroups with roots in the Arabic-speaking world. In addition to the Shia–Sunni divide, there are the Muslim–Christian and Kurdish–Arab divides. Chaldeans and other Christian Iraqis, some third-generation Americans, live side by side with their Muslim countrymen in Dearborn, Detroit, Chicago, and Los Angeles. Yemeni laborers began to arrive on U.S. shores in the 1960s. Many settled in Detroit, where they worked in auto assembly lines. Some in California, especially in Delano, have worked as farm laborers. Additionally, the 1990 Census shows small numbers of Moroccans, Saudi Arabians, and Algerians.

Iranians started coming to the United States in the 1950s, but emigration increased after the 1979 revolution. Although the INS had admitted 211,400 Iranians by 1990, the 1990 Census counted only 235,521. A large but unknown number of Iranian Muslims came before the revolution. Muslims also fled the political and economic upheavals that followed the revolution, although most of those who came were probably Zoroastrian, Armenian, Jewish, Christian, and Baha'i. The number of Iranian immigrants increased after 1990, with 89,000 people, mostly Muslim, arriving from 1991 to 1997. Now about 12 percent of all estimated Muslims of immigrant origins in the United States can trace their roots to Iran. They are especially visible in the car retail and rug businesses, but a number work in professional and managerial occupations. The largest concentrations of Iranians are found in Los Angeles, California, and Miami, Florida.

The Turkish group is the third major Middle Eastern ethnicity in the United States. Ottoman Muslims formed tiny enclaves in the Great Lakes region in the early 1900s. After World War II, most Turks migrating to the United States were sojourning students. By 1990 a total of 208,133 immigrants had arrived from contemporary Turkey and Turkey in Europe. But the 1990 Census counted only 84,000 people of Turkish descent. The huge disparity in the numbers could mean that many Turkish descendants were not counted, or that most of the early arrivals classified as Turks were not in fact Turkish. By 1997 the arrivals from Turkey totaled 223,833, and Muslims among them are estimated at 78,000, or 6 percent of the total number of all estimated Muslims. Turkish Americans are spread out across the country, with many residing in New York, California, New Jersey, and Florida and working in professional and technical positions.

SOUTH ASIANS

In the mid-1800s, harsh economic conditions led many people from the Indian subcontinent to work as indentured laborers in British sugar plantations in the Caribbean. And since the breakup of British-colonized India in 1947, the conflict over Kashmir among India, Pakistan, and the Kashmiri people has turned hundreds of thousands into refugees. The 1974 war between Pakistan and Bangladesh was another reason for many to flee the region. Most Indian immigrants, however, left for better economic opportunities in the United States and Canada. In all, Muslim immigrants hailing from the Indian subcontinent were estimated at about 194,900 by 1990, making their size on a par with their Arab counterparts. From 1991 to 1997 more Muslims of South Asian descent arrived from the Indian subcontinent and the Caribbean, raising their total to 321,443, or an estimated 29 percent of all Muslim immigrants.

The INS began to record Pakistani immigrants after 1965. Most Pakistani Americans live in California, New York, Illinois, Texas, and New Jersey. One small community of Pakistani Americans resides in Rochester, New York. The community includes physicians as well as cab drivers and mechanics. Pakistanis are ethnically diverse, the largest groups being the Punjabi and the Sindi. Other ethnic groups include the Pashtun and the Baluchi. The INS records Kashmiris as

Pakistanis or Indians, although they maintain a distinct ethnic identity. During the breakup of India, the region of Jamu and Kashmir, located between India and Pakistan, was supposed to undertake a plebiscite to determine its future. But India never allowed the vote, insisting that the state was an Indian territory. Consequently, two wars broke out between Pakistan and India over the status of the region. Kashmiri groups have fought Indian military rule seeking independence. Political turmoil rocked the region and many Kashmiris fled the ever-worsening conditions of their homeland.

South Asians also came from India, whose Muslim population is well over 130 million. Many hail from the Indian state of Gujarat and include a large number of professionals. Punjabi peasants settled on the West Coast as agricultural workers in the early decades of the twentieth century. A few of these immigrants married Mexican women and gave rise to a new group, the Punjabi Mexicans. Today they live mainly in Yuba City and San Joaquin Valley, California. Additionally, a small number of Malayalam Muslims migrated to America from Kerala, India. Indian Muslims in America are widely dispersed but live mainly in industrial and urban areas. Many of these immigrants have specialized in the hotel, real estate, retail, and wholesale trades.

Smaller numbers of South Asian Muslims came from the Caribbean and Bangladesh. The Bengalis (also called Bangladeshis), began arriving in the United States in sizable numbers after 1980. Many, seeking better economic opportunities, are coming through the immigration lottery program. A large number of Bangladeshi immigrants live in New York City. Some are taxicab drivers, while others hold white-collar occupations. Because of the high cost of living in New York, many of the recent immigrants have been moving to Detroit, Michigan. Now their number in Hamtramck rivals that of the city's Arab-origin residents. Immigrants from Guyana and Trinidad and Tobago (where Muslims of Indian descent make up 9 percent and 6 percent of the population, respectively) began arriving in the early twentieth century. Many live in Brooklyn and Queens, New York, and work in blue-collar jobs.

Other arrivals have come from Asia, including some groups whose numbers are not shown as separate categories in U.S. government records. Cham Muslims, for example, came from villages clustered in southeastern Vietnam and in central Cambodia. They fled the systematic suppression of the communists, who came to power in those countries in 1975. The United States has admitted thousands of these Asian Muslims on refugee and political asylum status. The INS classifies them as Vietnamese and Cambodian. Many Cham Americans now live in San Francisco, San Jose, Santa Ana, and Fullerton, California, and in Seattle, Washington.

The Afghans are among the latest arrivals of Muslim immigrants; they started coming in the 1980s. The Soviet invasion of Afghanistan in 1979 and the wars that followed ravaged the country and left four million refugees. INS records show that 26,600 Afghanis immigrated to the Unites States between 1981 and 1990. The 1990 Census counted about 31,000 Afghans. The Afghans have continued to arrive—between 1991 and 1997 about 13,600 Afghan immigrants were admitted. Most Afghans live in California, New York, and Virginia. Although many work in the service sector, some are professionals who fled the deteriorating economic and political conditions in their homeland.

AFRICANS

Muslims make up one-third of the inhabitants of Africa and are found in each of the continent's fifty-five nation-states. African countries never stabilized after colonial troops left the continent. Long series of coups in such countries as Nigeria, Ghana, and Uganda, accompanied by famine and drought in Ethiopia, the war between Ethiopia and Eritrea, and the civil war in Sudan, prompted many to look for a life elsewhere. Most recently, the tribal warfare in Somalia following the 1992 collapse of its communist regime left hundreds of thousands of refugees. Somali immigrants maintain a highly visible presence in Fairfax, Virginia St. Paul and Minneapolis, Minnesota, Columbus, Ohio, and Toronto, Canada.

The INS reports data on emigration from the African continent as a whole with country-specific information covering only three countries: Nigeria, Ethiopia, and South Africa. As shown in table 2.1, of the 298,419 African immigrants who arrived from 1820 to 1990, about 103,659 are estimated to be Muslims. They represent about 12 percent of all Muslim immigrants. In the 1990 Census 245,845 individuals identified their ancestry as African; others listed their countries of origin as Eritrea (4,270), Ghana (20,066), Nigeria (91,688), Ethiopia (30,581), Kenya (4,639), Liberia (8,797), Sierra Leone (91,688), Uganda (3,623), and Sudan (3,623). The largest concentration of African immigrants can be found in New York. Some sources suggest that most peddlers in New York City are African immigrants. California trails behind, followed by Texas, Florida, and Maryland.

BALKAN MUSLIMS

Balkan Muslims come from Albania, Bulgaria, and the former Yugoslavia, and represent about 3 percent of the estimated Muslim immigrant population, or about 40,645. In the former Yugoslavia, Muslims made up 19 percent of the population and lived largely in Bosnia and Kosovo. In 1908 several thousand emigrated when Austria-Hungary annexed Bosnia. In 1919 Muslims fled as the Kingdom of Serbs, Croats, and Slovenes expropriated land from Muslim landowners. Many of these Muslims settled in Chicago; others found employment in construction. In the post–World War II era, several thousand Muslims representing the entire spectrum of Bosnian society—many professional and well educated—immigrated to Chicago. Some of these early immigrants moved on to Los Angeles, California.

When an independence movement took hold in Bosnia following the 1992 collapse of communist rule in Yugoslavia, Serbian nationalists began repressive campaigns that ended in ethnic cleansing, killing an estimated quarter of a million people and displacing another million. As a result, many Bosnian Muslims came to the United States as refugees. About 32,000 immigrants came to the United States, with Chicago receiving the largest number of immigrants, followed by Detroit. Many work in low-paying, entry-level jobs because they lack English skills. Some Bosnian Muslim immigrants can be found in Cleveland, New York, San Francisco, San Jose, Santa Clara, Los Angeles, and Milwaukee.

Ethnic Albanians are the other main Balkan Muslim group. Like Bosnians, most ethnic Albanians came from the former Yugoslavia. The conflict over minority rights in Kosovo, a predominantly Muslim province, led to Serbian repression and civil war. Many refugees fled to Europe and eventually arrived on American shores. But historically, Albanians were among the first Muslims to come to America. In the early years of the twentieth century Albanian Muslims began to immigrate to the United States, primarily from Albania, an independent state. Most of these immigrants came before the communist takeover in 1944. The INS had admitted 2,232 Albanians to the United States by 1965. The early arrivals from Albania were street peddlers; more recent immigrants have included skilled laborers. About 70 percent of Albanians are estimated to be adherents of the Islamic faith, while the rest are members of the Eastern Orthodox Church. Small Albanian Muslim communities can be found in New York, Michigan, Illinois, Connecticut, and Pennsylvania.

SOCIAL PROFILE

Contrary to stereotypes that depict Muslims as foreigners sojourning in North America, most American Muslims are citizens, and many of them were born in the United States or Canada. While most Muslims are born into Muslim families, a large number are converts. The widespread perception of Muslims as black, Arab, and South Asian is not totally baseless; these are indeed the dominant ethnicities within the community. But, at the same time, the Muslim community is more diverse in terms of ethnicity. South Asians, who come from four distinct countries and represent a dozen ethnic groups, make up 25 percent of all North American Muslims. Arabs, who come mainly from about ten countries of origin, may make up 23 percent of the total. African Americans make up roughly 14 percent; Subsaharan Africans, 10 percent; Iranians, 10 percent; Turks, 6 percent; other Asians, 5 percent; Balkan Muslims, 2 percent. The remainder include Anglo Americans, Latinos, and Native Americans, among others.

Some Muslims have made it to the books of rich and famous. But these individuals are only a very small portion of the American Muslim community. While most of the early immigrants were unskilled workers, many of those who arrived after the immigration boom in the mid-1960s were highly educated professionals, including physicians and engineers. The latest arrivals from such countries as Afghanistan, Iraq, Somalia, and Bosnia have mainly been laborers. The 1990 Census, which represents the latest official data on ethnic populations, sheds some light on the social profile of ethnic groups with substantial Muslim populations. Of persons identified as Arab, about 60 percent are Native, or born in the

United States. The rest are foreign-born. (Half of them are naturalized U.S. citizens; the other half entered the country after 1980.) More than a third of the adults (twenty-five years of age or older) with Arab ancestry reported having a bachelor's or a higher college degree. Of the females in this age group, 27 percent reported having achieved this level of education. The average Arab-American household made $47,000 in 1989.

Most Iranians came to the United States after 1965—thus much of this population group is foreign-born. However, 44 percent were born in the United States or had acquired American citizenship by 1990, according to the 1990 Census. Of the Iranians older than twenty-four, those with a four-year college degree or higher represent 56 percent; of the females, 41 percent. Iranian household income in the United States averaged about $50,000 in 1989. Almost 44 percent of employed persons older than sixteen reported working in "managerial and professional specialty occupations." Almost all but a few of these were highly skilled recent immigrants.

Unlike Iranians, close to half of those of Turkish descent surveyed by the 1990 Census were born in the United States, with 70 percent of the total having acquired American citizenship. About 40 percent of all those of Turkish ancestry older than twenty-four had attained at least a bachelor's degree (35 percent among females). The average income of Turkish households in 1989 was calculated at about $52,000.

The 1990 Census did not reveal data on the social profile of most people with origins in the Indian subcontinent, except those who came from Guyana and Trinidad and Tobago. Muslims make up a very small segment of these groups, but there is no reason to believe that religion caused any disparity in income and educational levels of Indian immigrants. About 53 percent of the Guyanese and 42 percent of the Trinidadians in the United States because citizens by 1990. About 15 percent of those older than twenty-four in each group (including females) had attained higher education diplomas. In 1989 the Guyanese household income averaged $40,000; the Trinidadian, $36,000. Immigrants hailing from Pakistan, however, include many doctors and engineers.

About 65 percent of those with ancestry classified by the 1990 Census as Subsaharan African are U.S. citizens. Almost one-third of the persons older than twenty-four had attained higher education degrees (23 percent of females). The foreign-born African immigrants make up a disproportionate percentage of people with university diplomas. The average 1989 household income for this population category was calculated at $31,000.

Of the 38,361 Albanians counted by the census, 85 percent were U.S.-born or had acquired American citizenship by 1990. About 22 percent of Albanians reported the attainment of high degrees (18 percent of females). The Albanian average household income in 1989 was calculated at $45,000.

While the ancestors of some Muslims arrived in slave ships, most Muslims in North America migrated to escape war and other economic and political turmoil in their homeland. As evident in the 1990 Census, ethnic groups with substantial Muslim population have higher education levels than the nation as a whole. Very few Muslims own farms; most are city and suburban dwellers with white- and blue-collar jobs. Muslims come from all walks of life and have achieved varying standards of living. Most Muslims now live in low-to-upper-middle-class households. As the rest of this book will demonstrate, they have organized to attain the basic elements of dignified living. The next chapter explains how the establishment of places of worship has topped their priorities.

A CLOSER LOOK
HIGH-PROFILE MUSLIM AMERICANS

Through hard work many Muslim Americans have contributed to a number of occupational fields in the United States and Canada. In academia, the list of accomplished Muslims includes Farouk el-Baz in geology, Cherif al-Basyouni in international law, Ismail al-Farouqi in comparative religion, and Ali Mazrui in African history. In addition, thousands of Muslims have contributed their talents to research and practice in the fields of science and engineering. The architect who designed the Sears Tower in Chicago is local community organizer Fazlur Rahman Khan. Ahmed Zuweil, one of the world's leading experts on lasers, won the 1999 Nobel Prize in Chemistry.

Other Muslim Americans have excelled in business and technology, achieving considerable wealth and stature. Farooq Kathwari is chairman, president, and CEO of Ethan Allan, the world's largest home furnishing manufacturer. Rashid Chaudary is the founder and CEO of Raani Corporation, an international personal care manufacturing company that specializes in the production of toiletries, hair care, body lotions, body washes, antiperspirants, and baby products. Aside from being a respected businessman, Mr. Chaudary is also involved as a leader with many organizations. He is a board member of the American Refugee Committee and chairman of the Asian American Coalition of Chicago. In addition, Mr. Chaudary is a member of the Small Business Administration National Advisory Board and a member of the Democratic National Committee.

Safi Qureshey is cofounder, former CEO, and chairman emeritus of AST Research, Inc., a personal computer manufacturer. From a garage-based company in 1980, AST grew into a member of the Fortune 500 list of America's largest industrial and service companies, with more than $2.5 billion in annual revenue and operations in more than one hundred countries. With the phenomenal success of his business ventures well established, Qureshey is engaged in supporting and promoting philanthropic initiatives around the world. In May 1999 he established the Active Learning Initiatives Facility, a nonprofit organization promoting basic learning for underserved children in Pakistan, his country of origin.

A number of American Muslims have also risen to stardom in the sports world. These include the boxing legend Muhammad Ali, former boxing champion Rashid Rahman (also spelled Rochman), and basketball players Hakeem Olajuwon, Shareef Abdur-Rahim, and Mahmud Abdel Rauf.

Source: From American Muslim Databank Project.

THREE

MOSQUES AND
ISLAMIC CENTERS

Signs of Islamic religious practices in North America are centuries old. Several accounts are available about African slaves who practiced Islam in the east and south of the United States. Allan Austin's *African Muslims in Antebellum America: A Sourcebook* and Sylviane Diouf's *Servants of Allah* are replete with examples of slaves who prayed, fasted, and avoided pork. Some of these early Muslims on the continent are traced to the early days of the American republic. But the organized practice of Islam did not begin until almost a century and a half later—after slavery was abolished and immigration from non-European countries was allowed.

As the Muslim population grew in North America, the number of community organizations increased. The need for places of worship sparked the initial phase of Muslim institution-building. As soon as mosques were erected, they offered a venue for worshipers' alms giving. Soon Muslims recognized the need for religious education programs, especially for children being raised in predominantly Western Christian societies. As communities became larger and more resourceful, they expanded to provide for the general welfare of their participants.

This growth helped change the members' perception of Islamic centers from being places of worship to being service-oriented community centers. In naming their congregations, some communities use the terms *masjid* and *Jami'* or such derivatives because they appear in the Qur'an. Many local communities, however, prefer to use the word "center" rather than "mosque" in their name; others incorporate both words, signifying that they offer social, educational, and other services in addition to worship. Still other communities use the term "society" or "association" in reference to their mosque.

Muslims in North America established the first mosques in the early decades of the twentieth century. In 1915 Albanian immigrants in Maine established the first mosque community in the United States. While this prayer group remained informal and disintegrated when its founders moved, and while the physical facilities of community centers have changed rapidly, the communities of various Muslim population groups have maintained a continuous presence in the United States and Canada and have founded more stable organizations as they have grown. The oldest existing mosque community in North America was established by Arab immigrants from Syria in Cedar Rapids, Iowa.

Documenting the history of this community, Yahya Aossey, Jr. wrote in *Fifty Years of Islam in Iowa 1925–1975*,

> The Muslim immigrants in this particular area had the help of many of their Christian Arab Brothers [sic] who had immigrated before them. By the early 1920s, a small group of young men had started renting a building to serve as a temporary mosque. By 1925 they formed a group to bind themselves religiously, socially and culturally together. This was known as "The Rose of Fraternity Lodge." . . . In all they were less than twenty in number. Times were not easy for these humble but hardworking and faithful Muslims. They had no more than laid their plans for the construction of what was to be the first mosque in North America when the great depression of 1929 struck. . . . This demanded even more faith in the Almighty. They met the challenge! They started constructing the mosque even though the severe pains of the depression were already being felt. By 1934 it was completed.

Initially, the mosque was called Moslem Temple. It administered prayers, Arabic classes, and social activities. In 1949, the community dedicated the Muslim National Cemetery, which was the first Islamic graveyard in America, thanks to a generous donation by the Aosseys, who set aside six and one-half acres for the project. In 1972, the community completed its current mosque structure and renamed the organization Islamic Center and Mosque. The original structure, located at 1335 Ninth Street N.W. and nicknamed Mother Mosque, has been designated a historic landmark by the state of Iowa.

In Canada the first mosque, al-Rashid Mosque, was built in Edmonton, Alberta. Erected in 1938, it served the mushrooming Muslim population of the city. But the community outgrew its small size of thirty-by-fifty feet and in 1988 built a much larger structure. The old facility was nearly demolished for a parking lot before local Muslims fought city hall—and a local community that was, at times, overtly bigoted—to have the mosque declared a heritage building and moved into the Fort Edmonton Park historic site.

The development of local congregations has followed a typical pattern. These communities often start informally as prayer groups. Worshipers are hosted by members of the community. Sometimes prayer groups begin with Muslim foreign students whose schools provide them with places for meetings. Some students return home after graduation; others take job offers and settle. These burgeoning groups begin raising funds to rent facilities that are devoted to the activities of their emerging communities. As they continue to grow and add affluent members to their ranks, these congregations usually become resourceful enough to build their own places of worship.

The number of mosques in the United States increased sharply after the mid-1960s with the influx of Muslim immigrants. There are now more than 1,100 mosques located in every state of the American union, except Vermont.

Canadian mosques exceed 150 and are found in most provinces. The largest number of mosques can be found in California, New York, Texas, New Jersey, Illinois, Ohio, Pennsylvania, Michigan, Florida, and Ontario, Canada, where roughly 75 percent of North American Muslims reside. Most mosques have been built in urban centers, with large numbers in New York City, Newark, Philadelphia, Detroit, Cleveland, Chicago, Houston, Los Angeles, and Toronto.

Mosques are established through local initiatives and fundraising efforts. As shall be discussed in chapter 5, regional and national community development groups have ofen spearheaded mosque building projects. Gulf merchants, many of whom have studied and done business in the United States, made substantial donations toward the construction of some multimillion dollar mosques in the United States and Canada. Some of these mosques are in major capitals where embassies and consulates serve the national and diplomatic contingencies from Muslim countries. Some mosques in North America, still in their formative years, organize services from rental spaces, but hundreds of others are well established in owned facilities.

Sometimes local resistance to a new mosque is a factor in the Muslim community's choice of location and structure. As Kathleen Moore indicates in *Al-Mughtaribun: American Law and the Transformation of Muslim Life in the United States*, community decisions in some regions are shaped both by the restrictions of local building codes and by the apprehensiveness of local officials about the political cost of approving an Islamic presence. As a result, it is not unusual to find large mosques built in low-income residential areas or industrial zones.

Traditionally, Muslims prefer mosque structures with classical Islamic architectural designs. But other considerations frequently trump such preferences. Most communities have found the cost of building domes and minarets prohibitive. It is common for small or low-income Muslim communities to buy houses, churches, or other public buildings (such as warehouses, schools, and government facilities) to convert into Islamic centers. Some large and affluent communities would rather expand facilities and programs than invest in marvelous landmarks. Without building signs, most Islamic centers would be indistinguishable from their surroundings.

DEVOTIONAL ACTIVITIES

The main function of a mosque is as a location for the offering of the five daily prayers and the weekly Friday services, all of which are usually attended by men, women, teens, and children. Because the Muslim prayer schedule covers both day and night, many mosques are open from the early morning hours until late in the evening. This is especially true during Ramadan when special prayers are offered nightly. Many mosques close between services. While there are some mega-mosques, with thousands of regular worshipers, most centers are small.

Muslim religious practice in North America is almost identical to that in the rest of the world. In many Shia communities, some aspects of devotional activities that changed in Iran after the revolution were unaffected in many mosques in the United States and Canada because the formation of these mosques predated the revolution. For example, while in post-revolutionary Iran Shia mosques hold prayers in congregation, mosques in the United States and Canada follow the classical Shia position that the practice should be deferred until the return of Imam al-Mahdi.

Aside from prayer rituals, mosques are centers of learning. Some mosques offer full-time schools and day care as part of their services. Not surprisingly, whether a full-time school exists is strongly related to the size of the local community and its social profile. Suburban mosques whose membership includes a significant number of professionals are more likely to establish full-time schools than those in inner cities with membership drawn from blue-collar workers and small shop owners. Chapter 4 examines this finding in greater detail.

Religious education programs are found in almost all mosques. Teaching the faith to others comes under the general Muslim concept of *da'wa*, which means invite or call. A verse from the Qur'an reads, "Call to the path of your Lord with wisdom and good advice." Different Islamic call programs are found in mosques, but contrary to the mythical view of Islamic call as a missionary-like effort aimed at converting nonbelievers, most often Muslims preach to co-religionists. Even small centers offer weekend classes for children and religious discussion groups for adults. Sufi mosques offer weekly sessions of *dhikr* (remembrance of God), which usually include chanting the attributes of God.

Qur'an memorization is a favorite program in most mosques, because recitations from the Qur'an are part of the daily Muslim prayers. Along with Qur'anic studies comes the teaching of Arabic, the language of the Qur'an. Children are taught the basics of the language so that they can read the scriptures. The Prophet Muhammad said that Muslims are rewarded for every letter they read. Adults may also attend religious classes on the weekends. Other forms of Islamic call are less formal; *imams* and community members may give short talks after prayers, usually offering reflections on those verses of the Qur'an recited during prayer. These talks are of particular interest to worshipers without skills in classical Arabic. Also, weekly discussion groups are held in many mosques, offering a more interactive way of reflection on the meaning of the Qur'an and Hadith in the contemporary context.

Another type of call activity targets Muslims who do not practice the faith. A few dozen local groups in North America have been established for the purpose of distributing Islamic literature. Another more intense method is evident in the work of the *Tablighi Jamaa't* (Islamic Call Group). Members of the handful of mosques affiliated with the movement, often including visitors from overseas, go to homes and ask to address their hosts—similar to the method employed by American Mormon missionaries. Sometimes the preachers are turned away; other times they return with new worshipers. Most mosques, however, do not support the *Tablighi* approach—many Muslims believe it to be too intrusive and often counterproductive.

Instead, some mosque volunteers distribute educational pamphlets at ethnic stores and on street corners in neighborhoods with a visible Muslim presence. This material is handed out to Muslims who do not show up at mosques and to pedestrian non-Muslims. Sulayman Nyang noted in *Islam in the United States of America* that some of the immigrants who did not practice Islam in their country of origin rediscovered their faith after they arrived in the United States and Canada. Yet mosques do not offer special programs to these born-again Muslims. Because they were born Muslim, they are expected to blend in with the rest of the congregation and benefit equally from its educational programs. Little if any data are available about the impact of regular classes on this type of mosque participants.

Another form of Islamic call is directed to non-Muslims. Mosques with sufficient resources to hire instructors hold special classes for new Muslims. A 2000 survey of 416 U.S. mosques by Ihsan Bagby et al., *The Mosque in America: A National Portrait*, found conversion to Islam averages one per month per mosque. Most converts go to a mosque after they have made an initial study of the faith and decided to seriously consider accepting Islam. Mosque teachers hold sessions to answer their questions and, once converts declare *shahadah*, instruct them on the requirements of religious practices.

Some converts become regular participants in mosque activities; others frequent mosques only on occasions. Thus some mosques, especially those in African-American neighborhoods, have instituted support groups for new Muslims. The activities of the groups are designed to allow an informal atmosphere in which education can be more effective than the lecture format. The groups also offer emotional and social support for persons who usually change their lifestyles along with their creed.

Another form of Islamic call activities is prison outreach. Much like the work of preachers with Christian prison ministries, mosque activists take copies of the Qur'an and other material obtained from Muslim publishers and public affairs groups for distribution to inmates. They also volunteer to offer religious instruction to converts. Outside mosques a few groups have emerged for the purpose of providing counseling and religious literature to Muslim converts in prison. According to the Federal Bureau of Prisons, about 5 percent of federal prison inmates are Muslim—an estimated 85 percent of these converted to the faith after incarceration. Many of these converts have become community activists after their release.

Commemoration of Muslim religious occasions is an important part of the mission of mosques. The holy days draw not only the regular participants but also many ethnically inclined Muslims, who see such occasions as times of reflection on their own spirituality and religious identity. These special days not only include *Eid* and *Ashura*, but also *Lailatul Qadr*, or Night of Power in Ramadan, which commemorates the beginning of the Qur'anic revelation. Worshipers flock to mosques in large numbers, many praying all night. Other occasions include *Al-Isra' wal-Mi'raj*, the Night Journey and the Ascension, which commemorates the Prophet's miraculous journey from Mecca to Jerusalem and his ascension to the heavens. This event is mentioned in the Qur'an and is believed to have taken place in Rajab (the seventh month of the Muslim calendar).

Islamic centers also provide funeral and burial services. Large congregations often establish their own cemetery and funeral facilities. Other centers make such services available through partnerships with specialized local providers. For example, the Islamic Foundation in Columbus, Ohio, arranges for washing, shrouding, and *janaza* (prayer for the deceased), leaving community members to choose their own funeral home or cemetery. The foundation estimates the cost of these services can range from $3,000 to $3,850 per person. Because of such a considerable price tag, some centers must restrict these benefits. The Islamic Society of Greater Kansas City, for instance, owns a cemetery but offers burial space only to its members and those of an affiliated center. While the primary goal is to meet the demands of religious practices, mosques offer facilities and programs on the basis of expected revenues. When such revenues fall short, mosques must charge for their services.

SOCIAL ACTIVITIES AND OUTREACH

Although Mosques function mainly as places of worship, they have increasingly serve as community centers. Some mosques offer parenting and marriage counseling classes. They also provide mentoring and sports activities for children and young members. Some communities, such as the Islamic Center of Toledo, have formed soccer and basketball teams that compete in local tournaments. Summer youth camps and schools are also becoming popular programs in Islamic centers, although they are seldom offered free of charge.

Mosques are also hubs of activity for women, who usually form auxiliary committees running programs for mosque participants in general. Women's committees organize speaking events and discussion groups focusing on women's concerns. They also teach children the value of volunteerism and supporting one's mosque through a variety of fund-raising activities, including bake sales. Mosques with adequate facilities have offered fitness programs for women. Others have arranged for all-female sports events, such as swimming, in outdoor facilities.

Social events such as picnics and potluck dinners have become commonplace in many mosques. Communities with inadequate facilities hold them in public parks and rental halls. These events offer families and young people opportunities to meet informally in a community setting. Sometimes acquaintances initiated in such gatherings lead to eventual marriage proposals. Weddings increasingly take place in Islamic centers. Prophetic tradition supports a community-wide celebration on such joyous occasions. Such activity also brings much-needed revenue to the centers and usually saves the newlyweds the cost of renting expensive commercial halls.

Community fairs are usually held at Islamic centers with adequate space. These functions include merchandise booths for adults and entertaining shows for young people. Ethnic foods, clothing, crafts, and religious items exhibited by local religious and ethnic shops and civic organizations can be found. Such activities have also attracted non-Muslim neighbors, who buy items on sale and receive educational literature. Similar events are often lacking in small communities. In a few cases, leaders reason that Muslims should keep to themselves, but such self-imposed isolation results from an inward-looking style of leadership, or—in the case of recent immigrant *imams*—lack of confidence in their English language skills.

While many Mosques advise their members to look for welfare benefits from specialized social-service agencies, some centers provide such assistance. Community funds rest on alms and other charitable donations, but such contributions frequently fall short in the face of growing need. As a result, some communities welcome other private and public funding. The beneficiaries of these social programs are no longer limited to mosque participants. This new trend is emerging as Islamic centers are founding social-assistance offices.

The services offered by a mosque depend on the kind of talent offered by its participants. Some centers with highly skilled members conduct job training in specialized fields. Al-Sadiq Mosque in Pomona, California, has offered computer literacy classes. And because of the abundance of ethnic language speakers among mosque participants, some centers, such as the Islamic Education Center in Potomac, Maryland, have offered Urdu and Farsi in addition to Arabic classes. Some of the instructors are professionals who charge fees. In congregations with members in the medical profession, health awareness lectures are offered periodically.

Some centers increasingly target low-income people. They offer food pantries and soup kitchens, especially during Ramadan. Other centers collect food and clothes for distribution or donation to food banks and homeless shelters. Mobile units of the Red Cross visit mosques during community blood drives. Few centers even offer medical services to patients without health insurance. In a number of cases, these programs have become independent clinics tied to grants from public health sources. These include Crescent Clinic, which grew out of the Islamic Society of Greater Kansas City, and al-Shifa Clinic, which began in a small room in the V Mosque in Sacramento, California.

In some African-American neighborhoods, teens of various religious backgrounds frequent Islamic centers with their Muslim friends, taking advantage of the centers' tutoring, sports, exercise, and other activities. Some inner-city mosques have led their local communities in the fight against crime and drug abuse. Masjid al-Taqwa in Brooklyn, New York, and the West End Mosque in Atlanta, Georgia, are especially known for this sort of social activism. These efforts usually involve group marches with anticrime, antidrug messages as well as the distribution of literature. In Wilmington, Delaware, local Muslim activists used firm tactics against drug dealers around their mosque. In October 1999 members of the North American Islamic Foundation confronted young men using drugs outside the foundation's center. In most other centers emphasis is given to rehabilitation through counseling.

Marriage counseling is among the most popular services. Masjid Al-Islam in Washington, D.C., reports that the mosque's *imam* attends to one case of counseling each week. Neighborhood women, in particular, come to ask for intervention in cases of alcohol and domestic abuse. The mosque, which opened in 1996, accommodates two hundred Friday worshipers, about 25 percent of whom are recent converts. Community leaders believe that neighbors see converts as having undergone a process of change into a functioning family-centered social order. Those who accept Islam can restructure their lives around spouses and jobs and sometimes immediately stop going to bars and nightclubs. Community leaders believe the appeal of this personal transformation usually outweighs the impact of educational literature in individual decisions about conversion. Studies on the sociology of conversion, however, are still lacking.

As evident in the Islamic call activities, Muslims look at others as potential converts to the faith. Beyond that, Muslims share a social existence with neighbors and fellow citizens. Contact with others at the local community level is becoming commonplace, regardless of the size or affluence of the congregation. Most mosques are located in neighborhoods that are not predominantly Muslim. In addition, many students from area schools and colleges routinely visit mosques. Islamic centers also offer conference facilities, often hosting town meetings with elected officials and political candidates. Political activists regularly hold voter registration drives at mosques, with candidates to public office distributing election campaign literature.

Thus many centers engage non-Muslim persons and organizations at their localities. Some of the earliest contacts took place as neighboring churches allowed Muslims to use their parking facilities—particularly during high-traffic times on Friday afternoons and Ramadan nights. Some mosques have the resources to establish public relations offices, which provide media outlets and civic groups with information about the community and its events.

The September 11, 2001, attacks on New York City and Washington, D.C., were followed by a sharp rise in anti-Muslim hate crimes in the United States and Canada. When several mosques closed down in fear of threats and attacks, members of neighboring houses of worship in several counties held night vigils at mosques and offered to form watch groups to ensure security during prayer services. These dramatic events were also followed by a surge of public interest in learning about Islam and Muslims. Islamic centers holding "Open Mosque" activities swelled with visitors. To the surprise of Muslims, most of the people who showed up were ordinary citizens who talked candidly, asked questions about Islam, or expressed sympathy. For many attendees, this was the first time they entered a mosque.

Some mosques periodically conduct activities designed to invite neighbors. The Islamic Association of North Texas in Dallas, Texas, a mosque of about one thousand regular worshipers on Fridays used to attract about two hundred people on such events prior to September 11; their September 23 and October 14, 2001, events were attended by two thousand and sixteen-hundred prople, respectively. Centers that did not have an experience in such activities also drew large crowds. For example, the turnout was over one thousand attendees at the Islamic Center of the South Bay, Los Angeles, on September 16, 2001. Lower turnout was reported in towns with small Muslim populations. But even in places like

Masjid Al-Noor in Coachella, California, where the Muslim presence is hardly noticeable, the twelve people who showed up (twice the size of Muslims who attend daily prayers) represented a welcome surprise to local Muslims. Thus even in the face of tragedy, for many Muslim congregations September 11 may turn out to be the day in which their community became part of the local civic life in North America.

Some of the well-established Muslim communities had already been represented in interfaith councils. In some regions contacts between mosque leaders and others have reached a point in which mosque leaders have joined forces with other faith groups in order to defend shared values. For example, in October 1998 the Islamic Center of Long Island, one of the largest Muslim communities in New York, joined the Catholic League for Religious and Civil Rights and other local Christian congregations to protest *Corpus Christi*, a play that depicted a Jesus-like figure engaging in sexual acts with his disciples. The protest did not suggest a ban on the play, but it did assert that the denigration of religious values must be challenged.

LEADERSHIP

Because of the varied and increasing number of services provided by Islamic centers, Muslims increasingly see the centers not only as sacred spaces but as focal points of local social activism. While some mosques are registered as places of worship, others are chartered under laws regulating the operation of nonprofit organizations. As private entities, these centers answer to their own boards. Local community leadership typically includes boards of directors or trustees, usually including the founding members, executive officers, and *imams*. While *imam* is a gender-specific job, other mosque leadership positions are not. In most mosques women are allowed to serve on the board of directors, although this actually occurs in only a small number of communities. In addition to the directors and hired staff, most activities in Islamic centers are planned and supervised through volunteer committees, whose level of commitment usually determines the vibrancy of mosque life.

The general public does not make a distinction between mosques—all are Muslim houses of worship. Mosque leaders generally do not seek to publicize their particular orientation. To Muslims the variations are obvious in many ways. Large mosques and those with upper-middle-class participants may have full-time *imams*, usually graduates of Islamic studies programs from one of the Muslim world's colleges of religious learning. These colleges include Al-Azhar University in Cairo, Egypt, the Muslim world's oldest center of religious learning, and a number of Islamic studies colleges in Medina, Mecca, and Riyadh, Saudi Arabia. There are also schools in Shia centers in Qom, Iran, and Najaf, Iraq. Many other *imams* are self-taught, although some have obtained degrees in Islamic studies from American colleges.

The majority of congregations are not very large and usually do not have full-time *imams*; some hire part-time employees for the job. Communities that cannot afford to hire an *imam* usually assign these duties to the most learned mosque member willing to volunteer his time. These men generally earn their living through employment in other fields. In the management of a mosque's other functions, it usually develops a volunteer committee system to oversee its activities. When jobs require highly skilled persons, boards usually contract professionals.

After the mid-1970s oil boom, Saudi Arabia gained wealth and prominence in the Muslim world. A number of Sunni Islamic call organizations such as the Mecca-based Muslim World League have sponsored *imams* in the emerging mosques in North America. Some Shia *imams* serving in the U.S. and Canadian mosques are appointed by their *marji's* in Iran—an exercise of authority not very different from that of the relationship between the Vatican and the world's Catholic clergy. Also, several Sufi *imams* are commissioned by their overseas teachers, who could be either Shia or Sunni.

World political events have contributed to the rise of Shia–Sunni awareness in local congregations. As Abdul Aziz Sachedina noted in *The Case of the Shia in North America*, the Iranian revolution contributed to the awakening of religious sentiment in the Muslim world. But the political dynamics that followed witnessed a competition between Iran and Saudi Arabia for the hearts and minds of Muslims in North America. Supporters of both sides sent literature and speakers to Islamic centers. The debates associated with that period in mosque discussion groups faded away but left many Muslims with an increased awareness of similarities and differences between Shias and Sunnis.

Some mosques adopted the belief that it is better for all if the two groups maintain separate places of worship. Few would not even accept members of the other group. Masjid Annur in Sacramento, California, for example, requires that members be Sunni. Still, only a few *imams* follow a certain school of Sunni Islamic jurisprudence. Madina Masjid in Toronto, Ontario, is one of a small number of mosques whose *imams* follow the Hanafi school. Other Hanafi centers are located in Buffalo, New York, and Springfield, Virginia—all dominated by Muslims from South Asian ancestry.

Most Shia mosques in North America follow the Twelvers branch of Shia thought. Because of their small numbers in an already minority-faith community, Shia Muslims usually join Sunni mosques when they lack their own center. As Yvonne Haddad and Jane Smith observed in *Muslim Communities in North America*, when the numbers of people who share a particular orientation grew, the propensity to establish separate centers increased. In this regard, the Shia Muslims are no exception. Abdo El-kholy in *The Arab Moslems in the United States* and Linda Walbridge, in *Without Forgetting the Imam*, traced this tendency in the Shia community to 1949, thirty years before the Iranian revolution, when the first Shia mosques in the United States began to form in Dearborn, Michigan. Although the various mosques are distinct in ritual and other devotional activities, they usually hold similar social and outreach functions.

As for African Americans, a Hanafi center was established in Washington, D.C., in the 1960s, but it failed to attract a following and is now defunct. Most

African-American mosques use Sunni literature in their education, but their leaders publicly resent sectarian labels. Many *imams* in these mosques believe Muslims should distance themselves from the divisive political meanings usually attached to these group categories, especially at times of crisis. Yet in some mosques in which the *imams* graduated from the Islamic University of Medina, Saudi Arabia, the Sunni character is emphasized.

In mosques in which African-American or Shia Muslims are the majority, the *imam* is usually the established leader of the center. In many African-American mosques the *imam* is elected by mosque members and makes the final decisions about mosque programs. In most other Sunni mosques *imams* wield considerable influence, especially in directing devotional and educational activities. But ultimate authority rests with the boards of directors, which sometimes include *imams*. Officials of Islamic centers usually form consultation councils (*shura*) that set policies and priorities. Communication between mosque participants and board members is usually highly personal, especially in small communities. Large mosques often publish newsletters featuring board decisions and community news and events. Bulletin boards also are widely used for community announcements and other postings.

CONFLICT AND CHANGE

Mosque community dynamics often reflect the ethnic makeup of congregations. Most Muslims gravitate to mosques frequented by members of their own ethnicity or national origin. As a result, in most mosques the majority of participants come from a single ethnic background. But centers that draw members exclusively from one ethnic group represent only 10 percent of all U.S. mosques, according to *The Mosque in America: A National Portrait*. These mosques are located in all-African-American neighborhoods. Other patterns of ethnic distribution among the mosqued communities exist. Many mosques do not have a majority ethnic group in the congregation. Often board members come from the dominant ethnic group in a given center, but this is not uniformly the case. Therefore, the pluralism in the structure of mosque communities is manifest not only in the ethnic characteristics of individual Islamic centers but also in their leadership patterns and religious orientations. But, as Tamara Sonn accurately observed in *Diversity in Rochester's Islamic Community*, ethnic differences do not seem to be problematic in themselves.

Often the need for recent immigrants to communicate in their native languages explains the emergence of ethnic majorities in congregations. In some communities of recent immigrants there are not enough people from any single ethnic group to establish a mosque. People come together for a higher purpose despite language barriers. Their interactions, however, are usually conducted in English, which is the common language among them. Still, many have not mastered the language, sometimes resulting in misunderstanding and friction. Miscommunication is less likely to occur in mosques, whose participants include a significant number of English-fluent professionals. In these centers, leadership dynamics tend to be more interactive. The increasing proportion of North American Muslims whose first language is English has drawn more mosques toward all-English communication. Now English is increasingly prevalent during Friday sermons and social activities of Islamic centers.

The uncertainty inherent in a volunteer-based management has often given rise to disagreements about program priorities and policies. Teaching of the Arabic language has been debated and friction has ensued when its introduction was perceived as an attempt at ethnic domination by Arab members. At the Islamic Association of Raleigh, North Carolina, a center that was established in 1985 by Arabs and Pakistanis, Arab parents disagreed with a proposed mosque plan to deliver religious instruction at the Sunday school in English. The Arab parents insisted that all instruction must be conducted in Arabic. When mosque officials refused, parents started their own weekend school program outside the center.

But the appeal of all-Arabic instruction in religious education is not limited to Arab members. Proponents from different ancestries fear that future generations of Muslims in North America may lose the ability to even read the Qur'an should the next generation become unable to understand it in its own language. This rationale is so compelling that a number of mosques are instituting evening and Saturday Qur'anic Arabic classes in addition to the Sunday program. Disagreements, previously argued in ethnic terms, are now being solved through program diversification.

Mosques generally welcome new participants—much more so than congregations of other faith groups, according to the 2001 Hartford Seminary's report *Faith Communities Today*. Because of the continuing immigration, conversion, and mobility of Muslim people, the demographic composition of mosques continues to change. The constant need to absorb new participants is naturally ripe with tension, as comers who do not belong to the dominant groups often feel marginalized in decisions about activities and use of the center's facilities. These members may reduce their affiliation to participation in prayer services only. Sometimes dissatisfied members leave the mosque to form a new center. Such splits are often viewed as a realistic method of resolving irreconcilable differences.

Another means to deal with friction has been the growing tendency to formalize the relationship between mosques and their membership. Even though mosques welcome anyone to worship and take part in other activities, they are trying to instill a sense of responsibility among those interested in having a voice in decision making. These individuals must become members and pay dues, which are usually scaled according to income and may range from $10 to $50. Mosque officials hold periodic meetings with mosque participants to discuss their concerns. In some centers officers are elected by the membership.

An example of the trend toward formalizing the membership can be found in the Islamic Community of Bryan/College Station (ICBCS). The community was started by members of the Muslim Student Association at Texas A&M University in 1987 and operated in a rented space until the 1995 opening of a new two-story structure. ICBCS now consists of students and school faculty members and employees. Anyone can become a regular member by agreeing to respect the bylaws of the organization and by paying membership dues. A voting member, however, must agree to volunteer time in community functions.

Such changes did not come overnight or without cost. The trend toward institutionalization followed episodes of open confrontations over matters of authority and leadership. In a few cases, irreconcilable differences ended up in court. One of the most highly publicized instances is the case of Darul Islah in Tenec, New Jersey. The center's leadership was shared informally by a group of Pakistani and Hyderabadi–Indian descent Muslims since opening in 1986. In 1992 an altercation broke out between members of the two groups over leadership, splitting the congregation on national origin lines. The court ordered local authorities to supervise an election to determine legitimate leadership.

Notwithstanding the developmental challenges faced by local communities, Islamic centers link members to other religious and civic organizations, public and private social service agencies, and law enforcement authorities. The rise of Muslim multi-ethnic consciousness among the faithful in America has drawn many mosque leaders toward membership in national Muslim community organizations. Chief among these groups are the Ministry of Imam W. D. Mohammed and the Islamic Society of North America. The Ministry of Imam W. D. Mohammed represents mosques that are attended mainly by African Americans who converted to mainline Islam in 1975. The Islamic Society of North America is mainly composed of mosques that cater mostly to Arab and South Asian descent Sunni Muslims.

Nevertheless, a large number of Islamic centers do not maintain affiliation with national organizations. Local leaders today measure their interactions with other Muslims based on questions of purpose and effectiveness. This pragmatic tendency is leading local communities to think outside old boundaries—and even beyond national borders. The Muslim community in Windsor, Canada, for example, is drawn by social and economic ties to the large population of Muslims in Detroit and southeast Michigan. The Windsor Islamic Association, the main mosque in the city, decides on *Eid* celebrations after consultation with the Muslims of Michigan, not with those in other cities and provinces in Canada. Although many mosques are not formally affiliated with other organizations, they do work increasingly together under regional umbrella councils and have forged connections to various national groups. Chapter 5 sheds more light on this emerging trend. Locally, Muslim communities still struggle with educating young Muslims. Many congregations have pooled resources to develop institutional responses to this situation.

A CLOSER LOOK
SERVICES OFFERED BY IMAM AL-KHOEI FOUNDATION OF NEW YORK

- Full-time accredited Al-Iman elementary, junior high, and high school, from kindergarten to grade 12.

- Al-Iman Saturday school for religious education and Arabic language.

- Imam Al-Khoei Library, which provides services by trained personnel who
  - help in Islamic research and advancement of knowledge;
  - distribute Islamic literature to seekers of knowledge and to correctional facilities at no charge;
  - sell books, video, and audiocassettes, CD-ROMs, Islamic gift items, Islamic hijab, and more.

- Special religious ceremonies year round, including
  - month-long Ramadan programs (breaking-of-fast and *Dua'*;
  - *Eid-al-Fitr* and *Eid-al-Adha* congregational prayers;
  - *Ashura Majalis* in Muharram in Urdu, Arabic, Persian, and English;
  - celebrations of the birth and commemoration of the martyrdom of the Prophet and his *Ahlul Bayt* (People of the House), and such other occasions.

- Monthly newsletter, *Al-Huda*, in English and Arabic.

- Information on the sighting of the moon and prayer timetables.

- Wedding ceremonies, marriage counseling, and divorce procedures.

- Resolving family and communal disputes.

- Collecting religious dues (*khums*, *zakat*, *fitra*, and *sadaqhah*) and delivering them to the rightful recipients.

- Performing ceremonial baths and funeral services for deceased Muslims.

- Aid to Muslim refugees.

- Providing basic medical advice for community members at Imam Al-Ridha Medical Clinic.

- Facilitating *Zabiha* program and *Qurbani* programs.

- Responding to religious questions over the phone, mail, and the Internet.

Source: From www.al-koei-org.

FOUR

ISLAMIC
SCHOOLS

Muslim children make up a growing segment of the student population in North America. Private education is too expensive for most Muslim families, so the public school system has become the default choice for most. Nevertheless, public education has posed challenges to Muslim children and their parents. Although school curricula have become increasingly sensitive to diversity, this inclusiveness has not been extended to Muslims in many school districts. Many textbooks and teachers' lectures depict Islam and Muslims in grossly distorted ways. Muslims, like members of some other religious minorities, have had a difficult time persuading schools to accommodate their religious practices. Many girls have faced harassment for wearing a headscarf or for refusing—because of Islamic teachings regarding modesty—to wear T-shirts and shorts for gym classes.

Still, some Muslims believe public education offers the best chance for their children to socialize with their future coworkers, neighbors, and fellow citizens. Some also believe that the school experience will allow others to learn about Muslims firsthand—a process they see as crucial for Muslim integration into North American society. Muslim leaders encourage parents of public school children to participate more effectively in parent–teacher associations and school boards so that they may influence curriculum decisions and local regulations regarding religious accommodation.

The Council on Islamic Education in Fountain Valley, California, was established in 1990 to stimulate Muslim involvement in public school textbook hearings. The council formed a panel of education consultants to advise publishers of social studies and world history textbooks on their treatment of Islam. The organization has developed instructional materials on Islam and Muslims for use in public and private schools. The council also conducts workshops on Islamic history for social studies teachers. In conjunction with the First Amendment Center in Nashville, Tennessee, the council has recently developed guidelines for teaching about world religions in public schools. Other groups, including the Arab World and Islamic Resources and School Services, have developed social studies material focusing on Arab and Muslim history and culture.

The plight of Muslims in public education is so deeply felt that in one case in Toronto it became a hot political issue for Muslims. The Toronto District Muslim Education Assembly (TDMEA) was established in the mid-1990s to work with the Toronto District School Board and to address the general and particular concerns and needs of Muslim children. TDMEA noted that in the near future Muslim children will make up 20 percent of the school district's student population. They have also noted that Muslims lack representation on the school board's committees and the teaching and administrative staff of local schools. The group has established a website to inform community members about school regulations and have taken an active role in opposing what they considered a promotion of homosexual lifestyle by the school district.

The president of TDMEA stood before a Taric mosque audience in October 2000 and outlined the challenges before Muslims in public education. He concluded by urging Muslims to become more politically involved in municipal elections. Specifically, he urged Muslims to field candidates for school trustee positions. He also suggested that Muslims should support candidates who share similar values. He advised Muslim parents to participate in school councils and even to organize rallies to make administrators and officials pay attention to the concerns of Muslim parents.

Still, many parents are worried about fundamental problems with public education, including safety. In response, leaders in a number of Muslim communities have taken it upon themselves to set up Islamic schools, arguing that establishing Muslim schools should even be more important than building mosques. They believe that if the next generation of Muslims loses its attachment to religious values, there will be little use for the places of worship. Nizam Peerwani, a physician and director at Al-Hedayah Academy in Fort Worth, Texas, writes on the school's website:

> [F]or Islam to survive into the next century, Muslims in North America must take the challenge of building full-time Islamic schools seriously. . . . This is because it is very difficult for Muslim children attending public schools, where the curriculum is structured to promote both materialistic and secular values, not to be adversely influenced. And it is also natural for Muslim children attending such schools (with few exceptions) to experiment with alcohol, drugs, and pre-marital sex, despite the prevalence of strong Islamic value systems in their home environment.

FULL-TIME PRIVATE SCHOOLS

In some Muslim communities in North America, the focus on building Islamic schools almost immediately followed the establishment of Islamic centers. The number of full-time Islamic elementary and high schools in North America has risen steadily and in 2001 reached more than 200, of which 170 are located in the United States. Two dozen schools are located in California, while New York has twenty. The rest are dispersed throughout the country, with substantial numbers in Michigan, Illinois, New Jersey, Pennsylvania, and Florida. The cities with the largest number of Islamic schools are Houston and Philadelphia, each with seven, while Dearborn has four. Most Islamic schools have been established in the past decade, so the drive in favor of Muslim community education may have not yet have reached its peak. Each school serves an average of 150 students, for an estimated total of 30,000.

Some Muslims believe that the process of building Islamic schools has been too slow. Sometimes when a group starts a school in a densely populated Muslim community, the majority of parents in the community hesitate to enroll their children. Only when people realize that the school offers a stable educational environment do they begin to join in large numbers. Once neighboring communities become familiar with the school and have a model to follow, they often start planning their own schools. In the Toronto area, for example, Muslims began the Islamic Community School project in the early 1980s; now there are ten such schools in the area.

The Brighter Horizon School of Baton Rouge, Louisiana, is another successful Islamic school that has grown up from humble beginnings. Muslim community members started the school in 1994 in a small space in the back of the Islamic Center of Baton Rouge. In 1996 the Muslim community had raised enough funds to purchase the current school building, which includes eight classrooms, science and computer labs, a library, three lunch rooms, a general assembly room, two offices, and a small nursery. In its opening year, the school registered twelve students. By 1998 the number of students had grown to forty students enrolled in preschool through fifth grade. The 2001 enrollment jumped to seventy and the program was expanded to include students up to ninth grade.

Many Islamic schools stress the concept of Islamic identity in their mission statements and bylaws. This usually means acquainting students with the Islamic sources of knowledge and teaching them Islamic ethical values. In addition, Islamic schools conform to *halal* dietary standards and schedule classes and other school activities around the requirements of daily prayers, Ramadan, and other significant holidays.

Islamic schools also place an equally significant emphasis on the quality of their reading, math, and science programs. The initiatives of these schools may define high academic standards in terms of class size or special programs, such as technology courses. Some parents choose private Islamic schools for other reasons. In the view of some parents, for example, Islamic schools offer girls an education in a protected environment. For this reason, the enrollment of girls in some Islamic schools is higher than that of boys.

Parents who send their children to Islamic schools seek to ensure that their children are not only aware of their Muslim identity, but are also able to compete for jobs and college seats after graduation. The schools demonstrate sensitivity to such desire by participating in national and state standardized tests. Islamic schools typically utilize textbooks produced by such publishers as Scholastic, McGraw-Hill and Houghton Mifflin, whose material is widely used in public and private school systems. For social studies, Islamic schools usually select books that highlight the multicultural nature of the United States and Canada, so that children can develop their own sense of belonging to the larger society. In addition, the schools usually require readings of Islamic history. Muslim community publishers, such as Iqra International Education Foundation in Chicago, Illinois, offer Arabic and Islamic studies textbooks designed to reflect the diversity of the Muslim community and the particular sociopolitical environment in North America. However, a few schools with some ethnic bent still use language and religious textbooks from their countries of origin.

A growing number of schools distinguish between religion and history. Religion is presented in terms of beliefs, practices, and moral conduct. History is presented as events involving people. Increasingly, students of Islamic schools are exposed to textbooks that cover various times and places of the globe (as opposed to a selective focus on North America and the Muslim world). Students are also encouraged to appreciate diversity in Muslim life. For example, in Miraj Islamic School in Staten Island, New York, social studies curriculum requires students to compare the existing ethnic traditions associated with the observation of Ramadan and celebration of *Eid*. In addition, students are required to discuss material dealing with the various American holidays.

Most Islamic schools do not stress uniforms as a disciplinary measure; some do. At Madina Academy in Windsor, Connecticut, girls are required to wear navy jumpers, white shirts, and blue sweaters. Make-up is strictly forbidden, but earrings and necklaces are permitted. Girls must wear headscarves during school hours. The boys' uniform is navy pants, a white shirt, and a blue sweater. Boys are encouraged to wear *kufi*, but they are not permitted to wear any jewelry and the length of their hair must be kept below the earlobe. The school website states, "Not only does a uniform promote equality amongst students but it also fosters self-discipline and self-esteem."

Muslim schools generally decorate their walls with pictures of Muslim celebrities, past and present. While Islamic centers stress the Islamic lunar calendar, Islamic schools operate according to the local school district calendar, though they feature Muslim occasions more prominently. In a further attempt to stress and American Muslim identity, these schools also encourage research and writing assignments on American Muslim history.

PROGRAMS AND STANDARDS

Typically, Islamic schools adopt the local school district curriculum, adding to it subjects like Arabic and Islamic Studies. In setting academic goals, an Islamic school usually follows the standards of its local school board. There is wide variation in the goals and achievement expectations that Islamic schools set for themselves. For example, Al-Azhar School in Tamarack, Florida, states that its objective is to meet the achievement standards set by the state, ultimately developing students that can "successfully compete at the highest levels nationally and internationally and are prepared to make well-reasoned, thoughtful, and healthy lifelong decisions."

The Islamic character of the schools usually means that subjects are introduced with a faith-based approach to life. But it is not enough for a school to call itself Islamic to draw students. Parents carefully examine the school's facility, the teaching staff, and the education methods employed. A preschool program run by the Islamic School of Seattle has adopted the Montessori approach to teaching, a secular method that grew outside the religious school system and focuses on the development of self-directed individuals.

The performance of Islamic schools depends on a number of variables—most important are organization, quality of the teaching staff, community support, and revenue. Because the idea of Islamic schooling in North America is only beginning to take shape, many schools are run below state standards for a number of years before they can be fully accredited. For example many schools start without highly expereienced teachers. Many of the school buildings are well equipped, although some lack important facilities like gymnasiums.

Some Muslim schools set their criteria of excellence in terms of student-teacher ratio, test scores, and achievement awards. For example, Universal School in Bridgeview, Illinois, which enrolled 627 students in the 2000 academic year, has a faculty-student ratio of 1:12. The school's website claims that its "elementary school students, on average, performed better than 60 [percent] of America's second, fourth, sixth, and eighth graders on the Iowa Test of Basic Skills"; that in 1997, a Universal student scored 1570 on the SAT (out of a possible 1600); that the school has received several distinctive achievement awards, including the 2000 State Science Fair (in which all school participants receive outstanding awards in biochemistry and engineering), the 1999 National Merit Scholar (awarded to one in 250,000 high school seniors), and the 1997 and 1998 Illinois State Scholar (awarded to 1 percent of the state's high school seniors); and that Universal graduates have been admitted to Cornell University, the University of Chicago, and Northwestern University. Universal, however, is one of the highest-rated of all Islamic schools; its achievements do not represent the scholastic standard of the system as a whole.

In upper grades the attraction of some schools can hinge on their computer programs. For example, Granada Islamic School in Santa Clara, California, offers a computer lab. Many of the parents in this Silicon Valley school community are electrical engineers who want to offer their children early experience with cutting-edge learning tools. The school's website proclaims, "Our students have constantly scored well above the state averages on standardized tests." The Muslim Academy of Central Florida offers a laptop computer for every student. The children in this school community come from affluent families capable of paying for such costly equipment.

Some school programs in large Muslim communities involve students in community services, such as feeding the indigent, visiting nursing homes, participating in activities at homeless shelters, and sponsoring orphaned children. Other schools encourage student clubs to establish chapters of community organizations working in the fields of social service and public advocacy. For example, the first high school chapter of Inner-City Muslim Action Network

(IMAN), a group that offers mentoring and other youth programs in Chicago neighborhoods, was established at Universal School. In Al-Amal Islamic School in Minneapolis, Minnesota, social studies teachers include material received from national groups like the American Muslim Council on the role of citizens in petitioning their government.

Some schools stress religious teachings with the same vigor as other subjects. For example, Al-Qalam School in Springfield, Virginia, divides its curriculum into two main types of courses. The Islamic Education program teaches sixth through twelfth graders Arabic language arts, Islamic law, Qur'anic studies, comparative history, and comparative religion. The school's general education program offers courses in English language arts, math, science, and social studies.

Another academy, Rahmaniyyah School in Orlando, Florida, offers a regular academic curriculum during the day and religious education in the evening. There, children spend much of the day in school, which in essence means that the school takes on part of the child-rearing responsibility usually assumed by the family. Such an arrangement may fit the needs of households with two parents working in highly demanding occupations. Other Muslim families may believe that Muslim institutions do a better job than parents in transmitting Islamic values to their children.

RELIGIOUS EDUCATION SCHOOLS

Religious education programs represent another form of Islamic schooling. These schools have developed because many Muslim parents deem the weekend religion classes offered by Islamic centers inadequate for their children. Few weekend programs provide enough instruction time for children to become truly proficient in Arabic and Qur'anic studies. To fill this gap, religious education schools operate during evening and weekend hours. These programs are aimed at helping Muslim children read and understand the Qur'an, memorize parts of it for use in prayer, and gain acquaintance with Hadith.

Religious education programs typically operate on a part-time basis because attending children still have to meet the requirements of full-time schools in addition to their extracurricular activities. Gayong Academy in Paulsboro, New Jersey, is an exception. It is a boarding school for youth that was founded by a couple of Malaysian descent in 1999 to offer an intensive program in religious studies. The school targets orphans and Muslim youth from low-income and disadvantaged backgrounds.

Aside from inculcating religious values in children, these educational institutions aim to produce *imams* capable of serving American Muslims. Local communities are facing tough choices in selecting *imams*. Candidates with an English proficiency may not possess the religious education qualifications required for the job. Those with classical religious training overseas may not possess adequate English skills or may not be well acquainted with North American Muslim conditions.

For many communities, the model *imam* would combine English proficiency with religious knowledge and a good understanding of life in the United States and Canada. The School of Islamic and Social Sciences (SISS) was established in 1996 to meet this need. The master's program at SISS bears little resemblance to Islamic studies programs in Muslim countries. SISS aspires to emphasize the contemporary North American context in its courses. Its graduates must pass not only religious courses, but also a social studies curriculum. The assumption behind this academic training is that *imams* who are educated in the classical schools in Muslim countries emerge with little empirical, real-world knowledge. Graduates of SISS have worked as *imams* in mosques and chaplains in the various branches of the U.S. military and correctional institutions.

Also, in 1996 another seminary, American Open University, developed a college-level distance learning program that was accredited by al-Azhar University in Cairo. Applicants must have a high school diploma, be fluent in Arabic, and submit a recommendation letter from a director of an Islamic center or another Islamic leader. To graduate, students must pass 132 credit hours of coursework, memorize one and one-half of the thirty parts of the Qur'an, submit a research paper, and pass comprehensive exams. The school proclaims that it prepares its students to "relate Islamic studies to the present by discussing solutions to contemporary issues, with particular reference to the Western world." This promise, however, must be seen as an evolving process; the correspondence school continues to replicate al-Azhar's traditional programs of study.

Clearly Islamic education has grown in the past decade, primarily due to private initiatives and increasing demand. The goal of imparting faith-based concepts to children growing up in societies with highly complex value systems permeates all sorts of Islamic schools. Yet the experience has highlighted Muslims' appreciation of nonreligious sources of wisdom and domains of life. While some programs seek simply to prepare Muslims to better understand their scripture and conduct their religious duties individually and collectively, most programs aim to help students succeed in their future career as well.

ORGANIZATION AND DECISION-MAKING DYNAMICS

The Islamic school system in North America represents roughly a $100 million business and contributes to the economic life of local Muslim communities. Islamic schools provide several thousand jobs, especially for Muslim women, who occupy a large percentage of teaching positions. Although tuition is the main revenue source for Muslim schools, it usually falls short of expenses. To sustain their programs, schools seek local and federal funding whenever eligible. For example, many schools in the United States receive federal Title I grants, which pay for instructional materials. Also, community fund-raising efforts are conducted continuously. Many schools also participate in local supermarket certificate programs, which donate 5 percent of participants' grocery bills to the schools.

School decisions are usually made by local boards in conjunction with the principal. In the Clara Muhammed School system, the *imam* of the sponsoring local community is the principal in all but two of the twenty-two schools. To stimulate parental involvement, many schools develop committees under parent–teacher associations. These associations may wield influence in decision making, so long as they contribute to fundraising and program development.

Because broad community support is essential to the survival of Islamic schools, school boards usually include representatives of local, regional, and national Muslim organizations. For example, the Islamic School of Greater Kansas City maintains an assigned seat for a representative from the Islamic Society of North America (ISNA). Nonetheless, most Islamic schools are sponsored by local mosque communities many schools operate in classrooms within the premises of Islamic centers.

Thus the management of Islamic schools is usually tied to the sponsoring center. Such a situation is sometimes officially recognized in the schools. For example, the bylaws of London Islamic School Board (LISB) in Ontario, Canada, state that its board "shall consist of one Director from the London Muslim Mosque Board of Directors . . . the Imam of the London Muslim Mosque, four community-at-large members and three parents. The Imam shall serve on the LISB in a nonvoting, advisory capacity."

While affiliation with Islamic centers and national community development groups means that the ethnic orientation of those organizations may be reflected in the workings of Islamic schools, professional educational criteria tend to have a moderating impact on such influences. Arabic language teachers are not required to be Arab, but they must have a good command of Arabic and must have teaching credentials. While the schools usually hire only Muslims to teach Islamic studies courses, many employ qualified teachers in nonreligious disciplines, regardless of faith.

Also, because the ability to pay tuition is the main determinant in admittance, the student body of an Islamic school is often much more ethnically diverse than its sponsoring Islamic center. For example, the Muslim Community School in Potomac, Maryland, is housed by the Islamic Education Center, a Shia mosque, but it enrolls many Sunni students. Its website defines the school as nonsectarian, multicultural, and multi-ethnic. The school relies on a committee system run by staff and parents. These include an executive committee, along with subcommittees for fund-raising, revenue disbursement, programming, technology, and science.

Islamic schools did not immediately emerge as fully stable institutions. In the beginning, as quickly as new schools opened, others closed, falling victim to a multitude of obstacles. Most schools have developed through trial and error. Each community has put forth a curriculum that reflects the goals set by its own founders. Often Islamic schools work in isolation. Each school looks for resources and support wherever they can be found. The Muslim Academy of Central Florida in Orlando, for example, has maintained a long list of affiliations, mostly with educational associations outside the Muslim community.

The lack of support structures and standards for the development of Islamic schools has given rise to the formation of umbrella groups to strengthen the performance of school administrators. The Muslim American Society (MAS)–W.

Deen Mohammed established a national leadership body, called the MAS Board of Education, which offers networking activities for Clara Muhammad Schools.

OTHER EDUCATIONAL OPTIONS

Many Muslim parents seek other educational alternatives, because private schools are beyond their financial means and the moral climate in public schools does not meet their expectations. This is especially true for those who have been raised in North America and have attended public schools themselves. Many have pursued home schooling, which is a legal option in the United States and Canada—provided that certain guidelines are followed.

Many Muslims choose to school their children at home as a means of preserving religious values and of minimizing the negative influences of society. Many parents, however, hesitate to consider home schooling out of concern that they lack proper teaching skills. Some believe that the classroom setting must be strictly duplicated at home in order for instruction to be effective. Parents who choose home schooling focus instead on the core precepts of learning and character development. Parent-teachers tend to act like guides who direct their children to the proper resources, thus raising their children to become responsible for teaching themselves. These families believe that home schooling enables their children to grow with a great sense of self-respect.

Children schooled at home are usually offered a chance to develop friendships outside of the high-pressure environment of formal educational institutions. These circles of friendship include relatives, family acquaintances, neighbors, friends at local Islamic centers, and teammates in recreational sports. Home school parents believe such a wide variety of friends outside the home offers their children the chance to expand their minds and social skills. For highly educated, middle-class parents, the home schooling decision is a matter of commitment and the balancing of their own work with their children's education. Usually mothers stay home and assume the primary teacher's role, but sometimes they may work or run a business from home.

The Muslim Homeschool Network and Resource was founded in 1999 by parents in Massachusetts. It maintains a website designed to offer assistance to home schoolers. The group declared October Islamic History and Pride Month. The organization also holds the annual Muslim Home Schooling and Family Convention, which is another occasion for home school children to meet and for parents to share teaching experiences. The meeting links Muslim parents to the larger home school movement in North America.

Parents who believe they are not qualified to teach their children, or who maintain work schedules that rule out the option of home schooling, are inclined to explore other educational options. Because it can be expensive for parents to pay both local school board taxes and private school tuition fees, there has been great interest in the school voucher programs that began in the United States in 1990. Vouchers are tuition subsidies that students can use to attend private schools. Publicly funded voucher programs are currently in use in Milwaukee and Cleveland. Privately funded voucher programs are found in many other places, including most major cities. One problem with these programs is that while parents may choose a particular private or religious school, these schools do not have to admit those children.

For one Muslim community the voucher program has been a blessing. Salam School in Milwaukee which was established as a full-time Islamic School in 1992 with nine students in kindergarten through second grade, joined the public voucher program in 1996. At that time the school had 116 students in preschool through seventh grade. In 2001 the school had 352 students in kindergarten through eighth grade, a tripling of enrollment in just five years. Two-thirds of the student body is eligible for the $5,500 per year tuition vouchers. Eligibility is based on household income. Thus the Salam School voucher program has allowed children from low-income households to experience private Islamic education. The school, which once hired teachers on a part-time basis, now operates with a full-time teaching staff. All teachers have a bachelor's degree and 80 percent are certified by the state. The new funds allowed the school to add classrooms, hire a reading teacher, beef up the library book collection, and buy new equipment.

Other instructional options, such as charter schools, are also available, but Muslims have not considered them seriously because of their restrictions on religious instruction. Charter schools are publicly funded schools developed by parents and teachers with the flexibility to be innovative under fewer rules and regulations. The charter school movement has grown from one school in Minnesota in 1992 to about eleven-hundred schools across the country in 2001. Thirty-six states and Washington, D.C., have legislation authorizing the creation of charter schools. Charter schools might have a specific academic focus—math and science or the arts—and employ specific teaching techniques, or target a specific group of students, such as at-risk students. Both voucher and charter school programs have come under attack from teachers' unions and others who believe that they take funds away from public schools.

Generally, Islamic education suffers in the absence of quality control on curriculum and the lack of teacher development programs and instruction methods. There are no regional or national boards to help in the development of standards of learning, codes of conduct, and testing policies as there are, for example, in the case of Catholic schools. Such boards have affected the way Catholic families approach educational options. But the Catholic school system benefits from more than two centuries of experience in North America, while Muslim schools began to emerge only in the past two decades. Many Muslims, however, may continue the push for establishing and improving the performance of Islamic schools. A sign of such determination is that fund-raisers are held at Islamic centers to support schools experiencing shortage of revenue. In many communities local efforts have been strengthened by support from national and regional leadership groups. In some instances such groups have actually initiated a number of projects designed to build centers of learning and spiritual growth.

A CLOSER LOOK
CHERRY HILL CHILD DEVELOPMENT CENTER, MONTESSORI PRESCHOOL

General Information

Cherry Hill Child Development Center (CHCDC) is absolutely dedicated to the physical, mental, and spiritual health and happiness of the children (ages 3–6) in its care. Every effort is made to give the children a secure and homelike atmosphere. Our caregivers are chosen primarily for their ability to give the child genuine affection and expert attention.

Cherry Hill Child Development Center is sponsored by the Islamic School of Seattle and parents should be aware that the religion of Islam pervades the atmosphere of the school. CHCDC does not discriminate on the basis of ethnicity, religion, or handicap. Alternate activities will be provided for children whose parents choose that their children not participate in religious activities.

We Offer

- an Islamic environment;
- a challenging and balanced multicultural curriculum encompassing pre-academic and academic skills, as well as activities that foster creativity, social skills, and physical development;
- qualified, committed teachers;
- a spacious facility including gym and playground;
- central location with convenient bus access;
- gardening activities.

Curriculum

The curriculum includes and reflects the major areas of study described below:

PRACTICAL LIFE Children practice tasks of daily life such as spooning, pouring, sponging, grating, hand washing, lacing, buttoning, preparing and serving food. The activities in Practical Life are numerous, varied, and always a favorite of the children. These activities are designed to help the children gain a sense of order, concentration, coordination, independence, and refinement of their small motor skills.

SENSORIAL Children use and sharpen their five senses as they learn about the fundamental properties of the environment. They learn about shape, size, relationship, weight, texture, sound, and the like as they match, sort, or grade various materials according to their properties. These activities help prepare children for the tasks of mathematics and science, among others.

A Closer Look, continued on next page

A Closer Look, continued

MATHEMATICS The materials in this area are designed to lay the foundation for mathematical concepts and relationships. Children work with concrete materials that enable them to explore patterns, the properties of numbers and concepts of place value. The children carry out mathematical operations in a "hands-on," developmentally appropriate way.

LANGUAGE This area includes materials extending from pre-reading and pre-writing to reading, writing, and grammar activities. The classroom is a language-rich environment and we will nurture the children's innate interest and sensitivity to mastering language. We will help them develop the listening, decoding, and writing strategies they will need for future academic pursuits. In a Montessori classroom, the children learn the phonetic sounds of letters before they learn the alphabetical names in a sequence because these are the first sounds that children hear in words that they need to know in order to read. We enhance our language-rich environment with Arabic as a living language and Qur'an recitation.

ISLAM It is important that young Muslim children develop a strong foundation and sense of pride in their Islamic heritage. Islamic ideals and etiquette will pervade the atmosphere of the classroom through songs, stories, shelf activities, celebration of Islamic holidays, and the teachers being role models. The teaching of Islam complements our goals in achieving self-esteem, respect for self and others, and to become successful individuals.

SCIENCE Children learn about the environment as they study various kinds of plants, animals, inanimate objects, and events in nature. The children have the opportunity to carry out simple experiments and will be introduced to some of the basic classifications that they will encounter and develop in more depth as they grow academically.

GEOGRAPHY We nurture a curiosity about and build respect for the physical and cultural diversity of our planet as we learn through a variety of materials and activities about the solar system, planets, continents, cultures, and people.

HISTORY History helps children develop an awareness of time and the ways we measure time as they work with timelines. We also include activities designed to enhance children's awareness of themselves as beings that develop and change with time.

ART We strive to maintain the great joy the child finds in creating something of his/her own. This includes pre-writing activities, as well as a variety of opportunities for creative expression and experimentation with different media and processes. The importance of the process is stressed during this time, not the end product itself.

Source: From www.islamicschool-seattle.org.

FIVE

COMMUNITY
DEVELOPMENT GROUPS

A number of groups operating regionally or nationally have been organized to support the establishment of Islamic centers and schools. These groups convene annually to exchange ideas, intellectual materials, and business products. This effort dates back to the 1950s, when groups such as the Federation of Islamic Associations and the Council of Mosques sought to create umbrella organizations for Islamic centers. These earlier coordination councils fizzled at a time when the Muslim population was still very small. After the mid-1970s, several community development groups in North America humbly restarted and have redefined and expanded their roles as community conditions changed.

ISLAMIC SOCIETY OF NORTH AMERICA

Many activists who acquired organizational skills during their campus experiences with the Muslim Students Association (MSA) formed guildlike groups after settling into professional occupations. These groups include the Islamic Medical Association, the Islamic Association of Scientists and Engineers, and the Association of Muslim Social Scientists. The foundation of what is today the Islamic Society of North America (ISNA) began through the collaborative effort of former MSA members and has undergone several changes. In the early 1970s members of MSA who had recently arrived in the United States and Canada from Arab countries formed the Muslim Arab Youth Association (MAYA), while Malaysian students formed the Malaysian Islamic Study Group (MISG). Both these groups, along with the MSA and the other guild associations, have since joined ISNA.

While ISNA remains a forum for the members of its constituent groups, mainly through its annual convention, the organization has also taken on the task of facilitating the establishment and growth of primary organizations that work to preserve Muslim identity. Initially, much of what ISNA leaders had to offer was encouragement; they exhorted Muslims to pool their resources and meet this challenge. Aside from the annual convention, the Speakers Bureau of ISNA has been one of its most active departments.

Still, ISNA formed the North American Islamic Trust (NAIT) in 1971, which offered legal protections to affiliated properties designated for mosque use.

NAIT also manages an investment venture called the Islamic Centers Cooperative Fund (ICCF). About 8 percent of this fund goes annually to support local communities in the acquisition and improvement of mosques. The remainder of the money is placed in real estate and other investments, whose profits offset the cost of loans to Islamic centers.

Meanwhile, with the growth of the Muslim population in North America, the demand for Islamic literature has increased. In 1976 NAIT developed American Trust Publications (ATP) as a publishing house offering a wide spectrum of titles to introduce Islam to a new generation of American Muslims. ATP also translated religious books with worldwide popularity, including Yusuf al-Qaradawi's guide to practicing Muslims titled *The Lawful and the Prohibited in Islam*. The Islamic Book Service is another NAIT-sponsored organization. With more than twenty-five hundred titles, it has become one of the largest distributors of Islamic books in the West.

Throughout this period of growth, the various branches of ISNA were still being operated from homes and rental spaces. The leadership of the group realized ISNA itself had to become a stable institution before it could carry out its goal of facilitating the growth of Islamic centers in North America. In 1982 ISNA built its headquarters in Plainfield, Indiana, believing that the location was a central place between the Atlantic and Pacific coasts.

In 1985 ISNA leaders recognized the need for an organization aimed at young people born and raised in North America. The Muslim Youth of North America (MYNA) was formed to meet this need. The group offers an off-school national platform for Muslim teen activities. It has produced rap music with Muslim themes and conducted camps and other educational activities. MYNA attracts North American–born teenagers, who meet at its regional chapters' events and nationally during the annual ISNA convention.

By the 1990s ISNA had grown into an organization with significant assets and local roots. The organization began to formalize its work, placing emphasis on community development. The group adopted a mission statement that reads:

> ISNA is an association of Muslim organizations and individuals that serve the diverse needs of Muslims in North America. ISNA's mission is to provide a unified platform of expression for Islam, to develop educational, outreach, and social services that translate the teachings of the Qur'an and the Sunnah into everyday living, and to enhance Islamic identity in the society.

The organization is run by an administrative staff and a *shura* (consultative) council. Five of ISNA's consultative council members are elected from its affiliated Islamic centers and schools, which numbered more than three hundred by 2001—nearly one-fourth of all the Islamic centers on the continent. ISNA also accepts individual members, who receive discounts on the organization's products and services. These include matchmaking services, ad space in *Islamic Horizons*, *ISNA*'s bi-monthly magazine, and the annual convention. ISNA has a diverse ethnic character, although individual members are predominantly professionals of Arab and South Asian descent.

Through affiliation with ISNA, new Islamic centers enjoy immediate federal tax exemption. They also receive a free subscription to *Islamic Horizons*, and the group's endorsement of local fund-raising projects. This relationship, however, hardly implies a top-down command structure. Affiliates are not bound by any decision that the ISNA leadership makes. For example, when ISNA resolved to determine the start of Islamic months on the basis of astronomical calculations, the decision was not universally followed—and ISNA had no way to enforce its will on local centers. Many centers become affiliates simply to take advantage of the services offered by the various branches of the organization.

In the late 1990s ISNA instituted a series of specialized conferences designed to bring together activists and intellectuals involved in community organizations to address specific areas of importance. These areas included an annual education forum discussing the developmental needs of Islamic schools. Other conference programs focused on marriage counseling, conflict resolution, domestic violence, and outreach to prisoners and Latinos. ISNA also began administering an annual workshop on community development that trains administrators of local community centers and schools. The 2000 workshop was attended by leaders of sixty local community organizations.

ISNA's main activity is the annual convention. About thirty thousand people attended the 2000 event in Chicago, Illinois. A growing percentage of ISNA members, however, are men, women, and young people who are born and raised in North America, including both white and black converts. In conjunction with the annual convention, ISNA began in 2000 an international trade fair that allowed Muslim business leaders from around the world to network.

To address needs in training managers for community institutions, ISNA sponsors three students annually to study the management of nonprofit organizations at the Indiana University Center on Philanthropy. Each fellow receives a $9,000 stipend and housing allowance. Although the program does not offer a diploma, it offers a chance for rigorous theoretical and practical training, especially since fellows are required to maintain an internship with ISNA during their study.

With an eye toward ISNA's future security, an endowment fund was established in 1996. About 20 percent of the organization's collections are now deposited into the fund. In Canada ISNA has a structure parallel to that in the United States, with an added emphasis on programs of socioeconomic nature. The Canadian Islamic Trust Foundation is the counterpart of NAIT. It maintains a school board and a program designed to issue *halal* food certification. ISNA's successful Islamic Cooperative Housing Corporation in Mississauga, Ontario, is open to investors interested in buying cooperative shares.

ISLAMIC CIRCLE OF NORTH AMERICA

While ISNA has focused on local Islamic center development, the Islamic Circle of North America (ICNA) has concentrated on building a pool of Islamic activists who are willing to volunteer to work in *dawa* and social issues. The group was established in 1974 by a small group of South Asian students who were exposed to Islamic activism in their countries of origin. From these limited beginnings, the group has grown large enough to start sponsoring the establishment of organizations aimed at meeting the needs of Muslim living in North America. The Sister's Wing, which is ICNA's women's group, was established in 1979. Its website notes that the women's department was developed "to enable the sisters to work on the establishment of the [d]*een* [faith] freely and independently."

ICNA invests much of its energies in educating and supporting individuals who are highly capable of understanding the Qur'an, committed to living by its teachings, and interested in helping other people to experience Islamic life. In ICNA's view, neither Sunday schools nor the more intensive religious education programs offered by Islamic centers can accomplish this task. The core of ICNA's organization is the approximately one hundred study groups that meet monthly to study the Qur'an and discuss community issues. ICNA's members, or workers, are called to concentrate on reading the Qur'an with depth and recruit other Muslims into the organization. The workers are expected to dedicate at least an hour daily for their responsibilities. Every member is also required to devote at least two hours a week to a good cause. ICNA's national meeting is held annually and is attended by some six thousand participants. Headquartered in Jamaica, New York, it maintains two regional offices in Detroit, Michigan, and Oakville, Ontario.

In 1989 the organization started publishing a monthly magazine, *The Message International*, featuring news and analysis of Muslim issues. While the magazine today continues its affinity for Muslim world issues, it has paid increasing attention to the North American scene. The group's heightened recognition of the social problems facing the community has led ICNA to establish Muslim Family Services, an agency that aims to help families become self-sufficient. According to ICNA, the high divorce rate among American Muslim couples is a primary threat to the strength and unity of the Muslim family. The group has supported the construction of women's shelters and initiated a matchmaking program.

The March 2000 issue of *The Message International* featured an editorial lauding the idea that Islam in the twentieth century "got firm hold in North America . . . and Muslims became part of American mosaic." ICNA members are encouraged by the leadership to maintain a welcoming attitude toward Americans and Canadians, many of whom are seen to be neutral on matters of religion and have had little or no exposure to Islam and Muslims.

ICNA members are especially well known in the Muslim community for the volunteer hours they spend passing out pamphlets on Islam in public places. ICNA leaders have taken a special interest in social activism. In the mid-1980s they endorsed and organized participation in efforts to clean up the drug-infested neighborhood of Masjid al-Taqwa in Brooklyn, New York, and they have established soup kitchens to serve the poor. ICNA has so far refrained from taking any position on issues of political participation, leaving these matters to individual initiatives.

In the aftermath of the September 11 attacks on the Pentagon and World Trade Center, ICNA was among the most active Muslim groups. By September 21 it had compiled a list of fifty-five missing and twenty injured Muslims in the World Trade Center attacks. The group advised its members to donate blood to the victims and suggested that local leaders establish active contacts with local authorities. The group also increased its interfaith contacts. When an organization called Scarves for Solidarity was launched as a response to attacks on Muslim women with head scarves, ICNA featured the program prominently on its website.

ICNA's Sound Vision department has produced audio- and videotapes on various aspects of the Islamic faith. It has also developed *al-Qari* (the Reader), a multimedia program designed to teach any computer user how to properly read the Arabic language and recite the Qur'an. Overall, Sound Vision offers some fifteen hundred items that are sold over the Internet, via mail order, through local dealers, and in two stores in Chicago, Illinois, and London, England—where there is a large English-speaking population of South Asian ancestry.

The growth of ICNA's membership and financial resources has enabled the group to become active in the construction of mosques, a move that exemplifies the group's departure from its former focus on the building of individual character toward the development of service organizations. Now a dozen mosque communities are affiliated with ICNA. While ICNA's core membership has always been drawn from those of South Asian ancestry, it offers services and products to the public at large. The group has pioneered the production of English-language popular songs that are marketed in North America and Europe. The organization's sponsored documentary *Bosnia: The Untold Story* earned an international reputation and was aired on many television stations in the United States and Muslim countries.

MUSLIM AMERICAN SOCIETY

Like ICNA, Muslim American Society (MAS) is a group of dedicated Islamic activists, also called workers. Its founding members, however, were mainly foreign students of Arab descent—many born in the Middle East—who grew familiar with the discourse of Islamic movements in their homelands. After graduation, many settled in jobs and established businesses in the United States and Canada. MAS is an outgrowth of the Cultural Society that was established in Chicago, Illinois, in 1969 as a nonprofit organization focusing on the development of educated and spiritually enriched members. The group has grown into a body of Islamic workers who meet weekly in about three hundred small study groups. As such, much of the group's work is designed to shape the religious and intellectual character of its members. Leaders of the organization assert that its members have provided the impetus and a good amount of the volunteer work that has fueled the growth of mosques and Islamic schools in North America. These include such large projects as the Mosque Foundation in Bridgeview, Illinois, Daral-Hijrah in Falls Church, Virginia, and al-Iman School in Houston, Texas.

By the early 1990s a consensus had already developed among members and leaders of the organization about the future of the group. Most members had already experienced the emancipating effects of citizenship. They came to the conclusion that American and Canadian societies are diverse enough to accommodate Islam, that North America is a land in which Islam may grow. Because of the group's dedication to building Muslim religious centers in a Western society, MAS Leaders believe they have embarked upon a mission aiming at a coherent reconciliation of the Islamic and Western worlds. Because the group works with the grassroots, the leaders believe their journey must be seen as a long-term project of global nature. They also conceded that, rhetoric aside, the essence of the contemporary, mainstream Islamic movements has been largely educational.

MAS has also concluded that the goal of instilling an Islamic character in individuals and communities may not necessarily imply any set of political convictions. Thus the group pursued a path encouraging its members' full participation in American society and advocating local cultural preservation for converts to Islam. MAS only recently started to institutionalize its work, a move triggered by the fact that some of its leaders eventually left the organization to form specialized service organizations. In 1993 MAS registered under its new name in Chicago and opened its national office in Falls Church, Virginia, in 1998.

Recognizing the need to reach out to English-speaking Muslims and non-Muslims, in 1999 MAS started publishing a bimonthly magazine in English, *The American Muslim*, and began to publicize the challenges facing Islamic schools. The group also recognized the need to offer recreational programs to the rapidly growing Muslim teen population. In 2000 MAS Youth Center was launched in Brooklyn, New York. Moreover, MAS sponsored the establishment of the Islamic American University, a distant-learning program of classical Islamic studies with administrative offices in Southfield, Michigan, and Kansas, Missouri. The program offers bachelor's and master's degrees. Also in October 2000 the group convened an educational conference that was attended by teachers and administrators from thirty community schools.

MAS and ICNA have grown closer, as the two groups recognized that they share the mission of promoting a strong sense of Muslim identity. They also acknowledge that their ethnic and homeland differences are bound to become less important than their common destiny as Muslims of North America. In 2000, the two groups have unified their educational programs. Now members of ICNA and MAS undergo the same training, which is designed to develop a model Muslim who is health-conscious, devoted to his/her faith and community, well-versed in the Islamic sources of knowledge, and well-acquainted with the contemporary conditions of the Muslim world, especially in North America. The educational program recommends that members exercise regularly, fast often (beyond Ramadan), attend mosque prayers daily, and volunteer in community service organizations. In 2002 MAS and ICNA held their first joint convention, a step many believe will ultimately lead to merger.

Nevertheless, slogans of the Muslim world's two main Islamic revivalist groups, the Muslim Brotherhood in the Arab world and the Jama'ati Islami in South Asia, are found in the literature of MAS and ICNA. Their educational program, for instance, requires readings about "The Islamic System," a term used by Islamic writers referring to a vaguely defined political order based on Islam. A sign of the transitional nature of today's ICNA and MAS is their requirement that members be aware of the Muslim roots in North America, the history of Malcolm X, American Muslim community-building models, and the American political process. The groups also require the study of other religions, with emphasis on Christianity. They also include in their reading lists books written by non-Muslim thinkers.

MINISTRY OF W. DEEN MOHAMMED

The main national community development group among African-American Muslims is the Ministry of W. Deen Mohammed, also presently called the Muslim American Society. The group's identification with mainstream Islam began in 1975, when Imam Warith Deen Mohammed, son of NOI founder Elijah Mohammed, renounced his father's teachings in favor of the universal concepts of the faith. He created a new organization and called it the Muslim Community in the West before it assumed its present name. The *imam*'s website states the move was

> a clear and clarion public commitment to a religious investment reaching far beyond the accidents of the world today and tomorrow, and anchoring the well-being of his followers in the solid rock of classical Islam.

Since then, Imam Mohammed and the community under his leadership have been dedicated several projects. In 1997 the group name changed into Muslim American Society (MAS—no relation to the aforementioned group of the same name). The community consists of more than one hundred local congregations and three dozen schools. While ICNA performs *da'wa* through mail and personal contacts, the Ministry of W. Deen Mohammed hosts the television program *W. Deen Mohammed and Guest* and runs a nationally syndicated radio program. The ministry also sells audio and video items featuring the Imam's speeches and books. The *Muslim Journal*, a weekly that supports the ministry, carries national and international news articles and commentaries on Muslim life and issues. Recently it began covering local community events more closely.

Another organ affiliated with the community is the International League of Muslim Women, which was established in 1984 and now has thirty-three chapters, three of which are located in the West African countries of Togo and Ghana. To many Muslims, these African-American Muslim women are a good example of how American citizens in the age of globalism view the whole world as a natural domain for cultural and religious connectivity.

MAS–W. Deen Mohammed's annual conference, the Islamic Convention, draws members of all organs of the movement and about six thousand individuals annually, nearly all African American. The event features workshops, merchandise, and cultural performances. The convention also features an address by the Imam whose speeches are not tuned to a particularly religious Muslim audience. In his talks he crosses the lines of ethnicity and religion to call for unity. To some intellectuals, the substance of his speeches does not seem very rich. But the *imam's* audience is not the intellectual class, but the common people. The convention is attended by many non-Muslim African-Americans. The multifaith aspects of the event is a testimony that ethnicity has a natural appeal that religion cannot often capture.

But the leadership structure in the community is changing. A new generation of *imams* and activists are becoming part of the movement. In 1999 the community disbanded the old Shura Council, which was composed of *imams* of major mosques. In its place the MAS Monitoring Team was established to foster greater participation by professionals and business owners. Specialized committees were created under the new structure to cover health, housing, education, and business development. This move was coupled with the release of Imam Mohammed book *Islam's Climate for Business Success,* which encourages Muslims to become industrious. To set an example, Mohammed himself started a meat-packaging business in Chicago. His associates began exploring meat-business deals with Muslims here and around the world.

While institution-building efforts under the leadership of Imam Mohammed remain exclusively the domain of African-American participants, the Ministry and its affiliates have begun to build ties globally. In 1996 Imam Mohammed met with Pope John Paul II at the Vatican; in the following year he established close ties to the Roman Catholic Focolare Movement. He also visited several Muslim countries, including Malaysia, Syria, and Palestine. In November 1999 he attended a meeting of the World Conference on Religion and Peace in Amman, Jordan. He now serves on the executive committee of the organization.

There are a number of smaller community development groups among African Americans. The National Community is a loose affiliation of three-dozen local mosque communities and Islamic associations under the leadership of Imam Jamil al-Amin. Known as Rap Brown before converting to Islam in the 1970s, al-Amin was a leader of the Black Panther Party in the 1960s. Although he has had several run-ins with the police and was accused in the shooting of a law enforcement officer during the 1960s, the National Community has a long-standing reputation in Muslim and black America for its opposition to crime and drug use in inner-city neighborhoods. The group holds an annual *Riyadah* (sports) gathering attended by hundreds of men, women, and young people. Al-Amin is a member of the *Shura* Council, an ad-hoc Muslim forum that also includes Imam W. Deen Mohammed and representatives of ISNA and ICNA.

In August 1995 al-Amin was arrested and accused in a shooting incident in Atlanta. But later that year the alleged victim appeared with the *imam* in a press conference in Washington, D.C., saying that the police had pressured him to identify al-Amin as a suspect. To many Muslims the revelation shed serious doubt on the credibility of law enforcement in Atlanta. In community bulletins some expressed the view that the cops were pursuing him because of his radical past. The story became national news when members of ISNA and ICNA, among other groups, attended the press conference. A number of activists later developed a website with news articles about the case.

In March 2000 al-Amin was sought in Alabama for another shooting incident in which a police officer was killed. When the news media reported that the *imam* was in hiding, Muslim groups publicly called on him to surrender to the police, which he did. The organizations sought to underscore that defying the rule of law is not tolerable. Despite the severity of the charge against al-Amin, many Muslims believed his plea of innocence because of his community service record. A number of support groups were established in Atlanta and around the country to support a fair trial for him. When he was convicted in February 2002, Muslim activists supported his right to appeal the verdict.

SHIA COMMUNITY DEVELOPMENT GROUPS

There were only a few Shia centers in North America before the 1980s, and only one group that took up the task of institution-building. This group is the small Khoja Shia Ithna Asheri Community, which acts as a world body of local religious communities. Members of this association, whose leaders hail from East Africa, have formed four local communities, called *jama'ats*, in different parts of the North American continent. Delegates from these communities were among the members at a conference in 1976 in London, England, where the World Federation of Khoja Groups in the West was formed.

Other Shia Muslims have undergone major changes since the Iranian revolution. Not only has the Shia consciousness experienced an awakening worldwide, but the Iranian clergy has begun to restore its connections to all Shia communities in the world. In many Shia mosques, *imams* have been appointed by the religious authorities in Qom, a tangible support that gave a boost to the movement to build religious centers in the United States and Canada. However, many Shia Muslims, especially in the United States, have remained apprehensive ever since the 1979–1981 hostage crisis and the continued antagonism between the United States and Iran. Like other Muslims, especially those of Iranian heritage, they have endured demonization because of the widely held assumption that they sympathized with the politics and policies of Iran's revolutionary leaders.

To some extent, most Muslims of the world were supportive of the Iranian revolution's victory over the dictatorship of the Shah, although few agreed with the new government's policies. To Shia minorities around the world, the victory was a reassurance about their ability to shape their own future. But only a few community development groups started after the mid-1980s. The largest of the groups is the North American Shia Ithna-Asheri Muslim Communities (NASIMCO). This group was established in 1986 and now consists of eleven centers in Canada and thirteen in the United States. NASIMCO offers its member centers basic religious information via a website, including prayer timetables and a calendar of Islamic events. The organization has formed the Islamic Education Board (IEB), which issued a standardized manual for schools sponsored by local communities. IEB has also published resource material on Islam and the history of Shiism for the benefit of the schools and community centers.

In 1994 the Council of Shia Muslim Scholars in North America was created as a coordinating body *imams*, who also aspired to address the challenges facing the community. The council, however, must be seen as a guild association, for it only offers an opportunity for *imams* to network with each other. Another group that was established at the same time, the Islamic Group in Detroit, Michigan, consists of young immigrant professionals of Arab origin. It runs a bookstore and holds a annual convention, an event attended by several hundred individuals.

As for Sunni *imams*, chaplains working in prisons and the military have also formed associations. In August 2000 the Muslim American Military Chaplains Association held its first annual conference at the Graduate School of Islamic and Social Sciences, in Leesburg, Virginia. The school endorses Muslim chaplains in the United States military. There is also the National Association of Muslim Chaplains, another guild of members working for state and federal prisons, mostly in New York where the group was founded. Interestingly, the vast majority of Sunni *imams* do not have an organizational body to address their collective interests as religious figures. No such need has ever been identified. *Imams* are usually tied to their own congregations at mosques, where they receive recognition, support, and sustenance. In their capacity as community leaders, *imams* are found in many regional and national Muslim institutions. Some *imams*, especially those in volunteers or part-time positions, work outside their mosques at times, but they do so as individuals with talent in a particular area.

REGIONAL UMBRELLA GROUPS

Community development initiatives focusing on particular regions of the continent have formed along different organizational patterns. The degree of cohesiveness among leaders in these local settings has made a difference in what they have been able to accomplish. One reason these groups made a conscious choice to keep their scope of activity limited was the difficulties experienced by ISNA and the Ministry of W. Deen Mohammed in working in such a vast continental space. Simply put, a single national office can hardly cope with monitoring the ever-changing demographic structure and needs of local communities.

One of the best known of these groups is the Islamic Society of Greater Houston (ISGH), which was founded in 1968 before ISNA or other national community development groups stabilized their organizational frameworks. From the start, ISGH was structured to address the communal needs of Muslims in Houston, Texas, one of the largest cities in the United States. Today there are twelve mosques and three full-time schools under ISGH, which functions through an elaborate committee structure to maintain its existing facilities and to expand into other centers and programs.

The schools are managed by one board with established rules and procedures for running the programs. All of the local congregations pray together on *Eid*, an event that attracted nearly twelve thousand people in 2001. ISGH has its own funeral home and has negotiated with the state of Texas to procure a separate section of a local cemetery. The organization also maintains a bookstore that sells various literary items and a library that loans books to the public. Its educational activities include an annual symposium on topics related to challenges facing families, youth, and the Muslim community. To communicate with its members, ISGH publishes a monthly newsletter. It maintains a long list of volunteers on whom the group depends to assure the low administrative costs of its various programs.

While some regional councils in large cities experience occasional shortages of funds, ISGH usually maintains a surplus. The organization distributes *zagat* funds every Friday. Impressed by its level of sophistication and spirit of unity, Hakeem Olajuwon, the Muslim star professional basketball player, decided to sponsor the ISGH's communication scholarship. The beneficiaries of these awards are qualified graduate and undergraduate students in the fields of television/radio broadcasting and journalism at the University of Houston.

The Islamic Society of Central Florida (ISCF) is another notable regional community development organization. Based in Orlando, it runs six mosques, three schools, a day care center, a social service office, and a youth association. Its website contains valuable information about Islam and Muslim communities in the region and the United States. In 1997 the organization convened a conference on American Muslim community concerns. Like ISGH, ISCF is managed by a board of directors that is elected annually by community members.

Most other regional groups function as coordination councils; some offer informal forums for leaders of local communities to discuss shared issues of importance. This is especially true in highly diverse regions. For example, the Shura Council of Islamic Organizations in Southern California has brought together *imams* and leaders representing twenty-four Islamic Centers, including Sunni and Shia mosques with various ethnic representation, to discuss common concerns.

In other regions, coordination councils have brought local mosques and ethnic organizations together in the celebration of the two Muslim holidays of *Eid*. In the Washington Metropolitan Area, D.C. Eid Committee is composed of the area's highly diverse mosque communities, including Masjid Mohammed (African American), Manassas Mosque (ethnically diverse Shia), ADAMS (ethnically diverse Sunni), and Dar al-Hijrah (ethnically diverse Sunni). These local congregations held communal *Eid* prayers attended by twenty thousand Muslims in 2000 and thirty thousand in 2001.

Other Muslim groups attempting to shape the Muslim character have a smaller presence in the United States and Canada. There is the Islamic Assembly of North America, which follows the *Salafi* Sunni line. There is also the *Tablighi*

Jama'at, which has established a few centers around the country. *Tablighi* men often include South Asians, who go door to door to proselytize.

There are councils representing the various ethnic groups and their points of view on public issues (see chapter 9), many non-mosqued Muslims are left to fend for themselves in local community building. As we will see in chapter 7, some ethnic groups have managed to develop their own social service centers. These agencies, however, are few and far apart. In North America there are nearly fourteen hundred mosques, but only about three hundred ethnic associations and community centers. Spread across the continent, the ethnically oriented Muslims have not established community development forums or coordination councils. Surprisingly, this is true even in Canada, whose multicultural policy promotes the strengthening of ethnic communities. Although public schools in the United States and Canada encourage students to learn foreign languages, there is little impetus among the Muslim ethnic populations in favor of developing of ethnic-language programs.

The lack of ethnicity-based organizations dedicated to community building may explain the disparity in the number of well-established local ethnic associations. While there are only two major religious strands in Islam—Sunni and Shia—there are more than two dozen sizable national origin populations, and within these are various local, regional, and native tongues. With few exceptions, members of these ethnic groups are found in very small numbers throughout the continent.

The initiative to develop institution-building groups sometimes stems from an ethno-religious self-identification. The Albanian American Islamic Society fits in this prototype. It was established after a wave of immigrants arrived from the Balkans in the early 1990s, sparked by the need to maintain the dozen mosques in the United States and Canada that serve Albanians. Each year one of the centers hosts a meeting attended by leaders of the other member centers to discuss the needs of the community and raise funds to pay for the cost of agreed-upon improvements.

Another such group, the NOI, appeared to have been on the verge of transforming itself into a Muslim ethno-religious community-building organization. In February 2000 Imam Mohammed attended the NOI's Savior's Day event, where the Imam Mohammed and Louis Farrakhan declared their reconciliation of past conflicts. Farrakhan announced his faith in Muhammad the Prophet of Mecca. The Imam declared his acceptance of Farrakhan's intentions to join mainline Islam. Sayed Said, the general secretary of ISNA, said the step was indicative of the movement's growing interest in the Muslim faith. After the convention, however, NOI literature continued to print statements of belief contrary to the Muslim creed (such as the belief that God appeared in Detroit in 1930 in the person of Fard Muhammad, teacher of NOI Founder Elijah Mohammed).

Beyond conferences, local affiliates of the national development groups have experienced a growing level of interaction. Increasingly, they celebrate *Eid* together and hold joint youth programs. Such activities are mainly limited to concerns about preserving an Islamic character in a predominantly non-Muslim society. Accordingly, much of the work to build mosques and schools has been carried out independently, as regional and national groups have focused on working with affiliated communities and those which have already started on their own. Indeed, the affiliated Islamic centers and schools represent less than half of all such groups. As a result, local communities enjoy freedom in their decision making, but also must assume the burden of improving their services and growing in size to meet the needs of an increasing Muslim population.

The various regional and national groups have pursued different paths and targeted various constituencies. They have also begun to increase their interaction with one another. For example, the Ministry of W. D. Mohammed shares with the National Community, ISNA, and ICNA membership in the Islamic Shura Council, which has issued a number of statements during times of crisis but is all too frequently dormant. The Shura Council even issued a public rebuke of Shaykh Hisham Qabbani in 1999, when he charged in an address at the U.S. Department of State that 80 percent of the boards of directors of mosques are controlled by extremists. The Shura statement, which was joined by other community public affairs groups, was designed to set standards for intra-Muslim discourse. The groups resolved that no one, much less a Muslim leader, should use a broad brush to malign an entire community.

RESPONSES TO SEPTEMBER 11

Community development groups played a collective role in steering local communities into a united stance against terror and hate violence in the wake of the September 11 attacks. With counterparts in other faith communities, such as the U.S. Conference of Catholic Bishops, ISNA, ICNA, MAS–W. Deen Mohammed, and other groups issued a joint statement condemning the terrorist attacks. It read,

> We believe that the one God calls us to be peoples of peace. Nothing in our Holy Scriptures, nothing in our understanding of God's revelation, nothing that is Christian or Islamic justifies terrorist acts and disruption of millions of lives.

Similar joint statements with the National Council of Churches and other interfaith organizations were issued jointly by national and regional Muslim umbrella groups. But despite their previous experience with interfaith activities, the events of September 11 revealed a shocking lack of preparedness on the part of community development groups to cope with demands for literature and guidance from members of other faith groups. Citizens and media outlets alike began asking questions about Islam and Muslims more frequently and intensely than at any other time in North American history. It became obvious to Muslims that the media did not have a monopoly over shaping public opinion—and that it hardly exhibited a unified agenda in the portrayal of the faith and its adherents after the attacks.

Within two weeks of the attacks, ICNA began receiving more than a hundred letters and packages a day, a tenfold increase over the normal volume. Initially, the group experienced a shortage of the labor needed to meet this increase in demand for literature about Islam. Volunteers from local Islamic centers stepped in to help distribute more than ten thousand copies of the Qur'an in a matter of three months, and ICNA's pamphlets on Islam were reprinted several times. While ICNA does not keep a record of convert numbers, the group did not note any large increase in the months following the attacks.

There are signs that the event and its aftermath may lead to substantial changes in the amount of attention that Muslims give to interfaith relations. First, through interactions with others, Muslims realized that Americans are sophisticated in their social thinking and that their interest in learning about the faith was matched by their collective efforts to learn about its adherents. The December 2001 issue of *American Muslim* featured a report on 140 such exchanges involving MAS members in Texas, California, Maryland, Virginia, Michigan, North Carolina, Florida, Ohio, Oklahoma, Washington, D.C., Massachusetts, Illinois, Pennsylvania, and Alabama. The report shows that Muslims have identified their interlocutors by their affiliation to churches, synagogues, civic groups, and local and federal authorities.

September 11 was a tragedy that has led many people to self-reflection. Bookstores and Muslim publishing companies soon ran out of items on Islamic studies, most of which were meant for scholars. But the American public at large was also interested in reading material. Community development groups just could not keep up with the demand. Locally, mosques, Islamic schools, and Muslim parents of children in public schools were left to develop their own pamphlets and other materials to share with friends and neighbors.

To the institution-building minded leaders in the Muslim community, the event put them in a catch-up mode. All of a sudden, they realized how little they paid attention to interfaith relations. Non-Muslim groups, which have had a history of interdenominational dialogue, were also shaken by the realization that they had not paid adequate attention to reaching out to Muslims. Indeed many of the contacts that followed September 11 were initiated by churches seeking to change that state of affairs. Ethnic Muslims have still been struggling to organize themselves locally. Many have not been readily available to address church communities and other religious and civic associations.

A CLOSER LOOK
MUSLIM YOUTH
OF NORTH AMERICA

In today's society, youth face not only the pressures of young adulthood but also those of being Muslim in a largely non-Muslim environment. These pressures tend to draw Muslim youth into the temptations of Western society, leaving their Islamic values in the dark. If we, as Muslim youth, want to make a place in this complex society, we must establish our own Islamic identity.

A group of concerned young Muslims united to form an organization to deal with the challenges facing the Muslim youth of this continent. This unique organization is the Muslim Youth of North America (MYNA).

History

MYNA began as an idea in the minds of a group of dedicated Muslim youth who came to the conclusion that the situation of the youth programs in North America was, at the time, in desperate need of improvement. The first programs sponsored by these youth were held at the Islamic Society of North America (ISNA) conference and conventions. After the youth program of the 1985 ISNA Annual Convention, the ISNA Youth Committee felt that the time had arrived for Muslim youth to have a continental organization. The ISNA Majilis Ash-Shura (policy-making body) endorsed the idea and encouraged its development. MYNA was introduced, discussed, formatted, and approved at the First Annual Muslim Youth Winter Conference in December of 1985. With the grace of Allah and the efforts of the youth, a pioneering Muslim youth organization in North America was formed.

Structure

Coordinating activities throughout the continent can be quite a challenge, and MYNA developed a structure that divides the United States into three geographical zones: East, West, and Central. Canada is divided into East and West. Each zone has a youth representative that is elected by other youth in the zone at either the continental winter leadership conference or at a zonal event. Each zone also has an adult adviser that works with the representative. The five zonal representatives, along with the secretary, treasurer, and chairperson constitute the MYNA executive committee. The zonal advisors along with a chairperson of advisers constitute the MYNA advisory committee. Zones are further divided into regions, with their own representatives, and in some regions, they are again divided into metropolitan councils as well as local units.

A Closer Look, continued on next page

A Closer Look, continued

Affiliation
MYNA is affiliated with ISNA. It works in cooperation with ISNA and other Islamic organizations. MYNA makes its programs available to all interested Muslim organizations regardless of their affiliations.

The goals of MYNA are
1. To strengthen the faith and practice of Muslim youth, allowing them to develop an Islamic identity;
2. To help Muslim youth and communities plan and carry out educational training, and spiritual, recreational, and charitable Islamic activities;
3. To develop Islamic leadership for the future; and
4. To establish a positive and healthy image of Islam in North America.

Source: From www.jannah.org/myna/about.html.

SIX

ETHNIC
ASSOCIATIONS

The examination of groups functioning as facilitators for the building of schools and Islamic centers demonstrated that ethnicity has not been divorced from the very formation of faith-based community development organizations. In terms of the dominant ethnic composition of membership, MAS–W. D. Mohammed is African American; ICNA is South Asian; MAS is Arab; and ISNA is mainly Arab and South Asian. The various Shia groups exhibit a similar pattern of organization. These groups, however, embrace members who do not stress their ethnic heritage. For Muslims born in North America, the mosque has served as the natural hub of community life. Outside the mosque, ethnic affiliations are found in various forms, encompassing members of more than fifty national origins and subcultural entities. Again here, Middle Eastern and South Asian groups dominate the scene.

NATIONAL ORIGIN GROUPS

Arabs most prominently have claimed ethnic identities based on linguistic features. Persons who descend from Arabic-speaking countries, whether or not they acquire proficiency in the languages, are identified as Arab. Despite the long presence of Arab Americans in North America and their growing interest in national politics, the number of Arab-American ethnic organizations remains scant. Although there are no national or regional organizations dedicated to the preservation of the ethnic character of Arab Americans several local groups have emerged.

An example of such local ethnic formations is the Arab Cultural Center in San Francisco, founded in 1973 by Bay Area Arab Americans. It provides educational and cultural services for the local Arab community. The Cultural Center offers individuals and families the opportunity to meet, study, share, communicate ideas, and generally strengthen ties with their ethnic heritage. The Center offers Arabic language classes for children on Saturdays and English as a second language classes for adults. Arabic folk dance, called *debke*, and singing are also taught in the center. It frequently hosts programs featuring speakers and artists from around the world. Moreover, the center is furnished with a library, which contains books and instructional materials and is open to the public. Each year the center holds an Arab cultural festival for the city.

In Detroit, the Arab Community Center for Economic and Social Services (ACCESS), which is primarily a social service delivery system, sponsors several programs directed at promoting Arab-American identity. The organization offers youth educational and recreational programs through which a sense of ethnic belonging develops. ACCESS is a main sponsor of the annual Dearborn Arab International Festival, which features parades, international (not just Arab or Middle Eastern) food booths, and cultural performances. In addition, henna designs and traditional Arab crafts are displayed. For ACCESS, whose leaders are U.S.-born, maintaining a core Arab identity does not mean shutting out other influences.

While second- and third-generation Arabs now see themselves as Arab American, more recent immigrants exhibit attachment to a certain country of origin. The political turmoil in these countries reverberates outside, affecting ethnic group discourse and sense of identity. The plight of the Palestinian people, whose ethnic communities in the diaspora now exceed their numbers in the homeland, is a prime example. After the Palestine Liberation Organization (PLO)–Israel Oslo Accord in 1993, some Palestinian groups such as *Al-Awdah* (the Return), have translated their identification with the Palestinian cause into a public awareness campaign about the rights of Palestinian refugees. Presenting itself as an issue-oriented group, as opposed to a group of individuals who share an ethnic tradition, *Al-Awdah* has appealed to Arab Americans of all ethnicities and countries of origin. The group's cause resonates with Muslims and others who have participated in its marches for the plight of the Palestinians.

Turkish Americans maintain strong attachment to Turkey. They have formed associations in every state in America and some provinces of Canada. The Federation of Turkish American Associations, which was established in 1956, rents office space in the Turkish Consulate in New York and often hosts Turkish government officials coming to address the United Nations. The main function of the federation is the organization of the annual Turkish Day Parade in New York City, which usually takes place in May. The federation's member groups include the American Association of Crimean Turks, the Turkish Cypriot Cultural Association of New Jersey, and the Association of Balkan Turks of America. The Federation, in its efforts to unite Turks, has expanded to a worldwide level. In 1991 the Federation, along with sister organizations throughout the world, founded the World Turkish Congress, which represents ethnic Turks living in regions outside of Turkey, including North America, Europe, Asia, and Australia.

Most of the established local Turkish American groups are located in California, Arizona, Illinois, New York, and New Jersey. The local associations maintain websites and newsletters with links and news items from Turkey. They have also collected donations to assist victims of earthquakes that have hit Turkey. Turkish music and folk dance programs are universal elements in local group functions. The Kansas City Turkish Association website explains the emphasis on artistic expression as a way to make the "connection with Americans and their sub-cultures."

The Turkish American Association of Southern California (ATA-SC) is perhaps the oldest Turkish American local ethnic group. Established in 1953 as the Turkish-American Club, the group gathers to observe special occasions, such as *Eid* (*Byram* in Turkish) and other national days. The constant movement of Turks in and out of Southern California has caused the group to suffer periods of relative inactivity. In 1985, as the size of the community grew, the group adopted its current name. *Ata*, which means "father" in Turkish, refers to the Ottoman Turkish military leader Mustafa Kemal Ataturk, founder of contemporary Turkey.

Turkish American local associations, mainly organize recreational activities. The Minnesota Turkish American Association, for example, organizes backgammon tournaments. In New York, ATA-NY maintains facilities for ping-pong, foosball, and pool. The group also provides information about *Eid* and its rituals as well as Muslim prayer time schedules. In North Carolina, ATA-NC established a library of Turkish books, cassettes, and videos for people planning to visit Turkey. The Turkish American Cultural Association of Michigan organizes gatherings to allow members to watch Turkish soccer games through satellite television. The group's newsletter, *Anatolian Voice*, publishes quarterly and is filled with community news, obituaries, and advertisements. Among all local Turkish American associations only those in southern California, New York, and Maryland offer Turkish language training.

The Iranian–American Cultural Society of Maryland (IACS), founded in 1968, has been helping to educate others about the Iranian and Persian culture and language. The IACS offers evening Farsi classes at local elementary schools. It also sponsors a youth committee, which organizes such activities as camping, skiing, hiking and swimming throughout the year. For the older members, the group offers lectures that run the gamut of topics; everything from breast cancer to Persian poets are covered in this biweekly program. The IACS also sponsors a number of parties and cultural events, such as *Narooz*, or Spring Festival, for members of all ages. Still, for many Iranian American Muslims, especially since the Iranian revolution, the mosque remains the center of community life.

South Asian Muslims identify themselves by religion, lingual ancestry, and country of origin. The Bangladesh Association of Chicagoland was founded in 1980 by renowned Bangali American architect Dr. Fazlur Rahman Khan, who designed the Sears Tower and the John Hancock Center in Chicago. The organization brings Bangalis together in social and sports activities. It also raises funds to assist in relief efforts following natural disasters in Bangladesh. The group sponsored a national gathering of Bangladeshi Americans in 1992 and organized a conference in 1993 on Bangla literature. Its website reports that the Governor of Illinois proclaimed a Bangladesh Day on March 26, 1994, in honor of American citizens of Bangali origin.

The Bangladesh Association of North Texas in Dallas, Texas, was formed in

1988, seeking to promote Bangladeshi culture in north Texas and to facilitate Bangladeshi-American involvement in the welfare of American society in general. Sometimes, however, the group exhibits concern for the American Muslim community in general. On February 10, 2001, the group hosted Congressman Pete Session to speak about the recognition of Muslims in the United States.

The Federation of Bangladeshi Associations in North America was established in New York in 1987. But it has hardly galvanized a national Bangali American identity. With few resources, the organization has managed to conduct annual gatherings that bring members of local Bangali communities together. An editorial in the September 1995 issue of *Protiddhani*, a quarterly journal of the local affiliate Greater Washington–Bangladesh Association of America, suggested that the establishment of Bangali community centers must become a priority for all Bangalis. Yet the hope has not been matched by support from community members.

The Bangladesh Association of Central Ohio has celebrated Victory Day (February 24) and Bangladesh Day (April 21) and has organized an annual community picnic. In order to pass the Bengali culture to the youth, the group proposed an ethnic-language program in 1990. A few months later the association announced that the Bangla School project had been abandoned due to lack of interest from parents and volunteer teachers.

The Bangladeshi-Canadian Community Center is another example of unfulfilled hopes. Since 1997 a group of Canadian citizens of Bangladeshi origin set up an organizational structure of bylaws, committees, and officers, with the objective of raising funds to build a community center in Ottawa, Canada. The project never materialized because of a lack of community support. The group, however, has not abandoned its goal and has managed to build a website that contains useful links to Canadian government service agencies and Bangladeshi news sites.

The largest segment of North American Muslims of South Asian descent hails from Pakistan. The Pakistani-American Association in Raleigh, North Carolina, holds several events each year, including observances of *Eid*, Ramadan, and Pakistan Day (August 14). Family-oriented activities are designed to create an atmosphere in which Pakistani-American children can experience their cultural heritage. While the influence of religion is evident in some Pakistani groups, others, like the Pakistan Association of Greater Boston, states that it is committed to nonsectarian expressions of Pakistani-American identity. The group hosts Pakistani singers and organizes social events to allow families to meet.

Pakistani Canadians formed the National Federation of Pakistani-Canadians (NFPC) in 1982 in Ottawa—Canada's capital. This umbrella organization of the nation's Pakistani groups enjoys the official recognition of the national government. NFPC communicates with its members through an English-Urdu newsletter that features community news, Canadian news, and Pakistani government announcements. The Federation has several representatives in each of the various provinces. However, volunteer officers run the group;

it has no dedicated office to represent Canada's tens of thousands of ethnic Pakistanis. The NFPC's top-down approach to representing Pakistanis does not appear to have mobilized grassroots support among Canadian families descending from South Asia.

Despite the difficulty inherent in forming stable institutions for small clusters of people, many Muslim immigrants express ethnic pride even when they represent small minorities within these population groups. For example, the India Community Center in Indianapolis, Indiana, attempts to involve citizens of Indian origin in its activities. The center hosts an annual celebration of Indian Independence Day and a Spring Festival with music, dance, and Indian food. The group also hosts fund-raising activities to help victims of natural disasters in India. Muslims of Indian descent have taken part in the activities of the center, which allows them to use the facility to celebrate their own religious holidays. And when the center's youth participate in the national March of Dimes fund-raising walk, the Muslim youth members join in as well.

Ethnic affiliations instill in Muslims an appreciation for experiences that cut across religious boundaries. For example, Hindus, Buddhists, Sikhs, and Muslims from Bangladesh, India, Pakistan, and Kashmir share a special taste for spicy food, Indian movies (sold on videotape in ethnic stores), and Pakistani sitcoms (viewed on satellite television). While South Asian food has become an accepted, even ubiquitous, part of North America's international cuisine, ethnic films and television shows may not survive the pressures of assimilation. Young people are not well versed in their parents' ancestral languages, although they are exposed to these native languages at home. Also fading away is the ethnic clothing, which now usually is worn only during cultural events and during community observations of religious holidays and ethnic-pride days. Interestingly, cricket, a sport that was introduced to South Asia during the British colonial period, is followed by South Asians in the United States and Canada, and young South Asians have formed cricket teams in schools. Of course these students also follow basketball, football, and other popular American sports.

Recent immigrants from Africa have also established ethnic associations. This is true even in the case of newly established nations, such as Eritrea. The Eritrean Community Center of Minnesota (ECCM) is a nonprofit organization established in the Twin Cities (Minneapolis and St. Paul) in 1986 to work toward an increased understanding of Eritrean culture and heritage. ECCM sponsors Tigrigna language classes for children and adults, mentoring and tutoring programs for Eritrean youths, and cultural nights for the public. The center also runs weekly radio and television programs and publishes a quarterly newsletter in English and Tigrigna.

VILLAGE HOMELAND GROUPS

A subset of the national origin organizations is the affiliations based on a shared ancestral village or region of the homeland. Often such groups form in locales where a large number of people sharing a certain ancestral birthplace live in close proximity. For example, the Lifta Association, based in Burbank, Illinois, operates a community center that is open most evenings. The group's name is taken from a Palestinian village near Jerusalem where the founders were born. The village witnessed a wave of immigration after the Israeli occupation of the West Bank in 1967. The list of the group's recent speakers reveals civic links that are much broader than the limited attachment to the ancestral village. In 2001 the group hosted representatives of the Mosque Foundation in Chicago; a board member of the Lifta Arab Organization of Amman, Jordan; a former member of the Jordanian Parliament; a representative of the U.S. Bureau of the Census; and local Illinois-based *imams* and attorneys.

Deir Debwan Association was established in 1979 by Palestinian immigrants who named the group after their ancestral town. The organization aimed to support the Palestinian drive for self-determination. Most of the group's activities, however, promote Palestinian folk arts and culture. The group's Arabic language website contains traditional Palestinian folk songs, proverbs, stories, poems, and lullabies.

Another example of birthplace associations is the Bint Jbeil Club in Dearborn, Michigan. Bint Jbeil is a predominantly Shia village in southern Lebanon. Many of the village residents have immigrated to Dearborn, especially after the Israeli occupation of that part of Lebanon in 1982. When Israel withdrew from the village in 1999 the club joined other Arab-American community groups in organizing a parade in Dearborn. The club hosts Shia celebrations such as *Ashura*, but welcomes Arab and Muslim users of its community center facilities regardless of religious affiliations. The center's hall is a favorite place for wedding ceremonies in Dearborn, especially among low-income families. The club also offers scholarships for students.

From Africa there is the Gonja Association of North America (GANA), which was created in 1994 by people with roots in Ghana. Founded in Easton, Pennsylvania, this nonprofit organization works to enhance Gonjaland cultures and traditions, to support group members in times of crisis and other periods of need, and to offer a platform for communication. GANA acknowledges diversity among the Gonja people. While Muslims represent a minority among those with Ghanian origins, they are a majority among those from the northern part of the country. GANA maintains an open membership policy, allowing non-Gonja people to take part in its activities. It also informs members about jobs and investment opportunities them with provides immigration information. The group meets monthly and holds annual elections.

ETHNO-RELIGIOUS GROUPS

Few associations exhibit a mix of faith and ethnic sympathies. A notable exception is the Islamic Association for Palestine (IAP). Efforts to organize IAP started in the early 1980s by students working informally to offer each other support and to educate others about the Palestinian cause. The organization was formalized in the early 1990s with a headquarters in Chicago, Illinois—home to one of the largest Palestinian-American populations in North America. The group also maintains an office in Dallas, Texas, and operates chapters in Detroit, Michigan, and Paterson, New Jersey. Despite strong anti-Israeli statements from IAP, the group is open for news from all sources. Its website offers information about the Palestinian history of dispossession and current news updates of the conflict from American, Arab, Palestinian, and Israeli outlets, allowing members to view events from all sides.

The deterioration of the status of Palestinian communities around the world produced floods of immigrants to North America. To connect with these arrivals, the organization distributes literature to draw attention to the plight of the Palestinians. IAP also sponsors the Arabic *Al-Zaytuna*, a biweekly newspaper. In addition, two IAP-sponsored bands, the Stars and al-Isra, perform folk music at weddings and other community events. Despite IAP's fervent religious and historical view on the Israeli–Palestinian conflict, the group has engaged other Palestinian groups, including Arab Christians and secular ethnic Muslims.

In the 1990s many IAP members had already become citizens and a new generation of U.S.-born Palestinian Muslims have joined the organization. From the IAP's standpoint, maintaining the attachment of young Palestinian Americans to the Palestinian cause. For young people, the group organizes camps, picnics, and other recreational and educational activities, which are increasingly conducted in the English language. To keep youth-awareness high, IAP also organizes conventions, festivals, lectures, and exhibitions. Gradually the group has increased awareness of its American identity.

Therefore, pressing for the rights of Palestinians has gone hand in hand with expressions cherishing American citizenship. The growing identification with America is only rivaled by the revulsion many Palestinian Americans express to what they see as the U.S. government bias toward one side of the conflict. To Palestinian Americans, the global world under the leadership of the United States is a good in which they seek to partake. But it can improve if fairness is practiced toward their ethnic cohorts, who are also part of the human family and have suffered for so long.

Another ethno-religious association struggling to define its relevance to America is the North American Bangladeshi Islamic Community (NABIC). It began in 1990 in Tennessee, and since 1991 the group has held an annual meeting to discuss general Islamic topics and concerns of the Bangladeshi and Muslim communities in North America, the Bangali homeland, and the Muslim world. In 1993 the group started a bilingual newsletter, which is sometimes available at local Islamic centers.

NABIC calls itself an "*Ummah*-oriented, but Bangladesh-focused organization." Its website explains the group's name, ethnic allegiance, and the Bangali connection.

We are Muslims and as such we are part [sic] of the *Ummah*. Wherever Muslims live, their duties and responsibilities are manifold. At one level,

we are a part of the large Muslim community in North America. . . .
As Muslims we must share in the aspirations of a broader change of
the *Ummah*. As Bangladeshi Muslims we have certain special responsibilities. . . . However, *Ummatic* orientation should not be impractical or non-
functional. As a part of the *Ummah* we share the aspiration that someday
the Ummah will be united and, in whatever small way possible, NABIC
would like to contribute toward meeting that aspiration. . . . Those who are
closely associated with NABIC also actively participate in their respective
local Muslim communities. . . . To work with NABIC means, parallel to
the interaction with the larger Muslim community, to create the universal-
istic Islamic values among Bangladeshi Muslims; to help them build a better link with their respective local community and mosques; to tune their
hearts with the heart-beat of the *Ummah*.

Such an inward-looking definition of how the group relates to the North
American context includes a recognition of various levels of group formation:
Muslim Bangalis, mosqued-Bangalis, mosque community, and a continental
Muslim community—all part of an *ummah* guided by universal Islamic values.
But this NABIC statement is more focused on the group's role as an agent to foster the attachment between Bangalis and the *ummah*. By excluding references to
the non-Muslims of North America, NABIC is not necessarily suggesting that
its members should be disinterested in linkages with others; rather it is merely
acknowledging that this work is beyond the present scope of NABIC. But if the
group is to appeal to members who are exposed in their daily lives to so many
influences from outside the Muslim community, NABIC must develop a coherent conception of this surrounding and how it relates to its ethno-religious
worldview.

Activities at the Afghan Community Foundation (ACF) in Atlanta,
Georgia, offer a mix of devotion to religious observance, attachment to the country of origin, and enjoyment of cultural arts. In the foundation's 2000 celebration
of *Eid al-Adha*, a day of joy turned somber when members of the community,
including the U.S.-born youth, began discussing the state of the Afghan people
in their ancestral land. Popular Afghan musicians are frequently invited to enter-
tain the community. When an earthquake struck Afghanistan in 1998, ACF
raised relief funds in partnership with the International Red Cross. Most Muslim
contributions to the earthquake victims were channeled through the community's relief agencies.

Most ethnic organizations are small, with home-based officers who function
voluntarily as coordinators of social and educational events. For example,
NABIC claims only 120 members in seventeen states. The Turkish American
Cultural Association of Florida, founded in 1986, reported having 170 members
in 2000. The Bangladesh Association of Central Ohio claimed eighty-five members in 2000. The Bangladesh Association of North Texas in Dallas, Texas,
formed in 1988, claimed 500 members in 2001. *Shetubondhon* (bridge building in
Bangla) is a discussion group of Bangalis who meet on the basis of national ori-

gin, but stress similarities beyond religious distinctions. Formed in 1999, it has reported only 600 subscribers. Presently the Iranian American Cultural Society of Maryland reports a membership of 600 families. Most groups, however, do not publish their membership numbers.

Within most ethnic organizations, religion does not necessarily play a role in members' shared activities. For Muslim members, the extent to which faith is part of the experience is determined by their own ideology and interactions with non-Muslim members of their ethnic groups. In some cases—as in the Arab-American community or in communities of South Asian origin—Christians, Hindus, and Sikhs have influenced the way that Muslims express their ethnicity. While each religious subgroup maintains its own place of worship, members of various religious affinities have a chance to broaden their social circle in ethnicity-based forums.

ETHNICITY IN A COSMOPOLITAN WORLD

Multiculturalism is a federal policy in Canada and several federal agencies are dedicated to the preservation of traditional ways of life. In the United States, expressions of ethnic pride have increasingly been encouraged in many local and national forums. Since the start of the most recent wave of immigration in 1965, the Smithsonian in Washington, D.C., a federally funded institution, has been hosting an annual multicultural program called the Folklife Festival. The Smithsonian frequently holds events featuring musical instruments, storytelling, films, performances, and culinary arts of various ethnic groups. In major metropolitan areas immigrant groups hold annual ethnic pride days. Such events include the St. Petersburg, Florida, International Folk Festival, the Ethnic Enrichment Festival in Kansas City, and the Raleigh, North Carolina, International Festival—to name a few. The Texas Folklife Festival, which is sponsored by the Institute of Texan Cultures at the University of Texas at San Antonio, has been held annually since 1971.

The presence of new ethnicities in such metropolises as Chicago is so visible that local public agencies have decided to establish liaison offices to help communicate with the various groups. The Advisory Commission on Arab Affairs of the Chicago Commission on Human Relations deals specifically with Arab-American issues. The advisory council even works to educate teachers about Arab Americans and their contributions to America. The city celebrates Arab-American month in November.

Just as faith has been intertwined with ethnic identity, so have class, occupation, and gender. There are several Muslim women's groups that identify themselves with a certain ancestry, but very few of these groups, mainly Palestinian and Lebanese, have organized for the sake of gender and ethnic awareness. Rather, most of these groups are social-services oriented. In a number of cases, members of ethnic groups who share a certain profession have come together to form associations. Examples include the Iranian-American Film Forum, Arab Film Festival, the Radius of Arab American Writers, the Association of Egyptian

American Scholars, the Egyptian American Professional Society, the American Lebanese Medical Association, the Turkish American Neuropsychiatric Association, the Pakistani American Pharmaceutical Association, the Association of Pakistani Physicians of North America, the Bangladesh Chemical and Biological Society of North America, and the American Association of Bangladeshi Engineers and Architects. Typically, these groups facilitate networking among members and offer assistance to those beginning their careers.

The ethnic character of some guilds that drew membership from recent immigrant professionals may have been influenced by turmoil in the homelands and uncertainty about current and future career opportunities. The story of the Society of Afghan Engineers (SAE) is perhaps the clearest example thus far of the dynamic interplay between ethnic and occupational interests in the global scene. After the devastation of Afghanistan during the Soviet invasion and the failure of the tribal Afghan society to reconstruct, many Afghan professionals left the country. But these professionals never lost their attachment to their homeland, and they continued to believe that they will have ample job opportunities in any future rebuilding of Afghanistan. After all, these individuals constitute the human resource base whose qualifications are highly needed for rebuilding.

The engineers probably calculated that reconstruction will start someday and that they will be much in need. In the meantime they sought to acquire more skills and expertise while working in the West. In 1993 more than 120 engineers gathered in Northern Virginia to form the SAE and to discuss Afghan reconstruction. They came from the United States, Canada, Germany, and Switzerland and resolved that they would maintain their independence of any government. They also committed to respecting legal authorities while attempting to offer advice to governments or institutions interested in providing assistance for the reconstruction of their homeland. Soon after the overthrow of the Taliban, many of these engineers began relocating to Afghanistan to help in the rebuilding of the homeland.

Before such ethnic guilds came into existence, graduates of the Muslim Student Association established in the early 1970s the Association of Muslim Scientists and Engineers, the Association of Muslim Social Scientists, and the Islamic Medical Association. In 1999 young professionals of different ethnic backgrounds from the Chicago Metropolitan area established the Council of American Muslim Professionals, focusing on professional networking and development, along with community service activities. Their website recently announced the group's offering of two scholarships of at least $500 each to Muslim students demonstrating financial need and academic merit. Whether ethnic or religious, these guilds have helped their members land jobs and establish professional contacts in North America and in countries of the Muslim world.

Similarly, ethnic student associations have been formed ever since students from Muslim countries began coming to the United States and Canada for study. These student associations began as foreign student organizations, but as generations of North American–born students took over, the groups began expressing American and Canadian identities. They are usually sponsored by their colleges, which offer student groups rooms to hold meetings, as well as funds to offset the cost of activities. The groups usually offer tutoring to their members, and senior members usually act as mentors to freshman students. They also conduct ethnic-awareness programs and organize cultural activities and panel discussions on the concerns of their communities. In some cases, organized ethnic students have been able to assert some cultural influence on their campuses. For example, the Turkish Dance Association, whose performance troupe represents Turkish folk traditions from different regions of the country, is a student program at the Arizona State University.

As we have seen, ethnic life is centered around the quest to meet important needs: exploring social connections with familiar people, expressing pride in family heritage, maintaining relations with relatives, and teaching native languages. Still, few ethnic associations run ethnic-language programs. At community centers and in immigrant homes, most children are exposed to their parents' native tongues in the form of second-language learning. Few become competent speakers in this way; fewer still achieve competency in reading and writing. Thus for many immigrant Muslims, the acquisition of American and Canadian identities has often meant the dominance of English and French over native languages. Ethnic clothing, too, often is relegated to only occasional use. Despite these attachments in the lives of immigrants, the socioeconomic future of their children has taken precedence over the preservation of ancestral tongues and customs in the lives of ethnic Muslim families.

Clearly the priorities of group formation among the ethnically oriented communities are social and economic. But both religious and ethnic Muslims seek the material betterment of life. Nonreligious (some may say secular) interests are evident in the growth of the various ethnic and religious guilds. And while some groups have blended teachings of the mosque with the concerns of particular ethnic groups outside institutions of religious learning, the more numerous nonreligious ethnic groups have sometimes made accommodations for the religious requirements of their members. Indeed, in some cities lacking Muslim worship facilities, ethnic organizations have offered members information about the practice of their faith and have hosted religious functions in their facilities. The ethnic-religious Muslim discourse in North America is increasingly producing new terminology describing the attitude of members of the community: recent immigrant, first-, second-, and third-generation ethnic American, cultural Muslim, practicing Muslim. In group formation, ethnic associations can be strictly and consciously nonreligious or multireligious, or can blend religious values and memories with ethnic identity.

Most definitions of ethnicity are based on easily observable features such as skin color or complexion. In the case of many immigrant Muslims, however, ancestral homeland and language have formed the basis of ethnic identity. In addition, these immigrants have also found common ground with those who share their tastes in artistic expressions and foods, or those who share their practices in marriage customs and interpersonal mores. The most dominant ethnic group formation is the one based on country of origin, perhaps reflecting the continuing influence of the contemporary nation-state system in the dynamics of the global world.

While ethnic associations have identified with what they believed to be issues affecting the welfare of their worldwide ethnic community, they have not established national ethnic identities in North America nor have they invested significant resources in the teaching of ethnic languages. To the rest of Canadians and Americans these associations are only part of the cultural mosaic of this continent. Their special dishes and sweets have found a place in the American and Canadian restaurant industries. Patterns of both adaptation and religious preservation are found. While the South Asian *Shirwal Qamis*, the Arab *Thawb*, and the Turkish *palvar* and *mintan* have given way to contemporary North American clothing styles, *hijab* has survived because it is rooted in deeply held religious convictions rather than traditional ethnic customs. Because of this, in many instances involving issues of religious accommodation in the workplace, Muslim women wearing *hijab* is embracing the corporate world's preferences of style, fabric, and businesslike image. And for some in the professional class their know-how of modern world technology and homeland language and culture have meant opportunities for them across the globe.

Integrating into North American society has not meant shedding all aspects of one's cultural heritage. For one thing, the Canadian and American traditions are pluralistic in nature. In the Muslim immigrant experience, faith has created bonds among people of various ethnic backgrounds. Similarly, ethnic traditions have cemented bonds across religious boundaries. But worship and kinship are only two facets in the lives of people who intend to remain relevant to a dynamic worldwide web of economic, political, and cultural interactions. The next chapter will show that such ties have facilitated the delivery of assistance to those in need.

A CLOSER LOOK
THE SOCIETY OF AFGHAN ENGINEERS

The Society of Afghan Engineers (SAE) is a private nonprofit and nonpolitical corporation whose purpose is to encourage financial and technical assistance for the reconstruction and prosperity of Afghanistan.

Who We Are

The Society of Afghan Engineers was formed in 1993 by a group of Afghan engineers in Northern Virginia and surrounding areas who believe that they have a moral responsibility to help the grief-stricken people of Afghanistan. This Society is not an agency of the Afghan government or any other government. In addition, they are careful not to encroach upon, bypass, or circumvent the legal authority of the agencies of the Afghan government in advocating financial and technical aid from donor organizations. Rather, the Society is designed to serve as a catalyst or consultant to governments or institutions interested in receiving or providing financial and technical assistance for the reconstruction of Afghanistan. As a nonprofit, 501(c)(3) organization, the SAE is tax-exempt and is authorized to engage in cultural, educational, literary, and charitable activities.

Objectives

- To provide a forum for Afghan engineers to study and discuss technical problems related to the reconstruction of Afghanistan and to suggest appropriate solutions.
- To foster international support and solicit financial and technical assistance for the reconstruction of Afghanistan.
- To participate in the implementation of reconstruction programs in Afghanistan.
- To develop a network of engineers and advocates to promote the goals of the society and to create a center of guidance and counseling for young Afghans who want to pursue professional careers.
- To provide support and encouragement to Afghan engineers living abroad in order to enable them to accept job assignments in Afghanistan.

Organizational Structure

The structure of the SAE is the following:
- Board of Directors;
- Executive Committee;
- Technical Committees: Housing, Irrigation, Power; Transportation, Manufacturing, and Industry; Natural Resources;
- Administrative Committees: Planning, Publication, Translation, Membership, and Chapters.

A Closer Look, continued on next page

A Closer Look, continued

SAE Membership

There are two categories of members: regular and honorary. Regular membership is open to any Afghan who supports the purpose of the Society and who has completed at least four years of university-level education in engineering or architecture and/or an equivalent professional experience. Honorary membership is open to any individuals, regardless of national origin, who are able to make a significant contribution (monetary or otherwise) to the cause of the Society. Honorary members cannot vote or hold elective office.

Source: From www.afghan-engineers.org.

SEVEN

SOCIAL SERVICE AND CHARITY ORGANIZATIONS

Many Muslims give their *zagat* and *sadaquah* to mosque-run charitable funds. Others, perhaps because their community centers do not have the institutional infrastructure to manage the collection and distribution of donations, seek out independent charity groups instead. American Muslim community charities and social service agencies have proliferated in the past two decades. While many of these groups specialize in sending emergency help in the face of international crises, a growing number of programs provide services to the needy in local communities.

Overall, these charity groups are small in comparison to their counterparts in other faith communities. But most American Muslim aid societies were established after the mid-1980s, depend on a much smaller donor base, and, unlike other religious charities, receive little public funding. The groups conduct fund-raising activities through direct mail, charity dinners, advertisements in community publications, Internet sites, and participation in community conventions and other gatherings. Compared to the large religious and secular charities in the United States, Muslim aid societies seem marginal in terms of funds at their disposal—but that is how the larger organizations started many decades ago. Like other charities, Muslim charity groups provide services at home and abroad.

INTERNATIONAL RELIEF

Many American Muslims contribute a portion of their charitable donations to international relief efforts. Wars, natural disasters, and conflicts have afflicted many people in Asia, Africa, Europe, and South America, and all too often the victims are Muslims, who now are the majority of the world's refugees. Vivid images of destitution on television and in newspapers testify to the stark disparities in living conditions between North America and many parts of the Muslim world. For Muslims leading comfortable lives in the United States and Canada, being part of the *ummah* has meant identification with the plight of those helpless, voiceless fellow Muslims.

Initiatives to form charity organizations often come from individuals who recognize the dire need for assistance internationally. Sometimes the founders and staff of such groups have roots in service delivery regions. Many have known, sometimes first-hand, of the realities of destitution. International relief groups come in various religious and ethnic hues and often begin by focusing on particular problems or regions. Growing in resources and credibility, these groups expand their programs and, in cases of sudden disasters, aid people outside their area of focus.

The pioneer in the work of Islamic philanthropy in North America is Human Concern International (HCI) of Ottawa, Ontario. The group's establishment in 1980 followed the devastating Soviet invasion of Afghanistan. HCI, however, has also provided emergency assistance to victims of wars and natural disasters in Africa, Asia, Europe, and South America. Most of the staff and their offices are located among recipient populations, primarily in Peshawar, Pakistan—the location of a number of Afghan refugees and a place where the cost of hiring field workers is low. HCI has built Hope Village in the Pakistani region of Akora Khattak, with six primary schools, vocational training centers, income generation projects, and a child-sponsorship program.

To keep the administrative cost of aid delivery low, HCI depends on 250 volunteers from the Canadian Muslim community. The group has administered aid projects sponsored by the Canadian International Development Agency and other international bodies, including the Swedish Committee and the United Nations Development Program. Much of the assistance HCI distributes, an average of $2 million annually, has taken the form of emergency relief.

In the United States, the Indian Muslim Relief Committee was established in 1982 under the sponsorship of ISNA. With an average annual collection of $1.5 million, the committee funds a number of education projects in India. It has established training centers to help prospective college students prepare for entrance exams, provided scholarships for those who succeeded through the admission process, and it has built teacher-training centers for women. India is home to some of the world's poorest populations, including many Muslims.

The Islamic African Relief Agency (IARA) was established in 1984 with a focus on Africa, but it has provided emergency assistance elsewhere as well. In Timbuktu, Mali, the organization has implemented a health care program that combines extensive medical services with health education activities. Organization officials claim its grassroots approach has been more effective than the bureaucratic methods of its official partners, including UN agencies and the U.S. Agency for International Development (USAID). They claim that the key to its success has been the use of Malian local school graduates, who live among the people they serve. As a result, the group says, its educational program has introduced contemporary medical knowledge, challenging traditional beliefs and practices. On average, the group distributes $2.5 million in annual aid.

Benevolence International Foundation (BIF) was established in 1987 in Worth, Illinois. The organization started with the mission to help people emerging from the ruins of communism. BIF first provided short-term relief (such as emergency food distribution), and then moved on to long-term projects providing education and vocational training to children, widows, refugees, and the injured. These projects include providing vaccinations and clothing to new-born babies, as well as building toilets and showers in the largest refugee camps. The organization is currently conducting projects in Azerbaijan, Daghestan, and Tajikistan. More recently the group distributed emergency assistance in China, Palestine, and Pakistan. The organization disperses an average of $1.75 million in aid annually.

The Holy Land Foundation (HLF) was established in 1989 in Dallas, Texas, with a focus on providing aid to Palestinian refugees. The Palestinian American community is fairly large and the plight of Palestinian refugees draws strong sympathy, not only among American Muslims but also within the more established community of Arab-American Christians. HLF is perhaps the largest of the Muslim charity groups, collecting an average total of $10 million per year. The group maintains regional offices in California, Illinois, Michigan, and New Jersey.

HLF reports that it has developed wells in Lebanon serving 75,000 beneficiaries in the refugee camps of Al Rashediyah, Al Badawi, Ein El Helway, Al Jaleel, Wady El Jamous, and Al Rashediyah Al Jadeed. In addition the organization has funded the Rehabilitation Center for the Handicapped located in Amman, Jordan, and Dar Al-Salam Hospital in Gaza. In Hebron the group funded the establishment of the Al Anwar Al-Ibrahimiya Youth Education Center, where students can find books not available in school or at home. The center also offers computer-skills training and English language classes.

Life for Relief and Development (formerly the International Relief Association and popularly known as Life) was founded in 1993 in response to the humanitarian crisis that developed in Iraq in the wake of the 1990–1991 Gulf War. The United Nations has estimated that half a million Iraqi children die every year as a result of international economic sanctions. The group established its headquarters in Detroit, Michigan, which is home to a sizable Iraqi-American community. Life has built, renovated, and administered schools and rehabilitation centers in Iraq and has offered assistance in other countries. Life's annual collection has averaged $5 million, of which an increasing portion in recent years has been distributed as emergency aid to beneficiaries in Sierra Leone and Kosovo.

Other charity organizations, such as Mercy International, did not specialize in any particular region. The group, which is known as Mercy, was founded in 1986 with offices in Plymouth, Michigan, and Covina, California. It is registered with USAID and has consultative status with the UN Economic and Social Council. Although much of its funding comes from Muslim community sources, Mercy has implemented aid projects funded by USAID, the U.S. Department of Agriculture, the U.S. Department of Labor, the UN High Commissioner for Refugees, the World Food Program, UNICEF, the World Health Organization, and CARE International. With annual funds averaging $2.5 million, Mercy has assisted people in Afghanistan, Albania, Bangladesh, Bosnia and Herzegovina, Chechnya, Kosovo, Mozambique, Somalia, Kenya, and Turkey.

Mercy began as an effort to raise funds for Afghan refugees, and this remained its primary focus until 1989, when the group began providing emergency assistance to refugees and the poor in Kashmir, Lebanon, Somalia, Bangladesh, Cambodia, Ethiopia, Eritrea, and Sudan. To help in the delivery of development assistance, Mercy has established field offices in Somalia and Kenya, where the group runs primary schools, rural clinics, and a food convoy program that brings food directly to people in the drought-stricken horn of Africa. In addition Mercy provided aid to earthquake victims in Iran and the expatriate workers who fled Kuwait after the Iraqi invasion. The group also funded the building of the Afghan Surgical Hospital and three other clinics that serve Afghan refugees in Pakistan. In 1991 it built a clinic in Bangladesh and sponsored three mobile medical units in the West Bank. That same year Mercy also provided aid to Iraqi victims of war, including the Kurds in the north.

In 1992 Mercy sent emergency aid in the aftermath of an earthquake in Egypt and to the Burmese Muslims who faced extreme persecution and were forced from Burma into Bangladesh. When the genocidal war in Bosnia began in the same year, Mercy started providing aid, eventually establishing offices in Bosnia, Croatia, and Albania in 1994 to coordinate the effort. This aid included the distribution of food, medicine, firewood, and water purification kits. The assistance also included the delivery of agricultural seeds and fertilizer to farmers, as well as a poultry project that revived production at a local plant. That same year, Mercy also teamed with *Medecins sans Frontiers* (or Doctors Without Borders) to renovate an intravenous fluid production facility in Bosnia. The Bosnian programs also encompassed rape counseling and orphan care.

Global Relief Foundation (GRF) was established in Bridgeview, Illinois, in 1992 and later established offices in Kosovo, Chechnya, Afghanistan, Pakistan, and Kashmir. In Gokova, Kosovo, the group built vocational centers that provide training in foreign languages, computers, and sewing. In Afghanistan the group distributes poultry incubators to widows to encourage economic self-sufficiency. GRF has been registered with USAID as a private voluntary organization. The group's revenues average about $1.5 million annually.

In 1993 the ICNA established ICNA Relief, which was later renamed Helping Hand. The bulk of the organization's annual $4 million collection is used to fund programs in Pakistan, India, and Bangladesh, the homelands of most ICNA members. Like other agencies, Helping Hand has contributed to emergency relief efforts throughout the world during times of crisis.

All relief groups together—including the much smaller, ethnically oriented aid societies like Palestine Children's Relief Fund, the Jerusalem Fund, Palestine Aid Society, United Palestinian Appeal, Turkish Children Foster Care, Badr for Development and Relief (offering aid in Tunisia), Algerian Relief Fund, and Al-Ehssan Charitable Relief Organization (working in Somalia)—collect, on average, less than $35 million per year from all sources. In contrast, according to *The Chronicle of Philanthropy*, the top twenty-five U.S. charities alone received about $13 billion from private donors alone in 2000. A significant portion of this income has been distributed overseas. All the distributions, including those from Muslim charities, however, have alleviated little suffering for the world's poor.

While continuing to pursue grassroots approaches to refugee aid, Muslim relief groups have increasingly sought grants from government, international agencies, and private voluntary associations. Mercy, for example, is raising a growing percentage of its funds outside of the Muslim community. The group's 1998 financial statement showed that 21 percent of its funds came from federal government grants; 17 percent came from the United Nations and private foundations.

Some Muslims believe that these charity groups should stay away from government funding, lest they become dependent on it. Most, however, believe that these groups have established a track record of service and should have a fair chance at acquiring public funds, which are collected in part from Muslim taxpayers. After all, the charities are not religious institutions so they should welcome any assistance in the delivery of aid to the poor. Indeed, when the U.S. Department of State removed HLF and IARA from its list of recognized aid providers in 2000, the groups charged the government with religious and ethnic discrimination and initiated legal challenges.

The Muslim community's increased awareness of the rising need to deliver assistance in America has caused several aid societies to pay more attention to the home front. Indeed, several of the Muslim international relief groups have started sponsoring programs in North America. Mercy provided assistance to victims of Hurricane Hugo in South Carolina and Puerto Rico in 1989. In 1993 the group also assisted victims of the flood in Des Moines, Iowa. HLF and Mercy provided relief assistance to the victims of the Oklahoma City bombing in 1995. Since then HLF has opened a food pantry in Paterson, New Jersey, and has funded African-American youth activities in cooperation with Africa-Care. In 2000 GRF awarded $18,000 to the Stone Soup After School Tutorial Program, a youth program run by the North American-Islamic Foundation in Wilmington, Delaware. Helping Hand in New York has initiated a soup kitchen program for the city's homeless population. GRF and HCI have established programs to train the leaders of new community centers in fund-raising strategies and techniques.

A number of Muslim charities jumped in to help in the relief effort in the wake of the September 11 attacks. Helping Hand, based in New York, immediately formed an action plan. It identified affected families, assisted in funeral arrangements, and provided interpreters for victim relatives who did not speak English. HLF established a fund for the victims of the attacks. But after a flare up of violence in the Palestinian–Israeli conflict in December 2001, the Bush administration froze the assets of HLF, effectively shutting down the charity. A few days later the government also blocked the accounts of GRF and BIF. The two groups, as noted before, have been active in aid delivery to Afghanistan and Pakistan, where the United States has conducted a bombing campaign against the Taliban regime and its al-Qaedah allies three weeks after the September 11 attacks.

U.S. government officials charged that HLF services benefit supporters of Hamas—a group designated as terrorist by the U.S. Department of State. The frozen charity groups expressed disappointment, but agreed to comply with the government's decision. a BIF statement read,

> We join the rest of the country in mourning the loss of life caused by the terrorist attacks of September 11. We abhor terrorist activities and strongly deny any involvement in terrorism, including the funding of terrorist activities. We are a law-abiding United States charity, and have nothing to hide. We will fully cooperate with the government's investigation of our activities as well as the activities of the recipients of our funding.

HLF acknowledged that some of the beneficiaries of its assistance programs may be relatives to those implicated in violence against Israel, but insisted that it would be inhumane to exclude hungry refugees from food and medical assistance on account of suspected relatives. HLF pointed out that its projects have focused on the development of vocational, educational, and health care institutions, in addition to the delivery of food and clothing items.

The closure of the charities became part of the public debate over balancing security with civil liberties, as will be discussed in chapter 9. The government accompanied the closure decisions with awarding Mercy a grant worth $2 million to deliver school lunches for poor Albanian children. The move was widely seen as an attempt by the Bush administration to deflect charges of anti-Muslim bias. It was hardly a coincidence that this agreement with Mercy, along with the freezing of accounts of the other charities, all came within one week. The sanctioned charities filed lawsuits against the federal government, charging it with unconstitutional search and seizure.

Unlike large philanthropic institutions found in other American faith communities, Muslim charity agencies have not been active in social advocacy at home or in recipient nations overseas. Leaders of the charities usually argue that the aid they distribute is too small to bring about results anyway. The charities provide aid to poor people who are struggling to secure the basic needs of food and shelter. Donors usually regard any expenses other than deliverable benefits as administrative costs. And the charities have no choice but to abide by the donor preference to keep that cost at a minimum level.

Most of the community's international relief groups have emerged in ethnic communities. But most have increasingly delivered aid to areas of need outside their primary beneficiary group and have sought funding outside their core donor base. This came as a result of pressures from the growing multiethnic, faith-based consciousness, which tends to favor decisions of allocation on grounds of need and effectiveness. This in part explains misgivings expressed widely in the community about the government's charge that some of the charities have been entangled in political violence overseas. The decision of the government to keep the public in the dark about its investigation and the charities' track record of humanitarian work led many to believe that the Bush administration's judgment may have been clouded by anger in the wake of September 11.

Aside from the debate over the constitutionality of the government's sanctions, however, the various charities have hardly established standards of business
to place their organizations outside the politics of recipient nations. Regardless
of how the legal battle over the closure of HLF, BIF, and GRF, American
Muslims have learned that they cannot remain oblivious to the fact that any
socioeconomic activity they support overseas, even as mundane as charitable giving, is viewed by others in terms of its political implication. When such activity
targets areas of high political tension, the need for a clear demarcation between
humanitarian work and any appearance of partisanship becomes even more
urgent.

DOMESTIC SOCIAL SERVICES

Large social service programs targeting domestic beneficiaries in various ethnic
groups began even before the emergence of international relief groups. ACCESS,
which has been active since the mid-1970s, is perhaps the oldest and largest of
such agencies. Its multi-million-dollar programs include immigration, referral,
and liaison services. ACCESS offers community members information on available jobs, assists in the job application process, and offers job-training classes. In
addition to grants received from private foundations, the agency participates in
government programs designed to help poor families get off welfare, to match
the unemployed with work assignments, and to teach refugees computer skills
and basic English.

ACCESS also offers programs for immunization, health screening, infant
and child health care education, breast cancer prevention, AIDS education, and
smoking prevention. The organization offers an after-school program designed
to assist students lagging academically due to language difficulties. These services include tutoring and computer skills programs targeting at-risk Arab-
American children. ACCESS also manages a traveling exhibition illuminating
the lives of Arab Americans, a radio program featuring Arab and other ethnic
music, and an annual Arab culture street festival featuring performances of traditional dance and music.

Several other social service programs are run primarily with public funds and
target certain ethnic groups. Typically such programs are approved by government
agencies when there is a demonstrable need for them. Activists can make a good
case for funding if they can provide need-assessment studies—and if there is some
public recognition of the target beneficiary group. Such programs, however, end
with their funding. The reason that a program like ACCESS has stood the test of
time lies perhaps in the large size of the Arab-American community in Dearborn,
Michigan, which translates into leverage in the process of grant allocation.

Dearborn is home to other smaller Muslim community social service centers. Some of these organizations, like the Bint Jbail Cultural Center, are based
largely on community self-help action. The center provides about twenty $500
scholarships annually to students and rents out its facility for family social occasions at discounted rates.

Much smaller social assistance groups have emerged sporadically in local communities around the country, working along traditional concepts of social assistance—collecting and distributing food, cash, and clothing to those in need. One association operating in Maryland is the Islamic-American Zakat Foundation, which provides food, shelter, clothing, and transportation to the poor. While the group's beneficiaries are mostly Muslim, other eligible persons are also helped. Another small group working through local community centers is Islamic Services in Livonia, Michigan.

Muslim activists seeking to provide other kinds of assistance through community-based initiatives have established a number of new groups. In some instances social workers with first-hand encounters with the poor took on the initiative to assist the needy. One group established by social welfare workers is the Muslim Inter-Community Network, which began in Maryland in 1989. The group collects food and clothing donations and distributes these goods to needy Muslims in the Washington, D.C., area, as well as to area homeless shelters. In addition, the organization's answering service offers referrals that direct the needy to other social service providers. The agency often works as a liaison between Muslim families and government social service offices and assists Muslim parents interested in participating in foster-family programs.

ASSISTANCE TO REFUGEES

Aid initiatives targeting domestic beneficiaries have increased with the arrival of refugees and low-income immigrants. In Chicago the Bosnian Refugee Center (now called the Bosnian Community Center) was founded in 1994 with federal and state money to serve sixteen thousand refugees in the area. It provides post-settlement services, including employment counseling and English-language classes. Most of the center's beneficiaries are women victims of the Balkan war. To sustain its services, the center established a working relationship with the Islamic Cultural Center, a Bosnian majority-mosque community in Northbrook, Illinois.

On Chicago's south side, a group of DePaul University students formed the Inner-City Muslim Action Network (IMAN) in 1995 to counter trends they saw growing among Muslim youth: gang involvement, drug use, alcohol abuse, and sexual promiscuity. The group blends social service programs with interactive education. IMAN offers after-school programs, youth mentoring, as well as winter and summer camps. The group depends largely on local community centers and student organizations to host and run its activities, but it also secures meeting places outside the mosques. Some public funding has been used to help organize programs designed to keep teenagers off the streets.

Many other social aid initiatives from community leaders emerged outside the mosques and depend highly on government and corporate funding. For example, the Confederation of Somali Community in Minnesota (CSCM) in Minneapolis was incorporated as a nonprofit organization in 1994, three years after refugees from a brutal civil war in Somalia began to arrive in the area.

CSCM founders recruited members from all sectors of the refugee community and sought public and private funding for the rental of a service center. The organization offers recreational activities and tutoring for youth and job placement services.

Because of the language barrier with newly arrived Somali refugees, local and state government agencies find CSCM to be an appropriate social service delivery organization. Thus it has won contracts to implement a number of programs, including Special Supplemental Nutrition Program for Women, Infants and Children (known as WIC), the Safe School program, and assistance benefits for the elderly. CSCM also uses grants such as one from the Bush Foundation in 1996 to fund its work. Today, CSCM has ten full-time staff members who manage several programs. The Somali immigrant group acknowledges that private foundations like McKnight Foundation and United Way and governmental sources like Hennepin County and the State of Minnesota are the primary benefactors of the association.

Many Somalis settled in the Washington metropolitan area, where they often have a hard time finding jobs and housing. The Somali Rescue Agency (SRA) was formed in 1997 to assist these people in the resettlement process, to offer newcomers emergency food assistance and transportation to work or job training centers, and to conduct educational programs meant to help refugees adjust to their new cultural environment. Starting from a home-run office, the group raised only $5,000 in its first year. But by 1999 SRA was providing assistance worth $50,000.

HEALTH SERVICES

Health care is another area of dire need for many Muslims, especially for those without insurance. Members of mosque communities in the medical profession often spearhead such assistance projects. Since the early 1990s twelve doctors in Potomac, Maryland, have run the Ibn Sina, named after the revered eleventh-century Muslim physician (known in European classical literature as Avicenna). These doctors donate their time, on a rotating basis, to care for indigent patients. Ibn Sina doctors also deliver health education lectures at the local Islamic Education Center. In Falls Church, Virginia, the American Muslim Foundation has established a similar program in cooperation with Dar al-Hijrah Mosque and Islamic Center.

Other initiatives have developed beyond allowing low-income patients access to doctors. In 1994 two physicians started the Shifa Clinic in collaboration with the V Street Mosque in Sacramento, California. They realized that many local low-income Muslims did not have access to regular health care services. The clinic serves patients who either have no health insurance or have difficulty in obtaining health care in the traditional health system due to language or cultural barriers. The service has become particularly valuable for recent low-income immigrants after Congress phased out welfare service to noncitizens in 1996. The student-run program has slowly progressed from a location in an apartment to an increasingly well-equipped clinic. The clinic is open to all, but most patients are underserved recent immigrants who speak Urdu, Arabic, and Farsi. Educational programs are also stressed at Shifa, including preventative health-care measures. The clinic also conducts health fairs and health awareness seminars.

In some locations health clinics branched out of the mosque. The Islamic Society of Greater Kansas City runs the Crescent Clinic, which offers free medical care, including doctor visits and some medications. Two physicians, a male and a female, are available at the clinic for two hours every Sunday to see patients of any religious faith. In cooperation with the local health department, the clinic disburses WIC nutrition vouchers to those who qualify. In this government-funded program, services are provided to the general public, although most beneficiaries tend to be affiliated with the mosque community.

Some local service groups started through local, state, and federal grants. In 1996 University Muslim Medical Association (UMMA) at the University of California at Los Angeles (UCLA) established the UMMA Free Clinic. With six exam rooms and a lab, the clinic has provided care for patients who might otherwise have gone without regular medical attention. Although it was established by Muslim students proud of their faith, the UMMA Free Clinic states that it is not a religious organization. Rather, it was conceived as a vehicle to provide community service to the public at large by collaborating with other institutions and organizations. The group of students garnered the administrative and logistical support of the UCLA and Drew schools of medicine as well as City Councilperson Rita Walters. Located in the heart of South Central Los Angeles, one of the poorest and most medically underserved areas in the city, the clinic serves an impoverished population of Latinos and African Americans. The clinic serves the unemployed, the working poor who do not receive insurance or qualify for public assistance, and the homeless. The clinic reports an average of seventy-five patients are seen weekly and a beneficiary base of more than five thousand.

But there is a unique social aspect to the UMMA's treatment method. In addition to health care services, the program provides for lifestyle modification as a preventative measure against diseases like AIDS. The National Philanthropy Day Committee honored the clinic as an Outstanding Volunteer Organization on November 15, 2001. The clinic was selected as the award recipient for the entire Southern California region.

For several Muslim community centers and social service organizations—especially in Canada where multiculturalism is a state policy—securing public funds for employment, refugee settlement, and welfare to poor women and children have been less challenging. Religious and ethnic associations, along with specialized social service providers, have obtained funds for the exclusive benefit of their members. In the United States, where the Muslim community does not enjoy any official recognition, community groups compete for public funds. While some groups have successfully secured funding, many have not been as fortunate because of the lack of qualifications or influence in the decision-making process.

Muslims have also been required to demonstrate that public funds would not be distributed for the promotion of religious belief. As evident in the preceding examples, Muslim service providers have acted with sensitivity to this stipulation, as it is consistent with the First Amendment prohibition of governmental favoritism to any religion.

SERVICES TO WOMEN

A number of groups have targeted women exclusively. This type of service delivery, however, is only beginning. Muslim women's groups struggle to make the case that Islam has given women rights and that Westerners should not stereotype them. In Muslim community forums, these women have begun to make the case for inclusion. They have also asked for resources; and whenever community funds fell short, women's groups petitioned government agencies for support. Such activism by women has not been encouraged by Muslim community leaders. Muslim community forums have increasingly recognized that a gender gap exists between Muslim men and women. Although there are no religious objections to the involvement of Muslim women in public life, men are less interested in such prospects than women.

In the late 1990s a shift began to emerge that favored a focus on the human experience of women away from the ideological debates about the status of Muslim women in community and society. A number of groups began to identify areas of need by women that do not offend the sensibilities of the various sides of the ideological debate. Some of the emerging groups have predictably begun in the area of education. While some activities have been accommodated through the women's committees in mosques, some groups have organized independently.

The Canadian Council of Muslim Women may not have begun to formulate until the early 1980s, but it started its aggressive outreach to women in the mid-1990s. The group's reaction to the custom of female circumcision, which is practiced across religious lines in some African cultures, has been notable. Muslim religious scholars in Africa have not actively opposed the custom because it is not specifically prohibited by religious texts. But the council has dubbed it a form of female genital mutilation and called for an end to the practice. The winter 2000 newsletter of the council reports that their Peel and Toronto chapters have worked with health authorities to stem the practice among immigrants in Canada.

The Federation of Muslim Women (MFW) is another group of mainly South Asian women activists aspiring to enhance the quality of Muslim women's lives in Canada. The group holds social events for mothers and daughters and arranges sports activities. To support these activities MFW has instituted fundraising bazaars at Islamic centers. Such events are an opportunity for nonpracticing Muslim women to come to the mosque. The group has addressed international issues as well, conducting lectures at mosques on subjects like female victims of violence in Pakistan. In the aftermath of September 11, MFW organized a support team to offer counseling to Muslim women, especially those who were targeted in the backlash that followed the attacks. The team developed a network of educators and counselors to deal with the emotional distress of the victims.

In areas with a significant Muslim population, social service centers have paid special attention to domestic abuse. In Wood Dale, Illinois, the Hamdard Center for Health and Human Services has provided medical and counseling services for victims of abuse since 1994. The center's crisis hotline is staffed with multilingual workers who are able to communicate with recent immigrants from the Middle East and South Asia. The center's shelter assists women and children victimized by domestic abuse. Hamdard also provides court-ordered assessments in divorce and child-abuse cases, and serves as a facilitator for publicly funded social service programs. When the agency began, it was completely dependent on community support. While the demand for services grew over time, donations lagged. The agency is now well established and owns its own facilities, but it has become increasingly dependent on public funding.

Whether the beneficiaries of aid are here or abroad, community funds are extremely modest if measured against the actual need. Muslim communities are growing in many localities, although they are relatively small in much of North America. A lack of political clout has limited their access to public funds. Therefore, poor Muslim citizens depend largely on the public welfare system.

A CLOSER LOOK
CANADIAN COUNCIL OF MUSLIM WOMEN

The Canadian Council of Muslim Women is a national nonprofit voluntary organization established to assist Muslim women in participating effectively in Canadian society and to promote mutual understanding between Canadian Muslim women and women of other faiths.

The Organization

In 1982 Muslim women from across Canada attended the Founding Conference of the Canadian Council of Muslim Women in Winnipeg, Manitoba. The Council invites representation from across Canada, and has chapters across Canada.

Canadian Muslim women must develop their Muslim identity, make significant contributions to Canadian society, and provide positive role models for Muslim youth.

Vision and Objectives

- To attain and maintain equality, equity, and empowerment for all Canadian and Muslim women.
- To promote Muslim women's identity in the Canadian context.
- To assist Muslim women to gain an understanding of their rights, responsibilities, and roles in Canadian society.
- To promote and encourage rapprochement and interfaith dialogue between Muslims and other faith communities.
- To represent Canadian Muslim women at national and international forums.

Workshops

- Leadership Examples: Pioneer Women and Mentoring Program;
- Women's Equality Within the Islamic Framework;
- Women as a Force for Change.

Source: From www3.sympatico.ca/ccmw.london/ccmw.html.

EIGHT

COMMUNITY MEDIA

Community centers are the hubs of action for involved Muslims, but print and electronic media are becoming increasingly significant in shaping general Muslim education and discourse. Of course Muslims, like others in the United States and Canada, follow the news and programming of the major media networks. Muslim views are therefore influenced by the mainstream press, television, and radio. One of the favorite monthly magazines followed especially by activists and academics in the community is the *Washington Report on Middle East Affairs*, which was founded by former U.S. diplomats and covers much of the Muslim world. The magazine gives special attention to the coverage of political news involving Arab and Muslim Americans.

Muslim leaders have also recognized the need to develop their own media outlets to cover community news and views. This realization, however, does not translate into actual media outlets quickly. While mosques began to form in the early decades of the twentieth century, Muslim community media, with few exceptions, did not start to emerge until the 1970s. As the Muslim population in the United States and Canada grew, the demand for reading materials and entertainment products increased. The community's growing—and increasingly influential—professional class has demonstrated a taste for high-quality books and films. Now the most popular items are those materials oriented to the needs of families and Islamic schools. Muslim publishers have specialized according to the dictates of their more sophisticated core market.

PRESS MEDIA
BOOK PUBLISHERS AND DISTRIBUTORS

Prior to the 1970s Muslims imported all of their Islamic books from overseas, mainly Arabic and Urdu titles from distribution centers in Beirut, Lebanon, and Lahore, Pakistan. By the end of the 1980s this trend had begun to change. While ethnic stores continue to offer imported titles for sale, Muslim book publishers in North America now produce mostly English-language titles—and, increasingly, export them to Muslim communities around the world.

Kazi Publications is a Chicago-based nonprofit press and book distribution center. Since it was established in 1972, Kazi has published more than two hundred books in English. These include the translated nine-volume *Sahih al-Bukhari*, which Muslims regard as the most reliable collection of Hadith, and the one-volume *Noble Qur'an*. In addition, Kazi Publications produces children's books and textbooks that are used in universities throughout the world. The organization initially imported some one thousand Urdu titles, but these had been reduced to seventy by 2000.

Noting the demand for college-level books written by academics, Kazi Publications has relaxed its selective production and marketing policies. Motivated in part by business rationale, Kazi now focuses on acquiring for distribution any works on Islam and Muslims so long as the books are not clearly offensive to the Qur'an and Hadith. Its best-sellers have been books about Islam from a scholarly perspective. As a result, the company now stocks a total of two thousand titles, most published elsewhere. So in effect Kazi has been transformed into a large warehouse of books on Islam and Muslims, supplying items to such commercial bookstores as Borders, Barnes and Noble, and Baker and Taylor. Kazi also supplies university bookstores around the world. It contracts a wide variety of authors, including such highly regarded Muslim academics as Sayyed Hossein Nasr and Sulyman Nyang

As the public's conventional views on Islam and Muslims began to be seen as ethnocentrically biased, the demand for more objective analyses of non-European experiences grew. So did the number of Muslim community book publishers. However, most of the titles published by these firms continued to target the Muslim community market, which was also growing. In 1976 American Trust Publications was established as a branch of the North American Islamic Trust, producing titles for children and adults. Most of these books focus on the basic elements of the Islamic faith and its religious practices. The list also includes books targeting the growing convert audience, such as *Islam in Focus* by Hammudah Abdalati, and titles addressing the challenges of raising Muslim children in North America, such as *The Child in Islam* by Norma Tarazi.

In 1980 New Mind Productions was founded in Jersey City, New Jersey, and since has published about sixty English-language books. The topics include the Islamic creed, family, and marriage, African-American identity, and small business development. The company also distributes the major Hadith and Qur'an study titles. Like other Muslim publishers, New Mind Productions has produced only a small portion of what it distributes. New Mind Productions claims to be the largest publisher of Islamic literature by African-American Muslims in the country. The company advertises in the *Muslim Journal*, but so far has not tapped the base of Muslim immigrant readers, although it has distributed items produced by other Muslim publishers.

Iqra International Educational Foundation (better known as Iqra) was established in Illinois in 1983 as a nonprofit Islamic community trust focusing on the production of textbooks and instructional materials for Islamic schools. The elementary-level series *Our Prophet Muhammad* served as a pilot project for Iqra's future productions. In 1996 Iqra moved into its own spacious building, which provides ample office space and a research facility. Currently, there are nine full-time staff members and twenty part-time employees.

The staff of Iqra has undertaken the development of instructional material for Pre-K–12 in religious studies, Islamic history, Qur'anic studies, and Arabic language. The series' authors are specialized scholars and teachers whose works are peer-reviewed before publication. Iqra has also published curriculum guides for the preschool, kindergarten, elementary, and junior high levels. Since its inception, Iqra has published about 130 books. In addition, it distributes more than three thousand books on Islam and Muslim issues not only in English but also in Albanian, Arabic, Bosnian, Hindi, and Urdu.

Books and curriculum guides published by Iqra are used in full-time and weekend Islamic schools in North America. The books have also been sold in Muslim community markets in Australia, the Caribbean Islands, Europe, Indonesia, Malaysia, the Middle East, New Zealand, South Africa, South America, and South Asia. Iqra's outreach program serves teachers, administrators, and parents involved in Islamic schools, as well as public and private schools. The Iqra Library and Resource Center, a collection of donated books, is open to the public for research and reference purposes.

In 1986 Al-Sadawi Publications was established in Alexandria, Virginia, specializing in Arabic-language books. Al-Sadawi continues to import high-quality titles from Beirut that cover a wide range of interests, mainly classical Islamic heritage. The titles also include popular Western novels translated into Arabic, such as *Gone with the Wind* and the novels of Victor Hugo, whose books sell especially well in the Arab immigrant market. Although immigration from Arab countries has increased since then, the publisher has realized that children's books in English are most in demand. As a business, Al-Sadawi recognizes the rising demand for English-language books and now distributes fifty English titles, mainly religious-history books for children. The company claims that ethnic food eateries and bookstores make up half its customers; the other half are mainstream retailers in Canada, England, South Africa, and the Persian Gulf.

In 1990 Amana Publications was established in Beltsville, Maryland. It has published more than fifty titles in English and Arabic in various religious and other educational subjects for adult and child readers. In addition, the company has distributed nearly three hundred other titles. Among its bestsellers on Islamic modern discourse is Murad Hoffman's *Islam 2000*. Hoffman is a convert who had served as Germany's Ambassador to Algeria and Morocco. Also among the best-sellers is *Silent No More*, written by former Congressman Paul Findley, who shares his personal impressions and experiences in dealing with American Muslims active in public life.

Al-Basheer for Publications and Translations, founded in 1996 in Boulder, Colorado, offers translations of the Qur'an in English as well as fourteen other languages: Albanian, Aramaic, Bengali, Bosnian, Chinese, Farsi, French, Korean, Huasa, Indonesian, Somali, Spanish, Tamil, and Urdu. The company's website lists nearly six hundred books, mainly classical works on the Qur'an, Hadith,

Islamic jurisprudence, and Islamic history in Arabic and English. Of these titles the company has itself published less than two dozen, mainly English-language books by contemporary *Salafi* and other Gulf area authors.

Clearly, Muslim community book publishers have made the major sources of Islamic knowledge available in the market. They have also addressed some of the demand by schools and colleges for English-language Islamic studies books. Educational institutions continue to maintain a broad interest in Islam and Muslims, so the selection offered by the book publishers is equally broad. While Muslim publishing groups have maintained community ties, the need to remain financially sound has compelled them to broaden their pool of suppliers and consumers, thus becoming more involved in the distribution, as well as the production, of books.

MAGAZINES AND NEWSPAPERS

Books are consumed by students, researchers, and the intellectually inclined. Many others are simply too busy to read books. They may, however, be interested in reading newspapers and magazines to remain informed about events in their community and the world. These readers have a selection of publications offering different perspectives on Muslim issues. Newspapers and magazines from the Middle East and South Asia are available at newsstands in several major U.S. and Canadian cities and the two dozen universities with Middle Eastern and Islamic Studies departments. Periodicals with a community-based circulation are produced mainly by Muslim ethnic and religious groups in North America.

The most established and widely distributed periodicals are those sponsored by the national community development groups, especially *Islamic Horizons* and *Muslim Journal*. *Islamic Horizons* is issued six times per year with a declared circulation of 60,000. *Muslim Journal* claims to distribute 20,000 copies per week. Other Muslim periodicals have smaller circulation numbers. *Message International* of ICNA claims a distribution of 14,000 copies, while *American Muslim* of MAS has a declared readership of 10,000. In addition to news items and educational articles, these periodicals serve mainly to publicize the activities of their sponsors. Some magazines have been established under the tutelage by local Islamic centers. For example, *The Minaret*, which started in the late 1970s, grew out of the Islamic Society of Southern California. It is published monthly and claims a readership of 3,000.

In contrast to these periodicals, which have attempted to reach a broad-based audience, some newspapers exhibit a narrow interest in their coverage of events. An example is *Crescent International*. Founded in 1972, it is based in Markham, Ontario, and published simultaneously in South Africa, London, and Pakistan, claiming a circulation of 30,000. The editorial stance of this weekly newspaper usually posits the Muslim masses and opposition movements against Muslim-world governments and their Western government allies. To many Muslims this view is rooted in the colonial experience. As such, the view of this paper is not grounded in today's reality. Despite a number of troubled areas of conflict featuring a sharp disagreement between Western governments and Muslim nations, Muslim and Western societies and governments have become so much more diverse and interlinked; their relationships are mainly based on economic and political considerations that arise from the legitimate needs of people.

In a number of areas ethnic newspapers emerged to satisfy the need of recent immigrant populations, offering a variety of news and views in English and in the immigrants' native languages. *Arab American News* is one of the oldest of these. It started in 1984 as an Arabic-language paper covering the Arab-American community of Detroit, Michigan, and the Arab world as a whole. It is now published in tabloid form in both Arabic and English and is offered free of charge in many ethnic stores. Its declared circulation is 22,000.

Several other weeklies still publish in Arabic. *Al-Zaytouna* is an Arabic-language biweekly with a distribution of 15,000 published in Dallas, Texas, by the Islamic Association for Palestine. Founded in 1990, the newspaper is an ethno-religious voice in the Arab immigrant community. Several other non-English-language tabloids have started locally and are offered free of charge in Middle Eastern food stores and restaurants: *Sawt al-Uruba* in Paterson, New Jersey; *Akhbar Al-Jaliya* in Philadelphia, Pennsylvania; *Al-Akhbar Al-Mahjariya* in Los Angeles, California; *Al-Alam Al-Arabi* and *Al-Watan* in Anaheim, California; and *Al-Arab* in Glendale, California.

Immigrant journalists from the Middle East established *Al-Hewar* in 1989 in Washington, D.C. Now published quarterly in Arabic with an English supplement, it features presentations on a variety of contemporary issues but specializes in publishing presentations by Arab professionals, intellectuals, and diplomats at al-Hewar Center, a speaking forum established by *Al-Hewar* magazine in Vienna, Virginia, in 1994.

Pakistan Link, which publishes weekly editions in both English and Urdu, focuses on news from Pakistan. Recently, however, it has included a section on the American Muslim community. The coverage in this section is not limited to Pakistani Americans; it does, however, exhibit more interest in political news than in other aspects of American Muslim life. Its declared circulation is 35,000. Smaller Urdu-language newspapers can be found in ethnic stores, including *Sadae Pakistan* and *Urdu Times*, which address recent immigrants from Pakistan and India. These two weeklies are published in New York City.

Albanians established *Illyria* in 1991 as a weekly paper published in English and Albanian and claiming a distribution of 10,000. It contains news and editorials about Albanian Americans and Albanian communities in Europe. Despite the religious tone of the conflict in the Balkans, *Illyria*'s line remains strictly secular. The newspaper does not, however, suppress news from Albanian religious centers. It publishes bulletins from the mosques as well as from Albanian Orthodox and Catholic churches. Another Albanian weekly is *Dielli*, which has been published intermittently since the 1940s in Boston, Massachusetts.

The Muslim community experience shows that sustaining a newspaper over a long period of time is a tremendous challenge. Even some newspapers with impressive financial backing have not been able to survive. *Al-Sharq Al-Awsat*, an Arabic-language, Saudi-financed daily based in London, launched an American edition in 1991. It lasted only six months before the publisher decided that there was little interest among readers and advertisers to sustain it. Immigrant Arabs did not buy the paper because they were picking up Arabic language newspapers free of charge at community centers and ethnic stores.

While hopeful publishers attempt to start new independent periodicals, their efforts today are grounded in a more realistic concept: start small and address the broad concerns of an audience in a well-defined geographic zone. Some publishers have started English-language newspapers that target Muslim community readers in small local regions. In 1997 *Arizona Muslim Voice* began featuring headlines on events that affected Muslims in that state. It distributes 3,000 copies monthly through newsstands in community businesses, Muslim centers, and state colleges. Although it is free of charge, it profits from advertiser revenues—so much so that the newspaper now publishes a multicultural business directory for the state, which is also a moneymaker.

Following the example of the *Arizona Muslim Voice*, other local newspapers have begun to emerge. *Muslims USA*, founded in New York in 1998, covers city, national, international, and business news. The *Islamic Journal*, also started in 1998, targets community members in the states of Oregon and Washington. *The Muslim Observer*, launched in Michigan in 1998, covers health and sports in addition to national and international news. It prints 10,000 copies each week, most distributed at no charge. The *Observer*'s revenues come from advertising, mainly from businesses in the Detroit area. Much of the content of these local newspapers consists of reprints of stories and editorials that have previously appeared elsewhere. Still, several other states with substantial Muslim populations, including New Jersey, Pennsylvania, and Ohio, lack an English-language Muslim community paper with a local focus. Among the ethnic weeklies in English is *Arab American Views*, whose focus is the community in Chicago, Illinois.

A plethora of periodicals with very limited distribution representing a range of religious and political interests has also emerged in recent years. *The Voice of Islam* is published irregularly in Spanish. The Arabic-language *Al-Mashriq* offers opposition views on events in the Arab world. *Al-Jumah*, which publishes in English, and *al-Sirat al-Mustaqim*, which publishes in Arabic, represent *Salafi* religious concerns, while *Al-Muslimoon* is an English-language magazine with a Sufi perspective.

TELECOMMUNICATION
TELEVISION AND RADIO PROGRAMS

While Muslims are struggling to sustain a growing presence in the press, the community's experience with radio and television remains scant and is almost completely dependent on public access programs for airtime. For example, *Focus on Islam* is a weekly community access television program from Seattle,

Washington, that is broadcast throughout the Pacific Northwest. This talk show features various academics and religious scholars discussing Muslim issues.

While some leaders and *imams* in large cities have maintained weekly talk shows on radio and cable television since the mid-1980s, local programs featuring ethnic entertainment as well as news began multiplying in the 1990s. Examples of such efforts include Somali TV and Coalition for Action in Alexandria, Virginia; the Arabic Channel in New York City; Muslim Community TV in Oakland, California; Arabic Lebanese Newsline in West Roxbury, Massachusetts; Voice of Jerusalem and Voice of the Arab and Muslim Communities in Chicago; and Islamic Broadcast Network in Alexandria, Virginia.

A 1989 attempt by a Saudi businessman to develop a national radio and television audience through the Arab Network of America in the Washington, D.C., area foundered. Its radio program was scaled down in 1993 and eventually canceled in 2000. Its daily television program—now run by the Middle East Broadcasting Corporation (MBC) in London, England—offers Arabic entertainment and a weekly political talk show in English. The program is available through satellite and cable services.

There are several reasons for the limited use of the airwaves by Muslim community groups. Chief among them is the small reservoir of community members with broadcast production skills. This may be changing, however, with the community's increased attention to public relations and the encouragement that college students are receiving from national and local leaders to specialize in journalism and broadcasting.

AUDIO AND VIDEO

Islamic videos, audiotapes, and software programs have flourished because of their affordability and also because parents are attracted to this media's controled educational and environment. A number of wholesalers and retailers have competed to market audio and video programs featuring recreational speeches and lectures of popular scholars and *imams*. Some *imams*, including Hamza Yousef in Santa Clara, California, distribute their own lectures. Others license audio and videotape companies to record and market their speeches. There are dozens of popular speakers and educators at the continental, national, regional, and local levels. They come from different ethnic backgrounds and are valued for the depth of the their knowledge or their inspirational style. Some may appeal more to younger people than others. But almost all speakers whose tapes sell widely deliver in English.

In 1990 Sound Vision was established in Bridgeview, Illinois, as a nonprofit entity with a mandate to develop quality educational programs. It now offers songs, lectures, language training, and Islamic studies in a variety of media, including 163 audiocassette sets, 181 videos, and forty-four computer programs. The organization also sells a selection of more than 500 book titles, twenty-seven multimedia games for children, and 134 gift products. The items were either produced by Sound Vision or selected for distribution to consumers of all age groups—from infant to adult.

Several companies have begun to specialize in certain areas of program production. In 1991 ISL Software in Silver Spring, Maryland, launched the first version of *Alim*, which combines Qur'anic translations, commentaries, an extensive subject database with a host of other informational databases into one complete cross-referenced program. In 1997 ISL issued *Arabic Playhouse*, a software program designed to teach children and adults how to read Qur'anic Arabic.

Astrolabe in Sterling, Virginia, is now one of the largest distributors of Muslim multimedia products, offering more than 1,200 items. The company started in 1995 by producing Arabic language and religious-history videos for children, including *al-Fatih*, the story of Ottoman Sultan Muhammad; *Alif for Asad*, an elementary-level Arabic language program; and *Muslim Scouts Adventure*, the fictional story of an American Muslim scout group that solves mysteries. Astrolabe's best-selling items are in books, *Stories of Prophets* and *Mysteries of Jesus*; in audio, *The Jar Songs: Children of Heaven*; and in software, *Muallim*, a college-level Arabic language program.

THE INTERNET

With the advent of the Internet, the nature of Muslim community media has been revolutionized. Not only has every major group and resource-rich Islamic center established a presence on the World Wide Web, a large number of electronic magazines have emerged—superseding by far the number of print media items now available. Perhaps the most active Muslim website is IslamiCity.com, which reported receiving 42,624,586 hits (viewer visits) from January 2000 to May 2001. Of course those hits include Muslims and others from all over the globe. Another growing trend, especially among the technology-savvy North American Muslims, is audio webcast. Sound Vision began in 1999 to provide Internet radio broadcast at RadioIslam.com. Several organizations have followed the lead of Sound Vision, offering recitation and reflection on the Qur'an, Friday sermons, news, interviews, and commentaries.

Other popular sites include *Islam Online*, an electronic magazine with a network of reporters in the United States and several Muslim countries. At islam-online.net one can find introductory information on Islam, news, and commentary on current events. One can even send religious questions to *alims*. Several other Internet magazines, such as *iViews.com*, have been established where visitors can find news and commentary. Compared to print newspapers, Internet magazines are relatively inexpensive to produce, which explains their rapid proliferation.

As a result of the influence of the Internet, the information gap about Islam and Muslims has narrowed. Muslims have become better able to connect with one another and with others in their own communities and around the world. A case in point is the Scarves for Solidarity campaign, which was started as an idea by students at UCLA after attacks on Muslim women with *hijab* were reported following September 11. The campaign soon developed into an Internet site (interfaithpeace.org), and, in a matter of days, developed into a hub of activity connecting people in the United States and dozen other countries around the idea of condemning the September 11 attacks and the random violence against Muslim women. The website offered links to promoters of the campaign around the world. It also directed visitors to appropriate sites for purchasing solidarity scarves (for women) and solidarity ribbons (for men), donating to charitable organizations for the victims of the September 11 attacks, purchasing the *Eid* stamp from the U.S. Postal Service, and learning about Islam online.

Despite all these encouraging signs, Muslims have become aware of the existing class disparity in the use of the Internet. While basic access to the Internet is available through public libraries, those in low-income brackets without convenient access to the technology at home are left out the growing global network of communications. For these members of the community, the traditional media outlets are the main sources of news, views, and entertainment.

September 11 meant a sharp increase in business for Muslim community media, as the public tuned in to Muslims voices and demanded information about Islam. Kazi Publications in particular experienced a windfall of revenues as a distributor of books to the largest retail bookstores. The Qur'an itself was a best-seller—Kazi alone sold three thousand copies in the six-week bloom that followed the attacks. Suzanne Hanif's *What Everyone Should Know About Islam and Muslims* was also a best-seller. Media firms targeting the Muslim market also experienced an increase in the volume of sales, as Muslims began reading more and purchasing items to share with others. Astrolabe reports that demand on all items generally increased until it leveled off two months after the attacks. Also among the highest in demand were books written specifically for Christians, including Ruqaiyah Waris Maqsood's *What Every Christian Should Know About Islam.* To cope with the demand for literature about interfaith relations involving Muslims, Amana Publications released a new book entitled *The Cross and the Crescent.* The author, a former United Methodist Church minister, highlights the commonalities between Islam and Christianity.

In summary, the increasingly sophisticated market of community media consumers, both Muslims and those interested in learning about them, has demanded to learn about the basics of Islamic knowledge, especially the Qur'an. These consumers have also demanded educational materials that suit their specific needs. Community media producers have identified those consumers as parents, children, converts, Christians, Muslims, intellectuals, scholars, students, immigrants. The various audiences have also been identified by their ethnicity, whether or not native languages are used. In addition to educational books and news, there is also a demand for entertainment that is in tune with the communities' values.

Despite the evident mixture of cultural influences, ethnic language media is mainly limited to recent immigrant consumers. Popular speakers whose tapes sell in large volumes are less defined by their ethnicity and more by the inspiration and knowledge they offer. Another obvious trend is the increasing provision of media products in English. The only exception here is the revival of Qur'anic Arabic among Muslims of various backgrounds. To these observant Muslims, this is a matter of faith and practice. In order to be true to their religion, they must be able to read the Qur'an in Arabic.

While Muslim world news and events are featured in the various ethnic and religious media outlets, increasingly the focus is on the needs of families, schools, mosques, and local communities. While international Muslim investors have attempted to capture a wide base of information consumers in North America, only community-based media have persisted over time. Perhaps the only exception is television, which demands much greater resources than currently available to Muslim communities. As the circles of interaction have widened, the interests of community members and institutions have diversified. Thus information demanded by community members is not limited to knowledge about the faith, and their informers include many others besides *imams* and *alims*. Aside from community media networks, Muslim groups and leaders often address one another and the public through the major media outlets. Their goal, of course, is to establish a presence for the community in public discourse.

A CLOSER LOOK
AMERICAN MUSLIM HOUR

The following is an actual weekly television program schedule for February 17–20, 2001, for the *American Muslim Hour*, produced by Islamic Information Service for Southern California Channel 24.

February 17
- Part 1 Essence of the Qur'an (Dr. H. Hathout)
- Part 2 ISNA Appreciation Dinner
- Part 3 Issues: *Halal* Foods Part II
- Part 4 IIS Archive: Living Islam

February 10
- Part 1 Essence of the Qur'an (Ron El-Amin)
- Part 2 ISNA Fellowship Program
- Part 3 Issues: *Halal* Foods Part I
- Part 4 Interview with Hajj Bakr Shah

February 3
- Part 1 Essence of the Qur'an (Sayed M. Al-Qazwini)
- Part 2 *Aziza* magazine
- Part 3 The Environment

January 27
- Part 1 IIS Challenge Question
- Part 2 Essence of the Qur'an (Dr. H. Hathout)
- Part 3 History of Jerusalem Part IV—After Oslo
- Part 4 Ethiopia: The Face of Hunger

January 20
- Part 1 IIS Challenge Question
- Part 2 Essence of the Qur'an (Dr. Sa'dullah Khan)
- Part 3 History of Jerusalem Part III
- Part 4 Interview with Salam Al-Marayati

Source: From www.americanmuslimhour.com.

NINE

PUBLIC AFFAIRS
ORGANIZATIONS

Mosques, schools, ethnic associations, and charitable groups all demonstrate the Muslim desire to practice their faith or to assert cultural identities in an increasingly interdependent world. Community development groups and coordination councils work to promote the establishment of Muslim institutions at various levels. Community media organizations provide outlets for the transmission of Muslim news and views. But the well-being of Muslims is conditioned even more profoundly by federal and state laws and by everyday interactions between Muslims and non-Muslims.

At the formal level, the influence of government institutions in the United States and Canada on the lives of Muslims—and others, for that matter—is indeed tremendous. Through an elaborate system of federal and local taxation, government bodies place controls on the earnings and spending of all those who work, own property, or engage in any type of trade. Taxes are exacted to pay for programs, including education, the development of science and high-technology industries, transportation, social services, law enforcement, foreign policy, and national defense. While these benefits are formulated and implemented in the name of all citizens, U.S. and Canadian Muslim taxpayers are severely underrepresented in the decision-making process.

NORTH AMERICAN MUSLIMS, LAW, AND SOCIETY

Although Muslims have maintained a communal presence for nearly a century in the United States and not quite as long in Canada, they continue to face bias and denial of their right to practice their faith. Currently, Muslims address such concerns through the advocacy of religious tolerance and by seeking legal protections. The First Amendment to the U.S. Constitution states, "Congress shall make no law representing an establishment of religion, or prohibiting the free exercise thereof. . . ." This clause refers to the idea of separation between the state and religious institutions, and the idea that the government cannot favor one religion over another. The First Amendment prohibits the government from "abridging the freedom of speech, or of the press; or the right of the people peaceably to assemble, and to petition the Government for a redress of grievances." The Fourteenth Amendment prohibits the constituent states of the American union from making or enforcing any law that abridges "the privileges or immunities of citizens." This amendment also prohibits any state from depriving any person "of life, liberty, or property, without due process of law." It also commits the individual states to treat people equally under the law.

In addition to these safeguards, antidiscrimination laws have been enacted at the state and federal government levels. The Civil Rights Act of 1964, for example, stipulates that people should not suffer discrimination on account of their race, religion, or national origin. Individuals who believe that their constitutional and statutory protections have been violated can, and quite often do, seek legal remedy. Most complaints filed with the government are based on Title VII of that act, which applies to the employment sector. Corporations are required to extend "reasonable accommodation" for the religious practices of employees. But this stipulation excludes requests that may cause a business "undue hardship." The U.S. Supreme Court has defined this undue hardship as any monetary loss beyond ordinary administrative costs. Small businesses—a substantial segment of the U.S. economy—can, and do, exclude Muslims (and others) with legal immunity; the law applies only to firms with more than fifteen employees.

Yet Muslims have grown increasingly apprehensive about mistreatment by others, especially in the workplace. A large number of employment discrimination complaints has come from women who wear *hijab* and whose accommodation would imply no financial cost to businesses. Although in many cases the discriminatory treatment is overt and could conceivably be challenged in court, most potential plaintiffs are not willing to "make waves," cannot afford the usually high cost of legal counsel, or, in the cases of new immigrants, simply are unaware of their legal rights. In some cases, Muslim women denied their First Amendment right to wear *hijab* look for other jobs or relax their fulfillment of religious requirements to fit the demands of employers. Similarly, Muslim men often shave their beards or take off the *kufi* they wear for religious reasons in order to keep their jobs.

Some Muslim employees have successfully used the Equal Employment Opportunity Commission to settle complaints about job discrimination; others have taken their employers to court. In a number of cases the courts have affirmed the right of Muslims to exercise their religion's precepts. On October 4, 1999, the Supreme Court let stand a lower court ruling in favor of bearded Muslim police officers against the Newark Police Department's no-beard policy. This case handed the American Muslim community its most significant legal victory since the prisoners' rights movement of the 1960s. The ruling, issued by the United States Court of Appeals for the Third Circuit Court in *Fraternal Order of Police v. City of Newark* (App. No. 97–5542), stated:

> Because the Department makes exemptions from its policy for secular reasons and has not offered any substantial justification for refusing to provide similar treatment for officers who are required to wear beards for religious reasons, we conclude that the Department's policy violates the First Amendment.

The ruling encouraged Muslims to call for greater tolerance of Islamic religious practices in the workplace in general.

Still, many Muslim employees often face a choice between job and religion, as antidiscrimination laws are not self-enforcing. Despite the growing religious pluralism in the workplace, personnel policies in corporations all too frequently lack an appreciation for the religious requirements of employees. Companies usually deal with workers' rights on a case-by-case basis, so many firms resist modifying general corporate codes in favor of increased religious accommodation.

Evidence shows that economic factors can sometimes favor Muslim workers. Corporations with large numbers of Muslim employees or customers generally offer accommodations. In 2000, Sylvest Farms Inc., a chicken plant in Atlanta, Georgia, offered to bring an *imam* to the worksite so that workers would not have to leave the factory for Friday Prayer. Muslims in professional occupations are the least likely to complain about a lack of religious accommodation because their work environment allows them much more freedom of movement than, for example, assembly-line workers. Thus the actual experience of Muslims shows various patterns of treatment, mainly dependent upon the personal attitudes of bosses, the general work environment, and the worker's economic value to his or her employer.

As has been noted earlier in this volume, Muslim public school pupils are also vulnerable to mistreatment. In the public education system, local school boards formulate their own policies. Some districts have acknowledged their growing Muslim student population and have instituted various accommodations. For example, school districts close on *Eid* in Paterson, New Jersey, and Dearborn, Michigan, two communities in which Muslims are a large portion of the student body. In most other school districts, however, the Muslim student population is very small, thus its influence on school policy is minor. Mandatory exams often are scheduled on Muslim holidays, imposing on children a choice between school and religious observance. Additionally, as we have observed in a previous chapter, instructional materials are too frequently marred with misrepresentations of Islam and Muslims.

Nevertheless, some changes are occurring in other areas of religious accommodation. In 2000 the state of New Jersey passed the Halal Food Protection Act. Minnesota and Illinois followed suit in 2001, enacting their own laws to regulate the *halal* food industry. These laws identified *halal* food as a consumer commodity that has been subject to commercial abuse (some retailers have wrongly placed *halal* food labels on meat items to attract Muslim customers). The Illinois act, which has the most accommodating language, specifically defines the term *halal* food as being

> prepared under and maintained in strict compliance with the laws and customs of the Islamic religion, including but not limited to those laws and customs of zabiha/zabeeha (slaughtered according to appropriate Islamic code), and as expressed by reliable recognized Islamic entities and scholars.

This law makes it a misdemeanor for any person to make any oral or written statement that directly or indirectly tends to deceive or otherwise lead a reasonable individual to believe that non-*halal* food or food product is *halal*.

In Canada, the Canadian Charter of Rights and Freedoms was included in Canada's Constitution in 1982. The charter recognizes basic freedoms, similar to the first ten amendments of the U.S. Constitution known as the Bill of Rights. The charter came partly in response to the tension between the French and English communities, especially in the province of Quebec. In addition to the rights granted to individuals, the charter extends rights to citizens based on their communal identification. The document stipulates that the charter "shall be interpreted in a manner consistent with the preservation and enhancement of the multicultural heritage of Canadians." While declaring English and French as the official languages of the country, the charter recognizes Canada as a multicultural society. The "right to interpreter" clause reads, "A party or witness in any proceedings who does not understand or speak the language in which the proceedings are conducted . . . has the right to the assistance of an interpreter."

To many in the multiethnic, faith-based Muslim communities, however, language has not been the defining element in the way they have related to Canadian multiculturalism. Despite Canada's multicultural policy, the degree to which Muslims are tolerated and accommodated is not characteristically different from that in the United States. In both countries, education is administered through local boards and the workplace is primarily the domain of private sector corporations, which are recognized by law as entities with legal rights. Thus, outside the boundaries of family and community, the lives of children and working adults are greatly shaped by the dominant political and business interests.

Muslims have at times been subjected to reprisals by people who have not taken the time to understand them. Anti-Muslim violence reached a peak after the attacks on the Pentagon and the World Trade Center. Properties and persons who displayed Arab, Middle Eastern, or Muslim features were assaulted. These assaults included eleven hate-related killings. Among the victims were a Sikh, a Hindu, and a Copt mistaken for Muslims or Arabs because of their appearance. Most of the killers are still at large; in one case, however, the murderer was sentenced to death in Dallas, Texas, in 2002.

The Federal Bureau of Investigation (FBI) began in 1995 to release an annual report on hate crimes in compliance with the Hate Crime Statistics Act of 1990. The number of anti-Islamic assaults, threats, burglaries, and vandalism incidents noted in the reports has been steady. The publication, *Unified Crime Reports: Hate Crimes*, reported twenty-nine such incidents in 1995; twenty-seven in 1996; twenty-eight in 1997; thirty-two in 1998; twenty-one in 1999; and twenty-eight in 2000. In the three weeks following the September 11 attacks, however, media accounts indicated that more than 120 incidents were documented by the FBI.

Official monitoring of hate crimes in Canada has only recently become a matter of public concern, but there is no mandate to compile the data. Most notably after September 11, 2001, Canadian Muslims have suffered hate-based violence. Anti-Muslim violence is not limited to times of crisis. A suspicious

November 2000 fire caused heavy damage to the Surrey Masjid in Surrey, British Columbia. Community leaders believed the incident to be bias-motivated.

In Canada there have been no arrests specifically for violent attacks on Muslims. Nevertheless, one conviction was made after an incitement to violence incident in January 1999. Mike Harding was sentenced to 340 hours of community service in a case involving incitement to hatred against Muslims. Harding had distributed pamphlets calling Islam "a false religion" and Muslims "anti-Christ." Chief Judge Sidney Linden of Ontario Court's Provincial Division ruled these statements to be expressions of opinion. But the judge found another of Harding's statements—that Canadian Muslims are "like raging wolves in sheep's clothing . . . inside they are full of hate, violence and murder"—to contain "false allegations about the adherents of Islam calculated to arouse fear and hatred of them in all non-Muslim people." Canadian law criminalizes such hateful agitation.

To address the concerns of religious and ethnic Muslims in the public arena, a number of advocacy groups have emerged, working to carve a space for their members in the political systems of the United States and Canada. First came the secularly oriented, ethnicity-based Arab-American groups in the 1980s, followed by the multiethnic, faith-based Muslim groups in the 1990s.

ARAB-AMERICAN GROUPS

Chapter 2 illustrated that ethnic Arabs constitute the largest community of descendants from the Middle East. Many Americans miss the distinction between Arab and Muslim, although most Muslims are not Arab and more than half of Arabs in America are Christian. Yet Arab-American public affairs groups have developed as secular organizations. They have attracted both Muslims and Christians who identify themselves in terms of an Arab-American ethnicity, much like many Japanese Americans or African Americans view themselves not in terms of religion.

AMERICAN ARAB
ANTI-DISCRIMINATION COMMITTEE (ADC)

Arab-American academics and politicians have sparked the emergence of a number of public advocacy groups. In 1980 former U.S. Senator James Abourezk founded the American Arab Anti-Discrimination Committee (ADC) as a nonpartisan civil rights agency. Although it was started by Arab-American Christians, many Muslims have joined the organization as members and staffers. Working in an environment that is largely misinformed about Arabs, ADC has attempted to educate the public while advocating the rights of Arab Americans. The organization established the ADC Research Institute, which has launched such programs as Reaching the Teachers, an initiative aiming to ensure a fair portrayal of Arab history and culture in schools.

ADC has also worked to educate members of the Arab-American community, many of whom are recent immigrants to the United States. The group publishes *Educational Outreach and Action Guide: Working with School Systems*, which offers advice to parents on providing classroom resources, setting curriculum, and evaluating textbooks, as well as dealing with discrimination in schools. ADC's educational network has helped change some views. For example, well-known multicultural theoretician James Banks decided to include Arab Americans among the ethnic groups covered in his widely circulated textbook *Teaching Strategies for Ethnic Studies* as a result of ADC's work.

To promote greater participation of community members in public discourse, ADC issued in English and Arabic *Legal Guide: Your Basic Rights*, which describes the rights of citizens and residents in the United States, and *Political Action Guide: How to Write, Phone and Meet Your Legislators*, which offers practical tips on grassroots lobbying. In addition, ADC administers a year-round college internship program for students. Interns experience working at ADC national headquarters in Washington, D.C., convenient to organized visits to Congress and other institutions that influence national policy. Because of the impact of national and state media on the shaping of public opinion, ADC instituted an ongoing program in media monitoring. To help members of the community have their views heard by media outlets, ADC issued *Media Monitoring Guide: How to Voice Your Concerns to the Media*.

ADC's work also has been influenced by current events. Although the plight of the Palestinians has been a strong focus of the group since the inception, the Israeli invasion of Lebanon in 1982 marked a high point in ADC's mobilization efforts. The invasion was a turning point in American public opinion about the Arab–Israeli conflict. For the first time in history, Israel was seen on television screens as an invader. The role of the Israeli army in the massacre at the Sabra and Shatila refugee camps damaged the position of the pro-Israeli lobby, which in the past had had a de facto monopoly over America's Middle East policy. Since then, ADC's argument that Americans should become more sensitive to the other side of the conflict has had a better chance of being heard. After the Palestinian uprising, or *intifadah*, in 1987, ADC issued *Children of the Stones*, which featured stories of Palestinian children fed up with the Israeli occupation. Following the 2000 Aqsa *intifadan*, ADC launched a massive campaign in national media outlets to call for an end to the Israeli occupation of the West Bank and Gaza.

When ADC received reports that Arab-American and nonwhite travelers were being subjected to different treatment by the Israeli authorities, the group began to monitor Israel's treatment of American citizens. A report issued by ADC, *Harassment in the Holy Land: Israeli Discrimination Against Arab and Black Americans*, documented cases of mistreatment of Arab Americans and dark-skinned American citizens and demanded that the U.S. government take action against such abuses. As a result ADC became recognized as a credible source of information on Arab-American concerns as well as on civil liberties matters.

When in 1987 the Immigration and Naturalization Service (INS) began proceedings to deport eight activists in Los Angeles, California, for their alleged support of the Popular Front for the Liberation of Palestine (PFLP), ADC took the Justice Department to court. This action resulted in the immigrant rights case *ADC v. Reno*, which eventually reached the Supreme Court. The government contended that the individuals were engaged in fund-raising activities for the PFLP, an organization accused of involvement in terrorism by the Department of State. ADC charged that the government had singled out the defendants for deportation based on their political beliefs rather than for any criminal wrongdoing. The case dragged on until 1999, when the Supreme Court finally ruled that a 1996 immigration law did not allow immigrants facing deportation to go to district court and that their legal status did not allow them to raise a claim of selective enforcement. Still, none of the defendants in the original case was deported.

ADC has emerged as the premiere Arab-American civil and human rights organization, working to combat discrimination at home and to uphold human rights for Arabs overseas. When Palestinians in Kuwait came under pressure in the 1990–1991 Gulf War, ADC lobbied the Department of Justice to assist those of them with legal status in the United States to come back as citizens and immigrants. To document the overall Arab experience with discrimination, ADC has published a number of reports on hate crimes and discrimination against Arab Americans. The 2000 issue reported that Arab Americans face not only random violence, but institutionalized discrimination as well. Several cases describe how Arabs faced the use of secret evidence by federal law enforcement agencies, passenger profiling at airports, and bias in public school textbooks.

ADC has active chapters in several states, including Michigan, Ohio, Pennsylvania, New Jersey, Texas, and California. The group's annual convention is a major event in Arab America, drawing politicians, government officials, top journalists, business leaders, professionals, academics, and activists. Media and government agencies frequently consult ADC for assistance with issues impacting U.S. relations with the Arab world. In addition, community members often call upon the group for help in discrimination complaints.

The government affairs arm of ADC is National Association of Arab Americans NAAA–ADC. NAAA was an independent group established in 1972 to lobby for Arab foreign policy concerns in Washington, D.C. Although the group has not been able to pass any significant legislation through Congress, it has presented Arab-American views in public hearings. The pro-Israel lobbies outspend NAAA by a huge margin—consequently, they have won most legislative battles on foreign policy. But at least the views of pro-Israel groups no longer go unchallenged. In a number of instances they have had to retreat. When Israel closed down Palestinian universities in 1989, for example, NAAA was successful in passing H. Con. 315, a resolution sponsored by Representative Howard Nielson (R-Utah), which called on Israel to reopen Palestinian schools. In January 2000 NAAA merged with ADC.

ARAB AMERICAN INSTITUTE

The Arab American Institute (AAI) was organized as a nonprofit organization conducting educational and public relations activities, mainly with political candidates or leaders holding public office. AAI maintains a national directory called *Arab American Voters and Volunteers*, an information resource offered to local community activists. The institute provides training in voter registration and mobilization techniques, and sponsors get-out-the-vote functions for the Arab community. AAI also offers internships for college students and recent graduates in its Washington, D.C., office. This organization has placed Arab-American youth in several White House offices and at both national party headquarters. AAI also nominates Arab Americans for the American Council of Young Political Leaders and other college leadership outreach programs.

AAI also publishes a roster of Arab Americans in public service and political life. The 2001 edition lists individuals holding 110 elected offices and 237 appointed positions nationwide. Among the elected officials are the U.S. congressional representatives Darrel Issa of the 48th District of California; Ray LaHood of the 18th District of Illinois; Christopher John of the 7th District of Louisiana; John Baldacci of the 2nd District of Maine; John Sununu of the 1st District of New Hampshire; Nick Rahall of the 3rd District of West Virginia; New Hampshire Governor Jeanne Shaheen; Louisiana Attorney General Richard Ieyoub; five mayors; thirty-six judges; thirty-eight city and local council members; and nineteen representatives and senators in state legislatures.

These leaders are individuals who have made it to positions of power with only modest support from the Arab-American community. In the past candidates considered the mere association with Arab-American groups a liability. Now these candidates no longer shy away from publicly claiming pride in their heritage—sometimes actively soliciting the support of Arab Americans. Arab-American congressmen are particular about their independnce from the community, as they think of themselves representing all Americans, not only those of Arab heritage. Quite often these congressmen even vote against the recommendations of Arab-American organizations.

AAI conducts a number of educational activities as well. It sponsors U.S. delegations, including members of Congress, to Arab countries. AAI representatives participate in speaking tours, conduct interviews with Arabic-language media, and provide regular briefings for visitors from the Arab world. Also, the AAI website informs the public about the contributions Arab Americans have made to civic life, government, business, and education.

AAI has published a number of papers addressing the concerns of Arab Americans. In 1997 the organization issued *Life, Liberty and the Pursuit of Happiness: A Three-Decade Journey in the Occupied Territories*, which briefly discusses conditions in the Israeli-occupied territories. In 1998 AAI released *The Department of Justice and the Civil Rights of Arab Americans*, which explored the Department of Justice's efforts to examine civil rights violations against Arab Americans by federal agencies such as the FBI, the Federal Aviation Administration, and the INS.

While AAI has devoted much of its attention to high-level government dynamics, ADC has remained closer to the grassroots. When the news media broke the secret Oslo agreement between Israel and the PLO in 1993, the U.S. government supported the deal and invited both parties to a celebration at the White House. AAI participated in the ceremony and began to reach out to American Jewish groups, hoping to build a coalition between Arab and Jewish Americans in support of the agreement. Such a desire dissipated in 1996 when the hawkish Likud Party came to power in Israel and negotiations gave way to a spiral of violence and counterviolence.

In contrast to the AAI position, ADC supported a peaceful resolution to the conflict, but pointed out that the Oslo deal fell short of addressing core issues: Israeli settlements in occupied Palestinian lands, the right of self-determination for the Palestinian people, the right of return for Palestinian refugees, and the status of Jerusalem. Both groups draw members across religious and sectarian lines.

AMERICAN MUSLIM GROUPS

Many Muslims have joined a number of multiethnic, faith-based public advocacy groups. The attitudes of religious Muslims toward participation in the political process have evolved over the years. In the early decades of the Muslim experience in America, Muslims were too few to wield any political clout. Also, the community had to settle the debate over whether Muslims could take part in the political process in a non-Muslim country and remain true to their faith. The isolationist perspective is not very different from the view held by many in the Jehovah's Witnesses, who maintain that the true believer should not be concerned with government. For a few Muslims, however, political engagement itself is not sacrilege, but doing so in a predominantly non-Muslim society is.

In the 1990s it became clear that the majority of American Muslim citizens had decided in favor of participation. Former U.S. congressman Paul Findley, who addressed many local American Muslim forums in the 1990s, noted in his book *Silent No More* that

> People who have had anxieties in the past are reconsidering. Some of the doubters of yesterday are now active in politics and enjoying the experience. They recognize how open the U.S. political system really is, and have come to realize that if they do not speak up and try to be an influence themselves, they can't expect others to speak on their behalf.

Indeed, a national American Muslim identity did not begin to emerge until the 1990s. Organizations such as the ISNA and the Ministry of Warith D. Mohammed have actively encouraged Muslims to take part in the political process. Indeed, both of these groups maintain voter registration booths at their annual conventions.

AMERICAN MUSLIM COUNCIL

The American Muslim Council (AMC) was established in June 1990. Addressing the debate among Muslims about American politics, the group maintains the broad objective of increasing Muslim participation in the political process. Two months after AMC was launched, the Iraqi Army overran Kuwait, leading the organization to contemplate the whole spectrum of issues involving Muslims in the U.S. military and their participation in the war. The U.S.-led military alliance included several Muslim-majority countries against a single Muslim-majority state. AMC acknowledged that Muslims in the military must to follow their own consciences at a time when their country is at war with their coreligionists overseas. The organization sought to ensure that Muslims in the military would have access to Qur'an and Islamic books and be allowed to visit the holy places in Mecca. The Pentagon welcomed AMC's interest and proceeded to appoint a Muslim chaplain to lead prayers and to offer spiritual and religious advice.

AMC leaders also acknowledged that public officials know little about Muslims and resolved that it would be in the best interest of Muslims if a new atmosphere could be created to make American Muslims feel more welcome at government offices. To achieve this goal, leaders of AMC recognized the symbolic value of having Muslims take part in ceremonial functions of the various structures of government. The publicity and recognition such events yielded were obviously appealing. So the organization arranged for Imam Siraj Wahhaj of New York in 1991 and Imam Warith D. Mohammed in 1992 to deliver the first Islamic invocations before the House of Representatives and Senate.

After the war, the AMC complained that President George H. Bush had recognized Muslims abroad in his address on the occasion of *Eid*, but had not addressed Muslims as fellow American citizens. Six months later AMC received a videotaped *Eid* greeting message from the president. The White House continued to send these greetings to Muslims in the United States and around the world. AMC still lobbied the White House to conduct a ceremonial celebration of *Eid*, as it does for Christian and Jewish holidays. In 1996 First Lady Hillary Rodham Clinton conducted the first such celebration, inviting Muslim leaders and their families to attend. The first-ever Ramadan *Iftar* (Break-the-Fast) event on Capitol Hill was held in 1996 and was attended by congressional representatives, their Muslim aides, and AMC members.

At the 1992 and 1996 Republican and Democratic party conventions, AMC joined other Muslim organizations in hosting hospitality suites. AMC has also coordinated regular town meetings between members of local Islamic centers and elected officials. It also participated in meetings at the White House and at various government departments, offering advice on public policy issues. AMC's call for increased government appointments of American Muslims prompted the Clinton administration in 1999 to appoint Osman Siddiqui to be the first-ever Muslim ambassador, representing the United States in Fiji, Nauru, Tonga, and Tuvalu. Dr. Ikram Khan was also appointed in 1999 to serve as member of the

Board of Regents for the Uniformed Services University of the Health Sciences, a reputable medical school that trains military physicians.

The organization has issued several statements on domestic and foreign concerns. AMC position statements offer a perspective grounded in the promotion of peace and justice in the world, regardless of the religious identity of the parties in conflict. AMC condemned the bombing of the World Trade Center in 1993 as an unjustified attack in a country in which Muslims have experienced peaceful lives as citizens, residents, businessmen, visitors, and foreign students.

AMC campaigned against the genocide in Bosnia and lobbied for legislation that called for the lifting of the UN arms embargo against that country. The primary victims of the arms embargo were Bosnian Muslims—people who were also subject to genocidal attacks by the Serbs but denied any means of defense. AMC endorsed the Oslo agreement between the PLO and Israel, but later criticized Israel for reneging on withdrawal from the occupied territories and for violating the sanctity of the Aqsa Mosque. When Muslim mobs attacked the minority Timorese in Indonesia, AMC condemned the attacks and called on the the government of Indonesia to put an immediate stop to the violence. In 1991 when the Taliban in Afghanistan took control and began to institute a series of strict rules to keep women from schools and jobs outside the home, AMC criticized the policy as un-Islamic and oppressive.

In the legislative arena, AMC worked with Congressmen David Bonior (D-Mich.) and Tom Davis (R-Va.) to pass H.R. 174 in the House of Representatives in 1999, legislation which condemned prejudice against Islam and acknowledged the contribution of Muslims to American society. In 2000 Senator Spencer Abraham (R-Mich.) introduced and won the passage of a related bill under S. Res. 133. In the two versions of the legislation Congress acknowledged Islam as an Abrahamic faith, recognized that American Muslims have at times been treated unfairly, and condemned anti-Muslim intolerance.

At the local level in July 2000 the Minnesota chapter of AMC lobbied for the passage of state law H.F. 149, a law that offered measures against the abuse of *halal* food labeling. AMC has conducted numerous educational activities in connection with its objective of empowering Muslims. On September 29, 2000, the group convened a conference specifically for Muslim *imams*. The event drew 120 *imams*, who listened to speakers discuss the American political system and the role of *imams* in addressing American Muslim issues in the public arena.

MUSLIM PUBLIC AFFAIRS COUNCIL

The Muslim Public Affairs Council (MPAC) was established in 1992 as a nonprofit organization designed to dispel the stereotype of the fanatical Muslim as a central feature in popular discourse. The group's pamphlet, *An American Vision, An Islamic Identity*, states that its mission is to "offer the public a portrayal of Islam that goes beyond the stereotypes to elucidate that Muslims worship God, abhor terrorism, stand against oppression, and do not represent an alien existence." The group's pamphlet *Our Stand on Terrorism* defines terrorism as "using fear against noncombatants to achieve political or ideological goals," and notes that the Hadith instructs warring Muslims not to harm nonwarriors, children, women, the elderly, and people in their places of worship, among others.

MPAC acknowledges that terrorism exists in the Muslim world's troubled regions, but points out that it occurs in many other places in the world and as such has no national or religious affinity. To support this view, MPAC listed in 1997 a number of violent acts that meet its definition of terrorism, including the U.S. atomic bombing of Hiroshima in World War II; the bombing of Lebanese villages by Israel since the early 1980s; the 1985 killing of Arab-American activist Alex Odeh by suspected American-Jewish extremists; the Serbian genocide against Bosnians in the early 1990s; the World Trade Center bombing by followers of Shaykh Omar Abdul Rahman in 1993; the bombing of civilian buses in Israel by members of the military wings of Hamas and Islamic Jihad, which began after the 1994 Hebron massacre of Palestinians by a Jewish settler; the Oklahoma City bombing by Timothy McVeigh in 1995; and the Russian destruction and pillage of Chechnya since 1996. Based on this understanding, the group has monitored instances of terrorism and issued public statements condemning all such acts.

Although the group was founded in Los Angeles, California, it has exhibited more interest in national politics than in local concerns. In 1998 MPAC wrote to the U.S. Senate Subcommittee on Near Eastern and South Asian Affairs, proposing that the United States urge both the Palestinians and Israel to end human rights violations in that region. MPAC also called for a meaningful dialogue between the U.S. government and mainstream Islamic movements abroad. In the statement *Islamic Movements: Relationship and Rapprochement*, MPAC presented the following view on the relationship between the United States and the Muslim world's Islamic groups:

> Radical elements among the Muslims, acting against the dictates and principles of Islam, have engaged in acts of terrorism. However, we maintain that such fringe extremists should in no way dictate the debate between the U.S. and the Muslim world. . . . The U.S. should open dialogue with various Muslim groups seeking justice and human rights in their native countries. . . . The U.S. should work toward democracy for the Muslim peoples not represented by their governments. . . . The U.S. should join and support the various American and international Islamic groups in denouncing and fighting terrorism.

In 2000 MPAC opened an office in Washington, D.C. While supporting the fight against terrorism, the group has sought a fact-based appreciation of the problem. Prior to September 11 MPAC criticized the U.S. Department of State for an incoherent portrayal of the global threat of terrorism. The department's report *Patterns of Global Terrorism 2000* found that 172 anti-American terrorist attacks took place in Latin America, while two occurred in the Middle East and nine in Asia. Citing this government data in a statement issued on May 21, 2001,

MPAC concluded that the report reflected the department's unbalanced views on counterterrorism, noting that it "contains a section on the Middle East that is more than double that on Latin America." Also, since the report did not focus exclusively on anti-American attacks but purported to give a global picture of the violence that threatens civilians, MPAC pointed out that many occurrences of such violence in other parts of the world were missing from the document. These include Russian and Serbian attacks against their Muslim populations, India's genocidal suppression of the Kashmiri people, and Israel's systematic destruction of civilian Palestinian life and property in the West Bank and Gaza.

COUNCIL ON AMERICAN-ISLAMIC RELATIONS

From its outset, CAIR began addressing the most pressing concerns of Muslim individuals and communities. Established in June 1994, CAIR has worked largely as a service organization, defending Muslims against discrimination and defamation and providing information to the public on American Muslims and their concerns. CAIR's first advocacy campaign was directed at the greeting card company RPG Recycling for an offensive product that used the word Shiite (a misspelling of Shia) to refer to human excrement. CAIR issued action alerts to its network of volunteer activists to apply pressure on the company, which eventually decided to withdraw the product from the market.

In the wake of the false speculations almost universally aired by media outlets that Muslim terrorists had bombed the Murrah Federal Building in Oklahoma City on April 19, 1995, CAIR issued *A Rush to Judgment*, a report that logged more than two hundred incidents of anti-Muslim harassment and hate crime reported to the group by community members in the days after the explosion. The Oklahoma City bombing was a turning point for CAIR; the organization has gained national stature for its efforts to educate the public about religious and ethnic bias in America. The organization's report was featured in a front-page story in the *New York Times* on August 28, 1995, and it was prominently mentioned on *ABC World News Tonight* on the first anniversary of the incident.

Following anti-Muslim rhetoric after the crash of TWA Flight 800 on July 17, 1996, CAIR issued *The Usual Suspects*. The report was based on a search of the Nexis-Lexis computer database of stories from the United Press International, Associated Press, and Reuters during the forty-eight hours following the crash. The research identified 138 articles containing the words "Muslim" and "Arab" in connection to the tragedy, many containing unfounded speculations about a terrorist plot that had downed the plane. Of course, the United States determined later that the crash was caused by a mechanical failure

CAIR concluded that anti-Muslim bias in the news media remained a significant problem. The organization's approach toward a solution, however, remained educational. For one thing, CAIR observed that bias incidents against Muslims are mainly rooted in ignorance. CAIR prepared informational releases on major Muslim holidays and community events—Ramadan, *Hajj*, *Eid*, and other celebrations. Later CAIR established the Islam-Info e-mail list for journalists. The organization noted that media coverage of the Muslim community has improved as a result of CAIR's work.

CAIR's most notable advocacy cases involve large publishing and manufacturing corporations. In 1996 Simon and Schuster withdrew a textbook on world religions that depicted the Prophet Muhammad as a bloodthirsty killer; in 1997 the editor of *U.S. News and World Report*, Morton Zuckerman, published an apology for having offended the Prophet of Islam. In 1998 Nike, the multinational sports equipment manufacturer, agreed to remake a line of shoes with the word Allah scripted on the heel when, in response to a CAIR Action Alert, protests from Muslims mounted worldwide. Nike has a manufacturing plant in Indonesia and a lucrative consumer market in the Gulf region. When commentators in the Saudi press began raising the specter of boycott, Nike recalled the offensive shoes in 1999 and offered to construct five playgrounds in Islamic centers and community schools.

Prior to the 1996 elections CAIR launched a voter registration drive and released a poll on Muslim political attitudes in the United States. The poll showed American Muslims almost evenly split in support for the two major parties. Most Muslims found the Republicans closer to their own conservative views on such issues as family values, abortion, and the importance of faith in private and public life, but the Democrats seemed more inclusive and welcoming for religious and ethnic minorities. CAIR's increasing number of offices around the country began registering people to vote and reaching out to political candidates.

To address the regulatory aspect of religious accommodation in public schools, in 1999 CAIR released a study titled *Religious Accommodation Policies in Selected American School Districts*. This study compared local public school policies in a dozen school districts across the United States and offered proposals on how public schools might accommodate the growing religious and cultural diversity of their student population. At issue were such concerns as lunch menus, instructional material on human growth and development, student clubs and prayer, religious fasts, and other religious and ethnic observances. Thus far, there is no evidence that the paper has had any notable policy impact, but education activists and specialists use the resource to help them formulate their own views on these issues. The paper, however, was hoped to be a catalyst for a long-term process of attitudinal change.

In addition, CAIR has used moral persuasion and public pressure to resolve cases of discrimination complaints. Complementing this community service effort, CAIR produces educational material offering practical tips to employers, educators, correctional institutions, and health care professionals on how to accommodate Islamic religious practices. Since 1996 CAIR has issued *The Status of Muslim Civil Rights in the United States*, an annual report logging incidents of anti-Muslim discrimination and violence based upon such ethnic and religious features as beard, complexion, accent, name, birthplace, and national origin.

CAIR's 1999 report noted that, despite the persistence of discrimination in schools and at the workplace, an increasing number of employers have eased their objection to Muslim women wearing the *hijab* on the job. The 2002 release found a threefold increase in reported incidents, two-thirds of which seemed to have been triggered by perceived or actual ethnic of religious identity, and most followed the terrorist attacks of September 11.

Improvements were beginning to take hold at the workplace in a few corporations. On May 18, 2001, United Airlines, whose uniform policy was challenged by CAIR in a number of incidents, announced that its customer service employees across the United States would be "allowed to wear a company-sanctioned *hijab*, turban, or yarmulke as part of their uniform." Explaining the decision, the company stated, "We want our workforce to reflect the diversity of our global customer base." Because of this advocacy on behalf of women, CAIR earned tremendous support among them. Almost half of CAIR's staff is female.

As CAIR's credibility increased, contributions to the organization multiplied. By 2002 offices had sprung up in California, Ohio, New York, Michigan, Missouri, and Pennsylvania. Moving to its own building on Capitol Hill in February 2000, CAIR established a leadership training center and expanded its internship program. In 2000 the organization began hosting an annual workshop featuring experts on public speaking and grassroots mobilization. In 2001 CAIR–Los Angeles secured its own office building in Anaheim, where there is a growing Muslim community.

Occasionally, CAIR has given attention to foreign policy issues. The group argued for increased U.S. support of democratic reforms in Muslim countries and called for evenhandedness in the formulation and articulation of U.S. policy. In 1996 CAIR published a paper urging the Clinton administration to promote democratization in Egypt. The study followed the Egyptian government's arrest of political hopefuls running in that country's 1995 parliamentary election. Also, in the aftermath of Pakistan's test of a nuclear bomb in 1998, CAIR issued a statement describing the test as Pakistan's reaction to India's ongoing nuclear program. The statement maintained that the United States should view Pakistan's efforts with no more alarm than it had for India's attempts.

On the Middle East conflict, the group supports calls for the creation of a Palestinian state and the internationalization of Jerusalem. On June 5, 2001, the twenty-fourth anniversary of the 1967 Israeli occupation of the West Bank and Gaza, CAIR issued a release likening the Israeli control of the Palestinians to the old South African system of apartheid and asking the U.S. government to help dismantle it.

AMERICAN MUSLIM ALLIANCE

The American Muslim Alliance (AMA) was established in 1994 to foster Muslim participation in the American electoral process—both in voting and in running for public office. To achieve this mission, AMA has invested in political education and grassroots mobilization. Starting from an office in Fremont, California, AMA has grown into a network of ninety chapters, each led by one or two volunteer activists. Chapters conduct regular voter registration activities and organize events with political candidates and public officials.

AMA has produced training materials offering tips on how to organize communities for political participation, how to form a Democratic or Republican club, how to set up an internship program aimed at training young people in politics and lawmaking, and how to carry out successful voter-registration drives.

In the 1996 election AMA supported the drive to defeat Senator Larry Pressler (R-N.D.), the author of a controversial amendment that prohibited the sale of arms to Pakistan. The Pressler Amendment reads

> No assistance shall be furnished to Pakistan and no military equipment or technology shall be sold or transferred to Pakistan, pursuant to the authorities contained in this Act or any other Act, unless the President shall have certified in writing . . . that Pakistan does not possess a nuclear explosive device and that the proposed United States assistance program will reduce significantly the risk that Pakistan will possess a nuclear explosive device.

Members of AMA argued that Pressler had pursued an anti-Muslim policy by singling out Pakistan. Money from the Muslim community poured into the campaign of Democratic candidate Tim Johnson, who successfully unseated Pressler.

In many other states there were few, if any, contacts between Muslims and their representatives in Congress and in state legislatures. To tear down the psychological barriers between Muslims and public officials, AMA sought and won official recognition of its efforts. In 1999 Congressman Dennis Kucinich (D-Ohio) entered into the permanent record of the U.S. Congress a resolution that honored AMA on the occasion of its fourth annual national convention. At the state level, according to AMA, its chapters in New Jersey, Florida, California, Missouri, and Massachusetts have been recognized for public service by their state legislatures. And since the establishment of AMA, the organization has maintained hospitality suites at the conventions of both the Democratic and Republican parties.

As confidence in the promise of political participation grew after the 2000 election, AMA began to contemplate a legislative agenda. Its national office asked members to support the confirmation of attorney general nominee John Ashcroft, who had expressed concerns about the secret evidence clause in the 1996 antiterrorism law. The clause allowed the use of classified information in legal proceedings involving immigrants in a way that excludes such evidence from any kind of cross-examination. In practice, this clause has been used almost exclusively against Arabs and Muslims. Although civil rights leaders have criticized it for its violation of the constitutional requirement of due process, the passage of the law has not caused a public outcry; most Americans remain unaware of it.

Realizing that local and national challenges can only be met through multi-group collaborations, in 1998 Muslim public affairs groups established the American Muslim Political Coordination Council (AMPCC). In July 1999 a major action was taken by the AMPCC to endorse the establishment of American Muslims for Jerusalem (AMJ). This followed a number of local and national activities that highlighted the religious significance of Jerusalem in Islamic faith. A multiethnic Muslim coalition in California held the United for Al-Quds (Jerusalem) Conference in 1998, and the July/August 1999 issue of *Islamic Horizons* was devoted to Muslim concerns on Jerusalem. The issue featured an article by then-president of ISNA Muzammil Siddiqui who explained the religious attachment of Muslims to the city and its holy places.

AMJ, which is also endorsed by ISNA, ICNA, and the Ministry of Warith D. Mohammed, works to increase public awareness about Muslim religious sensitivities in Jerusalem. In 2000 AMJ opposed Burger King's plan to license a franchise in Maale Adomim, a Jewish settlement built on confiscated Palestinian land around the holy city. On June 5, 2001, AMJ organized a sit-in at the main entrance to the U.S. Department of State to protest what the group said was an American blind support to Israel.

Another major undertaking of AMPCC was to start a dialogue with the Council of Presidents of Arab-American Organizations (CPAAO). The two umbrella councils identified secret evidence, voter registration, and U.S. policy on Jerusalem as shared priorities. There was no unified plan of action, but each group agreed to focus on these concerns in their contacts with political candidates. As a sign of public unity, AMPCC and CPAAO declared September 2000 as Arab and Muslim American Voter Registration Month. Ethnic and ideological differences precluded the addition of other issues to the list of common concerns.

These divergent religious and ethnic tendencies converged on September 20, 2000. Muslims from Edmonton, Canada, to Miami, Florida, watched on television as other Arabs and Muslims died defending Islam's third holiest site, the Aqsa Mosque compound. This followed Ariel Sharon's entry with a thousand armed security guards to what is considered sacred space by Muslims worldwide. Sharon, a former general, is a right-wing Israeli politician who was implicated by the Israeli High Court for war crimes after the massacre of Palestinian women and children in the Sabra and Shatila refugee camps in Lebanon in 1982. For the Palestinians in the West Bank and Gaza, the 2000 Aqsa Mosque incident was the culmination of frustrations resulting from the expansion of Israeli control over their life after the Oslo Accord.

In grassroots Arab and Muslim America the status of Jerusalem and the Israeli occupation came to the forefront of public concern. American Muslim and Arab groups across all ethnic, religious, and functional divides issued statements asking the U.S. government to take a more active role in resolving the conflict. On October 29, 2000, more than ten thousand people rallied at Lafayette Park across from the White House to express identification with Jerusalem and solidarity with the Palestinians. The rally was sponsored by a coalition of twenty

American Muslim and Arab-American national, regional, and local organizations, including ISNA, ICNA, AMC, AMJ, MPAC, AMA, MAS, CAIR,
MAS–W. Deen Mohammed, MSA, Coordinating Council of Muslim
Organizations of Greater Washington D.C., ADC, and AAI. Bus caravans came
from as far away as Illinois, Ohio, Pennsylvania, Michigan, New York, and New
Jersey. The demonstrators included not only ethnic Arabs but also large numbers
of Pakistanis, African Americans, Anglo Americans, Shia, and women. The profound sensitivity toward Jerusalem and Palestinian liberation, however, did not
cause any immediate policy changes from the administration or Congress.
Clearly, substantive policy changes in a country that regularly sees demonstrations of tens, if not hundreds, of thousands, require much more substantial political mobilization over a long period of time.

When Israeli troops reinvaded Palestinian towns and refugee camps after a
Palestinian bombing attack in March 2002, polls showed a strong American public opinion in favor of Israeli withdrawal. Pro-Israel groups organized a massive
pro-Israel demonstration. Reports indicated that the forty thousand demonstrators, mainly American Jews, converged in Washington, D.C. on April 15, 2002
holding posters that read "We stand with Israel." Some Christian fundamental-
ists joined the rally invoking the Bible in their support for Israel. Several government officials participated. Among them was Deputy Secretary of Defense
Paul Wolfowitz, who spoke to the crowd affirming the long-standing policy of
support for Israel. When he called for a recognition of the Palestinian suffering
and spoke of a Palestinian state he was booed.

In response, fifty thousand Arab and Muslim Americans joined another
twenty thousand antiwar protestors in the capital on April 20, 2002 chanting
"Free Palestine. End the occupation." This protest was the largest pro-Palestinian
rally ever; it attracted religious and secular Muslims from various ethnic backgrounds, its message was orchestrated to reflect the common grounds between
the various groups sponsoring the event. Among them were civil rights advocates, Native Americans, opponents of U.S. military interventionism, and Jewish
rabbis opposing Zionism. The rally, however, was not attended by members of
Congress or Bush administration representatives. Muslims began to cultivate
relations with elected officials only recently.

AMERICAN MUSLIMS AND THE ELECTIONS

AMPCC is widely credited with organizing the Muslim bloc vote in the U.S.
national election of November 2000. It is now acknowledged that this bloc vote
was crucial to George W. Bush's victory in the presidential race. Writing in
Investor's Business Daily on February 13, 2001, Kerri Houston, an official with the
Conservative Union, observed,

> Underreported by the media and underacknowledged by the Republican
> Party, with the exception of the president and his staff, Muslim-Americans
> nationwide voted for Bush by an 80% margin—closer to 90% in Florida.

Without their thousands of votes in the Sunshine State, a newly inaugurated Al Gore would currently be proposing a new slate of excuses for picking the American pocket.

Although these numbers may be higher than can be confirmed by the actual voting record—and there was dissension in favor of Gore and Nader—Bush evidently garnered a majority among Muslim voters. A poll conducted by Zogby International in November/December 2001 found that 42 percent of Muslim voters cast their ballot for Bush; 31 percent for Gore; and 12 percent for Nader.

Gore and Nader both had local and national following among Muslims, however. In 2000 the Coalition for Good Government, which is affiliated with the Ministry of W. Deen Mohammed, had barely been launched with an office in the capital. The group conducted political education activities and took part in AMPCC for few months until it publicly rejected the council's endorsement of Bush. Locally, the Community PAC in Detroit, Michigan, an African-American political action committee, endorsed Al Gore and a slate of Democratic congressional candidates in the 2000 election. The Zogby International poll found that 55 percent of African-American Muslim voters supported Gore. Still, Bush voters in this group accounted for 20 percent—double the national number for African-American voters overall.

While the drive to develop a bloc vote among American Muslims and Arab-American groups has been tempered by partisan politics and ethnic divisions, Arab and Muslim voters have demonstrated their readiness to switch sides for particular candidates. This pattern was evident even before the 2000 election. In New Jersey, for example, Muslims first endorsed one senatorial candidate in the 1996 race, then changed their endorsement to his opponent after the first candidate slighted them. They were credited publicly by the winner, Democratic Senator Robert Torricelli, for his victory. Thus the American Muslim vote has become recognizable, which is a natural reflection of the growing Muslim population.

Although no Muslims currently serve in the U.S. Congress, some Muslim candidates have won electoral seats at the state and local levels. In 1994 Larry Shaw won a seat in the North Carolina House of Representatives; in 1996 he became a state senator—the first Muslim ever to occupy such a position in any state. Like many other elected officials, Shaw built his political career through business ties, not community connections.

Several other Muslims have won city council seats, including Yusuf Abdus-Salaam in Selma, Alabama; Lateefah Muhammad in Tuskegee, Alabama; Yusuf Abdul-Hakeem in Chattanooga, Tennessee; and Nasif Majid in Charlotte, North Carolina. Morshed Alam, a chemist of Bengali origin, won a seat on New York City's District 29 School Board; Nathaniel Ham (Najeeb Hameed) won a school board seat in Queens, New York.

In 2000 Aisha Abdullah-Odiase was reelected to Rhode Island State Assembly; North Carolina State Senator Larry Shaw also was reelected. Other Muslim candidates have won electoral seats at the state and local levels, some with support spearheaded by AMA. Saggy Tahir, a Pakistani-American member of AMA, was elected on the Republican Party ticket to represent the 38th district of the New Hampshire House of Representatives. AMA New Jersey activist Hassan Fahmy was elected to a city council post.

For Congress, Eric Vickers, an African-American lawyer from St. Louis and member of the board of directors of AMA, ran for the Democratic Party nomination in Missouri's 1st district. He received 6 percent of the vote in the primary election, while the winner, William Lacy Clay Jr., received 59 percent of the vote. Vickers was not expecting to win; he understood his defeat to be part of a learning process and has continued to campaign. AMA–Orlando reported that in June 2000 the group raised $10,000 for the Vickers campaign in a single event. According to AMA, in 2000 about 152 Muslims (mostly among its Texas members) won precinct committee and party delegate seats and other local and state offices, up from twenty-four such victories in 1996.

POLITICAL ACTION COMMITTEES

Financial contributions to political candidates serve as another measurement of involvement in the political process. While many individuals give their contributions directly to candidates, others channel their contributions through political action committees (PACs). The Federal Election Commission maintains public files on those contributions.

As table 9.1 shows, Arab-American PACs, which have been around for a longer period of time, have contributed the largest amounts of political financial contributions. The Arab American Leadership PAC, which works closely with AAI, was established in the 1980s but became active only after the mid-1990s. It contributed $77,550 in 1997–1998, and $99,329 in 1999–2000. The Arab American Political Action Committee (AAPAC) filed as an independent political committee with the State of Michigan in January 1998. It aims to encourage Arab-American involvement in the American political process and to support qualified Arab Americans who wish to run for political office. AAPAC also supports candidates who are deemed to be friendly to the concerns of Arab Americans. Besides direct political contributions, AAPAC functions as a lobbying group open to Democrats, Republicans, and independents alike. In the 2000 election season the group contributed $10,500 to political candidates. The National Arab American Association PAC, which is the oldest on the list, spent only $6,150 in 1997–1998 and $2,470 in 1999–2000.

Albanian and Pakistani Americans have also formed PACs. The Pakistanis donated $2,500 in each election cycle, while the Albanians donated $50,100 in 1997–1998 and $17,300 in 1999–2000. These ethnicity-centered organizations are not highly vocal in public forums, but this does not make them less effective. Contributions from Pakistani-American Physicians, for example, were essential in defeating former North Dakota senator Pressler. There are several other newer community PACs that have not reported any contributions. These include

TABLE 9.1

ETHNIC COMMUNITY POLITICAL ACTION COMMITTEES
BY FINANCIAL CONTRIBUTIONS TO FEDERAL CANDIDATES
(IN DOLLARS)

Political Action Committee	1997–1998	1999–2000
Arab American Leadership PAC	77,550	99,329
American Task Force for Lebanon Policy Council PAC	36,000	41,800
Albanian American Public Affairs Committee	50,100	17,300
Arab American PAC	—	10,500
National Arab American Association PAC	6,150	2,470
Pakistani American Physicians Public Affairs Committee	2,500	2,500
American League of Muslims PAC	—	147
Total	172,300	174,046

Source: www.fec.gov, information taken on May 23, 2001.

American Muslim Alliance PAC, AMPCC–PAC, CAIR–PAC, Pakistan-American Friendship Society, U.S.–Pakistan PAC, and the Arab American Empowerment Committee.

PAC contributions do not include those from individuals given directly to candidates. Community members have often contributed to political candidates whom they have met in public and private events. For example, Congressman David Bonior (D-Mich.) and former member of the House Tom Campbell (R-Calif.), the main sponsors of the 1999 Secret Evidence Repeal Act, each received about $20,000 from Muslim donors in events held in Santa Clara, California, and Falls Church, Virginia, in June 1999.

Some contributions to congressional candidates are driven by local concerns, such as zoning permits for mosques and the resolution of parking and traffic problems. As an example, Virginia Congressmen Jim Moran (D-Va.) and Tom Davis (R-Va.) have continuously received contributions from local Muslims, both having established a relationship with the Dar al-Hijrah Islamic Center in Falls Church. These congressmen have written letters to Fairfax County officials to oppose a motion by Falls Church residents to revoke the mosque's user permit. They have also supported Dar al-Hijrah's request that Fairfax County install a traffic light to facilitate safer street crossing in front of the mosque.

LOCAL LEVEL PARTICIPATION

Several Islamic centers and other local religious and ethnic associations have launched their own public relations initiatives, sending informational material each year to local newspapers and radio and television stations about Muslim celebrations. Muslim activists noted that, similar to the national trend, local media coverage of American Muslim celebrations has increased in recent years. Still, in much of the United States the local character of American Muslim public involvement has yet to emerge—although in some instances community groups have addressed Muslim issues in the local context. For instance, the Muslim Education Council in Fairfax County, Virginia, has successfully lobbied the county school board to mark pork items on school lunch listings, to offer Arabic-language classes, and to issue a directive allowing Muslim students to wear more modest clothing during gym classes.

Before 20th Century Fox released the film *The Siege* in 1998, community activists nationwide went into action. ADC and CAIR leaders who read the film's transcript as it was being produced criticized it for its anti-Arab, anti-Muslim stereotypes. The film's director refused to modify the alleged defamatory content. This included a scene showing Muslim worship rituals immediately preceding footage of exploding bombs which implied a false association between Muslim religious practices and acts of violence. CAIR called on community members to organize educational activities to counter the damaging effects of the film.

Local and national media picked up on the Muslim campaign. Movie critic Roger Ebert wrote in the *Chicago-Sun Times* on November 6, 1998,

> In its clumsy way, [*The Siege*] throws in comments now and then to show it knows the difference between Arab terrorists and American citizens. But the prejudicial attitudes embodied in the film are insidious, like the anti-Semitism that infected fiction and journalism in the 1930s—not just in Germany, but in Britain and America.

For the first time the stereotyping of Muslims in the entertainment industry became a matter of public debate. The *New York Times* published editorials opposing the film's controversial content. Community activists distributed literature about Islam and invited moviegoers to open house activities at local Islamic centers. An event at the Islamic Society of Ann Arbor, Michigan, drew four hundred mostly non-Muslim residents. Working with the media had already attracted a number of activists to form local groups to explore media resources for public outreach. The Islamic Media Foundation began such work in Detroit, Michigan. Among its achievements have been the notable "Message from Your Muslim Neighbor" public service announcements in local radio and television stations.

Despite their fledgling status, state and local groups are emulating the efforts of their national counterparts. They have pushed for greater inclusion of the American Muslim community. Michigan's state legislature opened its first session after the 1999 summer recess with an invocation by a Muslim spokesperson from the Islamic Center of Ann Arbor. The Islamic Council of Ohio organizes an annual "Islamic Day in Ohio" event with the cooperation of other Islamic centers. The day is celebrated in a different Ohio city each year, allowing Muslims to meet with state and local officials, media representatives, and other members of the interfaith community. In New Jersey, the state senate began its winter session with Islamic prayers on December 16, 1999.

Often when the public relations infrastructure in local communities was lacking, Islamic centers and regional umbrella groups stepped in to fill the vacuum. In 1999 the Newark-based Majlis Ash-Shura of New Jersey (Council of Mosques and Islamic Organizations) produced a handbook designed to educate New Jersey's twenty-six hundred public schools about Islamic religious practices. The New Jersey Department of Education agreed to allow the Muslim council to distribute this booklet to public schools. Later, the Paterson County school board voted to close public schools on the two main Muslim holidays. *Imams* also have often led such efforts. Prince George's County Public Schools in Maryland, for instance, decided to include Ramadan, *Eid-al-Fitr*, and *Eid-al-Adha* on the school district's calendar of religious holidays after the *imam* of Masjid al-Taqwa wrote a letter to the district administration for the schools.

Regardless of the type or level of public advocacy, community groups in this field have seized upon public issues that appeal to the majority of their members. When the U.S. government began in 1996 to implement the computerized automated passenger screening program, also known as passenger profiling, Muslim travelers complained that they had been singled out for extra scrutiny. In response, Muslim public affairs groups issued critical statements and called on their members to report profiling incidents to them and to the Federal Aviation Commission.

CANADIAN MUSLIMS IN THE PUBLIC SQUARE

As the Canadian Muslim population grew, the interest of Muslims in public policy has increased—even though they have not yet been involved in any major electoral campaign in Canada. In 1997 the Canadian Islamic Congress (CIC) was founded, producing an annual report that looked at media bias in Canada's major newspapers. CIC has sought to underscore the pervasive sentiment among Muslims in North America that the latter part of the twentieth century saw systematic extermination campaigns against Muslims. The group asked the UN to support an internationally recognized day of remembrance for all Muslims who have been killed as a result of genocidal policies. CIC also has entered into a partnership with Jewish and Hindu groups to pressure a Canadian airline to stop charging for special meals that conform to specific religious dictates.

CAIR–CAN was founded early in 2000 and has modeled its activities on its sister group in the United States, although it is independent from the American organization. CAIR–CAN opposed a challenge by anticircumcision advocates who sought to go to court to make the case that male circumcisions should be treated like female circumcisions, which are banned under Canadian law. Male circumcision is a practice sanctioned by both Jewish and Muslim religious teachings. The Association of Genital Integrity had hoped to receive funding from the federal government's Court Challenges Program to prepare their legal challenge. Opposing the funding request were CAIR–CAN and several Canadian Jewish groups. In 2001 the Association of Genital Integrity lost its bid in front of a program panel, which ruled against the merits of the proposed litigation.

CAIR–CAN and CIC have been at the center of the battle over the 1999 Federal Government's Bill C-16, otherwise known as the Charities Registration Act. This law is designed to unmask charities with ties to terrorist groups overseas. CAIR–CAN argued before a Parliamentary hearing panel in June 2001 that the goal of the bill was commendable, but that the secrecy attached to its implementation may violate legal guarantees to equality under the law and thus might hamper the ability of Muslim groups to raise funds for legitimate causes locally and overseas. CIC issued a statement pointing out that the bill might allow the use of potentially biased secret evidence from Canada's spy agencies and foreign governments in court cases that would establish whether a particular charity is guilty of supporting global terrorism.

After the September 11, 2001, attacks in the United States, CAIR–CAN was joined by one hundred other national, regional, and local religious and ethnic associations in condemning the terror and in calling for swift justice against the perpetrators. Much like the reaction of U.S. Muslims, Canadian Muslim groups held prayer services for the victims of the attacks and encouraged members to donate blood and contribute to charities for the benefit of the victims. Soon, however, it became evident that Canadian Muslims and their community facilities had become subject to bias-motivated reprisals. CAIR–CAN, along with an affiliate group called the Canadian Muslim Civil Liberties Association, issued a report on November 20, 2001, describing anti-Muslim hate crimes in the wake of the terrorist attacks.

In December 2001, a coalition of Muslim community organizations endorsed a briefing to the Canadian Senate on Bill C-36 (Anti-Terrorism Act). The testimony, prepared by the Muslim Lawyer's Association, a Canadian Muslim guild, criticized the bill for its lack of balance between the need to ensure security and the need to respect the constitutional guarantees in the Canadian Charter of Rights. The group argued that the bill's definition of what constitutes a terrorist activity is too loose, that it may leave security agencies the room to act on the basis of questionable intelligence from foreign governments. The bill also allows the government to seize private property, arrest people, and imprison them for excessive terms based on classified information.

Like in the United States, Canadian Muslims at the grassroots level have been increasingly involved in media relations. Some of the media campaigns that began in the United States have been joined usually by Muslim Canadian groups. In certain respects, Muslims in Canada have been even more successful in winning apologies from major networks—including the *National Journal*, the *Toronto Star*, and the Canadian Broadcasting Corporation—for stereotypical coverage of Muslims. Locally, as it has been noted earlier, the Toronto District Muslim Education Assembly represents a pioneering effort in lobbying for Muslim education issues in North America.

MUSLIMS AND INTERGROUP RELATIONS
PUBLIC PERCEPTIONS OF MUSLIMS

Public opinion surveys have shown that large numbers of people in North America have little knowledge about Muslims. To some, Muslims appear to have many similarities with other groups whose women wear scarves on their heads and whose men have long beards. Sikhs, Hindus, Orthodox Christians, and members of other groups are sometimes mistaken for Muslims. But Muslims with such appearances represent only a small portion of the Muslim community. Many people in North America report to pollsters that they have little or no contact with Muslims. Because there is no one set of common characteristics identifying all Muslims, and because Muslims come in all shades of skin color and styles of dress, it is quite probable that many of these people have actually met Muslims without knowing it.

Indeed, Muslims as a whole are indistinguishable from the multitude of ethnic groups to many in the U.S. and Canada. But Americans and Canadians have been accustomed to Muslim stereotypes. The Nation of Islam, for example, is widely identified in the Muslim community as an "outsider" organization interested only in aspects of their own faith. In mass media, its members are often referred to as Black Muslims. In the movies, Arab Americans and Muslims are often portrayed by headdressed actors with a Mediterranean complexion, further adding to the confusing blend of stereotypes that have been applied to so many different people. As a further example, the terms "Pak" and "Desi" have been applied not only to Pakistanis but also to Indians, Bengalis, Iranians, Afghans, and Kashmiris—all of whom happen to share some of the same physical features but who are of many different ethnic and religious backgrounds. Even Latinos sometimes have been mistaken for Middle Easterners and South Asians.

Anti-Muslim expressions have often been linked to violent attacks against Muslims. As we have seen, following the bombing of the Murrah Federal Building in Oklahoma City in 1995, Muslims were subjected to verbal and physical abuse when reporters initially—and erroneously—attributed the incident to Middle Easterners and Muslims. Suad al-Musawi, a pregnant Iraqi immigrant with *hijab* living in Oklahoma City, lost a baby to stillbirth when an angry man attacked her at her house on April 20, a day after the bombing. Also in 1995 the Islamic Society of Greenville, South Carolina, was set ablaze. Similar anti-Muslim incidents were reported in 1996 following the crash of TWA Flight 800, when some pundits speculated that the disaster might have been the result of a terrorist attack led by Middle Easterners.

But Muslim symbols have been attacked in noncrisis times, as well. Perhaps the first spectacular arson attack on a mosque took place in Yuba City, California, in 1994 when a multi-million-dollar mosque was burned to the ground. Random attacks against Arabs and Muslims increase during times of crisis involving Muslims, such as the Iranian hostage crisis in 1979 and the Gulf War of 1990–1991.

Still, public opinion in the United States and Canada is as pluralistic as the societies are. Moreover, public opinion often is sensitive to dramatic events and to statements made by political and religious figures. After the 1993 World Trade Center bombing, Zogby International conducted a poll that found the nation split into three almost equal parts: those favorable toward Muslims, those unfavorable, and those neutral. In 2000 the National Conference for Community and Justice released a poll in which 13 percent of those polled said they felt close or very close to Muslims; 25 percent said they felt far or very far from them; 27 percent said they felt neutral; and 36 percent said they simply did not know.

In contrast, a poll commissioned by the Pew Forum on Religion and Public Life released on December 6, 2001, showed that 59 percent of Americans held a favorable view of American Muslims, up from 45 percent the previous March. Surprisingly, the greatest boost to these numbers was among conservative Republicans—in March only 35 percent had had a favorable view, but by November that number had risen to 64 percent. Two factors contributed to the change in the public mood. First, unlike the aftermath of the 1993 World Trade Center bombing and the 1995 Oklahoma City bombing, an overwhelming majority of Muslim groups took swift, high-profile actions to condemn the September 11 attacks. Several national groups published statements in major newspapers like *The Washington Post, The New York Times* and *The Los Angeles Times*. Local Islamic centers took similar steps and increased their outreach activities to civic and religious groups. The news media featured Muslim-world governments taking the same position. Second, national leaders, especially President Bush, stressed the distinction between Muslim terrorists and their coreligionists and warned against ethnic and religious reprisals.

And yet Muslims in general are more driven by the quest to articulate their concerns on public policy than by apprehensions and fears stemming from their minority status. Muslims enter the domain of politics with a major disadvantage: they lack experience. This fact will change with time, as it has with other groups that once lacked political clout. Because of the fractured nature of interest group politics, the willingness and ability to form coalitions with a wide variety of partners is a key to effectiveness. Likewise, any reasonable assessment of the relations between Muslims and others must account for areas of convergence and divergence. So far, political interaction and alliance-building involving Muslims as core participants has been sporadic.

ALLIES

Muslim groups have joined in alliances on such strategic issues as the promotion of tolerance. On occasion, Muslims and Arab Americans have taken the initiative in forming such coalitions. For example, when Pat Robertson, the founder of the Christian Coalition, said in 1997 "To see Americans become followers of quote Islam is nothing short of insanity." Muslim community groups joined the Interfaith Conference of Metropolitan Washington and People for the American Way in denouncing Robertson's remarks.

In another campaign in October 1999 Muslims and others asked the Senate Republican Policy Committee to rebuke anti-Muslim policy analyst James Jatras, who called the presence of Muslims in America a "population infiltration" and suggested that NATO's policy in the Balkans was foolish because it offered aid to Muslims. The General Board on Church and Society of the United Methodist Church, the Interfaith Alliance, and the Catholic League for Religious and Civil Rights, a conservative group, joined Muslim advocacy groups in asking Senate majority leader Trent Lott (R-Miss.) to take a stand on the issue.

Muslim and Arab-American groups have also worked in partnership with a wide spectrum of allies on issues of civil rights and freedom of speech. They joined the American Civil Liberties Union (ACLU)–led coalition opposing the 1996 Anti-Terrorism and Effective Death Penalty Act, which contained the secret evidence clause. After the bill passed, the coalition monitored its implementation and publicly noted that it was used against Arabs and Muslims almost exclusively. The coalition then lobbied Congress to introduce the Secret Evidence Repeal Act in 1999. Several Arab and Muslim activists testified before the House Judiciary Committee, which passed the bill few weeks before the end of the 1998–2000 session. The bill did not go through a vote and was reintroduced by Democratic Representatives David Bonior and John Conyers (both of Michigan) and Republican Representatives Bob Barr (Ga.) and Tom Davis (Va.) as soon as the new Congress convened in January 2001.

After September 11 the tide reversed in favor of tougher security measures, allowing not only detention based on classified information but also spying on suspected individuals—and even religious and political organizations. The USA Patriot Act of 2001 was rushed through Congress to back this campaign. Civil libertarians and their supporters were cowed, limiting their criticism only to the most blatant abuses. Behind closed doors, however, Muslims, Arabs, African Americans, Irish Americans, and other minority and religious groups have met to monitor the situation and coordinate a public education campaign on civil rights. In one January 2002 incident, a security screener forced a passenger to remove her headscarf in full view of the public at Baltimore–Washington International Airport. A number of groups protested, including CAIR, which filed a complaint with the security company and asked for an apology.

Another profiling incident in Chicago led to the filing of a discrimination lawsuit by the ACLU in a federal district court. Muslim groups offered public support for the ACLU action, which charged that an Illinois National Guardsman and three private security personnel at O'Hare International Airport engaged in an unnecessary, unjustified, illegal, and degrading search of a twenty-two-year-old U.S. citizen of Pakistani descent on November 7, 2001. The woman, Samar Kaukab, is a resident of Columbus, Ohio, and wears *hijab*. She was traveling home when she was pulled out of a group of airline passengers and subjected to a strip search based on her ethnicity and her religion. The lawsuit charged that the woman's freedom of religion and constitutional protections against unreasonable search and seizure were violated.

Groups that have taken Muslims as allies and friends are mainly secular, Catholic, politically liberal, or mainline Protestant. Conservative groups have maintained varying views on Muslims. Accommodationists, such as Libertarians, consider Muslims a great asset to the Republican Party. After the 2000 elections Grover Norquist, head of Americans for Tax Reform, publicly credited Muslim political activists for the Bush victory. Norquist had already cofounded the Islamic Institute in 1998, with a group of Muslims, in an attempt to win Muslims to the Republican Party. Another conservative group that has reached out to Muslims with enthusiasm is the Catholic League for Religious and Civil Rights. This league has collaborated with Muslim groups to combat anti-Catholic, anti-Muslim bias. In a joint symposium in October 1998 the league and CAIR underscored their commonalities in these causes.

Although Muslims and Catholics share many traditional values, most Muslim and Arab-American public affairs groups have no functioning political dialogue with the U.S. Conference of Catholic Bishops (USCCB), the main Catholic lobby in America—although USCCB leaders on several occasions have made joint appearances with Muslim groups and leaders in interfaith events. Still, Catholic–Muslim relations have been warming since the Second Vatican Council in 1965, when the church recognized non-Christian religions as genuine, respectful expressions of faith. The most recent example of cooperation between U.S. Catholics and Muslims took place during the 1994 UN population conference, when delegates from both camps joined forces to fight for a family-centered vision of society.

On foreign policy issues, among the oldest allies of Muslim community organizations has been the Council on National Interest (CNI), a group that has been particularly interested in U.S. Middle East policy. The group was founded by former ambassadors and elected officials and had called for cutting U.S. aid to Israel, and for support to the creation of a Palestinian state as a solution to the Israeli–Palestinian conflict. In 2001 CNI conducted a campaign to persuade the U.S. Department of State to pressure the Israeli government to address reports of the Israeli torture of Palestinian Americans visiting relatives in the West Bank and Gaza. CNI has also worked in collaboration with American Muslim and Arab-American groups in public education campaigns regarding this policy area.

DETRACTORS

Among the ideologically oriented interest groups are those who believe in a cosmic war between Islam and the West. As such they do not even envision a place for the Muslim community in the American body politic. In contrast to the view of the mainline National Council of Churches and its affiliated study centers, which have sought an understanding of Islam and Muslims, some conservative Protestants have only resorted to selective, segmented views of Muslims and Islamic ideas and religious events. James Phillips, an analyst with the right-wing Hoover Institution, contributed an article in *Urban Terrorism* in 1996 suggesting that immigrant Muslims pose a potential "security threat" after half a dozen Muslim men were convicted in the 1993 World Trade Center bombing. Muslims have argued that this broad-brush generalization was never applied to Christian, white men—or even to the antigovernment militia groups—in the aftermath of the 1995 Oklahoma City bombing.

Other leaders believe that America is, or ought to be, an exclusively Christian nation. These advocates include Reverend Jerry Falwell, who in 2000 told the Internet magazine *Beliefnet.com* that when it comes to applying for federal funds under President Bush's proposed faith-based initiatives program, "Islam should be out the door before they knock." Such intolerant speech is constitutionally protected in the United States, despite its divisive tone. National Muslim organizations have become accustomed to challenging such rhetoric in public, and they have won friends to their side in spite of it.

Anti-Muslim rhetoric in the conservative, white Christian camp has increased substantially after the collapse of communism, as some sought to identify a new enemy for the West to fight. In the summer of 1993 Samuel Huntington wrote an article in *Foreign Affairs* predicting a new fault line in world conflicts based on culture. Conservative pundit Richard Neuhaus, the editor of *First Things*, who believes in a Judeo-Christian America, published several commentaries promoting the idea that Islam is the new global enemy.

Another group that believes in a Judeo-Christian America is the Free Congress Foundation. This group has never offered exchanges with religious and ethnic Muslims. Yet Paul Weyrich, president of the foundation and founder of the far-right-wing Heritage Foundation, suggested in 2001 that the recently released *Eid* Greetings stamp should be recalled by the U.S. Postal Service and "overprinted with the image of the twin towers," because "America's most notable experience with Islam was the attacks on September 11." Muslims countered that they, too, were outraged by the attacks and expressed resentment over Mr. Weyrich's dismissal of the contributions of millions of fellow citizens and the linkage of the Islamic faith to the actions of terrorists.

Indignation and call for dialogue was the response of Muslims when Franklin Graham, son of mainstream evangelist Billy Graham, shocked television viewers by stating that "The God of Islam is not the same God. He's not the son of God of the Christian or Judeo-Christian faith. It's a different God, and I believe it is a very evil and wicked religion." In the same NBC report, Graham said, "I don't believe this [Islam] is this wonderful, peaceful religion." Responding to Graham's comments, evangelist Charles Colson, the founder of Prison Fellowship Ministries, said: " . . . I agree that Islam is a religion, which, if taken seriously, promotes violence." Colson is seen as a mainline pastor who has spoken publicly against Jerry Falwell's Moral Majority. He has, however, expressed the view that the whole idea of Western liberal democracy rests upon Christian premises. Still, Graham and Colson do not call for the exclusion of Muslims from government, as Falwell and Robertson do.

Nevertheless, anti-Muslim rhetoric appears sometimes to be politically motivated. Even congressional representatives have used Muslim bashing to appeal to Robertson and Falwell supporters in the south. In the aftermath of September 11, Representative Saxby Chambliss (R-Ga.), chairman of the House Subcommittee on Terrorism and Homeland Security and a candidate for the Senate, told Georgia law enforcement personnel they should "just turn [the sheriff] loose and have him arrest every Muslim that crosses the state line." Another congressman, John Cooskey (R-La.), mocked Muslim head-wear days after the attacks. He stated, "If I see someone that comes in that's got a diaper on his head and a fan belt wrapped around the diaper on his head, that guy needs to be pulled over and checked." Faced with public criticism, the two congressmen later apologized.

To some analysts, confrontations between faith-based Muslims and the religious right seem bizarre, because both occupy socially conservative niches in America's pluralistic society. But the spat underscores the fact that the two groups are still in search of a cohesive, informed vision of the public square. While groups in the two blocs exchange attacks and apologies through the press, neither camp has invested seriously in developing a multifaith perspective on public policy alternatives. For groups on the extreme right, such possibility is inconceivable anyway.

The relationship of American Jewish groups with Muslims has been the most tenuous, although both minority groups recognize that they share some common ground in a predominantly Christian society. A short list of shared concerns includes combating hate crimes and promoting the free exercise of religion. Nevertheless, Jewish–Muslim relations in North America, especially in the United States, have been dominated by disagreement over the Palestinian–Israeli conflict.

Many Muslims believe that U.S. policy in the Middle East is tilted unfairly in support of Israel, whose occupation of Palestinian territories is increasingly viewed by many as an inhumane apartheidlike regime. Ethnic and religious Muslims have rallied locally and nationally in support of the Palestinians. While ethnic Arab Americans have been most vocal in favor of a Palestinian state, faith-based Muslim groups have expressed particular interest in the issue of Jerusalem for its religious significance.

Sensing the potential challenge, the entrenched pro-Israel groups have taken a series of actions widely seen in the Muslim community as attempting to curtail

Muslims' access to government. In 1998 and 2001 Jewish groups objected to the inclusion of officials from CAIR in panel discussions organized by the U.S. Commission on Civil Rights—even when it was evident that their opposition would fail. The Anti-Defamation League (ADL), an American jewish public advocacy organization, criticized New Jersey Republican gubernatorial candidate Bret Schundler for meeting with members of AMA in April 2001. The candidate rejected what he called an attempt to keep Muslims out of the political process. He issued a statement stating, "to shun the organization would be caving in to anti-Muslim bigotry."

Furthermore, pro-Israel groups have attempted to block the appointments of American Muslims to public office several times. In 1999 major Jewish groups, including the Council of Presidents of Major Jewish Organizations, opposed the nomination of Salam Al-Marayati, executive director of MPAC, to the National Commission on Terrorism. Al-Marayati stated that Israeli repression of the Palestinian people has bred violent responses. His condemnation of attacks against noncombatant Israelis was deemed insufficient evidence of his opposition to terrorism.

For some American Jewish groups, bullying is not new. In 1993 ADC accused the ADL of illegally gathering information on Arab-American activists. In 1996 the ADL agreed to sign a legal document to turn over the gathered data and to refrain from directly or indirectly obtaining any document or other information about individuals in violation of the law. To Muslim activists, the ADL's renewed interest in harassing opponents is only a testament that the organization's leadership has resisted change; it seemingly has moved from one fight to another.

Despite the fractious nature of the Jewish–Muslim relationship, there have been instances when the two groups have come together. For instance, AMC endorsed a statement cosigned by the American Jewish Congress and other groups on religion in public schools. Also, AAI and AMC, along with the Israel Public Affairs Committee endorsed the 1993 Oslo Accord between the PLO and Israel. Afterward, AAI joined a Jewish group named the Foundation for Middle East Peace, with the blessing of Vice President Albert Gore, in establishing Builders for Peace, a group that hoped to promote American private investment in the West Bank and Gaza. Even prior to the Oslo accord, AAI had been exchanging views on peace between Israelis and Palestinians with Americans for Peace Now—the equivalent of the Israeli Peace Now Party.

Moreover, the American Jewish Committee in Los Angeles, California, joined the Women's Coalition Against Ethnic Cleansing. Leading the effort to formulate this alliance was the city's Muslim Women's League. The group compiled information and testified in Congress on the rape of Muslim women during Serbian attacks on Bosnian towns. In 1998 a dialogue between Muslims and Jews in California led to a draft of a code of ethics, which decried rumor-mongering and prejudice and called for a fact-based discourse.

Even in the midst of the row between Muslims and Jews over political nominations and foreign policy options the two camps are hardly unified in the opposition to one another. When the Washington-based American Jewish Committee (AJC) opposed the nomination of Salam al-Marayati to the terrorism commission, Rabbi Alfred Wolf of the Skirball Institute—linked administratively to AJC—along with three other West coast rabbis, disagreed with the view of the East coast Jewish leaders. The rabbis argued that it was not in the best interest of the Jewish community to block the nomination of al-Marayati. On the Muslim side, several local Muslim groups and *imams*, especially those affiliated with the Ministry of Imam W. D. Mohammed, have maintained contacts with a variety of Jewish American groups—this despite the sharp disagreement over Jerusalem and the Palestinians.

MUSLIMS AND THE BUSH ADMINISTRATION

The most perplexing relationship to Muslims has been theirs with the George W. Bush administration. During the Bush electoral campaign, he challenged the use of "secret evidence," and the AMPCC cited this as a reason for endorsing him. After the election, however, the Muslim community has felt ignored by his administration. No action was taken to address domestic and foreign policy issues of concern to Muslims, for instance. September 11 witnessed a sudden shift in the administration's outreach to American Muslims. In a matter of days after the event several meetings took place between government officials and Muslim community leaders at various levels, from the White House down to low-level officials in the Department of State, Department of Justice, and EEOC. Some of the meetings were televised, especially the president's visits to the Islamic Center in the nation's capital. Muslims appreciated the publicity, especially coming in the midst of the worst anti-Muslim, anti-Arab, and anti–South Asian violence in U.S. history.

At the same time, Muslim and Arab community members complained about racial and religious profiling at airports and in shopping centers, schools, and workplaces. Federal and local authorities, acting on tips from private citizens, detained and interrogated many individuals—and in few instances high school pupils—of Middle Eastern and South Asian descent. Also, hundreds of noncitizens were detained for visa violations; many were neither deported nor released with an adjusted legal status. An unknown number of legal residents were also taken into custody as material witnesses (in April 2002, a federal judge in New York ruled that the detention of material witnesses was unconstitutional). Al-Badr Al-Hazmi, a San Antonio doctor with a last name similar to that of one of the September 11 hijackers, was held for two weeks and denied a lawyer for several days during his detention. Even individuals with a mundane association with suspected terrorists were detained; some were deported.

Nevertheless, national Muslim community groups kept their civil rights concerns separate from their views on the September 11 attacks. All of the Muslim community's public affairs groups issued statements in support of the war against terrorism. The only public dissent to the president's policy was a call by a number of community groups for a pause and reassessment of the bombing in Afghanistan after reports of civilian casualties. Many argued that after all, the United States had not accused any Afghani citizen in the September 11 attacks. Still, some American Muslim leaders pointed out that the U.S. government has not maintained a coherent definition of the term "terrorism" in its declared war on it and have expressed concern about the president use of the term "crusade" in referring to a pending worldwide, open-ended response.

The Bush administration's investigative campaign moved to a new phase with the government decision to interview eight thousand Arab and Muslim noncitizens who live legally in the United States. Civil rights activists said this action constituted racial profiling. The chief of police in Portland, Oregon, said that he would not cooperate in gathering information on noncitizens who did not violate any laws under the jurisdiction of the police. Muslim community leaders expressed disappointment over the increasingly sweeping nature of what has become known as a dragnet of arrests, detentions, and investigations. Some of the released detainees and their relatives complained that federal agents had even asked about their religious and political views.

The ACLU-led coalition sent a letter to Attorney General John Ashcroft requesting the disclosure of information about the detainees and their legal status. When the government ignored the requests, ADC charged the Bush administration with violating the Freedom of Information Act. Later the media published some information on the national origin of detained foreign students. The reports, however, were not inclusive of all detainees. Legal expert David Cole criticized the duplicity in actions taken by the government—pleading for assistance from Arabs and Muslims while alienating them by religious and ethnic profiling. Government officials repeated the standard response that the country was at war and that law enforcement must be allowed all the tools needed to assure security. Officials with CAIR publicly acknowledged the duty of the government to prosecute anyone who breaks the law, but pointed out that the selective enforcement of the law on Arabs and Muslims was a form of discrimination that only gave the public a false sense of security. Although most of the detainees were released within six months, a few hundred remain incarcerated—none has been charged with terrorism.

Intellectuals began to question the Bush administration's commitment to the Constitution. Some pointed out that the government's actions cast doubt over the moral integrity of resolutions made by Congress, which previously apologized to citizens of Japanese descent for internments during World War II. American Muslim spokesmen pointed out that this official apology by the representative body of the American people amounted to a collective declaration that the detention of people due to their heritage or ethnicity is morally wrong. American Muslims believed that if they did not stand up for their rights in this atmosphere of suspicion, they would lose them altogether. But realizing that the public remains wounded after the terrorist attacks, many Muslims toned down their rhetoric.

On December 4, 2001, the Bush administration blocked the assets the Holy

Land Foundation (HLF) in the wake of a violent flare-up in the Palestinian–Israeli conflict. The government charged that HLF programs in the West Bank and Gaza benefit families of Palestinians linked to Hamas—which was listed as terrorist by the Department of State in 1997. HLF, however, does not work solely in the occupied territories; the group has offered assistance in Lebanon, Bosnia, and Turkey. In the United States, the HLF sponsored a number of social service programs and helped in the relief effort after such disasters as the Oklahoma City bombing and the September 11 terrorist attacks.

Because of the secrecy with which the U.S. government has moved against the organization, Arab-American and Muslim commentators suggest that the action taken against HLF is another case of religious and ethnic profiling. HLF founders, they claimed, are American citizens who hail from Palestine and are known best for being religiously observant Muslims. ADC President Ziad Asali issued a statement that "Arab Americans are committed in the fight against terrorism at home and abroad, but all Americans should have a chance to defend themselves when accused of crimes by the government and punished through seizure of assets." Asali added "ADC expects the Justice Department to pursue all those suspected of illegal activities, present its evidence against them in open court, and prosecute them according to American legal norms."

A week later, two more charities—Benevolence International Foundation (BIF) and Global Relief Foundation (GRF)—were placed under blocking orders by the government. No public accusations were made in the freezing of the accounts of these two groups, except a general accusation of the linkage to terrorism. Religious and ethnic community groups locally and nationally have criticized these actions and called for the charities to be allowed to either resume their important work or face a fair trial. The three charities denied the accusations of terrorism and filed law suits seeking to clear their names and regain their legal status.

Nevertheless, Muslim community groups hailed the vigilance of law enforcement authorities when they foiled a bombing attack by the Jewish Defense League (JDL) in California in 2001. JDL chairman Irv Rubin and another member of his group were arrested on December 11, 2001, on suspicion of plotting to blow up a mosque in Culver City, California, and the offices of MPAC and Arab-American Congressman Darrell Issa (R-Calif.). Rubin was arrested after bomb-making components were allegedly delivered to his co-conspirator's home. Other bomb components were reportedly seized at Rubin's home, as well.

In meetings with the Department of Justice, MPAC and other groups called on the government to freeze the assets of JDL and close down its offices. But the government seemed disinterested in heeding the request with any urgency. Muslim leaders later charged that there is disparity in the government's treatment of Muslim and Jewish groups implicated in violence. Some spokesmen suggested that the Bush administration maintains two tiers of standards in its law enforcement, one for Arab and Muslim Americans, another for all others.

Meanwhile, discrimination reports from Arabs and Muslims in the United States mounted. ADC went before the U.S. Commission on Civil Rights on December 11, 2001, to testify about 115 cases of employment discrimination complaints that the group received since September 11. CAIR went before the Judiciary Committee in the House of Representatives on January 24, 2002, to testify on the impact of racial and religious profiling faced by Muslim residents and citizens in the aftermath of September 11, outlining more than seventeen hundred complaints that the group received from community members. CAIR asked Congress to hold civil liberties oversight hearings on the implementation of the USA Patriot Act and to assure that any new laws or regulations issued in connection with the events of September 11 are narrowly tailored to true terrorism activity and rescinded when no longer needed.

Clearly, American Muslim public advocacy groups have struggled for improved status and inclusion. As a result of the community's encounters with American political institutions and the public sphere in general, Muslims have gained greater acquaintance with the political process and some of its key players. Robert Fowler and Alan Hertzke, authors of *Religion and Politics in America: Faith, Culture, and Strategic Choices*, predicted in 1995 that many Muslims may join like-minded groups in what is known as the "religious right" in opposition to the forces of secularism. Evidence shows that more and more Muslims have entered into alliances with groups on both the conservative and liberal ends of the American political spectrum. Muslims have found room to work with conservative Catholics on pro-family policies; with liberals, mainline Protestants, and social conservatives on tolerance and fact-based public discourse; with civil libertarians, African Americans, and other minority groups on civil rights. Relations with Jews have fluctuated and have become increasingly confrontational with the break down of negotiations in the Palestinian-Israeli conflict.

The main objective of Muslim participation in mainstream politics in both Canada and the United States is empowerment. Muslim public affairs groups have made the sterotyping of Muslims a matter of public debate, have resolved many incidents of discrimination and defamation, and have demonstrated their ability to mobilize support for their concerns. These efforts, as modest as their accomplishments may be, have decidedly shifted political attitudes among Muslims in favor of integration in North American political institutions. The mainline view recognizes non-Muslim groups as social entities with rights and duties that can be considered as allies on matters of common good. An attitude of engagement—identifying actions and views with specific groups rather than with broad religious communities—has increasingly characterized Muslim interactions with others.

To some Muslims, community public affairs groups may seem to engage in soft press-release politics and photo-op events, with little to show for all the funds they collect. Such sentiment is usually held by recent immigrants who have not had much experience in their homelands in grassroots development and political mobilization. To many Muslims who appreciate the difficult and time-consuming task of developing a grassroots consensus, however, the community's public affairs organizations have rendered valuable service in communicating their communities' concerns about domestic and foreign policy. These groups have also educated community members about their rights and have helped them gain access to the political process. For now, the main thrust of American Muslim public advocacy is the effort to combat prevailing prejudice and ignorance.

A CLOSER LOOK
KARAMAH—MUSLIM WOMEN
LAWYERS FOR HUMAN RIGHTS

The Qur'an states that God has endowed human beings with dignity [*karamah*]. This dignity extends to us all, regardless of race, status, or gender.

As Muslim women, we cherish our God-given *karamah*.

Karamah is a reciprocal concept. It is a claim that each one of us makes upon society, but it is also a claim that society rightfully makes upon us. We must live up to the expectations of *karamah*.

Karamah: Muslim Women Lawyers for Human Rights is a charitable, educational organization which focuses upon the domestic and global issues of human rights for Muslims. Karamah stands committed to research, education, and advocacy work in matters pertaining to Muslim women and human rights in Islam.

Karamah is founded upon the idea that education, dialogue, and action can counter the dangerous and destructive effects of ignorance, silence, and prejudice.

Karamah seeks to support Muslim communities in America and abroad in the pursuit of justice. When we talk of human rights abuses, we often direct our attention to governments and institutions. We must not forget, however, that the most basic of our rights emerges within our private and our domestic spheres.

Mission Statement

KARAMAH has four key goals:

1. Increase the familiarity of the Muslim community with Islamic, American, and international laws on issues of human rights;
3. Advise and assist individuals, institutions, and organizations on matters of human rights as seen from the perspective of Islamic law;
4. Advise and assist Muslims, particularly women, on matters adversely affecting the free exercise of their religion, freedom of expression, and other constitutional rights in the United States;
5. Provide educational materials on legal and human rights issues to American Muslims.

A Closer Look, continued on next page

Activities

- Karamah at the United Nations Fourth World Conference on Women (September 1995)
- Supreme Court Frieze Controversy (March 1997)
- Karamah hosts presentation by Bahraini women's activist at Library of Congress (July 2000)
- Karamah asserts right to education for Muslim schoolgirls in France (October 2000)
- Karamah responds to *Atlantic Monthly* article (January 1999)
- Karamah sponsors workshop "Human Rights Advocacy: From Theory to Practice" (February 2001)
- Karamah endorses Islamic Scholar's analysis of the Taliban's destruction of Buddhist statues (March 2001)
- Karamah issues a statement raising concerns on Taliban's edict on religious minorities (May 2001)

Source: From www.karamah.org.

TEN

RESEARCH ORGANIZATIONS

Many Muslim academics hold positions at North American universities, but most work in medical, engineering, and other applied sciences careers. Some Muslims fill positions in teaching ethnic and Islamic studies in dozens of centers and college departments specializing in the Middle East, Africa, and Asia. For historical reasons, of course, much of the scholarship on Islam and Muslims has paid little attention thus far to North American Muslims.

Interest in the Muslim world has focused primarily on language and history. Until recently, studies that ventured into exploring Muslim societies have been mainly concerned with political power. Academic research examining the social conditions of Muslims around the world has been largely based on abstract typologies that reveal little information about the dynamics of Muslim life. As one example, researchers examining the status of Muslim women have been most interested in the theoretical and polemical aspects of the issue, while scant attention has been paid to the fact-based inquiry of women's lives and struggles.

Outside academia, some think tanks funded by political and corporate interests have also focused on the development and politics of the various parts of the Muslim world. The Washington, D.C.–based Middle East Institute is perhaps the oldest private research organization devoted to studying the Middle East. It was established in 1946 on the basis of its founders' prediction that the oil-rich region would have a significant role in world affairs. Its flagship publication, *The Middle East Journal*, covers a wide variety of topics—including politics, economics, culture, ethnicity, and religion—from Morocco to Pakistan. The quarterly includes a bibliography of U.S. government publications relating to the Middle East. The institute offers language instruction to Washington-area government employees, academics, business people, and university students. It also maintains a library on Islam and Islamic art, as well as a rare-book collection of the works of early Muslim scholars and Middle Eastern travelers.

Other private study programs are found within the well-established public policy–oriented think tank community. These organizations—such as the Center for Strategic and International Studies, the Brookings Institution, the Cato Institute, and the Rand Corporation—offer foreign policy study programs focusing on the Middle East, South Asia, and Africa. Their works are influential in policy-making circles, although these organizations have rarely represented Muslim community perspectives. Muslim intellectuals who occupied positions in these establishments contribute their talents to the public debate on matters of concerns to Muslims, but overall they tend to be ambivalent toward policy questions expressed in Muslim community forums.

A number of organizations have been established to illuminate the religious and political concerns of Muslim community members. The goals and endeavors of these research groups vary: some examine matters of jurisprudence; others venture into intellectual reform; while still others address more specific political challenges. These groups have been able to attract career-oriented professionals and have targeted academics, political leaders, and policy makers.

EDUCATIONAL RESEARCH

Research groups with intellectual products serving educational purposes have developed various ideological orientations and areas of focus. The Fiqh Council of North America aims at advancing knowledge of Islamic law in North America, although it has only recently begun to routinize its activities. The council traces its origins to the early 1960s, when the Muslim Students Association established the Religious Affairs Committee of the United States and Canada. This group became the Fiqh Committee of ISNA in the early 1980s, and in 1986 it was named the Fiqh Council of North America. The council remained largely dormant, however, until the late 1990s.

The council answers inquiries from members of the community. Its website lists questions and rulings as researched by members of its board of scholars. The concerns range from matters of ritual to philosophical inquiries about the Islamic tradition and its applicability in North America. For example, one question addressed to the council was whether or not it would be religiously permissible to use lottery money in the building of Islamic centers. The council replied negatively in this case, because lotteries have been traditionally likened to gambling, which the Qur'an explicitly prohibits, and are therefore considered unlawful economic activities. The council, however, has no legal authority and thus serves as an advisory panel striving to reach sound opinions regarding the moral dilemmas of the day.

The council also has explored contemporary issues with implications for public policy. In order to perform its task proficiently, the council has consulted Muslim legal and religious experts in the areas under examination. Most recently, the council examined the issue of capital punishment when public debate arose over suggestions that the government issue a moratorium on executions. Reviewing testimony from a law professor, the council issued a recommendation in favor of an interim moratorium. This opinion was primarily based on a finding that there is evidence of racial and social class discrimination in the implementation of the death penalty.

On another occasion, the council examined the issue of postdivorce financial settlements and concluded that a divorced woman has the right to receive compensation from the husband adequate enough to secure a decent living after divorce. The council's recommendation stated that the Qur'an and Hadith offer support for the idea of equitable compensation, but Muslim world scholars in the past did not emphasize this idea because a safety net was offered to divorced women through the prevailing custom of extended family support. Such tradition has changed in modern times—in North America, the extended family structure is almost nonexistent. Hence the ruling in favor of reviving the requirement of equity stated in the Qur'an and Hadith was an important one.

In 1997 a group of African-American Muslim lawyers and academics began publishing the *Journal of Islamic Law*, which since has acquired the title *Journal of Islamic Law and Culture*. The journal appears biannually with articles addressing a range of Muslim concerns, both practical and theoretical. Some articles addressed American Muslim concerns blending Islamic values with contemporary U.S. law. Other pieces deal with Islamic law from a classical jurisprudence perspective. Several contributors to the journal are specialized in Islamic studies, a field of inquiry that has traditionally focused on Islam as expressed in classical texts.

Other research groups have been struggling to bridge the gap between medieval Islamic literature and modern realities. In 1977 North American and European Muslim activists and intellectuals who had been affiliated with Islamic revival movements held a seminar on Islamic thought in Lugano, Switzerland. There they decided that the Muslim *ummah* was experiencing an intellectual crisis that debilitated progress in all domains of Muslim life. The meeting resolved that an institute for Islamic thought should be established to address this predicament. In 1984 the Institute of International Islamic Thought (IIIT) was established in Herndon, Virginia.

Because of the global nature of the reform mission, the organization established branch offices and representatives in the United Kingdom, France, Egypt, Pakistan, Bangladesh, Indonesia, Morocco, Nigeria, Sudan, Iran, Jordan, and Lebanon. IIIT has conducted more than 150 seminars, conferences, and training programs. It has also produced several hundred books in Arabic, English, and other languages—many concerned with issues of intellectual inquiry. Many of the works center around the themes that social research is not value-free and that Islamic ideas can relate to intellectual speculation in the various disciplines of social studies.

In *The Qur'an and the Sunnah: the Time–Space Factor*, IIIT authors suggest that a proper understanding of religious scripture must account for the circumstances of the time of revelation. Another title, *Toward an Islamic Theory of International Relations*, concludes that classical Islamic thought cannot possibly produce an adequate understanding of contemporary relations between Muslims and non-Muslims. Yet another book, *Toward Islamic Anthropology*, discusses the various approaches to the study of the dynamics between individuals and societies. It concludes that no individual or society is value-free and that Muslims can add to the inquiry their own set of assumptions about human behavior.

Critics of IIIT note that the group has been hesitant to take its reform agenda to a logical end by actually examining Muslim behavior and Islamic values in real-life settings. Although the group has made the call for appreciating the social sciences a core objective, IIIT has not promoted the production of studies that are based on empirical research. So its efforts must be seen as a general contribution to the intellectual debate in the Muslim world over religion, rationality, and leadership. In this connection, IIIT can be described best as an Islamic outreach to Muslim intellectuals, challenging them to remain true to their faith.

Nevertheless, there is uniqueness in the IIIT experience. Unlike other contemporary Sunni institutes, IIIT has consciously involved Shia intellectuals in its activities. Also, IIIT work has given rise to the School of Islamic and Social Sciences, which now proposes to establish a training program for *imams* that is centered around an American Muslim consciousness. Also, IIIT scholars have been instrumental in rejuvenating the Islamic Fiqh Council in North America. Moreover, IIIT has sponsored the Association of Muslim Social Scientists (AMSS) and that organization's publication, the *American Journal of Islamic Social Sciences* (AJISS).

AMSS mainly attracts Muslim graduate students, new college professors, and activist scholars interested in contemporary intellectual Muslim discourse. AJISS has been a forum for intellectuals to exchange ideas on issues ranging from the examination of classical Muslim discourse to the exploration of such contemporary challenges as modernity, human rights, and the status of women in Muslim societies. The area of educational challenges facing Muslim communities around the world also has been a constant theme in AJISS published articles.

Another voice in this intellectual discourse is the Center for the Study of Islam and Democracy (CSID). Founded in 1999 by a group of Muslim activists and academics of various faith affiliations, this association of intellectuals promotes the idea that democratic principles are compatible with Islam. The group holds an annual conference where members present their views on theoretical and practical themes about the relationship between Islam and democracy. CSID also organizes lectures discussing the future of democracy in the Muslim world. In February 2001 CSID cosigned a letter with the AMC to newly elected President George W. Bush, urging him to revamp U.S. policy toward the Muslim world, to nurture respect for Islam as a world religion, and to encourage authoritarian Muslim governments to reform themselves on the basis of American democratic values.

Other research groups focus on the contemporary social and political conditions of specific ethnic groups or countries. For historical reasons Arab-American academics, including many Christians, dominated this area. The most prominent group they established was the Association of Arab-American University

Graduates (AAUG), which was founded in 1968 to bring together Arab-American intellectuals in annual conferences, cultural events, and summer study visits to Arab countries. The group began shortly after the June 1967 Israeli occupation of Arab lands in Egypt, Syria, Lebanon, and the West Bank and Gaza. AAUG promised to contribute well-researched educational material to the development of the Arab world.

AAUG offers internships to college students and organizes panels on public issues. The group's main activity is the publication of *Arab Studies Quarterly*, which since 1978 has offered analytical perspectives on politics and development in the Arab world. The group's publications also include books and papers that analyze the evolution of Arab-American identity, especially in connection with Israel's occupation of Arab lands and U.S. support for the state of Israel. Contributors to AAUG publications are mostly academics specialized in Middle Eastern studies. With the rise of Islamic movements in the Arab world, AAUG literature has allowed an increasing coverage of faith-based perspectives to the Arab world heritage and contemporary dilemmas.

The mission of other groups are even more specific. The Institute for Palestine Studies (IPS), whose Arab branch was founded in Beirut in 1963, started a satellite office in Washington, D.C., in 1983 and has continued to function as a nonpartisan research group. Palestinian-American academics helmed the project, whose main product is the *Journal of Palestine Studies*. IPS has also published books and produced documentaries on the Arab–Israeli conflict and Palestinian affairs. IPS maintains offices in Jerusalem, London, Nicosia, and Paris, and publishes in Arabic, English, and French. IPS has offered a close monitoring of the Palestinian national movement and the peace process. However, the journal and the institute have given only scant attention to internal Palestinian dynamics and their impact on the Palestinian struggle for liberation or on the implications for the future of the conflict.

Other groups have addressed even narrower concerns. The United Association for Studies and Research (UASR) was founded in 1989 in Chicago, Illinois, and moved to Annandale, Virginia, in 1991. UASR has focused on relations between Western countries and Islamic movements and the Israeli–Palestinian conflict. UASR's papers and its quarterly, the *Middle East Affairs Journal*, present perspectives on regional and country-specific dynamics. The group has also sponsored a number of roundtable discussions featuring Muslim leaders, academics, and other think tank professionals. Despite the thematic interest in challenges facing Muslim Palestinians in the current conflict, UASR has only attempted to shed light on the views of this segment of Palestinians. Although the group gives special attention to the rise of Hamas within Palestinian society, this examination lacks any assessment of the political future of the group in any serious political settlement to the conflict.

UASR actively facilitates a dialogue between Islamic leaders and Western analysts through seminars and writings. Even though Islamic movements owe much to the work of grassroots social groups and civic associations, UASR literature pays little attention to this civic life in the relationship between Western and Muslim-world nongovernmental organizations. And although much of the contribution of Muslim revivalist groups has been in the domain of education, UASR's literature instead emphasizes the political aspects of these developments. These issues aside, the group has produced valuable information on politics and change in the Arab world, the Gulf War of 1990–1991, and Palestinian political Islam—all of which is much in demand by specialists in Middle Eastern studies.

Another Middle Eastern study group is the Washington Kurdish Institute (WKI), a nonprofit research and educational organization working to inform the public about the plight of the Kurds, an ethnic group of thirty million people left stateless when the British and the French carved up the Middle East in the middle of the twentieth century. Although the political implication of research on such a messy history is quite obvious, WKI has refrained from producing policy proposals. The largest group of Kurds lives in southeastern Turkey, where their culture and language are actively being suppressed. Another large Kurdish minority is found in Iraq, where Kurds represent the majority in the north of that country and have suffered ethnical attacks by the Iraqi regime. Other substantial Kurdish minorities live in Syria and Iran. Many Kurds, especially in Iraq and Turkey, have become refugees as a result of violent conflicts in the region. Despite the suffering of the Kurds, there is little publicly available information about their condition.

Through educational activities the WKI seeks to increase public awareness of Kurdish concern. The group's forums bring government officials together with academics and representatives of nongovernmental organizations to discuss policy matters affecting the Kurds. The group also provides news updates from the region and its own analysis of political developments. In 1998 WKI sponsored a conflict resolution conference cosponsored by the Carnegie Endowment for International Peace. Panels considered local, regional, and international approaches to conflict resolution in Iraq, Iran, and Turkey. WKI issues *Zagros*, a newsletter sent to members and to U.S. officials concerned with Kurdish policy. The institute also offers Kurdish language classes.

PUBLIC POLICY RESEARCH

Aside from the groups that offer specialized research on Islam and the conditions of religious and ethnic communities, a number of groups have emerged to influence U.S. public policy through research. The Center for Policy Analysis on Palestine (CPAP) was established in 1991 as the educational program of the Jerusalem Fund, a charitable organization. CPAP examines the Arab–Israeli conflict and U.S. Middle East policy, focusing on the Israeli military occupation of the Palestinian territories. CPAP offers information and analysis to key individuals, institutions, and media outlets. The center conducts symposia and press briefings. These proceedings are published as *For the Record* summaries. In addition, the center produces policy briefs, and as special reports written by leading international experts.

CPAP also provides a library open to researchers, students, media, and the community. The library contains more than two thousand books, periodicals, and films that relate to Palestine, Arab culture, the conflict, and other regional issues. CPAP has been pointedly geared toward exploring a peaceful settlement of the Palestinian–Israeli conflict on the basis of a two-state solution. Its speakers have included several Jewish and Israeli academics and politicians, often bringing them together in panels with Palestinian representatives.

Aside from the plight of the Palestinians, the status of Jerusalem has always attracted the attention of Arab and Muslim Americans. In 1995 the American Committee on Jerusalem (ACJ) was founded to develop educational activities and materials that focus on the heritage of the city and its future. As the group contends,

> Such activities in the past have generally been one-sided, offering the
> views exclusively of the Israeli government, and pro-Israeli groups in the
> United States. The ACJ will present an Arab-American consensus position
> on Jerusalem in clear and unambiguous terms, to provide the American
> public and policy-makers with a balanced viewpoint on the issues involved.

ACJ contends that Christians, Muslims, and Jews in the city can live together peacefully if given the chance. The group has put forth three conditions for a successful resolution of the status of the city: (1) that there can be no monopoly of Jerusalem's sovereignty by either the Israelis or the Palestinians; (2) that there can be no relation of conqueror and conquered; and (3) that there can be no privileged or dominant religious or nationality group in Jerusalem. In support of these views, ACJ has published a number of books, including *Two Capitals in an Undivided Jerusalem*, *Jerusalem in History*, and *Islam, the West, and Jerusalem*. ACJ has also conducted a number of briefings in the U.S. Congress on the situation in Jerusalem—and the Arab opinion of it. The group has instituted a Christian outreach program to raise awareness of these issues in American churches.

The research material published by CPAP and AJC has added the informational background for community outreach. One activist group that has utilized the studies is American Muslims for Jerusalem (AMJ). Also, thanks to facilitation by CPAP, AMJ has held joint meetings with such Jewish groups as Jews for Peace in Palestine and Israel, the Israeli Committee Against House Demolitions, and the Israel Policy Forum. Pushing for a viable peace settlement through education and outreach may have had an impact on American public opinion. In January 2001 AJC commissioned a poll on the future status of Jerusalem and found that 47 percent of the American public supported the idea of a shared or divided Jerusalem as opposed to 23 percent who favored keeping the city under Israeli control.

In addition to groups that focus on the Middle East, other organizations have sought to illuminate other causes in hot spots in the Muslim world. There is the Kashmiri-American Council (KAC) that was established in 1990 in Washington, D.C., to raise awareness in the United States about the plight of the Kashmiri people. This issue remained unresolved since the end of the British colonial rule in the late 1940s. As the Indian subcontinent split into India and Pakistan, two-thirds of the Muslim-majority state of Jammu and Kashmir remained under Indian rule. UN resolutions stipulated that the Kashmiris should decide their own future through a plebiscite, to which India publicly assented but never allowed. Now the Kashmiri people are split between India and Pakistan and have repeatedly expressed the desire to exercise their right to self-determination.

Although the U.S. government has not taken keen interest in this issue, KAC maintains that U.S. policy makers will be likely to take a stand if they are better informed. KAC supports a peaceful end to the Kashmir conflict through a settlement negotiated by the governments of India and Pakistan and the leadership of the people of Jammu and Kashmir. In the meantime, KAC has issued reports on human rights violations in Indian-held Kashmir and criticized the terrorist attacks of militant Kashmiris on civilian Indian targets. In Canada the Kashmiri-Canadian Council (KCC) functions along the same lines as KAC. KCC publishes periodical updates on developments in the Kashmir region.

In short, research groups with implicit or explicit public policy interest have focused on the most intractable conflicts of the Muslim world, dealing primarily with population groups (the Palestinians, Kashmiris, and Kurds) that remained stateless in a world of nation-states. Most of these intellectual endeavors developed within the ethnically oriented communities. Faith-based Muslim think tanks have devoted their energies to the reform challenges facing Muslim contemporary life.

Despite the growth of ethnic and religious community organizations in North America, there has been a lack of research-support facilities focusing on these groups and the domestic concerns they raise. Likewise, the phenomenal rise of American Muslim interest in the political process has not been matched by the development of research institutions that specialize in the sociopolitical conditions of American Muslims. Thus, by default, foreign policy priorities have dominated the discourse of researchers and activists.

Contacts are growing between Muslim community research groups and others working closely with the intellectual and academic establishments in the United States. In 1993 the Center for Muslim-Christian Understanding (CMCU) was founded at Georgetown University to foster a better understanding of Islam and Muslim–Christian relations. CMCU is distinguished in its focus on the development of contemporary Islamic thought and its impact on politics and development in Muslim countries. In several books, CMCU professors have argued that Islamic activism is not necessarily anti-Western or anti-democratic and that Muslim grassroots movements must be understood through careful attention to the sociopolitical environment that has conditioned their growth.

CMCU has distinguished itself in its increasing attention to Islam in the West, particularly in the United States. In 1999 CMCU, with a grant from the Pew Charitable Trusts, began hosting a research project known as Muslims in the American Public Square (MAPS) to study the increased involvement of Muslims in American public life. The project has conducted various seminars bringing local and national Muslim leaders to discuss their role in America's civil society. MAPS also solicited the writings of two-dozen Muslim specialists to explore the various aspects of Muslim civic involvement. In November 2001 the organization released the first-ever national survey of American Muslim political attitudes. The poll, which was conducted in the aftermath of September 11 showed that an overwhelming majority of Muslims were in favor of the war against terrorism, but were strongly critical of U.S. government positions on major foreign policy concerns—particularly the Middle East.

Developments in the Muslim intellectual community after September 11 have received scant coverage in the media, so the public remains unaware of the profound debates that have taken place. The most critical response came from the Fiqh Council in North America. Prior to the attacks the council had received a question from U.S. Captain Abd al-Rasheed Muhammad about the religious permissibility of serving in the U.S. military. Dealing with the thorny issue of a possible collusion between faith and patriotism, this question was perhaps the most difficult of all inquiries presented to the council. Essentially it asks whether an American Muslim soldier should join in combat against other Muslims. During the 1990–1991 Gulf War two Muslim soldiers were discharged from the military after claiming conscientious objector status.

The council's deliberations on this issue after September 11 became a matter of worldwide discussion in Muslim circles. The council's *fatwa* approved of Muslim participation in the U.S. military, but stipulated that lawful combat must conform to just war standards. A just war from the Muslim perspective, the council argued, stipulates that military actions should comprise a proportionate, self-defensive response that avoids civilian targets. The *fatwa* also indicated that stopping those who perpetrate mischief on earth, as in the September 11 attacks and bringing them to justice would meet the definition of a just war.

As for individual American Muslim soldiers, the council advised that they must discharge their duties with unequivocal expression of allegiance to their country while being true to their own consciences. If these soldiers are in doubt about taking part in combat, the *fatwa* pointed out that the U.S. military has in the past offered accommodation options, including serving in noncombat duties and accepting a discharge on grounds of conscientious objection.

This *fatwa* affair could have significant meaning for the development of Islamic jurisprudence in the contemporary world. The reputable *alims* who issued the ruling essentially backed the idea that citizenship in contemporary states such as the United States is a form of covenant of rights and obligations between the individual and his government. The Qur'an places great emphasis on keeping contracts. In other words, Muslim citizens are morally obligated to defend their country against aggressors—regardless of the religious composition of that country or the party committing the aggression against it. This understanding, of course, is a clear rejection of the medieval political thought that classified the world into three categories: the Abode of Islam—where law and order must be preserved in lands under Muslim control, the Abode of War—where conflict and warfare is the norm, and the Abode of Treaty—where there are peace agreements between Muslims and non-Muslims.

The *fatwa* also recognized the narrow authority of Muslim jurists in the lives of Muslim citizens. The jurists acknowledged their role as advisers and replied to the specific concerns presented to them; they chose not to comment on the Bush administration's declaration of war on terrorism and the role of the various parties involved in it. This is understood in the community as an indication that the jurists prefer to leave such matters to political analysts and groups specialized in public policy. According to this formulation, Muslims seeking guidance in meeting today's challenges would only expect to receive a partial feedback from *alims*. They will have to look to specialists in other fields to be able to reach well-informed conclusions.

A CLOSER LOOK
KASHMIRI–CANADIAN COUNCIL

The Kashmiri–Canadian Council (KCC) is a nonprofit organization dedicated to promoting the Kashmiri cause, both within Canada and internationally. In Canada the KCC is working with NGOs, media, academicians, students, and conscientious Canadians to raise the level of awareness about the Kashmiri people's struggle for their right of self-determination as enshrined in successive United Nations resolutions. It is also dedicated to promoting and encouraging the association of Kashmiris in Canada.

KCC's Objectives

1. To promote a better understanding of the Kashmiri situation to Canadian people and organizations.
2. To strive at all levels of the Canadian framework to build a favourable public opinion for implementation of the United Nations resolutions of 1948 and 1949, which gave the people of Jammu and Kashmir their right of self-determination.
3. To draw the attention of the government of Canada and the Parliamentarians to the plight of Kashmiris, and the need for Ottawa to show its proactive leadership role on the issue, support a peaceful settlement of this conflict by bringing all concerned parties to the dispute to the negotiating table—namely, India, Pakistan, and the accredited leadership of the people of Jammu and Kashmir.
4. To urge the G–7 leaders, the Commonwealth Heads of Government and the Secretary General of the United Nations to act more quickly and effectively in halting massive violations of human rights in Indian Occupied Kashmir (IOK) and to assist parties to find a peaceful and lasting solution of the world's oldest dispute.
5. To publicize the tragedy of IOK and to uphold and defend the human rights of the people of Jammu and Kashmir.

To achieve its objective the KCC will use all peaceful, moral, and political means within the framework of Canadian legality.

Articles

- White Paper on Elections in Kashmir
- Indian Pledges on Kashmir
- The Killing Field of Kashmir
- Kashmir Dispute: A Nuclear Hot-Spot in South Asia
- Situation of Human Rights in Indian Occupied Kashmir
- Kashmir: An Unresolved Dispute

Source: From www.kashmiri_cc.ca.

CONCLUSION

Estimates of the Muslim populations in North America range widely—from four to seven million. There is no scientific count, but there is no disagreement that the Muslim population is growing. American and Canadian Muslims are descendants from all continents of the world and are represented in all racial and ethnic populations, although most are South Asian, Middle Eastern, African American, African, and Eastern European. In terms of their introduction to the faith, some are converts to Islam, while most are born into Sunni or Shia Muslim families. Religiously, Muslims exhibit various attitudes, from the strictly observant to those who do not practice the faith. In terms of economic class, few Muslims are rich, some come from low-income households, and many are middle-class wage earners.

Still, Muslims constitute only a small minority of the more than three hundred million inhabitants of the United States and Canada. But Muslims are hardly isolated; in addition to racial and ethnic bonds, they maintain kinship ties with other Americans and Canadians through marriage. Individually and collectively, Muslims seek to maintain their religious and ethnic identities while working for the betterment of their lives and the lives of their children—goals that are embodied in the assertion of the U.S. Declaration of Independence that all people should be free to enjoy "life, liberty, and the pursuit of happiness."

MAINSTREAM MUSLIM COMMUNITY

To address the needs of their communities, North American Muslims have established faith-based and ethnicity-based organizations. Ethnicity-based groups strive to maintain kinship ties, provide mutual aid, and educate others about their shared experiences and concerns. Ethnic groups conduct activities and sponsor publications expressing pride in their heritage. They also promote educational and social organizations and businesses that sell particular ethnic products. Clusters within these groups are made up of professionals who have established guilds to improve their career chances.

Much more numerous than ethnic organizations are faith-based institutions. They are most evident in the established mosques and Islamic schools. While Islamic centers offer educational and devotional services, they also have become gravitation points of local community activism. They provide social services to members and conduct interfaith relations. As we have seen after September 11, 2001, Muslims have conducted outreach programs for secular purposes—mainly to allay the fears of neighbors and to seek their support following the anti-Muslim hate crimes.

Time and again Muslims in North America learned that they—and those who look like them—will be subjected o reprisals after episodes of political violence involving Muslims anywhere in the world. This produced a shared feeling among Muslims of threat emanating from profiling, stereotyping, and secret evidence laws, especially since the mid-1990s and most notably after September 11, 2001. In the United States and Canada, public affairs groups on both sides of the faith-ethnicity spectrum have worked together to address such common issues. Yet for the most part America is the land of promise for Muslims. Islamic centers and ethnic associations have held joint festivals, parades, bazaars, and political demonstrations. They also have joined functions held by other public and private entities to reinforce common bonds among the various ethnic and faith groups. Across the borders of Canada and the United States several groups maintained close cooperation while respecting the laws of the land in each country.

INTERDEPENDENCE AS A FEATURE OF MUSLIM DEVELOPMENT

In the formation and administration of Muslim community organizations several patterns of interdependence have emerged across religious, intellectual, and geographical boundaries. Muslims have raised funds to build community organizations from any number of legitimate sources—be it public funds or private Muslim international donors who have studied or have done business in North America. Also, while there are dozens of North American *imams* sponsored by the Saudi-based Islamic call groups, dozens more chaplains are employed by state and federal institutions in the United States. Moreover, non-Muslims are part, and sometimes founders, of groups working to serve Muslims. Although North American Muslims have often appeared to be on the receiving end of funds, they have increasingly given to charitable organizations that provide assistance to those in need here and abroad. To fulfill their missions, these charities have raised funds from American and Canadian private foundations and have received matching funds from public agencies.

Links are found sometimes in the very administration of religious institutions. In the case of the Shia community, whose religious structure is semi-hierarchical, connections extend from North America to the Middle East and South Asia. Sunni *imams* with training in Muslim religious learning centers overseas have been hired in many American and Canadian mosques. However, a number of Islamic studies colleges have sprung up in the United States because of the realization that locally trained *imams* can serve their communities better. But the training of community leaders often involves institutions and instructors outside of the Muslim community. Islamic schools teach Islamic studies and North American history and have introduced into their curriculum textbooks developed by mainstream publishers. Community development groups (such as ISNA) train Muslim activists in public institutions of higher education. MAS and ICNA include in their training books written by non-Muslim authors. Community public affairs groups have sought to influence public officials through cooperation with others.

IMMIGRANTS AND TRADITIONAL ISLAMIC MOVEMENTS

Some immigrants came to America with prior exposure to Islamic revivalist movements. Due to the global nature of today's communications networks, ideas flow in all directions. With America frequently the center of the world's attention, Muslims across the globe visit North American Muslim websites as major media outlets in Muslim countries cover American Muslim news. But if the institutional development of American Muslim organizations is any indication, it demonstrates that American Muslims may change the very nature of Islamic activism.

Muslim leading organizations are increasingly expressing views based on their own strategic interests as American Muslim citizens who earn a living in North America and whose children are growing up on the continent and are socialized in its educational systems. Experiencing the sophisticated institutional make-up of North America has broadened the views of many Islamic activists. Many now believe that traditional Islamic movements offer a meaningful contribution only at the social and educational spheres. Although these movements have been drawn to politics in Muslim countries, their experience in that domain, much like that of most ruling parties, has left much to be desired. American and Canadian Muslims report from their own experience in pluralistic societies that a key problem in Muslim countries has been the lack of political structures capable of addressing their societal cleavages. Hence, faith-based American Muslim groups in the immigrant community are departing from the often-amateurish Islamist discourse and the oppressive political rhetoric of one-party rule in many Muslim countries.

The emerging American Muslim faith-based discourse exhibits sensitivity to the difference between norms and facts. Norms are expressed in terms of viewpoints about acceptable or desirable behavior. In this regard religious values inform the choices of individuals and groups. In community forums, however, practicing Muslims increasingly interact with nonpracticing Muslims, whose active organizations usually maintain ethnicity-centered perspectives. As a result there is a growing recognition among religious and ethnic Muslims that, despite their difference, they share a reality of life that is pluralistic. The fact that the faith-based community has supported the establishment of organizations focusing on public affairs is a clear indication that Muslims view the political arena as a sphere of life that is distinct from other domains. And this tends to reinforce the understanding that community organizations of various orientations can only be effective if they focus on their shared ground. Facilitating this prospect is the emerging communications culture resting on a language of facts about Muslims and their relations with others.

IMMIGRANT MUSLIM INTEGRATION IN NORTH AMERICA

Immigrant Muslims in the United States and Canada have made substantial adaptations to ease their cultural integration into North American societies. The tendency to support English as the language of instruction and communication at mosques, schools, and community conventions has become the norm. The only ethnic language that has remained of significant relevance to the younger generations of Muslims is Arabic—and that is due to its religious character as the language of the Qur'an. But thanks to economic globalism, ethnic languages remain important in the lives of many people who study, work, and do business throughout the world.

There is further evidence of adaptation in the very structure of North American Muslim institutions. They have increasingly internalized the norm of functional specialization, which has been a significant feature of the development of Western societies. In part, the rise of the professionals in the leadership of community groups has pushed groups into a focus on substantive action away from ideological rhetoric. This tendency is particularly apparent in the decisions made by the Ministry of W. D. Mohammed and ISNA to move away from their old vague postures as national movements to the more specific role of community building. Such development is bound to make groups with specific functional definitions more effective and may help to smoothen interactions with their counterparts in other faith and ethnic communities.

The growing involvement of Muslims in the public square leaves no doubt that the Muslims of North America are seeking to situate themselves within their countries' civic and political structures. Some Muslims remain adamant in opposition to such involvement, opting instead for isolationism. But such voices have been increasingly marginalized by the rising tide of participatory American Muslim politics. Muslims generally see the United States and Canada as pluralistic societies offering them a chance not only to prosper and live in freedom but also to become a bridge of understanding between North America and the Muslim world.

MUSLIMS IN THE PUBLIC SQUARE

To many Muslims, the experience of American Muslims in public life during the past two decades has demystified the political process. Despite the growing sense of empowerment, politics has been full of uncertainties. Muslims have seen political candidates befriending them at voting time, only to give them a cold shoulder once in office. President George W. Bush did not feel the urgency to fulfill his campaign promise to do away with the secret evidence clause of the 1996 antiterrorism law. After September 11, the Bush administration used secret evidence in the detentions of Arab and Muslim men while freezing the funds of a number of Muslim charities chartered under U.S. law as American corporations.

Realistically, the whole Muslim community is barely beginning to appear on the radar screens of the major power players. So far the community's largest grassroots conventions together attract fewer than 50,000 participants (at ISNA, 30,000; MAS–W. D. Mohammed, 6,000; ICNA, 6,000). As for public affairs groups like ADC, CAIR and AMC, each has a membership base of several thousand individuals. While these groups maintain a visible Internet presence and increasingly garner a global audience, this does not supplant a substantive number of registered voters, volunteer activists, and financial contributors to political campaigns. Whatever political clout Muslims may have in the near future rests with empowering members of the fifteen hundred local Islamic centers and ethnic associations. Indeed, evidence shows that at this point much of what the community's public affairs groups have done is education—and much of that effort has been directed to their own community.

Three structural factors shape the options now before Muslims as they consider their role in American public life. First, although the Muslim population in America is increasing, it is still relatively small and young. The largest Muslim group is perhaps the one under voting age. Second, the political experience of Muslims is nascent, ranging from three to twenty years—depending on the group. Third, the Muslim community's current social profile is dominated by wage earners who can provide a decent or comfortable living for their families but cannot wield sufficient financial resources to cause any significant effect in Washington.

Thus, the call for a political involvement strategy based on participation in local political and civic processes is gaining support. This is particularly true because the necessary financial and organizational resources for achieving local results are not as large as they are in the high-stakes national arena. Nevertheless, practical steps in the focus on grassroots development so far have been largely limited to the emphasis on voter registration and participation in political party precinct meetings. A consolidated drive for involvement with school boards, local councils, and local civic organizations is yet to gain momentum.

In the area of charitable work, Muslim groups that have worked in international relief are now increasingly turning their attention to the home front. A growing number of such charities are actively promoting and establishing "local programs"—services targeting domestic beneficiaries. It is unlikely, however, that international relief work will become less significant. North American Muslims may continue to empathize with the plight of the poor in countries where they may have ancestry or business interest, as America and Canada continue to deliver aid to several parts of the Muslim world.

American and Canadian Muslims continue to face misunderstanding and, sometimes, intolerance. The religious accommodations Muslims have received thus far, in the view of many Muslims, fall short of what is required to assure

Muslims security and dignity in a constitutional framework that professes liberty and freedom for all. Muslims have often noted with frustration that their complaints are usually handled on a case-by-case basis, even though their experiences of Muslim community members indicate a clear pattern of discrimination. But changing the situation through tougher prosecution of the civil rights laws or by adding more legal teeth to current statutes will require political will beyond the wishes and capabilities of most Muslims.

The growing activism of American Muslims has engendered diverse responses among other groups. Some Catholic, Methodist, Irish, African-American, and secular liberal groups have welcomed Muslims into America's multicultural experience. Some politically oriented evangelists have expressed intolerance, while other conservatives have embraced Muslims as a potential Republican Party constituency. Friction between Muslims and Jews over the Middle East conflict is at an all-time high, there have been positive local interactions among members of the two communities.

DEVELOPMENTAL PRIORITIES

Internally, Muslims face many challenges to strengthening their organizations. Most groups have been established within the past two decades and continue to struggle with the institutionalization of their work. Even mosques, which historically have had a clearly defined role in Muslim life, continue to search for solutions as they grow in size and become more diverse and service-oriented. While some organizations have managed to define their functional roles and gained legitimacy, some continue to struggle in identifying specific, achievable goals, securing financial resources, and generally improving their effectiveness. September 11 brought to public light the extent to which many groups are lacking resource development, especially in the areas of interfaith outreach. Student organizations, which are numerous and active in all major campuses and now consist of mainly U.S.- and Canadian-born members, have traditionally supplied community groups with volunteers in cases of urgent circumstances. The community's inability to cope with the sudden rising demand revealed a weak linkage between student groups and other community organizations. Indeed, the whole institutional structure of Muslim communities in the United States and Canada lacks connectivity mechanisms between organizations involved in similar functions and between groups across the ethnic divide.

The role of women in the community is evolving. Evidence shows that there continues to be a gender gap between Muslim men and women regarding the social and political role of women. More women than men would like to see women involved in activities outside the house. But the reality is that Muslim women participate in community life in a variety of ways: some have formed Islamic call groups, others have pooled resources to extend social services, and others chose activism in public life. Most Muslim women, however, serve mainly within Islamic centers. While women work with schools and other educational, social, and fund-raising programs—and even staff public affairs agencies—they still lack representation in the community's decision-making bodies. Some national groups (such as ISNA, AMC, and CAIR) have acknowledged the problem and moved to appoint women in their boards. Other groups (such as ICNA and the Ministry of W. Deen Mohamed) have opted for the model found in many local Islamic centers: to establish parallel leadership structures for women within the organization.

DOMESTIC AND FOREIGN POLICY CONCERNS

American Muslim concerns include many domestic and foreign policy issues. While the 1990s witnessed a heightened attention to the domestic agenda of civil rights and political inclusion, a number of events thrust community groups into the world arena. In the early 1990s the main issue was the genocide of Muslims in the Balkans. In the late 1990s the issue of Kashmir came to the forefront of foreign policy concerns, especially in light of the nuclear race between India and Pakistan. The Israeli–Palestinian conflict has continued to capture the attention of Muslims, especially after the dramatic deterioration of peace efforts and the growing concerns about the rights of non-Jews in Israel and in Jerusalem. Also, since September 11, 2001, Muslims have been hard-pressed to make sense of America's relations with Muslim-majority states. Community groups are increasingly vocal in favor of an American policy promoting participation, accountable governance, and human rights.

American–Islamic relations changed in meaningful ways after September 11, 2001. National community organizations came out forcefully against the terrorist attacks, conducting far-reaching public relations campaigns and identifying with the victims. Several groups highlighted the fact that their ethnic and religious cohorts perished in the attacks. Muslim religious scholars with the Fiqh Council of North America encouraged Muslims to join the U.S. military in taking up arms against the perpetrators. At the grassroots level, Muslims and others met in houses of worship and community centers to express a united stand against terror. Due to the global character of the world's human interactions and the Muslims' preoccuation with misperception and discrimination, the Muslims of North America are increasingly adding their voices to the idea that all people of good will should share the responsibility of making the world just, secure, and free for all.

REFERENCES

AbuSulayman, AbdulHamid. *Toward an Islamic Theory of International Relations.* Herndon, VA: International Institute Islamic Thought, 1993.

Ahmad, S. Akbar. *Nahwa Ilm al-Insan al-Islami* (Toward Islamic Anthropology). Herndon, VA: IIIT, 1990.

al Alwani, Taha Jabir et al. *The Quran and the Sunnah: The Time–Space Factor.* Herendon, VA: IIIT, 1991.

Al-Faruqi, Ismail Raji. *Islam and Other Faiths.* Leicester, United Kingdom: Islamic Foundation, 1998.

Aossey, Yahya Jr. *Fifty Years of Islam in Iowa 1925–1975.* Unity Publishing, Cedar Rapids, IA: n.d.

Arab American Anti-Discrimination Committee (AD.C.). *Educational Outreach and Action Guide: Working with School Systems.* Washington, D.C., 1993.

———. *Legal Guide: Your Basic Rights.* Washington, D.C., 1988.

———. *Political Action Guide: How to Write, Phone and Meet Your Legislators.* Washington, D.C., 1984.

———. *Media Monitoring Guide: How to Voice Your Concerns to the Media.* Washington, D.C., 1986.

———. *Children of the Stones.* Washington, D.C., 1988.

———. *Harassment in the Holy Land: Israeli Discrimination Against Arab and Black Americans.* Washington, D.C., 1988.

Arab American Institute (AAI). *Arab American Voters and Volunteers.* Washington, D.C., n.d.

———. *Life, Liberty and the Pursuit of Happiness: A Three-Decade Journey in the Occupied Territories.* Washington, D.C., 1997.

———. *The Department of Justice and the Civil Rights of Arab Americans.* Washington, D.C., 1998.

Austin, Allan D. *African Muslims in Antebellum America: A Sourcebook.* New York, NY: Garland Publishing, 1984.

Bagby, Ihsan, Paul M. Perl, and Bryan T. Froehle. *The Mosque in America: A National Portrait.* Washington, D.C.: Council on American-Islamic Relations (CAIR), 2001.

Banks, James. *Teaching Strategies for Ethnic Studies.* Boston, MA: Allyn & Bacon, 1991.

Ba-Yunus, Ilyas. *Muslims of Illinois: A Demographic Report.* 2002. Unpublished.

Ba-Yunus, Ilyas, and Moin Siddiqui, *A Report on the Muslim Population in the United States.* Center for American Muslim Research and Information (CAMRI). Richmond Hill, NY, 1998.

Council on Arab-Islamic Relations. *The Status of Muslim Civil Rights in the United States,* Washington, D.C., 1996, 1997, 1998, 1999, 2000, 2001, 2002.

———. *American Muslims and the 1996 Elections: A Poll of Political Attitudes on Selected Issues.* Washington, D.C., August 1996.

———. *A Rush to Judgment,* Washington, D.C., 1995.

———. *The Usual Suspects.* Washington, D.C., 1996.

———. *Religious Accommodation Policies in Selected American School Districts.* Washington, D.C., 1999.

Diouf, Sylviane A. *Servants of Allah: African Muslims Enslaved in the Americas.* New York: New York University Press, 1998.

Dirks, Jerald F. *The Cross and the Crescent.* Beltsville, MD: Amana Publications, 2002.

El-kholy, Abdo. *The Arab Moslems in the United States: Religion and Assimilation.* New Haven, CT: College and University Press, 1966.

Findley, Paul. *Silent No More.* Beltsville, MD: Amana Publications, 2001.

Fowler, Robert, and Allen Hertzke. *Religion and Politics in America: Faith, Culture, and Strategic Choices.* Boulder, CO: Westview Press, 1995.

Ghayur, Arif. "The Muslim Population in the United States." *Annals of American Academy of Political Science.* March 1981.

Haddad, Yvonne, and Jane Smith, eds. *Muslim Communities in North America.* New York: State University of New York Press, 1994.

Haddad, Yvonne, ed. *The Muslims of America.* New York: Oxford University Press, 1991.

Hartford Seminary. *Faith Communities Today.* Hartford: CT, 2001.

Huntington, Samuel. "Clash of Civilizations." *Foreign Affairs.* Summer, 1993.

McCarus, Ernest. *The Development of Arab American Identity.* Ann Arbor: MI: University of Michigan Press, 1994.

McCloud, Aminah. *African-American Islam.* New York: Routledge, 1995.

Mohammed, W. Deen. *Islam's Climate for Business Success.* Chicago, IL: W. Deen Mohamed Publications, 1994.

Moore, Kathleen. *al-Mughtaribun: American Law and the Transformation of Muslim Life in the United States.* Albany, NY: State University of New York Press, 1995.

Muslim Public Affairs Council (MPAC). *An American Vision, An Islamic Identity.*

———. *Our Stand on Terrorism.*

———. *Islamic Movements: Relationship and Rapprochement.*

Muslim World League, Canada Office. *Muslim Guide to Canada*. Etobicoke: Ontario, 2000.

Nyang, Sulayman. *Islam in the United States of America*. Chicago, IL: Kazi Publications, 1999.

al-Qaradawi, Yusuf. *The Lawful and the Prohibited in Islam*. Indianapolis, IN: American Trust Publications, 1999.

al-Qazwini, Mustafa. *Inquiries about Shi'a Islam*. Islamic Educational Center of Orange County, Costa Mesa, CA, n.d.

Sachedina, Abdul Aziz. "The Case of the Shia in North America," in *Muslim Communities in North America*.

Sonn, Tamara. "Diversity in Rochester's Islamic Community," in *Muslim Communities in North America*.

Stone, Carol. "Estimate of Muslims Living in America," in Haddad, Yvonne, ed., *The Muslims of America*. New York: Oxford University Press, 1991.

Walbridge, Linda S. *Without Forgetting the Imam: Lebanese Shi'ism in an American Community*. Detroit, MI: Wayne University Press, 1996.

Waugh, Earle and Baha Abu-Laban and Regula B. Qureshi, eds. *The Muslim Community in North America*. Edmonton, Alberta: University of Alberta Press, 1983.

Weekes, Richard, ed. *Muslim Peoples: A World Ethnographic Survey*. Westport, CT: Greenwood Press, 1978.

Weeks, John. *Counting the Number of Muslims in the United States: Estimates for the U.S. and Results From a Pilot Project in San Diego*. Unpublished document. San Diego, 1996.

Winters, Paul A. *Urban Terrorism*. San Diego, CA: Greenhaven Press, 1996.

U.S. GOVERNMENT DOCUMENTS

Central Intelligence Agency. *World Factbook 2000*. Washington, D.C.: Brassey's, 2000.

Federal Bureau of Investigation. *Unified Crime Reports: Hate Crimes*. Washington, D.C.: 1995–2001.

U.S. Department of State. *Patterns of Global Terrorism*. Washington, D.C., 2000.

U.S. Bureau of the Census. *Statistical Abstract of the United States*. Washington, D.C., 1966, 1987, 1997, 1999.

———. 1990 Census of Population: Ancestry of the Population in the United States. Washington, D.C., 1990.

NEWSPAPERS AND MAGAZINES

American Muslim. December 2001.

Chicago-Sun Times. November 6, 1998.

The Chronicle of Philanthropy. November 1, 2001.

Investor's Business Daily. February 13, 2001.
Islamic Horizons. July/August 1999.
The Message International. March 2000.
The New York Times. August 28, 1995.

WEBSITES

Al Basheer for Publications and Translations, Boulder, CO.
    <http://al-Basheer.com>
Al-Hedayah Academy, Fort Worth, TX. <www.hedayah.com>/mission/html>
Amana Publications, Beltsville, MD. <www.amana-publications.com>
American Committee on Jerusalem, Washington, D.C. <www.acj.org>
American Arab Anti-Discrimination Committee, Washington, D.C.
    <www.ad.c.org>
American Muslim Alliance, Newark, CA. <www.amaweb.org>
American Muslim Council, Washington, D.C. <www.amconline.org>
American Muslims for Jerusalem, Washington, D.C. <www.amjerusalem.org>
Arab American Institute, Washington, D.C. <www.aaiusa.org>
Association of Arab-American University Graduates, Washington, D.C.
    <www.aaug.org>
Astrolabe Pictures, Sterling, VA. <www.astrolabepictures.com>
Bangladesh Association of Chicagoland, Chicago, IL. <www.bacusa.org>
Bangladeshi-Canadian Community Center, Ottawa, Canada.
    <www.iprimus.ca/nmayeena>
Beliefnet.com, New York, NY. <www.Beliefnet.com>
Council on American-Islamic Relations, Washington, D.C. <www.cair-
    net.org>
Council of American Muslim Professionals, Chicago, IL. <www.campnet.net>
Federal Election Commission, Washington, D.C. <www.fec.gov
Federation of Muslim Women, Oakville, Ontario <www.fmw.org>
Fiqh Council of North America, Leesburg, VA. <www.fiqhcouncil.org>
Granada Islamic School, Santa Clara, CA. <www.granadaschool.org>
Institute of International Islamic Thought, Herndon, VA. <www.iiit.org>
International Book Centre, Inc., Shelby Township, MS. <www.ibcbooks.com>
IQRA International Educational Foundation, Chicago, IL. <www.iqra.org>
Islamic American Relief Agency, Columbia, MO. <www.iara-usa.org>
Islamic Association for Palestine, Chicago, IL. <www.iap.org>
Islamic Circle of North America, Jamaica, NY. <www.icna.org>
Islamic Research Foundation International, Louisville, KY. <www.irfiweb.org>
Islamic Relief Worldwide, London, England (HQ), Burbank, CA.
    <www.irw.org> <www.islamic-relief.com>
Islamic Society of Central Florida, Orlando, FL. <www.Islam.org>/iscf
IslamiCity.com, Culver City, CA. <www.IslamiCity.com>
Islamic Video Productions, Rancho Palos Verdes, CA. <www.islamic-
    video.com>

IslamOnline.net, Alexandria, VA. <www.islamonline.net> <www.isna.net>
Kansas City Turkish Association, Kansas City. MO.
    <www.members.aol.com>/taalfkc
Kazi Publications, Inc., Chicago, IL. <www.kazi.org>
London Islamic School, Ontario, Canada. <www.londonmosque.com/school>
Madina Academy, Windsor, CT. <www.madinaacademy.com>
Mercy-USA for Aid and Development, Plymouth, MI. <www.mercyusa.org>
New Mind Publications, Jersey City, NJ.
    <http://home.earthlink.net/~hanan/newmind.html>
Muslim American Society, W. Deen Mohammed, Chicago, IL.
    <www.wdmonline.com>
Muslim Community School, Potomac, MD. <www.muslimcommunityschool.com>
Muslim Homeschool Network and Resource, Attleboro, MA.
    <www.muslimhomeschool.com>
Muslim Public Affairs Council, Los Angeles and Washington, D.C.
    <www.mpac.org>
National Community, sit for Imam Jamil al-Amin.
    <www.mindspring.com>/~altafb/ImamAlAmin.html>
North American Bangladeshi Islamic Community, Oak Ridge, TN.
    <www.nabic.org>
Radio Islam.com, Bridgeview, IL. <www.RadioIslam.com>
Scarves for Solidarity, UCLA, Los Angeles, CA. <www.interfaithpeace.org>
Toronto District Muslim Assembly (TDMEA), Toronto, Canada.
    <www.members.tripod.com/tdmea/content.htm>
Universal School, Bridgeview, IL.
    <www.universalschool.org>/School_Profile.html>

DIRECTORY OF ORGANIZATIONS

This directory includes mosques, Islamic schools, and other Muslim organizations arranged by state for the United States and by province for Canada. It has been assembled without interpretations, recommendations, or judgments. Any omissions are unintentional.

UNITED STATES

ALABAMA

Audio / Video Producer
Muslim Youth Television
PO Box 55118
Birmingham, AL 35255
(205) 879–4247
arabicphonics.com

Ethnic Association
Turkish American Cultural Association of
  Alabama
11116 Hillwood Drive SE
Huntsville, AL 35803
(256) 881–8788

Magazine
Muslimah Mini Magazine
PO Box 691
Camp Hill, AL 36850
(205) 896–4663

Mosques / Islamic Centers
Masjid Al-Islam
903 Columbus Road NW
Aliceville, AL 35442
(205) 373–2046

Masjid An-Nur
312 E B Street Rear
Anniston, AL 36207
(205) 238–9041

Anniston Islamic Center
1928 Christine Avenue
Anniston, AL 36207
(256) 238–8613

Islamic Center at Auburn
338 Armstrong Street
Auburn, AL 36830
(334) 821–8307
almarab@auburn.edu

Masjid As-Saabiqoon
3501 Jefferson Avenue SW
Birmingham, AL 35221
(205) 925–3525

Muhammad Mosque
2404 33rd Avenue N
Birmingham, AL 35207
(205) 323–2404

Masjid Al-Qur'an
3424 26th Street N
Birmingham, AL 35207
(205) 324–0212

Birmingham Islamic Society
1810 25th Ct S
Homewood, AL 35209
(205) 879–4247

Huntsville Islamic Center
814 Lee Drive NW
Huntsville, AL 35816
(205) 534–4117

Mobile Masjid of Al-Islam
PO Box 6353
Mobile, AL 36660
(205) 473–4100

Masjid Baitul Haqq
509 Aurelia Street
Mobile, AL 36604
(334) 432–2609

Islamic Society of Mobile
63 East Drive
Mobile, AL 36608
(205) 343–4695

Islamic Society of Montgomery
2425 Lark Drive
Montgomery, AL 36108
(205) 281–8474

Selma Islamic Center
230 Franklin Street
Selma, AL 36703
(205) 875–4264

Tuskegee Islamic Community
PO Box 830668
Tuskegee, AL 36083
tnainc99991125@aol.com

Masjid Ash-Shura
1902 Franklin Rd
Tuskegee Institute, AL 36088
(334) 724–9827

Schools
Sr. Clara Muhammad School
PO Box 5442
Birmingham, AL 35207
(205) 320–1300

Islamic Academy of Alabama
1810 25th Ct S
Homewood, AL 35209
(205) 870–0422
haiderb@hotmail.com

Islamic Academy of Huntsville
1645 Sparkman Drive NW
Huntsville, AL 35816
(256) 722–9838
fsaafi@hotmail.com

Tuskegee School
1610 Hunter Street
Tuskegee, AL 36083
(205) 724–0580

Student Groups
Muslim Students Association
University of Alabama–Birmingham
Birmingham, AL 35294
(205) 934–8224

Tuskegee Muslim Students Association
1508 Adams Street
Tuskegee, AL 36088
(205) 727–8011

ALASKA

Mosques / Islamic Centers
Islamic Community Center
3901 Taft Drive
Anchorage, AK 99517
(907) 248–7333

Islamic Center of Alaska
4141 Ingra Street, Suite 202
Anchorage, AK 99503
(907) 562–4241

Islamic Society of Alaska (Fairbanks)
PO Box 35362
Fort Wainwright, AK 99703
(907) 356–1574
mustafa@mosquitonet.com

ARIZONA

Ethnic Association
Turkish American Association of Arizona
PO Box 373
Tempe, AZ 85280
(602) 766–4895
www.futureone.com/~graphic/turkish.html

Mosques / Islamic Centers
Masjid Ibrahim
2075 Airway Avenue
Kingman, AZ 86401
(520) 757–8822

Mosque
4025 E Chandler Boulevard # 70C-28
Phoenix, AZ 85048
(602) 254–2583

Islamic Community Center of Phoenix
7516 N Black Canyon Highway
Phoenix, AZ 85051
(602) 249–0496
iccp@abacusnet.net

Muslim Community Mosque
1818 N 32nd Street
Phoenix, AZ 85008
(602) 306–4959
mcmphoenix@aol.com

Islamic Center of North Phoenix
9032 N 9th Street
Phoenix, AZ 85020
(602) 371–3440

Masjid Jauharatul-Islam
102 W South Mountain Avenue
Phoenix, AZ 85041
(602) 268–6151

Islamic Cultural Center
131 E 6th Street
Tempe, AZ 85281
(602) 894–6070
icctempe@msm.com

Islamic Center of Tempe
616 S Forest Avenue
Tempe, AZ 85281

Islamic Center of Tucson
901 E 1st Street
Tucson, AZ 85719
(602) 624–3233

Yousef Mosque
250 W Speedway Boulevard
Tucson, AZ 85705
(520) 624–4100

School
Al-Huda School
901 E 1st Street
Tucson, AZ 85719
(520) 624–8182

ARKANSAS

Ethnic Associations
Pakistani Cultural Club at University of
    Arkansas
1263 W Mount Comfort Road
    Apartment 13
Fayetteville, AR 72703
(501) 442–6520
waste_inn@hotmail.com

Mosques / Islamic Centers
Islamic Center of Northwest Arkansas
1420 W Center Street
Fayetteville, AR 72701
(501) 442–4155
muslim@uark.edu

Islamic Center of Jonesboro
118 N. Rogers Street
Jonesboro, AR 72401
(870) 935–2658

Islamic Center of Little Rock
4223 Anne Street
Little Rock, AR 72205
(501) 565–4930

Masjid Al-Bayina
1219 W 20th Street
Little Rock, AR 72206
(501) 374–1841

Masjid Ameen Zakariyya
1717 Wright Avenue
Little Rock, AR 72202
. (501) 372–1942

Schools
Sister Clara Muhammad School
1219 W 20th Street #16429
Little Rock, AR 72216

Huda Academy
3224 Anna Street
Little Rock, AR 72204
(501) 565–3555

CALIFORNIA

Book Publishers / Distributors
Golden Horn Publishing
2120 Dwight Way
Berkeley, CA 94704
(510) 530–6394

Islamic Book Center
2900 W Florence Avenue
Los Angeles, CA 90043
(323) 758–4547

Islamic Research and Publications
30024 Via Rivera
Rancho Palos Verde, CA 90275
(310) 212–5854
ivprod@earthlink.net
www.islamic-video.com

Sufi Islamia–Prophecy Publications
65 Norwich Street #A
San Francisco, CA 94110
(415) 285–0562

Cemetery
The Islamic Cemetery
18927 Bellflower Street
Adelanto, CA 92301
(760) 246–8842

Charity Groups
Islamic Relief Worldwide
1919 W Magnolia Boulevard
Burbank, CA 91506
(818) 238–9520
info@irw.org
www.irw.org

Afghanistan Relief Organization
PO Box 10207
Canoga Park, CA 91309
(818) 724–0430
Afgrelief@aol.com
www.afghanrelief.com

International Relief
PO Box 8035
La Verne, CA 91750
(909) 596–4284

Indian Muslim Relief Committte
800 San Antonio Road Suite 1
Palo Alto, CA 94303
(650) 856–0440
manzoor@aol.com

Palestine Children's Relief Fund
PO Box 15404
San Diego, CA 92175
thepcrf@aol.com

Coordination Council
Islamic Shura Council of Southern
    California
10573 West Pico Boulevard #35
Los Angeles, CA 90064

Ethnic Associations
Palestine Democratic Youth Organization
PO Box 4758
Anaheim, CA 92803
(714) 520–5309

South Asian Network
18000 Pioneer Boulevard
Artesia, CA 90701
(562) 403–0488
saninfo@onebox.com

Persian Center
2029 Durant Avenue
Berkeley, CA 94704
(510) 848–0264
sepass@yahoo.com

Women Concerned About the Middle
    East
PO Box 7152
Berkeley, CA 94707

Pakistani American Association
1511 3rd Street
Duarte, CA 91010
(818) 357–7101

Egyptian Cultural Club
PO Box 4080
Foster City, CA 94404
(415) 967–6900

Ramallah Club
2525 Hartford Avenue
Fullerton, CA 92835

Arab-American Affairs
PO Box 3684
Glendale, CA 91221
(818) 507–0333

Turkish American Association of
  Southern California
PO Box 53024
Irvine, CA 92619
(714) 806–7720
atasc2000@aol.com
www.atasc.org

Council of Pakistan American Affairs
895 N Holly Glen Drive
Long Beach, CA 90815
mshahmd@aol.com
www.copaa.org

Turkish American Association of
  California
2053 Grant Road Suite 123
Los Altos, CA 94024
(415) 646–0946
taac@taaca.org
www.taaca.org

Arab American Press Guild
PO Box 291190
Los Angeles, CA 90029

Arab Community Center
4121 Santa Monica Boulevard
Los Angeles, CA 90029
(213) 669–9966

Tunisian Club
7445 1/2 W Sunset Boulevard
Los Angeles, CA 90046

Kashmir Human Rights Foundation
1835 Apex Avenue
Los Angeles, CA 90026
(323) 662–6163
rafikhan@aol.com

Birzeit Society–Southern California
  Chapter
500 N Garfield Avenue Suite 110
Monterey Park, CA 91754
(714) 996–3389
www.birzeitsociety.org

Islamic Education Institute
1901 Old Middlefield Way Suite 19
Mountain View, CA 94043
(650) 428–0752

Egyptian Club of Orange County
PO Box 7792
Newport Beach, CA 92658

Eritreans United Association
PO Box 10657
Oakland, CA 94610
eua@egroups.com

The Iranian-American Film Forum
4096 Piedmont Avenue Suite 153
Oakland, CA 94611
(510) 547–1350
iaff2000@jps.net

Egyptian American Association
349 San Carlos Avenue
Piedmont, CA 94611

Institute of Islamic Education of
  Southern California
1447 Old Settlers Lane
Pomona, CA 91768
(909) 623–6144

Persian Performing Arts Institute
3306 Gibson Place
Redondo Beach, CA 90278

Ethiopian Sports Federation in North
  America
3150 Hilltop Mall Road
Richmond, CA 94806
(510) 970–7617
asceng@msn.com

Fiji Jam'atul Islam of America
373 Alta Vista Drive
South San Francisco, CA 94080
(650) 876–9763

Palestine Solidarity Committee
PO Box 27462
San Francisco, CA 94127

National Association of Yemeni
   Immigrants
PO Box 6414
San Francisco, CA 94101

Yemeni Benevolent Association
145 Turk Street Floor 2
San Francisco, CA 94102
(415) 776–8088

Deir Debwan Association
201 Jones Street
San Francisco, CA 94102

Cham Refugee Community of San
   Francisco
435 14th Street
San Francisco, CA 94103
(415) 864–4368

Arab Cultural Center
2 Plaza Street
San Francisco, CA 94116
(415) 664–2200

Ramallah Club
1951 Ocean Avenue
San Francisco, CA 94127
(415) 239–9115

Bosnian-Hercegovinian Center
1294 6th Avenue
San Francisco, CA 94122
(415) 242–9500

Sahel Club of San Francisco
2450 21st Avenue
San Francisco, CA 94116

Society of Iranian Professionals
PO Box 590968
San Francisco, CA 94159
officers@anjoman.org

Bosnian American Association
3410 Stevens Creek Boulevard Suite 104
San Jose, CA 95117
(408) 244–6989
baasj@ca.freei.net

Arab American Club College Union
PO Box A
San Jose, CA 95151

Afghan Cultural Center
60 Senter Road
San Jose, CA 95111
(408) 285–1619

San Jose Afghan Islamic Association
32 Rancho Drive
San Jose, CA 95111
(408) 224–8655

Arab Film Festival
416 Park Avenue
San Jose, CA 95110
(415) 564–1100
info@aff.org

Indo-Chinese Muslim Association of the
   United States of America
1001 E Grant Street Apartment B2
Santa Ana, CA 92701
(714) 547–8513

The Eritrea Advancement Association of
   Santa Clara County
1800 Stokes Street
Santa Clara, CA 95126
vp@warsai.org

Bay Area Bangladesh Association
PO Box 1080
Santa Clara, CA 95052
(408) 246–4371
baba@baba1.com

Persian Student Association at Stanford
   University
PO Box 19734
Stanford, CA 94309
(650) 736–4772
psa-admin@lists.stanford.edu

Bethlehem Association
16259 Aurora Crest Drive
Whittier, CA 90605
(213) 926–9293

Guilds
Arab Grocers Association
116 Valley Oaks Drive
Alamo, CA 94507

Arab American Lawyers Association
8907 Wilshire Boulevard
Beverly Hills, CA 90211
(213) 271–1911

Society of Palestinian Engineers and
    Scientists
PO Box 2661
Daly City, CA 94017
(415) 997–3104

Association of Professors and Scholars of
    Iranian Heritage
PO Box 4175
Diamond Bar, CA 91765
(213) 740–4458
pedram@ceng.usc.edu

Arab American Dental Association
215 N Harbor Boulevard
Fullerton, CA 92832
(714) 680–6767

Arab American Historical Foundation
RD Box 3684
Glendale, CA 91201

Association of Arab American
    Oceanographers
2504 Ellentown Road
La Jolla, CA 92037
(714) 453–0163

Turkish American Chamber of
    Commerce
4801 Wilshire Boulevard Suite 305
Los Angeles, CA 90010
(323) 937–3872

American Lebanese Medical Association
3654 E Imperial Highway
Lynwood, CA 90262
eayoub@hotmail.com
www.almamater.org/alma/default.html

Arab American Medical Association
1605 Avocado Avenue
Newport Beach, CA 92660
(949) 719–6373

Iranian Trade Association
1250 6th Avenue Suite 211
San Diego, CA 92101
(619) 368–6790
Afshar@IranianTrade.org

Housing Cooperative
Ameen Housing Cooperative of
    California
800 San Antonio Road
Palo Alto, CA 94303
(650) 856–0440
ameencoop@aol.com
Ameenhousing.com

Islamic Call Groups
Darul-Uloom Falah-e-Darain
720 N Fairview Street
Santa Ana, CA 92703
(714) 547–9107

Islamic Education and Information
    Center
1667 Langport Drive
Sunnyvale, CA 94087

Magazines
The Minaret
434 S Vermont Avenue
Los Angeles, CA 90020
(213) 384–4570
aslam1958@aol.com
www.theminaret.com

The Muslim Magazine
PO Box 391660
Mountain View, CA 94039
(650) 968–7007

Mosques / Islamic Centers
High Desert Islamic Center
18927 Bellflower Street
Adelanto, CA 92301
(760) 246–8842

Islamic Center of Alameda
901 Santa Clara Avenue
Alameda, CA 94501
(510) 521–8201

Alameda Mosque
707 Haight Avenue
Alameda, CA 94501
(510) 523–9866

Muslim Community Center
922 E Mendocino Street
Altadena, CA 91001
(818) 791–7290

Masjid Al-Taqwa
2181 Lake Avenue
Altadena, CA 91001
(818) 398–8392

Muslim Center
3184 Olive Avenue
Altadena, CA 91001
(818) 791–7290

Islamic Center of Anaheim
1136 N Brookhurst Street
Anaheim, CA 92801
(714) 999–2800

Islamic Institute of Orange County
1839 S Mountain View Avenue
Anaheim, CA 92802
(714) 740–1911

Islamic Institute of Orange County
1221 N Placentia Avenue
Anaheim, CA 92806
(714) 533–6271

Muslim Community of Cerritos
130 S Ridgeway Street #1
Anaheim, CA 92804

West Coast Islamic Society
708 N Valley Street Suite T
Anaheim, CA 92801
(714) 635–3113

Islamic Center of East Bay
311 W 18th Street
Antioch, CA 94509
shakeeb_79@hotmail.com

Masjid Al-Ihsan
1115 East Plaza Road
Bakerfield, CA 93307

Bakersfield Muslim Center
1221 California Avenue
Bakersfield, CA 93304
(661) 634–0518

Masjid Al Farooq
615 Kentucky Street
Bakersfield, CA 93305
(805) 324–7526

Islamic Society of San Joaquin Valley
701 Ming Avenue
Bakersfield, CA 93307
(805) 836–9055

Bell Islamic and Cultural Center
4651 Gage Avenue
Bell, CA 90201
islampathca@aol.com

Jafaria Islamic Society
7333 Wilcox Avenue
Bell, CA 90201
(213) 560–9304

Islamic Center of Berkeley
2254 Dwight Way
Berkeley, CA 94704
(510) 642–2876

Muslim Mission Center
2365 San Pablo Avenue
Berkeley, CA 94702

Muslim Association of Berkeley
245A Hesse Hall
University of California
Berkeley, CA 94720

Risale-i Nur Institute
PO Box 2192
Berkeley, CA 94702
(510) 845–4355

Berkeley Masjid
2510 Channing Way
Berkeley, CA 94704
(415) 549–9465

Muslim Brothers of America
128 S Wetherly Drive
Beverly Hills, CA 90211
(213) 274–2925

Fatima Islamic Society
7252 Remmet Avenue Suite 209
Canoga Park, CA 91303
(818) 992–9608
arastu@earthlink.net

Islamic Center of Santa Cruz
4401 Capitola Road Suite 2
Capitola, CA 95010
(831) 479–8982
mzayed@ave.net

Islamic Center of Castroville
11080 Cooper Street
Castroville, CA 95012
(831) 632–0905

Islamic Center of Chico
1316 Nord Avenue
Chico, CA 95926
(916) 342–5889

Islamic Society of Palm Springs
84650 49th Avenue
Coachella, CA 92236
(760) 398–7609
twassil@hotmail.com

Compton Masjid Al Rasheed
2212 E Compton Boulevard
Compton, CA 90221
(310) 537–3146

Bait Ul Hameed Mosque
11941 Romona Avenue
Chino, CA 91710
(909) 628–4699

Concord Masjid
4145 Concord Boulevard #43
Concord, CA 94519
(925) 755–5558

Concord Afghani Mosque
1545 Monument Boulevard Floor 2
Concord, CA 94520
(925) 825–2533

Islamic Center of Corona and Norco
1820 Fullerton Avenue Suite 330
Corona, CA 92881
(714) 371–2971

Islamic Society of Corona–Norco
500 West Harrington Street Suite L
Corona, CA 92880
(909) 736–8155
iscn@hotmail.com

Islamic Educational Center of Orange
    County
3194 Airport Loop Drive Suite B
Costa Mesa, CA 92626
(714) 432–0060
mqazwini@pacbell.net

Jafria Islamic Society
7333 Wilcox Avenue
Cudahy, CA 90201
(213) 560–9304

Islamic Society of West Los Angeles
4117 Overland Avenue
Culver City, CA 90230
(213) 837–5512

Islamic Foundation of Ibn Taymiyah
11004 Washington Boulevard
Culver City, CA 90232
(310) 204–1250

Islamic Center of Cypress Inc
5900 Ball Road
Cypress, CA 90630
(714) 220–1786

Davis Islamic Center
539 Russell Boulevard
Davis, CA 95616
(916) 756–5216

Yemeni Association Mosque
1122 High Street
Delano, CA 93215
(805) 725–9940

Islamic Center of Midcity
12428 Benedict Avenue
Downey, CA 90242
(562) 940–1995

Islamic Center of El Cajon
511 S Magnolia Avenue
El Cajon, CA 92020
(619) 401–2692
almadina-almunawara@hotmail.com

Imperial Valley Islamic Center
1560 Ocotillo Drive Suite B
El Centro, CA 92243
(760) 370–5880
LKR@trianglevision.com

Islamic Society of West Contra Costa
5666 San Pablo Dam Road
El Sobrante, CA 94803
(510) 669–0737

Islamic Society of California
781 Bolinas Road
Fairfax, CA 94930
(415) 454–6666

Masjid Al-Noor
902 Union Avenue
Fairfield, CA 94533
(707) 434–9280

Islamic Society of Folsom
99 Cable Circle Apartment 81
Folsom, CA 95630
(916) 985–0356

Islamic Society of Folsom
311 Market Street
Folsom, CA 95630
(916) 984–9002

Islamic Society of East Bay
PO Box 8422
Fremont, CA 94537

Fremont–Ibrahim Khalillillah Islamic
    Center
4938 Paseo Padre Parkway
Fremont, CA 94555
(510) 796–6761

Islamic Center of Freemont
4039 Irvington Avenue
Fremont, CA 94538
(510) 661–0352

Bilal Mosque
18248 Glenmoor Drive
Fremont, CA 94536
(510) 797–7336

Islamic Society of East Bay
3535 Capitol Avenue
Fremont, CA 94538
(510) 795–7137

Muslim Society of Central California
PO Box 25481
Fresno, CA 93729
(559) 449–1463

Masjid Muhammad
1329 B Street
Fresno, CA 93706

Masjid Al-Aqaba
1468 Fresno Street
Fresno, CA 93706
(559) 498–0401
muslimeen@webtv.net

BaD Islamic Center
4222 W Alamos Avenue Suite 101
Fresno, CA 93722
(559) 274–0906
masjidbadr@homestead.com

Mosque of Fullerton
413 West Avenue Apartment A
Fullerton, CA 92832
(714) 552–5092

Islamic Society of Indochina, Inc.
737 Gage Avenue
Fullerton, CA 92832

The Islamic Center
9392 Weldon Drive
Garden Grove, CA 92841

Islamic Society of Orange County
9812 13th Street
Garden Grove, CA 92844
(714) 531–1722

Islamic Society of Santa Barbara
PO Box 714
Goleta, CA 93116
(805) 968–9940
worshipallah@hotmail.com

Islamic Center of Granada Hills
11439 Encino Avenue
Granada Hills, CA 91344
(818) 360–9963

Masjid Abdullah
1540 C Street
Hayward, CA 94541

Islamic Association of Afghans
1172 W Tennyson Road
Hayward, CA 94544

Masjid Abu Bakr Al-Siddiq
24806 Mission Boulevard
Hayward, CA 94544

Masjid Muhajireen
185 Folsom Avenue
Hayward, CA 94544
(510) 786–0313

Islamic Society of Hemet
41456 Collegian Way
Hemet, CA 92544

The Islamic Society of Palm Springs
PO Box 1581
Indio, CA 92202
(760) 775–8892
adnan2@worldnet.att.net

Jamat-E-Masjid-Ul-Islam
820 Java Avenue
Inglewood, CA 90301
(310) 374–9898

Pathfinders and Community Leadership
    Organization
560 Saint John Place
Inglewood, CA 90301

Islamic Educational Center
17945 Sky Park Circle
Irvine, CA 92614
(949) 222–0320

Islamic Education Center of Irvine
14795 Jeffrey Road Suite 102
Irvine, CA 92618
(949) 786–4264
syedjafrey@home.com

Imam Ali Ibn Abi Talic Center
10390 Mountain View Lane
Lakeside, CA 92040
(619) 596–0020
alqazwini@aol.com

Islamic Center of North Valley
42554 4th Street E
Lancaster, CA 93535
(661) 726–4749
islamic@hughes.net

Islamic Center of Northern Valley
2763 W Avenue L # 274
Lancaster, CA 93536

Islamic Center of Live Oak
2825 Fir Street
Live Oak, CA 95953
(916) 695–8945

Islamic Center of Livermore
379A S Livermore Avenue
Livermore, CA 94550
(510) 373–6499

Mosque of Lodi
210 Poplar Street
Lodi, CA 95240
(209) 333–9619

Islamic Center of South Bay Los Angeles
25816 Walnut Street
Lomita, CA 90717
(310) 534–1363

Masjid Al Sharif
PO Box 267
Long Beach, CA 90801
(562) 591–5320

Islamic Center of Southern California
434 S Vermont Avenue
Los Angeles, CA 90020

Al-Quddus Mosques
5524 W Pico Boulevard
Los Angeles, CA 90019
(323) 930–1345

Masjid Al-Momin
1635 S St. Andrews Place
Los Angeles, CA 90019
(213) 737–8682

Masjid Salaam
2900 W Florence Avenue
Los Angeles, CA 90043
(213) 758–4033

Masjid Umar Ibn Al Khattab
1025 Exposition Boulevard
Los Angeles, CA 90007
(213) 733–9938

Masjid Ibdullah
2310 W Jefferson Boulevard
Los Angeles, CA 90018
(626) 398–3900

Masjid Al-Rasul
11211 S Central Avenue
Los Angeles, CA 90059
(323) 567–7114

Iranian Muslim Association of North
  America
3376 Motor Avenue
Los Angeles, CA 90034
(310) 202–8181
info@iman.org

Masjid Bilal Ibn Rabah
5450 Crenshaw Boulevard
Los Angeles, CA 90043
(323) 291–0105

Masjid Bilal
4016 S Central Avenue
Los Angeles, CA 90011
(213) 233–7274

Masjid Al-Tawheed
2244 Westwood Boulevard
Los Angeles, CA 90064

Ksit Jamaat of Los Angeles
11322 Idaho Ave., Suite 208
Los Angeles, CA 90025
(213) 836–1850

Madera Islamic Center
16634 Road 26
Madera, CA 93638
(559) 675–9100

Islamic Center of Merced
2322 Ashby Road
Merced, CA 95348
(209) 725–8167
Islamiccentermerced@muslimemail.com

Islamic Center of Mill Valley
62 Shell Road
Mill Valley, CA 94941
(415) 383–0617

Al Hilal Center
90 Dempsey Road
Milpitas, CA 95035
(408) 526–1475
web@alhilaal.org

Orange County Islamic Foundation
23581 Madero Drive
Mission Viejo, CA 92691
(949) 595–0480

Islamic Center of Modesto
PO Box 815
Modesto, CA 95353
(209) 576–8149
alabbasi3@hotmail.com

Masjid Qurtaba
1121 E Huntington Drive
Monrovia, CA 91016
(626) 305–0077

Al-Fatiha Islamic Center
1125 Orange Avenue
Monrovia, CA 91016
(818) 357–0465

Islamic Center
PO Box 3021
Monterey, CA 93942
(408) 375–0692

Islamic Society of Monterey County
1151 10th Street
Monterey, CA 93955
(831) 644–9332

Islamic Development Center
24436 Webster Avenue
Moreno Valley, CA 92553
(909) 247–8581
terrym@unocal.com

Morgan Hill Islamic Center
16725 Monterey Street Suite K
Morgan Hill, CA 95037
(408) 782–9142
mosquemh@juno.com

Islamic Center of Mountain View
607–A W Dana Street
Mountain View, CA 94041
(831) 644–8332

Darul Ulum
2012 Mallory Street
Muscoy, CA 92407
(909) 595–4246

North Hollywood Islamic Center
5114 Vineland Avenue
North Hollywood, CA 91601

Islamic Center of Conejo Valley
2700 Borchard Road
Newbury Park, CA 91320
(805) 499–2106
asif@datastreet.com

Islamic Center of Northridge
8424 Tampa Avenue
Northridge, CA 91324
(818) 360–9963

Masjidul-Waritheen
1652 47th Avenue
Oakland, CA 94601
(510) 436–7755

Masjid Al-Islam
8210 Macarthur Boulevard
Oakland, CA 94605
(510) 635–5277

Abubaker Mosque
948 62nd Street
Oakland, CA 94608
(510) 653–8028

Oakland Islamic Center
515 31st Street
Oakland, CA 94609
(510) 547–4768

Masjid As-Salam
1005 7th Street
Oakland, CA 94607
(510) 451–8110

Islamic Cultural Center of Northern
    California
1433 Madison Street
Oakland, CA 94612
(510) 832–7600

Masjid Al-Iman
4606 Martin Luther King Jr. Way
Oakland, CA 94609
(510) 652–5271

Muhammad Mosque
5277 Foothill Boulevard
Oakland, CA 94601
(510) 436–0206

S. Jamaludeen Afghan Islamic Center
546 W Katella Avenue
Orange, CA 92867
(714) 288–9655

Islamic Center of Oxnard
525 S A Street
Oxnard, CA 93030
(805) 486–8886

Masjid of Antelope Valley
PO Box 902846
Palmdale, CA 93590
(661) 224–1111
mav@muslims.net

Jamil Islamic Center of California
427 S California Avenue
Palo Alto, CA 94306
(650) 326–7450
jamil@best.com

Masjid Imam Bukhari
8741 Van Nuys Boulevard
Panorama City, CA 91402
(818) 894–3025

Islamic Foundation of Pasadena
2116 E Colorado Boulevard
Pasadena, CA 91107

Islamic Center of Petaluma
222 Bassett Street
Petaluma, CA 94952
(707) 773–1576
masjid_petaluma@hotmail.com

Petaluma Musala
317 Greenbriar Circle
Petaluma, CA 94954
(707) 773–1576

Shia Ithna-Asheri Islamic Jamaat of Los
   Angeles
PO Box 1207
Pico Rivera, CA 90660
(562) 942–7442

Pittsburg Islamic Center
8 Cambria Court
Pittsburg, CA 94565
(928) 439–3894

Masjid al Sabireen
805 S Garey Avenue
Pomona, CA 91766
(909) 865–7833
cham525@yahoo.com

Islamic Center of Claremont
3641 N Garey Avenue
Pomona, CA 91767
(909) 593–1865

Ahlul-Beyt Mosque
2155 Murchison Avenue
Pomona, CA 91768
(714) 622–0988
bismihi001@aol.com

Islamic Center of North County
14034 Poway Road Suite G
Poway, CA 92064
(858) 513–2733
www.spaceports.com/~paca/isctr.htm

Islamic Center of Inland Empire
9212 Baseline Road
Rancho Cucamonga, CA 91701
(909) 944–1836

Jerrahi Order of America
3644 Hoover Street
Redwood City, CA 94063
(845) 352–5518
info@jerrahi.org

Islamic Center of Reseda
18206 Victory Boulevard
Reseda, CA 91335
(818) 996–9116

Islamic Center of Rialto
755 E Foothill Boulevard #C and D
Rialto, CA 92376
(909) 875–7456
icor@aol.com

Masjid Aisha
1369 N Willow Avenue #B-11
Rialto, CA 92376

Islamic Society of West Contra Costa
1110 36th Street
Richmond, CA 94801
(510) 236–8130

The Mosque of Riverside
1038 W Linden Street
Riverside, CA 92507
(909) 684–5466

Masjid Muhammad
4104 Park Avenue
Riverside, CA 92507

The Islamic Society
2530 Thayer Court
Riverside, CA 92507

Islamic Center of San Gabriel Valley
19164 E Walnut Drive N
Rowland Heights, CA 91748

Islamic Center of Sacramento
2011 4th Street
Sacramento, CA 95818
(916) 444–6323

Sacramento Islamic Mosque
411 V Street
Sacramento, CA 95818
(901) 644–3316

Masjid As-Sabur Islamic Dawah Center
4911 15th Avenue
Sacramento, CA 95820
(916) 422–5472

Baitul Llah Islamic Information Center
4123 12th Avenue
Sacramento, CA 95817
(916) 455–2902
slaveof1@deepsell.com

Sacramento Area League of Associated
  Muslims
4531 College Oak Drive
Sacramento, CA 95841
(916) 451–7650

Masjid Annur
6990 65th Street
Sacramento, CA 95823
(916) 457–3233

Sacramento Area League of Muslims
PO Box 19905
Sacramento, CA 95819
(916) 451–7650

Masjid Ibrahim
3449 Rio Linda Boulevard
Sacramento, CA 95838
(916) 925–4191

Masjid An-noor
7320 14th Avenue
Sacramento, CA 95820
(916) 457–3233

Masjid Al-Noor/Islamic Association and
  Foundation of San Diego
3872 50th Street
San Diego, CA 92105
(619) 282–0037

Al Ribat Al-Islami Center
7173 Saranac Street
San Diego, CA 92115
(619) 589–6299
Affnan2@prodigy.net

Masjid Hamza
9494 Black Mountain Road #C
San Diego, CA 92126
(858) 271–1691

Masjidul Taqwa
2575 Imperial Avenue
San Diego, CA 92102
(619) 239–6738

Islamic Society of San Francisco
20 Jones Street
San Francisco, CA 94102
(415) 343–3818

The Mosque and Islamic Center of San
  Francisco
400 Crescent Avenue
San Francisco, CA 94110
(415) 282–9039

Masjid Al-Tawheed
1227 Sutter Street
San Francisco, CA 94109
(415) 776–8088

Masjid Muhammad
1805 Geary Boulevard
San Francisco, CA 94115

Anjaman Fidayan Rasool
1411 Thomas Avenue
San Francisco, CA 94124
(415) 822–1000

Islamic Community of Northern
   California
PO Box 410186
San Francisco, CA 94141
(415) 552–8831

Masjid Al-Falah
PO Box 421424
San Francisco, CA 94142

Masjid Al-Noor
3004 16th Street Suite 102
San Francisco, CA 94103
(415) 552–8831

Muslim Community Center
850 Divisadero Street
San Francisco, CA 94117
(415) 563–9397

Multaqa Alsiddiq
311 S Mission Drive
San Gabriel, CA 91776
(626) 457–1491
multaqa@egroups.com

Masjid Gibrael
1301 E Las Tunas Drive
San Gabriel, CA 91776
(626) 285–2573

South Bay Islamic Association
325 N 3rd Street
San Jose, CA 95112
(408) 947–9389

Shia Association of Bay Area
2725 S White Road
San Jose, CA 95148
(408) 238–9497
saba@saba-igc.org
saba-igc.org

All Muslim Islamic Community Center
160 E Virginia Street Suite 201
San Jose, CA 95112
(408) 236–3308

The Islamic Education and Information
   Center
1440 Koll Circle Suite 109
San Jose, CA 95112
(408) 453–1970

Islamic Center
514 Lanfair Ar
San Jose, CA 95136

Masjid San Jose
126 Viola Avenue
San Jose, CA 95110
(408) 246–9822

Al Hilal Islamic Center
2625 Zanker Road
San Jose, CA 95134
(408) 526–1475
frydhan@jps.net

San Jose Evergreen Islamic Center
2486 Ruby Avenue
San Jose, CA 95148
(408) 247–0706

Yaseen Foundation
PO Box 1312
San Mateo, CA 94401
(650) 572–9152
yaseen@yaseen.org

San Mateo Al-Haq Mosque
228 N Ellsworth Avenue
San Mateo, CA 94401
(650) 579–0429

San Ramon Valley Islamic Center
2232B Camino Ramon
San Ramon, CA 94583
(510) 866–7088

Masjid Santa Ana
1301 Halladay Street
Santa Ana, CA 92707

Muslim Community Association
3003 Scott Boulevard
Santa Clara, CA 95052
(408) 970–0647
www.mca-sfba.org
cr@mca-sfba.org

Islamic Center of Santa Cruz
PO Box 3126
Santa Cruz, CA 95062

Islamic Society of Santa Rosa
2654 Mendocino Avenue
Santa Rosa, CA 95403
(707) 538–8810
said_mansour@ocli.com

Islamic Center of Santa Clarita Valley
26477 Golden Valley Road #D
Saugus, CA 91350
(805) 251–1501

Masjid An-Nur
764 N Mount Vernon Avenue
San Bernardino, CA 92411

Masjid Makki
1959 N Macy Street
San Bernardino, CA 92411

Masjid Aisha
1594 Hancock Street
San Bernardino, CA 92411
(909) 887–1605

Islamic Society of San Luis Obispo
108 Mustang Drive Apartment 104
San Luis Obispo, CA 93405
(805) 541–6298

Islamic Society of the Central Coast
679 Santa Rosa Street
San Luis Obispo, CA 93401
(805) 541–6298
iscc@muslimsonline.com

Azzahrah Islamic Center
8152 Seville Avenue
South Gate, CA 90280
(323) 589–3510

Islamic Society of Stanford
Stanford University Old Building #19
    Box 2067
Stanford, CA 94309
(510) 657–0223

Masjid-Us-Sadiq
PO Box 690991
Stockton, CA 95269
(209) 941–4915

Assiddiq Muslim Center
2065 E 8th Street
Stockton, CA 95206
(209) 941–4915

Stockton Islamic Center
1130 S Pilgrim Street
Stockton, CA 95205
(209) 466–9101

Islamic Center of Temecula Valley
28900 Old Town Front Street Suite 103
Temecula, CA 92590
(909) 694–5666
mahmood@PE.net

Dar-ul-'Uloom Torrance
18093 Prairie Avenue Suite F
Torrance, CA 90504
(310) 921–2786
imam@darululoom.org

Masjid Alfalah
2681 Dow Avenue Suite C
Tustin, CA 92780

Vallejo Islamic Center
726 Sonoma Boulevard
Vallejo, CA 94590
(707) 554–0122

Musalla-Victorville
14036 Hesperia Road
Victorville, CA 92392

Dar-ul-Islam Mosque
2822 W James Avenue #A
Visalia, CA 93277
(209) 732–6402

Masjid Visalia
1317 S Divisadero Street
Visalia, CA 93277
(209) 732–6402

Islamic Movement of North America
925 Anza Avenue
Vista, CA 92084
(760) 945–9544
malik@home.com

Islamic Education Center
659 Brea Canyon Road
Walnut, CA 91789
(909) 594–1310

Mosque of Woodland
1023 North Street
Woodland, CA 95695
(916) 666–4706

Yuba City Mosque
2910 Nuestro Road
Yuba City, CA 95993
(530) 674–7371

Islamic Center of Yuba City
3600 Tierra Buena Road
Yuba City, CA 95993
(916) 674–7371
mosque@juno.com

Newspapers
al-Jadid
PO Box 24DD2
Los Angeles, CA 90024
(323) 957–1291
aljadid@jovanet.com

Muslim Monitor
PO Box 3477
San Dimas, CA 91773
(714) 599–3131

Periodicals
Iqra
325 N 3rd Street
San Jose, CA 95112

Azerbajan International
PO Box 5127
Sherman Oaks, CA 91413
(818) 785–0077
www.azer.com

Prison Outreach Groups
Al Haqq Publications
PO Box 338
Compton, CA 90223

California Muslim Prisoners' Foundation
8448 Reseda Boulevard Suite 207
Northridge, CA 91324
(818) 886–1463

Public Affairs Organizations
Council on American-Islamic
    Relations–Southern California
2115 W Crescent Avenue Suite 228
Anaheim, CA 92801
(714) 776–1847
cair@nayzak.com

American Arab Anti-Discrimination
    Committee
(West Coast)
9355 Chapman Avenue Suite 205
Garden Grove, CA 92841
(714) 636–1232
shehadeh@worldnet.att.net
www.adc.org

Consultative Committee of the Indian
    Muslims
5035 W 137th Street
Hawthorne, CA 90250
(310) 675–7554

American Muslim Alliance (HQ)
39675 Cedar Boulevard, Suite 220–E
Newark, CA 94560
(510) 252–9858
info@amaweb.org
www.ama.org

American Muslim Alliance PAC
39675 Cedar Boulevard, Suite 220–E
Newark, CA 94560

American-Arab Anti-Discrimination
    Committee –San Diego Chapter
4386 Jutland Drive
San Diego, CA 92117

United Muslims of America
PO Box 878
San Gabriel, CA 91778
(818) 285–5890

Arab American Silicon Valley Congress
416 Park Avenue
San Jose, CA 95110
(408) 279–2722
arabcenter-sj@yahoo.com

Islamic Networks Group
2136 The Alameda Suite 2F
San Jose, CA 95126
(408) 296–7312
ini@ing.org

Muslim American Voter Association
6640 Barnsdale Court
San Jose, CA 95120

Council on American-Islamic
    Relations–Northern California
3000 Scott Boulevard Suite 104
Santa Clara, CA 95054
(408) 986–9874
cair@av.net
www.cair-net.org

Radio / TV
Islamic Communications Center
514 Lanfair Circle
San Jose, CA 95136
(408) 995–0551

Schools
Bilal Ibn Rabah Institute
PO Box 4487
Berkeley, CA 94704
(510) 582–6550

Fatimah Girls' Academy
PO Box 8059
Fresno, CA 93747
(209) 338–0203

Happy Horizons Pre-School
3516 W Commonwealth Avenue
Fullerton, CA 92833
(714) 870–0403

Orange Crescent School
9802 13th Street
Garden Grove, CA 92844
(714) 531–1451
Kbaig@delphi.com

Al-Najm Islamic School
820 Java Avenue
Inglewood, CA 90301
(310) 672–0773
MTaj201252@aol.com

Qurdobah School
3420 W Jefferson Boulevard
Los Angeles, CA 90018
(213) 731–2581

New Horizon School–Los Angeles
    Campus
434 S Vermont Avenue
Los Angeles, CA 90020
(213) 480–3145
newhorizon@worldnet.att.net

Islamic Middle School
2105 41st Avenue
Oakland, CA 94601
(510) 436–0232

Sr. Clara Muhammed School
1652 47th Avenue
Oakland, CA 94601
(510) 436–7755

New Horizon School
626 Cypress Avenue
Pasadena, CA 91103
(818) 795–5186
newhorizon@worldnet.att.net
www.islam.org

Claremont Islamic School
3619 N Garey Avenue
Pomona, CA 91767
(909) 392–9692
azzamascha@hotmail.com

City of Knowledge School
3285 N Garey Avenue
Pomona, CA 91767
(909) 392–0251
cityofkn@aol.com

Islamic Academy of Riverside
1038 W Linden Street
Riverside, CA 92507
(909) 682–1202

School of Islamic Center of San Gabriel
    Valley
19164 E Walnut Drive N
Rowland Hghts, CA 91748
(626) 964–3596

Darul Uloom Al Islamiyah Sacramento
7285 25th Street
Sacramento, CA 95822
(916) 424–4770

Al-Basit Academy
9921 Cormel Mountain Road Suite 137
San Diego, CA 92129

Islamic Madrassa of America
PO Box 151112
San Diego, CA 92175

Islamic School of San Diego
7050 Eckstrom Avenue
San Diego, CA 92111
(858) 278–7970
nobarr1@juno.com

Sister Clara Muhammad School
2575 Imperial Avenue
San Diego, CA 92102
(619) 232–5910

School of San Francisco—Masjid
    Darussalam
20 Jones Street Floor 3
San Francisco, CA 94102
(415) 863–7997

Granada Islamic School
3003 Scott Boulevard
Santa Clara, CA 95054
(408) 980–1161
gis1@ave.net
www.granadaschool.org

Darul Uloom Al-Islamia of America
2012 Mallory Street
San Bernardino, CA 92407
(909) 880–0201

Darul Hikmah–Silicon Valley Academy
1095 Dunford Way
Sunnyvale, CA 94087
(408) 243–9333
sva@mailexcite.com
www.jamil.com/sva

Social Services
National Islamic Society of Women of
    America
PO Box 1403
Lomita, CA 90717
(310) 782–2482
info@niswa.org

University Muslim Medical Association
711 W Florence Avenue
Los Angeles, CA 90044
(323) 789–5610
info@ummaclinic.org
www.ummaclinic.org

Muslim Burial Service
3872 50th Street
San Diego, CA 92105
(619) 527–9999

Student Groups
Muslim Student Union of University of
    California–Berkeley
300 Eshlaman Hall
Berkeley, CA 94720

University of California–Berkeley Arab
    Student Union
PO Box 40408
Berkeley, CA 94704
qasem@ieor.berkeley.edu

Muslim Students
    Association/Cresent–Monta Vista
    High School
21370 Homestead Road
Cupertino, CA 95014
(408) 253–6257
youssuf@mvhs.fuhsd.org

Muslim Students Association–PSG Los
    Angeles
PO Box 4884
Downey, CA 90241
(213) 960–5073

Muslim Student Association
17500 Rinaldi Street
Granada Hills, CA 91344
(818) 363–2765
husnain2@hotmail.com

Muslim Students Association–California
State University of Long Beach
6101 E 7th Street
Long Beach, CA 90840

Muslim Student Association–USC
830 Childs Way, Suite 222
Los Angeles, CA 90089

Muslim Student Association at University
of California–Los Angeles
308 Westwood Plaza
Los Angeles, CA 90095
(310) 206–9124

California Polytechnic Pomona Muslim
Student Association
3801 W Temple Avenue
Pomona, CA 91768
(626) 286–3207
msa@csupomona.edu
www.csupomona.edu/~msa

Muslim Student Association–University
of California at Riverside
Student Life and Leadership
Riverside, CA 92521
(909) 686–8343
interest9@hotmail.com

Muslim Students Association–San
Francisco State University
1600 Holloway Avenue Student Union
B139
San Francisco, CA 94132
(415) 552–8831

Muslim Students Association–University
of San Francisco
2130 Fulton Street Room 402
San Francisco, CA 94117
(415) 666–2817
banguraa@stu.admin.usfca.edu (Ahmed
Bangura)

Arab Students Association
California State Poly College, Box ASI
San Luis Obispo, CA 93401

Muslim Student Association–University
of California–Santa Barbara
PO Box 13845
Santa Barbara, CA 93107
(805) 967–9495

Muslim Students Association–Mission
College
2382 Sutter Avenue Apartment 7
Santa Clara, CA 95050
(408) 249–2557

Islamic Society of Stanford University
Stanford University, Old Union Club
House, Room 19
Stanford, CA 94305
(650) 497–7951
issu-officers@cs.stanford.edu

Stockton Student Mosque
1219 W El Monte Street
Stockton, CA 95207
(209) 474–3184

Student Newspaper
Al-Talib
118 Kerckhoff Hall
308 Westwood Plaza
Los Angeles, CA 90024
(310) 206–7877
altalib@media.ucla.edu
www.altalib.media.ucla.edu

Sufi Groups
The Haqqani Trust
23150 Mora Glen Drive
Los Altos, CA 94024
(415) 941–7916

As-Sunnah Foundation of America
607A W Dana Street
Mountain View, CA 94041
(310) 253–5363
staff@sunnah.org
www.sunnah.org

Sufi Islamia Ruhaniat Society
410 Precita Avenue
San Francisco, CA 94110
(415) 285–5208

School for Islamic Sufism
PO Box 1135
San Rafael, CA 94915

Textbook Consultant
Council on Islamic Education
9300 Gardenia Avenue Suite B3
Fountain Vly, CA 92708
(714) 839–2929
info@cie.org
www.cie.org

TV Programs
Muslim Community TV
4122 Macarthur Boulevard
Oakland, CA 94619
(415) 530–8502

Arabic Broadcast Network Inc.
4660 La Jolla Village Drive Suite 500
San Diego, CA 92122
(858) 625–4690

Women's Groups
Palestine Democratic Women's
    Organization
225 Coronado Avenue Apartment 320
Daly City, CA 94015
(415) 756–1142

Council of Muslim Women
7902 Gerber Road #140
Sacramento, CA 95828
(916) 689–6249

United Muslim Women's Association
790 Lucerne Drive #39
Sunnyvale, CA 94085
(408) 730–9977

Youth Groups
United Islamic Youth Organization, Inc.
18927 Bellflower Street
Adelanto, CA 92301
(760) 246–8842

Al Hussein Youth Center
4313 Gage Avenue
Bell, CA 90201
(323) 562–8087
hajaliayoub@aol.com

COLORADO

Book Publisher / Distributor
Al Basheer
PO Box 17533
Boulder, CO 80308

Ethnic Association
Turkish American Cultural Society of
    Colorado
PO Box 260435
Littleton, CO 80163
(303) 708–4408
cevdet@worldnet.att.net
www.tacsco.org

Islamic Call Group
Islamic Assembly of North America
    Chapter
13918 E Mississippi Avenue #240
Aurora, CO 80012
(303) 338–0638
iana@iananet.org
www.iananet.org

Mosques / Islamic Centers
Al-Muslims Service Center
PO Box 31143
Aurora, CO 80041
(303) 366–4666

Islamic Center of Boulder
1530 Culver Court
Boulder, CO 80303
(303) 579–4666

Islamic Society of Colorado Springs
2121 N Chestnut Street
Colorado Springs, CO 80907

Mountain States Islamic Association
2715 Humboldt Street
Denver, CO 80205
(303) 296–0948

Islamic Center of Alh-Al-Beit
201 S Lowell Boulevard
Denver, CO 80219
(303) 999–3658
center14@juno.com

Denver Islamic Society
2124 S Birch Street
Denver, CO 80222
(303) 759–1985

Colorado Muslim Society
2071 S Parker Road
Denver, CO 80231
(303) 696–9800

Fort Collins Islamic Center
900 Peterson Street
Fort Collins, CO 80524
(970) 493–2428

Greenley Islamic Center
1600 8th Avenue
Greenley, CO 80631
(970) 356–8448

Pueblo Islamic Society
30 Martha Lane
Pueblo, CO 81001
(719) 546–0137

Schools
Denver Education Islamic Center
10958 E Bethany Drive
Aurora, CO 80014
(303) 745–2245
www.crescentview.org

Denver Islamic School
2071 S Parker Road
Denver, CO 80231
(303) 696–9800

Student Group
Muslim Students Association–Metrostate
Student Activities Campus 39 #173362
Denver, CO 80217
(303) 399–4461

CONNECTICUT

Ethnic Associations
Albanian League of Prizren
1 Walker Court
Greenwich, CT 06831
(203) 531–0592

Turkisk Islamic Cultural Associates
560 Middletown Avenue
New Haven, CT 06513
(203) 786–4752

Turkish American Cultural Association of
    Southern New England
291 Vine Road
Stamford, CT 06905
(203) 225–4784
gbiro@mail.dnb.com

Association of Nigerians in Connecticut
PO Box 26465
West Haven, CT 06516

Turkish Community Club
727 Campbell Avenue
West Haven, CT 06516
(203) 931–0330

Guilds
Turkish American Physicians Association
645 Beaver Dam Road
Stratford, CT 06614
(203) 378–4178
ymnaci@aol.com

Iranian Chemists Association of the
    American
Chemical Society
35 Meadowbrook Lane
Woodbury, CT 06798
mohahmad@omni.cc.purdue.edu
www.ica-acs.org

Islamic Call Group
New England Muslim Sisters Association
PO Box 595
Hartford, CT 06141

Mosques / Islamic Centers

Islamic Association of Greater Hartford
1071 Wilbur Cross Highway
Berlin, CT 06037
(203) 829–6411

Masjid Al-Aziz
679 Fairfield Avenue
Bridgeport, CT 06604
(203) 375–3619

Bridgeport Islamic Society
1300 Fairfield Avenue
Bridgeport, CT 06605
(203) 579–2211

Dar ul Ihsan
739 Terryville Avenue
Bristol, CT 06010
(860) 585–9742

Islamic Society of Western Connecticut
388 Main Street
Danbury, CT 06810
(203) 744–1328

Islamic Center
290 Tahmore Drive
Fairfield, CT 06432
(203) 371–1979

Muhammad Islamic Center
PO Box 260607
Hartford, CT 06126

Masjid Al Islam
624 George Street
New Haven, CT 06511
(203) 777–8004
info@deeninc.com

Islamic Institute of Ahl'albait
82 Somerset Street
West Hartford, CT 06110
(860) 232–8954
rbachir@ziplink.net

Albanian American Muslim Community
38 Raymond Street
Waterbury, CT 06706
(203) 757–6123

Albanian Islamic Center
106 Columbia Boulevard
Waterbury, CT 06710
(203) 754–4993

New Haven Islamic Center
2 Prudden Street
West Haven, CT 06516
(203) 933–5799

Islamic Center of Connecticut
PO Box 624
Windsor, CT 06095
(860) 728–9637
imam1@aol.com

Madina Masjid
1 Midian Avenue
Windsor, CT 06095
(203) 249–0112

Albanian Community Center
21 Longmeadow Drive
Wolcott, CT 06716

Religious Education Program

Jafaria Association of Connecticut
3 Fowler Drive
West Hartford, CT 06110
(203) 468–2961
nraza@aol.com

Student Groups

Muslim Students Association–University
   of Bridgeport
Carstensen Hall 247 University Avenue
Bridgeport, CT 06601
(203) 576–4531

Islamic Student Association–Yale
PO Box 204933
New Haven, CT 06520
(203) 436–1568

Muslim Students Association–University
   of Connecticut
Student Union Room 344S
Stross, CT 06268
(203) 427–7501

Youth Group
National Islamic Committee on Girl
  Scouting
31 Marian Street
Stamford, CT 06907
(203) 359–3593

DELAWARE

Guild
The International Society of African
  Scientists
PO Box 9209
Wilmington, DE 19809
isas@dca.net

Islamic Call Group
Islamic Dawah Endeavors in America
2812 Baynard Boulevard
Wilmington, DE 19802
(302) 652–2237

Mosques / Islamic Centers
Masjid Ibrahim
28 Salem Church Road
Newark, DE 19713
(302) 733–0373

The Islamic Society of Delaware
133 Garrett Road
Newark, DE 19713
(302) 733–0373

The Muslim Center of Wilmington
301 W 6th Street
Wilmington, DE 19801
(302) 571–0532

North American Islamic Foundation
2215 N Washington Street
Wilmington, DE 19802
(302) 654–4758
naifinco@aol.com

DISTRICT OF COLUMBIA

Charity Groups
Jerusalem Fund
2435 Virginia Avenue NW
Washington, DC 20037
(202) 338–1958

United Palestinian Appeal
2100 M Street NW #409
Washington, DC 20037
(202) 659–5007
upa@cais.com
www.cais.net\upa

Coordination Council
Coordination Council of Muslim
  Organizations of the Washington
  Metropolitan Area
PO Box 5593
Washington, DC 20016

Ethnic Associations
Arab American University Graduates
4201 Connecticut Avenue NW Suite 303
Washington, DC 20008
(202) 237–8312

Palestine Aid Society
203 I Street NW #120
Washington, DC 20001
(202) 728–9425

Platform International
3413 Wisconsin Avenue NW
Washington, DC 20016
(202) 244–3555

Iran Teachers Association
PO Box 6257
Washington, DC 20015
mehregan@ig-dc.com

Nigerian Muslim Council in the United
  States
1800 11th Street NW
Washington, DC 20001
(301) 887–0901

Assembly of Turkish American
   Associations
1526 18th Street NW
Washington, DC 20036
(202) 483–9090
assembly@ataa.org
www.ataa.org

Guild
National U.S. Arab Chamber of
   Commerce
1100 New York Avenue NW Suite 550
Washington, DC 20005
(202) 289–5920

Islamic Call Group
Association of Latin American Muslims
PO Box 57285
Washington, DC 20037
(202) 483–3467

Mosques / Islamic Centers
Community Mosque
770 Park Road NW
Washington, DC 20010

Jamaat Al-Qawiyy
1830 11th Street NW
Washington, DC 20001
(202) 332–4976
jamaat@aol.com

Islamic Center of Washington, D.C.
2551 Massachusetts Avenue NW
Washington, DC 20008
(202) 332–8343

Masjid Muhammad
1519 4th Street NW
Washington, DC 20001
(202) 483–8832

Masjid Al-Madrasa
5931 Georgia Avenue NW
Washington, DC 20011
(202) 723–3744

Ivy City Educational Center and Mosque
2001 Gallaudet Street NE
Washington, DC 20002
(202) 529–3100

Masjid Al-Islam
4603 Benning Road SE
Washington, DC 20019
(202) 581–0004

Masjid Ush Shura
3109 Martin Luther King Jr. Avenue SE
Washington, DC 20032
(202) 574–8417
gkashif@salaam.net

Prison Outreach Groups
National Islamic Prison Foundation
6424 8th Street NW
Washington, DC 20012
(202) 291–7772

American Muslim Council National
   Prison Project
1212 New York Avenue NW Suite 400
Washington, DC 20005
(202) 789–2262

Public Affairs Organizations
National Albanian American Council
2000 L Street NW Suite 200
Washington, DC 20036
(202) 416–1627

Arab American Leadership PAC
1600 K Street NW Suite 601
Washington, DC 20006

Palestine Affairs Center
1730 K Street NW Suite 703
Washington, DC 20006
(202) 785–8394

Solidarity International for Human
   Rights
1220 L Street NW
Washington, DC 20005
(202) 347–9801
sihr@sihr.net

American Muslim Council (HQ)
1212 New York Avenue NW Suite 400
Washington, DC 20005
(202) 789–2262
amc@amconline.org
www.amconline.org

American Muslims for Jerusalem
208 G Street NE Suite 100
Washington, DC 20002
(202) 548–0913
amj@amjerusalem.org
www.amjerusalem.org

Palestine Human Rights Information
Center
4201 Connecticut Avenue NW Suite 500
Washington, DC 20008
(202) 685–5116

Council on American-Islamic
Relations–National
453 New Jersey Avenue
Washington, DC 20003
(202) 659–2247
cair@cair-net.org
www.cair-net.org

Muslim Public Affairs Council
(Washington D.C.)
529 14th Street NW Suite 923
Washington, DC 20045
(202) 879–6726
mpac1@aol.com
www.mpac.org

Arab American Institute
1600 K Street NW Suite 601
Washington, DC 20006
(202) 429–9210
aai@aaiusa.org
www.aaiusa.org

National Coalition to Protect Political
Freedom
3321 12th Street NE
Washington, DC 20017
(202) 529–4225

American Task Force of Lebanon
2213 M Street NW Floor 3
Washington, DC 20037
(202) 223–9333
codytennis@aol.com
www.atsl.org

American Arab Anti-Discrimination
Committee
4201 Connecticut Avenue NW Suite 300
Washington, DC 20008
(202) 244–2990
adc@adc.org
www.adc.org

Research Groups
Arab American University Graduates
4201 Connecticut Avenue NW Suite 303
Washington, DC 20008
(202) 237–8312
aaug@aaug.org
www.aaug.org

Institute for Palestine Studies
3501 M Street NW
Washington, DC 20007
(202) 342–3990
ips-dc@cais.com
www.cais.net/ipsjps

Center for Policy Analysis on Palestine
2425–35 Virginia Avenue
Washington, DC 20037
(202) 338–1958
info@palestinecenter.org
www.palestinecenter.org/framecpap.html

Washington Kurdish Institute
605 G Street SW
Washington, DC 20024
(202) 484–0140
wki@kurd.org
www.kurd.org

Kashmiri American Council
733 15th Street NW Suite 1100
Washington, DC 20005
(202) 628–6789
Info@kashmiri.com
www.kashmiri.com

School
Clara Muhammad School
2313 Martin Luther King Jr.
Avenue SE #15
Washington, DC 20020
(202) 610–1090
cmschooldc@aol.com

Social Services
Ahlul Bayt Assembly of America
PO Box 33007
Washington, DC 20033
majmaa@hotmail.com
www.nabaa.com

Islamic Community Services
6705 2nd Street NW
Washington, DC 20012
(202) 882–7364

Naim Foundation
3000 Connecticut Avenue NW
Washington, DC 20008
(202) 462–5715

Student Groups
Muslim Student Association George
  Washington University
9 Marvin Center
800 21st Street
Washington, DC 20052
(202) 994–0929

Muslim Student Association Georgetown
  University
SAC 6863 Georgetown University
Washington, DC 20007
(202) 687–1756

Howard University Muslim Community
2395 6th Street NW
Washington, DC 20059
(202) 806–7930

Muslim Students Association–Operations
  Office
PO Box 18612
Washington, DC 20036

Muslim Student Association of American
  University
4400 Massachusetts Avenue
N. Kay Spiritual Life Center
Washington, DC 20016
(202) 342–6043

Muslim Students Association–University
  of the District of Columbia
3636 16th Street NW Apartment A725
Washington, DC 20010
(202) 462–0733

Muslim Student Association Catholic
  University
620 Michigan NE Union Center
West #200
Washington, DC 20064

Sufi Group
Islamic Supreme Council of America
1201 Pennsylvania Avenue NW Suite
  300
Washington, DC 20004
(202) 661–4654

FLORIDA

Charity Groups
Health Resource Center for Palestine
1313 S Military Trail Suite #283
Deerfield Beach, FL 33442
(954) 941–4727
president@hrcp.org

Bosnian Refugees Relief Fund
145 Suncrest Drive
Safety Harbor, FL 34695
(813) 725–2686

Ethnic Associations
Turkish American Cultural Association of
  Florida
PO Box 3303
Brandon, FL 33509
(727) 799–2501
tacaf@tacaf.org
www.tacaf.org

Iranian-American Society
PO Box 10541
Daytona Beach, FL 32120
info@iranianamericansociety.org

Florida Turkish American Association
PO Box 50021
Lighthouse Point, FL 33074
(954) 975–3384
guneyadak@aol.com

Islamic Call Group
Bilal Muslim Mission of
Americas–Florida
1973 Corporate Square
Longwood, FL 32750
(407) 831–7912
bilalmuslim@altavista.com

Mosques / Islamic Centers
Assalam Center
21218 Saint Andrews Boulevard Unit 147
Boca Raton, FL 33433
(561) 347–0938
ieom@aol.com

Nurul-Islam Masjid
10600 SW 59th Street
Cooper City, FL 33328
(954) 434–3288

Islamic Center of Daytona Beach
PO Box 1903
Daytona Beach, FL 32115
(904) 252–0843

Islamic Center of South Florida
3337 Broadway
Fort Myers, FL 33901
(941) 768–1207

Islamic Center of Fort Pierce
1104 W Midway Road
Fort Pierce, FL 34982
(561) 465–9200
icfp@aol.com

Masjid Tawhid
1557 NW 5th Street
Fort Lauderdale, FL 33311
(954) 581–6295

Masjid Al Sultan Sallah Deen
2822 Griffin Road
Fort Lauderdale, FL 33312
(954) 986–1373

Masjid Al-Iman
2542 Franklin Park Drive
Fort Lauderdale, FL 33311
(954) 581–6295

Islamic Dawa Center of Fort Walton
6A Hollywood Boulevard SW
Fort Walton Beach, FL 32548
(850) 863–9215

Islamic Movement of Florida
3201 NW 74th Avenue
Hollywood, FL 33024
(954) 894–9110

Masjid Al-Salaam
1625 N Pearl Street
Jacksonville, FL 32206
(904) 355–7001

Islamic Center of Northeast Florida
2333 Saint Johns Bluff Road S
Jacksonville, FL 32246
(904) 646–3462

Jacksonville Masjid of Al-Islam
2242 Commonwealth Avenue
Jacksonville, FL 32209
(904) 358–1969

Islamic Center of Osceola
715 Oak Commons Boulevard
Kissimmee, FL 34741

Darul-Ulum
2350 Old Vineland Road
Kissimmee, FL 34746
(407) 390–1100

Aisha Masjid
1161 Blossom Circle S
Lakeland, FL 33805
(863) 686–4713

Almunineen Masjid
1507 N State Road 7
Margate, FL 33063
(954) 917–9588

Islamic Society of Brevard County
550 E Florida Avenue
Melbourne, FL 32901
(321) 952–2008

Muslim Community Center
7350 NW 3rd Street
Miami, FL 33126
(305) 261–7622

Nigerian Islamic Society Inc.
2410 NW 93rd Street
Miami, FL 33147

United Muslim Organization
10180 SW 168th Street
Miami, FL 33157
(305) 259–0042
masjidalihsan@aol.com

Masjid Al-Ansar
5245 NW 7th Avenue
Miami, FL 33127
(305) 757–8741
yousif3316@yahoo.com

Masjid Annoor
13774 SW 84th Street
Miami, FL 33183
(305) 383–6668

Masjid Miami Gardens
4305 NW 183rd Street
Opa Locka, FL 33055
(305) 624–5555

Islamic Center of Orlando
11543 Ruby Lake Road
Orlando, FL 32836
(407) 238–0266

Islamic Society of Central Florida
1320 N Semoran Boulevard Suite 112
Orlando, FL 32807
(407) 173–8363
iscf@aol.com

Masjid al-Haqq
545 W Central Boulevard
Orlando, FL 32801
(407) 835–9600

Islamic Center of Downtown Orlando
312 S Parramore Avenue
Orlando, FL 32805
(407) 481–4393

Islamic Society of Central Florida
1089 N Goldenrod Road
Orlando, FL 32807
(407) 273–8363
iscf@aol.com

Masjid Al-Rahim
4962 Old Winter Garden Road
Orlando, FL 32811
(407) 523–7882

Masjid Al-Ihsaan
4326 S Semoran Boulevard
Orlando, FL 32822
(407) 381–8203

Bay County Islamic Society
3312 Token Road
Panama City, FL 32405
(850) 785–8085

Islamic Society of Pinellas County
8800 49th Street Suite 304/305
Pinellas Park, FL 33782
(813) 546–3162

Darul Uloom Institute and Islamic
    Center
7020 Hollywood Boulevard
Pmbk Pines, FL 33024
(954) 963–9514

Islamic Center of South Florida
507 NE 6th Street
Pompano Beach, FL 33060
(954) 946–2723

Islamic Community of Southwest Florida
24148 Harbor View Road
Port Charlotte, FL 33980
(941) 625–8855

Islamic Society of Sarasota
4350 N Lockwood Ridge Road
Sarasota, FL 34234
(941) 351–3393

Islamic Center Inc.
PO Box 1779
St Augustine, FL 32085

Masjid Al Muminin
3762 18th Avenue S
St. Petersburg, FL 33711
(727) 327–8483

School of Islamic Studies at Broward
4505 NW 103rd Avenue
Sunrise, FL 33351

Masjid Al Nahal
115 Bragg Drive
Tallahassee, FL 32305
(904) 878–2943

Islamic Education of Tampa
6450 Rockpointe Drive
Tampa, FL 33634
(813) 884–0847

Islamic Community of Tampa
5910 E 130th Avenue
Tampa, FL 33617
(813) 985–9433

The Islamic Society of the Tampa
Bay Area
7326 E Sligh Avenue
Tampa, FL 33610
(813) 628–0007

Masjid Al-Mumin
1101 S Washington Avenue
Titusville, FL 32780

Muslim Community of Palm Beach
County
4893 Purdy Lane
West Palm Beach, FL 33415
(561) 969–1584

Muslim Community of Palm Beach
PO Box 18003
West Palm Beach, FL 33416
(407) 969–1584

Public Affairs Organizations
Institute for Islamic Education and
Research
PO Box 248384
Miami, FL 33124
(305) 666–9590
mtapia@miami.edu

Council on American-Islamic
Relations–Florida
PO Box 245446
Pembroke Pines, FL 33024
(954) 797–7493
florida@Council on American-Islamic
Relations-net.org

Religious Education Programs
Islamic Jaffaria Association Inc.
10554 NW 132nd Street
Hialeah, FL 33018

American Muslim Association of North
America
15969 NW 64th Avenue, #210
Miami, FL 33014
(305) 898–9314

Schools
Nurul-Islam Masjid School
10600 SW 59th Street
Cooper City, FL 33328
(954) 434–3288

Sr. Clara Mohammad School
2242 Commonwealth Avenue
Jacksonville, FL 32209

Melbourne Islamic School
550 E Florida Avenue
Melbourne, FL 32901
(321) 952–2008

Masjid Al-Ansar School
5245 NW 7th Avenue
Miami, FL 33127
(305) 757–8741
yousif3316@yahoo.com

Buena Vista Muslim Academy
Incorporation
11551 Ruby Lake Road
Orlando, FL 32836
(407) 465–1200

Muslim Academy of Central Florida
1021 N Goldenrod Road
Orlando, FL 32807
(407) 382–9900

Al Azhar School
7201 W McNab Road
Tamarac, FL 33321
(954) 722–1555
alazhar@bellsouth.net
www.alazharschool.org

Islamic Academy of Florida
5910 E 130th Avenue
Tampa, FL 33617
(813) 987–9282

Universal Academy of Florida
7320 E Sligh Avenue
Tampa, FL 33610
(813) 664–0695
uaftampa@yahoo.com
www.geocities.com/At hens/8943/

Student Groups
Southwest Florida Muslim Student
Association
14540 Cortez Boulevard Suite 116
Brooksville, FL 34613
(904) 596–7203

Muslim Students Organization–Miami
PO Box 248623
Coral Gables, FL 33124
(305) 598–2295

Muslim Student Association of
University of Florida
1010 W University Avenue
Gainesville, FL 32601
(352) 372–1980
msa@grove.ufl.edu
grove.ufl.edu/~msa

Muslim Students Association
PO Box 338
Goldenrod, FL 32733
(407) 273–8363

Muslim Student Association–University
Central of Florida
PO Box 163240
Orlando, FL 32816
(407) 823–5107

Muslim Student Association Florida
State University
1020 W Pensacola Street
Tallahassee, FL 32304
(904) 681–9022

GEORGIA

Audio / Video Producer
Taqwa Productions Incorporated
PO Box 18211
Atlanta, GA 30316
(404) 378–0306
taqwatv@juno.com

Book Publisher / Distributor
Al Noor Islamic Book Center
420 14th Street NW
Atlanta, GA 30318
(404) 874–5629

Charity Group
Somali Refugee Family Foundation
750 Dalrymple Road NE Apartment D2
Atlanta, GA 30328
(770) 730–5853

Community Development Group
The National Community
1128 Oak Street SW
Atlanta, GA 30310
(404) 758–7016

Ethnic Associations
Bengali Association Pujari Group
4515 Holliston Road
Atlanta, GA 30360
(770) 451–8587
priyadas@msn.com

Afghan Community Foundation, Inc.
PO Box 893
Atlanta, GA 30301
acf1@mail.com

Persian Community Center of Atlanta
6890 Peachtree Industrial Boulevard
Atlanta, GA 30360
(404) 409–8966

Turkish American Cultural Association of
    Georgia
PO Box 190013
Atlanta, GA 31119
(770) 457–8177
tacaga@mindspring.com
www.mindspring.com/~tacaga

Gonja Association of North America
PO Box 403
Lithonia, GA 30058
sibrahim@ba-ld.com
www.geocities.com/Athens/4495/

Halal Food Services
Georgia Halal Consortium
2711 Glenwood Avenue SE
Atlanta, GA 30317
(404) 377–4834

Islamic Legal Services
Shura Law Center
74 Belemonte Circle SW
Atlanta, GA 30311
(404) 755–2303

Mosques / Islamic Centers
Al-Huda Islamic Center Inc.
2022 S Milledge Avenue
Athens, GA 30605
(706) 548–4620

Zainabia Islamic Educational Center
1100 Hope Road
Atlanta, GA 30350
(770) 645–5413
zainabia@hotmail.com

Masjid al-Mujahidden
1281 McPherson Avenue SE
Atlanta, GA 30316
(404) 533–5154

Atlanta Masjid of Al-Islam
560 Fayetteville Road SE
Atlanta, GA 30316
(404) 378–1600

Al-Farooq Masjid of Atlanta
442 14th Street NW
Atlanta, GA 30318
(404) 874–7521
pr@alfarooqmasjid.org.

Community Mosque
547 W End Place SW
Atlanta, GA 30310
(404) 758–7016

Masjid al-Muminun
1127 Hank Aaron Drive SW
Atlanta, GA 30315
(404) 586–9562

Masjid Ahl as Sunnah
1231 Simpson Road NW
Atlanta, GA 30314
(404) 753–5544

Muslim Community Center of Augusta
912 Laney Walker Boulevard
Augusta, GA 30901
(706) 724–9739

The Islamic Society of Augusta
3503 Lost Tree Lane
Augusta, GA 30907

Masjid Al-Momineen of Stone Mountain
837 N Indian Creek Drive
Clarkston, GA 30021
(404) 294–4058

Masjid Al-Noor (WD)
837 5th Avenue
Columbus, GA 31901
(706) 327–1794

Masjid ul Jannah
6550 Forest Road
Columbus, GA 31907
(706) 568–6750
sheik159@aol.com

Muslim Community Center
E Butler Road
Gainesville, GA 30506
(404) 536–5306

Griffin Muslim Center
315 N 3rd Street
Griffin, GA 30223
(404) 228–7924

Bilal Ibn Rabah Islamic Center
120 Hamilton Drive
Lagrange, GA 30240

Masjid as-Nur
2618 Max Cleland Boulevard
Lithonia, GA 30058
(770) 484–8898

Muslim Center
2031 E Napier Avenue
Macon, GA 31204

Islamic Center
4525 Bloomfield Road
Macon, GA 31206
(229) 788–6917

Muhammad Mosque
1695 3rd Street
Macon, GA 31201
(229) 744–0913

Masjid Al-Hedaya
968 Powder Springs Road SW
Marietta, GA 30064
(770) 795–9391

Masjid Al Islam
402 Augusta Drive SE
Marietta, GA 30067
(770) 423–7413

Islamic Society of Augusta
3416 Middleton Drive
Martinez, GA 30907
(706) 868–7278

Masjid Omar Abdul Aziz
955 Harbins Road
Norcross, GA 30093
(770) 279–8606

North Atlanta Islamic Center
6014 Goshen Springs Road
Norcross, GA 30071
(404) 441–2955

Islamic Society
4082 Macedonia Road
Powder Springs, GA 30127

Sahebozzaman Islamic Center
4853 Old Mountain Park Road
Roswell, GA 30075
(770) 642–9411

Masjid Jihad
117 E 34th Street
Savannah, GA 31401
(229) 236–7387

Al-Iman Center
465–C Pat Mell Road SE
Smyrna, GA 30080
(770) 437–9065

Jafari Center
562 Doyal Mills Court
Stone Mountain, GA 30083

Public Affairs Organization
The Ahad Foundation
2221 Peachtree Road NE #D-109
Atlanta, GA 30309
(770) 493–7470
syedn19@mail.idt.net

Schools
Warith Deen Mohammed High School
735 Fayetteville Road SE
Atlanta, GA 30316
(404) 378–4219

West End Primary School
573 W End Place SW
Atlanta, GA 30310
(404) 766–8878

Islamic School Madrassa Al-M
1127 Hank Aaron Drive SW
Atlanta, GA 30315

Dar un Noor School
434 14th Street NW
Atlanta, GA 30318
(404) 876–5051

Social Services
Muslim Social Service
750 Dalrymple Road NE Apartment D2
Atlanta, GA 30328
(770) 730–8157

Student Groups
Muslim Students Association at Emory
3232 Gables Way
Atlanta, GA 30329
(404) 315–8105

Muslim Student Association–Georgia
   Tech
Student Center Program Area
Atlanta, GA 30332
(404) 874–7521

Pakistani Student Association–Georgia
   Tech
Student Services Building
Atlanta, GA 30332
psa@gatech.edu
cyberbuzz.gatech.edu/psa/main.html

Women's Groups
Alnisa
1282 McPherson Avenue SE
Atlanta, GA 30316
(404) 533–5154

al-Muslimah Publishing Co.
480 S Howard Street SE
Atlanta, GA 30317
(404) 377–0104

HAWAII

Ethnic Association
Turkish American Friendship Association
   of Hawaii
1330 Ala Moana Boulevard Apartment
   1506V
Honolulu, HI 96814
(808) 593–0500
turkalp@lava.net

Mosques / Islamic Centers
Muslim Association of Hawaii
1935 Aleo Place
Honolulu, HI 96822
(808) 947–6263
maha@iio.org

IDAHO

Mosques / Islamic Centers
Islamic Center of Moscow
PO Box 4025
Moscow, ID 83843
(208) 882–1590

Student Groups
Muslim Students Association–Boise State
   University
1910 University Drive
Boise, ID 83725
(208) 343–0455

Muslim Students Association–University
   of Idaho
PO Box 4025
Moscow, ID 83843
(208) 882–8312

Muslim Students Association–Idaho
   State University
PO Box 8781
Pocatello, ID 83209
(208) 232–4342

ILLINOIS

Audio / Video Producer
Community Productions
1632 Meyer Street
Elgin, IL 60123
(708) 741–1631

Book Publishers / Distributors
Qur'anic Literacy Institute
PO Box 1467
Bridgeview, IL 60455

W. Deen Mohammed Publications
PO Box 1944
Calumet City, IL 60409
(708) 862–7733

Kazi Publications
3023 W Belmont Avenue
Chicago, IL 60618
(773) 267–7001
kazibook@kazi.org
www.kazi.org

The Qur'an Society
810 73rd Street
Downers Grove, IL 60516
(630) 969–6755

Islamic Society of North America
    International Educational Foundation
7450 Skokie Boulevard
Skokie, IL 60077
(847) 673–4072
iqra@aol.com
www.iqra.org

Charity Groups
Relief International
PO Box 59202
Chicago, IL 60659
(312) 561–6644

The Bosnia Relief Fund, Inc.
PO Box 91825
Elk Grove Village, IL 60009
(708) 616–8223

United Holy Land Fund
6000 W 79th Street Lower Level
Burbank, IL 60459
(708) 430–9731

College
American Islamic College
640 W Irving Park Road
Chicago, IL 60613
(773) 281–4700

Community Development Groups
Islamic Circle of North
    America–Chicago Chapter
PO Box 484
Bellwood, IL 60104
(312) 226–0205

Ministry of Imam W. Deen Mohammed
266 Madison Avenue
Calumet City, IL 60409
(708) 862–5228

Coordination Councils
Council of Islamic Organizations of
    Greater Chicago
7260 W 93rd Street
Bridgeview, IL 60455
(708) 599–3200

Midwest Association of Shia Organized
    Muslims (MASOM)
6111 W Addison Street
Chicago, IL 60634
(773) 283–9718
info@mason.com
www.mason.com

Education Consultants
Islamic Educators Program
212 Deer Creek Road
Rochester, IL 62563
(217) 498–8472

Ethnic Associations
Albanian American Culture Association
5825 Saint Charles Road
Berkeley, IL 60163
(708) 544–2609

Radius of Arab American Writers
PO Box 2164
Bridgeview, IL 60455
idiab@aol.com

Nigeria Islamic Association of United
    States of America
932 W Sheridan Road
Chicago, IL 60613
(773) 665–2451

Bosnian Refugee Center
4750 N Sheridan Road Suite 353
Chicago, IL 60640
(773) 506–1179

Gujarati Muslim Association of America
5806 N Octavia Avenue
Chicago, IL 60631
(312) 775–2254

Arab American Action Network
3148 W 63rd Street
Chicago, IL 60629
(773) 436–6060
aaan@aaan.org

Turkish American Cultural Alliance
3845 N Harlem Avenue
Chicago, IL 60634
(773) 725–3685
info@tacaonline.org
www.tacaonline.org

Turmus Siya Palestine Club
1257 N Milwaukee Avenue Floor 3
Chicago, IL 60622

Ramallah Club
4041 N Francisco Avenue #1
Chicago, IL 60618

Palestinian American Congress
7905 S Cicero Avenue Suite 205
Chicago, IL 60629
(773) 735–7755
www.palpac.org

Consultative Committee of Indian
   Muslims
4380 N Elston Avenue
Chicago, IL 60641

Lifta Association for Charity
PO Box 528247
Chicago, IL 60652
(773) 445–3736

Nigerian Progressive Organization
PO Box 2332
Chicago, IL 60690
www.npo.org

Chicagoland Arab Professionals and
   Students Interactive
6544 S Kilpatrick Avenue
Chicago, IL 60629
(773) 585–0227
khaledesq@aol.com

Ethiopian National Congress
PO Box 59636
Chicago, IL 60659
(623) 561–6625
pr@ethiopiannationalcongress.org

Ethiopian Community Association of
   Chicago
4750 N Sheridan Road Suite 249
Chicago, IL 60640
(773) 728–0303

Palestine Congress of America
5809 Francis Avenue
Countryside, IL 60525

Foundation for Palestinian Culture
1801 Oakton Street
Evanston, IL 60202
(708) 368–0523

Pakistani American Congress
525 Aberdeen Road
Frankfort, IL 60423
(815) 469–8444

Iran House of Greater Chicago
3741 W Morse Avenue
Lincolnwood, IL 60712
(847) 673–0614

Turkish American Association for
   Cultural Exchange
825 Jaipur Avenue
Naperville, IL 60540
(630) 416–9820
faruk_oksuz@parsons.com

Islamic Association for Palestine
10661 S Roberts Road Suite 202
Palos Hills, IL 60465
(708) 974–3380
rafiqjady@aol.com
www.iapinfo.org

Association of Pakistani Physicians of
North America
6414 S Cass Avenue
Westmont, IL 60559
(630) 968–8585
appna@appna.org
www.appna.org/

Guilds
Arab American Association of Engineers
and Architects
PO Box 2160
Bridgeview, IL 60455
(312) 214–0393
aaaea@aaaea.org
www.aaaea.org

Council of American Muslim
Professionals
P.O. Box 543613
Chicago, IL 60654
www.campnet.net

Arab American Bar Association
PO Box 81325
Chicago, IL 60681
(312) 946–0110
arabbar90@aol.com
www.arabbar.org

North American Association of Muslim
Professionals and Scholars
PO Box 6083
Macomb, IL 61455
(309) 298–1326
m-siddiqi@wiu.edu

Jordanian Arab American Business
Association
PO Box 671
Oak Lawn, IL 60454
(708) 599–1300
vojnews@aol.com

American Association of Physicians of
Indian Origin
17W300 22nd Street Suite 300A
Oakbrook Ter, IL 60181
(630) 530–2277
info@aapiusa.org
www.aapiusa.org

Arab American Journalists Association
15139 Windsor Drive
Orland Park, IL 60462
(708) 403–3380
rayhanania@aol.com

Halal Food Services
Islamic Food and Nutrition Council of
America
5901 N Cicero Avenue Suite 309
Chicago, IL 60646
(773) 283–3708
comments@ifanca.org
www.ifanca.org

Muslim Consumer Group
PO Box 8538
Rolling Meadows, IL 60008
(847) 392–8971
halalfood@juno.com

Islamic Call Groups
Institute of Islamic Information and
Education
4390 N Elston Avenue
Chicago, IL 60641
(773) 777–7443
iiie@essm.net
www.iiie.net

National Da'wah Committee of United
States of America
5440 N Sawyer Avenue
Chicago, IL 60625
(318) 478–5997

Islamic Information Center of America
830 Willow Hills Lane #107
Prospect Heights, IL 60070
(847) 541–8141
iica1@home.com
www.iica.org

Mosques / Islamic Centers
Fox Valley Muslim Community
1187 Timberlake Drive
Aurora, IL 60506
(630) 801–7729

Islamic Community of Illinois
8 Ohare Court
Bensenville, IL 60106
(630) 766–6466

Albanian American Islamic Center
5825 Saint Charles Road
Berkeley, IL 60163
(708) 544–2609

Muslim Association of Bolingbrook
593 Piccadilly Lane
Bolingbrook, IL 60440

Mosque Foundation
7360 W 93rd Street
Bridgeview, IL 60455
(708) 430–5666
themosque@aol.com

Islamic Center of Carbondale
511 S Poplar Street
Carbondale, IL 62901
(618) 457–2770
islamic.center511@hotmail.com

Islamic Center of Centralia
224 S Broadway
Centralia, IL 62801
(618) 532–0698
morsy35@yahoo.com

Champaign Masjid
1035 Baytowne Drive
Champaign, IL 61822
(217) 352–5298

Muslim Reading and Study Center
504 E Eureka Street
Champaign, IL 61820
(217) 352–6689

Masajid Umar, Inc.
11405 S Michigan Avenue
Chicago, IL 60628
(312) 821–6221

Northside Mosque
1017 W Roscoe Street
Chicago, IL 60657
(312) 935–9786

Chicago Islamic Center
3357 W 63rd Street
Chicago, IL 60629
(708) 906–7405
abubaidah@hotmail.com

Masajid Umar of North America
11365 S Forest Avenue
Chicago, IL 60628
(312) 821–6221

Masjid Noor
6151 N Greenview Avenue
Chicago, IL 60660
(773) 743–9364

Al-Ansaar Masjid
2506 W 63rd Street
Chicago, IL 60629
(312) 778–5614

Masjid Al-Fatir
1200 E 47th Street
Chicago, IL 60653
(312) 268–7248

Downtown Islamic Center
218 S Wabash Avenue
Chicago, IL 60604
(630) 961–0705

Masjid Muhammad
7351 S Stony Island Avenue
Chicago, IL 60649

Jamia Masjid
6340 N Campbell Avenue
Chicago, IL 60659
(312) 743–9364

Al Shaheed Mosque
5135 S Carpenter Street
Chicago, IL 60609
(312) 373–0189

Wallen Masjid and Madrasah
1709 W Wallen Avenue
Chicago, IL 60626
(312) 764–8056

Ephraim Bahar Cultural Center
2525 W 71st Street
Chicago, IL 60629
(773) 476–8825

Muslim Community Center
4380 N Elston Avenue
Chicago, IL 60641
(312) 725–9047
iiie@essm.net

Inner City Islamic Center
5301 S Justine Street
Chicago, IL 60609
(773) 768–5136

Islamic Center of Chicago
4035 N Damen Avenue
Chicago, IL 60618
(312) 989–9330

Al-Haqqain Community Center
461 83rd Street
Chicago, IL 60649
(773) 768–1879

Masjid Al-Latif
5033 N Clark Street
Chicago, IL 60640
(773) 293–2387

Asr Islamic Dawab Center
3847 W Flournoy Street
Chicago, IL 60624

Masjid Wali Hasan
1807 N Edward Street
Decatur, IL 62526
(217) 827–2963
kursdr@webtv.net

Islamic Community Center of Des
   Plaines
480 Potter Road
Des Plaines, IL 60016
(847) 824–1100

Islamic Community Center
345 Heine Avenue
Elgin, IL 60123
(847) 695–3338

Elmhurst Group
621 N Michigan Street
Elmhurst, IL 60126
(312) 530–4070

Center of Islamic Education
PO Box 834
Elmhurst, IL 60126
(708) 941–9255

American Islamic Association
8860 W Saint Francis Road
Frankfort, IL 60423
(815) 469–1551

Islamic Education Center
2N121 Goodrich Avenue
Glendale Heights, IL 60139
(630) 469–5533
najafi@hotmail.com

Muslim Society Inc.
1785 Bloomingdale Road
Glendale Hts, IL 60139
(630) 893–7860

South Suburban Islamic Center
15200 Broadway Avenue
Harvey, IL 60426
(708) 331–4165

Harvey Islamic Center
15406 Turlington Avenue
Harvey, IL 60426
(708) 333–1823

Islamic Foundation North
PO Box 7284
Libertyville, IL 60048
(847) 604–2365

Islamic Center of Macomb
334 W Wheeler Street
Macomb, IL 61455
(309) 833–3875

Islamic Center of Quad Cities
3061 7th Street Suite C
Moline, IL 61265
(309) 762–0768

Islamic Center of Naperville
450 Olesen Drive
Naperville, IL 60540
(630) 983–4210

Bosnian American Cultural Association
1810 Pfingsten Road
Northbrook, IL 60062
(847) 272–0319

Islamic Center
120 E High Point Road
Peoria, IL 61614

Muslim Education and Community
   Association
817 W Armstrong Avenue
Peoria, IL 61606

Islamic Foundation of Peoria
2200 W Altorfer Drive Suite B
Peoria, IL 61615
(309) 691–8195
amfmmalik@prodigy.net

Islamic Society of Peoria
1716 N North Street
Peoria, IL 61604
(309) 688–4605

Naqshbandi Foundation for Islamic
   Education
PO Box 3526
Peoria, IL 61612
(309) 655–7979

Muslim Community Center of Greater
   Rockford
5921 Darlene Drive
Rockford, IL 61109
(815) 397–3311
mccrockford@hotmail.com

Muslim Association
3458 Sage Drive
Rockford, IL 61114

Islamic Society of Northwest Suburbs of
   Chicago
3890 Industrial Avenue
Rolling Meadows, IL 60008
(847) 776–5902

Midwest Islamic Center
1081 W Irving Park Road
Schaumburg, IL 60193
(708) 894–9650

Central Illinois Mosque and Islamic
   Center
106 S Lincoln Avenue
Urbana, IL 61801
(217) 344–1555
cimic@prairienet.org

Islamic Foundation–Villa Park
300 W Highridge Road
Villa Park, IL 60181
(630) 782–6562

Al-Huda Center
38622 N Sheridan Road
Waukegan, IL 60087
(847) 244–8920

Islamic Cultural Center
848 North Avenue
Waukegan, IL 60085
(847) 249–4069

Periodical
Voice of Islam Newsletter
300 W Highridge Road
Villa Park, IL 60181

Prison Outreach Groups
Islamic Prison Outreach
10326 S Hoyne Avenue
Chicago, IL 60643
(773) 445–3516
booksink@email.msn.com

Islamic Correctional Reunion Association
PO Box 774
Tinley Park, IL 60477
(708) 429–1985
mafardausi @juno.com
islam-correctional.org

Public Affairs Organizations
Muslim Americans for Civil Rights and
   Legal Defense
7260 W 93rd Street
Bridgeview, IL 60455
(708) 829–8786

American Muslim Alliance–Midwest
6246 N Western Avenue Suite 1
Chicago, IL 60659
(773) 507–5335
director@ama-midwest.org
www.ama-midwest.org

Arab American Anti-Discrimination
    Committee–Chicago
6815 W 95th Street
Oak Lawn, IL 60453
(708) 974–3655

Arab American Institute–Chicago
4700 W 95th Street Floor 2
Oak Lawn, IL 60453
(708) 952–0274

Religious Education Programs
Islamic Guidance Society
7735 Lotus Avenue
Burbank, IL 60459
(618) 529–5960

American Islamic Association
8860 W Saint Francis Road
Frankfort, IL 60423
(815) 469–1551

Islamic Foundation
356 Brainerd Avenue
Libertyville, IL 60048
(414) 552–8239
khaliqbutt@hotmail.com

Muslim Association
122 W Coventry Lane
Peoria, IL 61614
(309) 745–8410

Schools
Universal School
7360 W 93rd Street
Bridgeview, IL 60455
(708) 599–4100
universalschool@aol.com
www.universalschool.org

Ramallah Arabic School–Chicago
2700 N Central Avenue
Chicago, IL 60639
(773) 237–2727

Islamic African-American Historical
    Academy
10326 S Hoyne Avenue
Chicago, IL 60643
(773) 445–3516
booksink@email.msn.com

Islamic Open School
P.O. Box 53398
Chicago, IL 60653

Muslim Society Inc. School
1785 Bloomingdale Road
Glendale Hts, IL 60139
(630) 893–7860

College Preparatory School of Illinois
331 W Madison Street
Lombard, IL 60148
(708) 889–8000
cpsaer@muslims.net
www.muslims.net/cpsa

Muslim Community Center Elementary
    School
8601 Menard Avenue
Morton Grove, IL 60053
(847) 470–8801
mmecc@msn.com

Bosnian American Cultural Association
1810 Pfingsten Road
Northbrook, IL 60062
(847) 272–0319

Islamic Academy
PO Box 754
Skokie, IL 60076
(313) 665–8882

Islamic Foundation School
300 W Highridge Road
Villa Park, IL 60181
(708) 941–8800
ifvp@islamicfoundationvp.org
www.geocities.com/soho/museum/5225

Social Services

Muslim American Community
Assistance Fund
PO Box 1061
Calumet City, IL 60409
(708) 862–5228

Inner City Muslim Action Network
3344 West 63rd Street
Chicago, IL 60629
(773) 434–4626
iman@imancentral.org
www.imancentral.org

Muhammad Ali Foundation
1136 E 49th Street
Chicago, IL 60615

Student Groups

Muslim Student Association of
Carbondale
419 S Washington Street #1
Carbondale, IL 62901
(618) 529–9560

United Muslims Moving Ahead–DePaul
University
2320 N Kenmore Avenue
Chicago, IL 60614
(312) 363–0917

Muslim Students Association—Harold
Washington College
30 E Lake Street
Chicago, IL 60601
(312) 553–5600

Muslim Students Association–Northeast
Illinois University
5500 N Saint Louis Avenue
Chicago, IL 60625
(312) 583–2259

Muslim Women's Association-University
of Illinois
3115 N Sawyer Avenue
Chicago, IL 60618
(312) 996–7000

Muslim Students Association at
University of Illinois
750 S. Halstead 300 CCC
Chicago, IL 60607
(312) 455–0336

Muslim Students Association–East West
University
816 S Michigan Avenue
Chicago, IL 60605
(312) 939–0111
chancellor@eastwest.edu

Islamic Society of Northern Illinois
University
721 Normal Road
Dekalb, IL 60115
(815) 756–9640
isniu@hotmail.com

Muslim Student Association–Southern
Illinois University at Edwardsville
PO Box 1168
Edwardsville, IL 62026
(618) 692–5492

Muslim Students
Association–Northwestern University
1999 Sheridan Road
Evanston, IL 60607

Muslim Cultural Students Association
1936 Sheridan Road Suite B5
Evanston, IL 60208
(847) 467–5739
t-salikuddin@nwu.edu
www.studorg.nwu.edu/mcsa

Muslim Student Association of
Naperville
420 Prairie Knoll Drive
Naperville, IL 60565
(630) 961–1815
nabilattaya@yahoo.com

Islamic Student Society of Bradley
University
1315 W Main Street
Peoria, IL 61606
(309) 673–5117

Muslim Student Association–University
of Illinois
106 S Lincoln Avenue
Urbana, IL 61801
(217) 344–6667

Sufi Group
The Jerrahi Order of Illinois
612 Hannah Street
Bloomington, IL 61701
(309) 828–6599

Women's Groups
Midwest Muslim Women's Association
1448 E 52nd Street #204
Chicago, IL 60615
(312) 268–8070

Arab American Ladies Society
8926 Oakdale Court
Orland Park, IL 60462

Youth Groups
National Islamic Committee on Scouting
PO Box 64863
Chicago, IL 60664

Young Men's Muslim Association
1154 Brighton Street
Glen Ellyn, IL 60137
(708) 790–9205

Muslim Youth of Chicago
5228 Fargo Avenue
Skokie, IL 60077
(847) 933–9695

INDIANA

Audio / Video Producer
Islamic Society of North America Vision
PO Box 38
Plainfield, IN 46168

Charity Group
Somali Relief Fund
PO Box 51534
Indianapolis, IN 46251
(317) 839–7563

Community Development Group
Islamic Society of North America
PO Box 38
Plainfield, IN 46168
(317) 839–8157
info@isna.net
www.isna.net

Coordination Council
Council Islamic Schools in North
America
PO Box 38
Plainfield, IN 46168
(317) 839–8157

Ethnic Association
American Jordanian Social Center
7130 Belmont Avenue
Hammond, IN 46324

Guild
Association of Muslim Scientists and
Engineers
PO Box 38
Plainfield, IN 46168
(313) 593–5028

Mosques / Islamic Centers
Angola Islamic Center
PO Box 191
Angola, IN 46703

Bloomington Islamic Center
1925 E Atwater Avenue
Bloomington, IN 47401
(812) 333–1611
islam@indiana.edu

Northwest Indiana Islamic Center
9803 Colorado Street
Crown Point, IN 46307
(219) 756–7622

Islamic Society of Michiana
25831 Lily Creek Drive
Elkhart, IN 46514
(219) 291–4236

Islamic Society of Evansville
1332 Lincoln Avenue #8055
Evansville, IN 47714
(812) 425–9801

Al-Fatihah Dawah Center
511 E Leith Street
Fort Wayne, IN 46806
(219) 456–6826

Islamic Center of Fort Wayne
1111 Chute Street
Fort Wayne, IN 46803
(219) 423–2432
islam1usa@aol.com

Masjid-Al-Amin
3702 W 11th Avenue
Gary, IN 46404

Gary Muslim Center
1473 W 15th Avenue
Gary, IN 46407
(219) 885–3018

Nur Allah Islamic Center
2040 E 46th Street
Indianapolis, IN 46205
(317) 251–9796

Islamic Society of Greater Indianapolis
    Islamic Center
PO Box 51623
Indianapolis, IN 46251
(317) 839–8157

Indianapolis Muslim Communtiy
    Association
2846 Cold Spring Road
Indianapolis, IN 46222
(317) 923–2847

Masjid Muhammad
2405 N College Avenue
Indianapolis, IN 46205

Islamic Center of Michigan City
PO Box 710
Michigan City, IN 46361
(219) 879–9667

Islamic Center of Greater Indianapolis
PO Box 38
Plainfield, IN 46168
(317) 839–8157

South Bend Islamic Dawah Center
PO Box 3678
South Bend, IN 46619
(219) 272–0569

Great News Islamic Center
431 Dundee Street
South Bend, IN 46619
(317) 233–7933

Valparaiso Islamic Community Center
402 Sturdy Road Apartment 1A
Valparaiso, IN 46383

Public Affairs Organization
Islamic Media Foundation
6742 Dunn Way
Indianapolis, IN 46241
(317) 240–4200

Schools
Islamic School of Fort Wayne
1117 Lagro Drive
Fort Wayne, IN 46804
(219) 432–6605

Al-Amin School
PO Box 4797
Gary, IN 46404
(219) 949–1854

Madrassa-Tul-Ilm
2846 Cold Spring Road
Indianapolis, IN 46222
(317) 923–0328

Student Groups
Muslim Students Association of
    IUPUI
2846 Cold Spring Road
Indianapolis, IN 46222
(317) 925–0682

Islamic Student Association–Ball State
    University
1717 N Ball Avenue
Muncie, IN 47304
(317) 288–8014

Muslim Students Association
PO Box 38
Plainfield, IN 46168
(317) 839–8157

Muslim Students Association–Terre
    Haute University
1319 S 6th Street
Terre Haute, IN 47802
(812) 237–7562

Muslim Students Association–Purdue
    University Masjid
1022 1st Street
W Lafayette, IN 47906
(317) 743–8650

Trust / Endowment
North American Islamic Trust
2622 E Main Street
Plainfield, IN 46168
(317) 839–9248

Youth Group
Muslim Youth of North
    America–National
19921 Overlook Circle
Lawrenceburg, IN 47025

IOWA

Coordination Council
Islamic Council of Iowa
PO Box 5813
Cedar Rapids, IA 52406
(319) 366–0473

Ethnic Association
Friends of Nigeria
1203 Cambria Court
Iowa City, IA 52246
(319) 351–3375
pjhansen@ia.net
www.ultranet.com/~gregjonz/fon/

Halal Food Services
Islamic Services
1105 60th Avenue SW
Cedar Rapids, IA 52404
(319) 362–3711

Mosques / Islamic Centers
Muslim Community of the Quad Cities
2115 Kimberly Road
Bettendorf, IA 52722
(319) 243–8421

Islamic Cultural Center
1335 9th Street NW
Cedar Rapids, IA 52405
(319) 366–3150

Islamic Center of Iowa
PO Box 213
Cedar Rapids, IA 52406

Islamic Center of Cedar Rapids
2999 1st Avenue SW
Cedar Rapids, IA 52405
(319) 362–0857

Islamic Society of Clinton County
3223 Tower Court
Clinton, IA 52732
(319) 243–8421

Muslim Community Organization
1087 25th Street
Des Moines, IA 50311
(515) 277–7111

Islamic Center of Des Moines
6201 Franklin Avenue
Des Moines, IA 50322
(515) 255–0212

Masjid Muhammad
1430 University Avenue
Des Moines, IA 50314

Islamic Society of Iowa City
PO Box 1502
Iowa City, IA 52244
(319) 354–6167
mabhatti@uiowa.edu

Masjid Al Noor Islamic Community
    Center
728 W 2nd Street
Waterloo, IA 50701
(319) 233–2671

Student Group
Muslim Students Association–Iowa State
    University
1221 Michigan Avenue
Ames, IA 50014
(515) 292–3683

KANSAS

Mosques / Islamic Centers
Islamic Center of Lawrence
1917 Naismith Drive
Lawrence, KS 66046
(785) 749–1638

Islamic Center of Manhattan
1224 Hylton Heights Road
Manhattan, KS 66502

Islamic Center of Topeka
1117 SE 27th Street
Topeka, KS 66605
(785) 478–4930
shorty4272.com

Masjid Muhammad
1007 Cleveland Street
Wichita, KS 67214

Islamic Society of Wichita
3104 E 17th Street N
Wichita, KS 67214
(316) 687–4946

Islamic Association of Mid-Kansas
3406 Taft Street
Wichita, KS 67213
(316) 945–0472

School
Annoor Islamic School
PO Box 21272
Wichita, KS 67208
(316) 686–5152
annoor@noornet.com
www.noornet.com

KENTUCKY

Audio / Video Producer
Sounds of Ultimate Life
PO Box 11582
Lexington, KY 40576

Mosques / Islamic Centers
Masjid Al-Karim
336 Byrd Street
Covington, KY 41011
(606) 491–5986

Muslim Community Center
940 Whitney Avenue
Lexington, KY 40508

Masjid Bilal Ibn Rabah
572 Georgetown Street
Lexington, KY 40508
(606) 255–9374

Islamic Society of Lexington
649 South Limestone Street
Lexington, KY 40508
(859) 255–0335

Islamic Center of Louisville
1715 S 4th Street
Louisville, KY 40208
(502) 634–1395

Islamic Cultural Association of Louisville
1911 Buechel Bank Road
Louisville, KY 40218
(502) 499–0334

Abdullah Muhammed Islamic Center
1917 Magazine Street
Louisville, KY 40203
(502) 774–3208

Faisal Mosque
4007 River Road
Louisville, KY 40207
(502) 893–9466

Islamic Center of Eastern Kentucky
684 Big Branch of Abbott
Prestonsburg, KY 41653
(606) 889–0626
icek786@hotmail.com

Schools
An-Nur Islamic School of Louisville
1911 Buechel Bank Road
Louisville, KY 40218
(502) 459–9447
nanang01@gwise.louisville.edu

Sr. Clara Muhammed School
1917 Magazine Street
Louisville, KY 40203
(502) 772–7076

Student Groups
Muslim Students Association University
    of Kentucky
649 S Limestone Street
Lexington, KY 40508
(606) 255–0335

Muslim Students Association–Louisville
1715 S 4th Street
Louisville, KY 40208
(502) 534–1395

LOUISIANA

Ethnic Associations
Turkish American Association of
    Louisiana
PO Box 55112
Metaire, LA 70055
(504) 461–8018
taalouisS@hotmail.com

Organization of Nigerian Professionals
PO Box 29524
New Orleans, LA 70189
(919) 255–1771
www.onp-usa.org

Mosques / Islamic Centers
Islamic Association of Arabi
7527 W Judge Perez Drive
Arabi, LA 70032
(504) 277–9222
akhan272@aol.com

Islamic Complex
740 E Washington Street
Baton Rouge, LA 70802

Islamic Center of Baton Rouge
820 W Chimes Street
Baton Rouge, LA 70802
(225) 387–3617
icbr@webrouge.com

Muslim Community Center
5684 Packard Street
Baton Rouge, LA 70811

West Bank Muslim Association
448 Realty Drive
Gretna, LA 70056
(504) 392–3425

Islamic Society of Lake Charles
4320 Auburn Street
Lake Charles, LA 70607
(337) 474–4519

Jefferson Muslim Association
4425 David Drive
Metairie, LA 70003
(504) 887–5365

Masjid Muhammad
2414 Oak Street
Monroe, LA 71201
(318) 387–8596

New Orleans Masjid of Al-Islam
2626 Magnolia Street #32
New Orleans, LA 70113
(504) 895–6731

Bilal Ibn Rabah Islamic Center
1401 Teche Street
New Orleans, LA 70114
(504) 367–5322

Masjidur-Rahim
1238 N Johnson Street #40
New Orleans, LA 70116
(504) 827–0017

New Orleans Islamic Center
1911 Saint Claude Avenue
New Orleans, LA 70116
(504) 944–3758

Islamic Center of North Louisiana
203 S Homer Street
Ruston, LA 71270
(318) 255–6902
alsharek@alphao.gram.edu

Masjid Ul-Taqwa
2510 Morningside Drive
Shreveport, LA 71108
(318) 636–1215

Islamic Association of Greater Shreveport
3769 Youree Drive
Shreveport, LA 71105
(318) 861–7990

Islamic Center of Greater Shreveport
PO Box 52433
Shreveport, LA 71135
(318) 861–7990

Slidell Masjid al-Islam
37482 Brownsvillage Road
Slidell, LA 70460
(504) 649–3693

Islamic Society of Lake Charles
501 Miller Avenue
Westlake, LA 70669
(318) 439–3783

Schools
Brighter Horizon School
1896 Wooddale Boulevard
Baton Rouge, LA 70806
(504) 927–2521
bhsbr@yahoo.com
www.webrouge.com/bhs/

Abu Bakr al-Sideeq
4425 David Drive
Metairie, LA 70003
(504) 887–5365

Sr. Clara Muhammed School
2700 Magnolia Street
New Orleans, LA 70113
(504) 895–6731

Student Group
Muslim Students Association–Louisiana
    State University
820 W Chimes Street Suite 100
Baton Rouge, LA 70802
(504) 387–3617

Muslim Students Association–University
    of N.E. Louisiana
1700 165 S. Bypass
Monroe, LA 71202

Muslim Students Association–Tulane
    University
7103 Burthe Street
New Orleans, LA 70118
(504) 866–3879

Muslim Students Association University
    of New Orleans
6244 Waldo Drive
New Orleans, LA 70148
(504) 282–0700

Muslim Students Association–Ruston
203 S Homer Street
Ruston, LA 71270
(318) 255–6902

Muslim Students Association–Southern
    New Orleans University
PO Box 3218
Slidell, LA 70459
(504) 649–3194

MAINE

Mosques / Islamic Centers
Islamic Center of Maine
PO Box 267
Orono, ME 04473
(207) 942–1930
ikhuwa31@maine.maine.edu

Islamic Society of Portland, Maine
PO Box 10294
Portland, ME 04104
(207) 934–7812

MARYLAND

Book Publisher / Distributor
Amana Publications
10710 Tucker Street
Beltsville, MD 20705
(301) 595–5777
igamana@erols.com
www.amana-publications.com

Ethnic Associations
Iranian American Cultural Association
PO Box 71171
Bethesda, MD 20813
(301) 656–4222

Maryland Turkish American Association
10176 Baltimore National Pike Suite 211
Ellicott City, MD 21042
(410) 750–7735
mfomer@aol.com

Association of Indian Muslims
11649 Masters Run
Ellicott City, MD 21042

Indonesian Muslim Association in
America
13113 Holdridge Road
Silver Spring, MD 20906

Rediscover Iran
13115 Ideal Drive
Silver Spring, MD 20906
(301) 962–1581

Eritrean Development Foundation
911 Silver Spring Avenue Suite 202
Silver Spring, MD 20910
(301) 589–9440
Nuhad@edfonline.org

The Iranian American Cultural Society of
Maryland
PO Box 9844
Towson, MD 21284
(410) 720–4507
mjahangiri@v2pop.hst.nasa.gov

American Turkish Association of
Washington, D.C.
205 E Joppa Road Apartment 2105
Towson, MD 21286
(410) 828–8222
gkarahasan@aol.com
www.ata-dc.org

Guilds
Nigerian Professional Network
PO Box 426
Columbia, MD 21045
npnetwork@npnetwork-inc.org
www.npnetwork-inc.org

Ethiopian Pharmacists Association in
North America
13208 Bellevue Street
Silver Spring, MD 20904
(202) 806–4214
bhailemesekl@howard.edu

Halal Food Services
Islamic Center for Halal Certification
14660 Good Hope Road
Silver Spring, MD 20905
(240) 350–6909

Mosques / Islamic Centers
Masjid Al-Inshirah
6004 Liberty Road
Baltimore, MD 21207
(410) 669–0655

Masjid As-Saffat
1335 W North Avenue
Baltimore, MD 21217
(410) 669–0655

Jammat al-Muslimeen
4624 York Road
Baltimore, MD 21212
(410) 435–4046

Islamic Society of Baltimore
6631 Johnnycake Road
Baltimore, MD 21244
(410) 747–4869
info@isb.org

Ummat West
500 N Caroline Street
Baltimore, MD 21205
(410) 276–0306

An-Nur Foundation of Maryland Inc.
10012 Harford Road
Baltimore, MD 21234
(410) 663–9637

Masjid Ul-Haqq
514 Islamic Way
Baltimore, MD 21217
(410) 728–1363
ahakim@msn.com

Muslim American Society of Baltimore
3401 W North Avenue
Baltimore, MD 21216
(410) 945–0413

Dar-Adh-Dhikr Masjid
4323 Rosedale Avenue
Bethesda, MD 20814
(301) 951–0539

Mosque Emmanuel
12804 5th Street
Bowie, MD 20720
(301) 262–1146

Dar-us-Salam
5301 Edgewood Road
College Park, MD 20740
(301) 982–9848
safi@alhuda.org

Dar Al-Taqwa
10740 Route 108
Ellicott City, MD 21042
(410) 997–5711

Islamic Community Center of
    Gaithersburg
18404 Flower Hill Way
Gaithersburg, MD 20879
(301) 977–6614

Islamic Center of Maryland
19401 Woodfield Road
Gaithersburg, MD 20879
(301) 840–9440

Germantown Mosque of Maryland, Inc.
PO Box 543
Germantown, MD 20875
(301) 972–5510

Masjid Taqwa An Nur
8000 Martin Luther King Jr. Highway
Glenarden, MD 20706
(301) 772–5969

Islamic Soceity of Western Maryland
2036 Day Road
Hagerstown, MD 21740
(301) 797–0922

House Al-Touba
7604 Wells Boulevard
Hyattsville, MD 20783
(301) 422–8440
alaa@cheerful.com

Prince George's Muslim Association
9150 Lanham-Severn Road
Lanham, MD 20706
(301) 459–4588

Turkish American Islamic Foundation
9704 Good Luck Road
Lanham, MD 20706
(301) 459–9589

Islamic Community Center of Laurel
7306 Contee Road
Laurel, MD 20707
(301) 317–4584

Southern Maryland Islamic Center
PO Box 3366
Prince Frederick, MD 20678
(301) 535–0000

Islamic Society of Del Marva
PO Box 2053
Salisbury, MD 21802
(410) 341–4023

Islamic Society of Maryland
601 E Franklin Avenue
Silver Spring, MD 20901
(301) 588–3650

Muslim Community Center
15200 New Hampshire Avenue
Silver Spring, MD 20905
(301) 384–3454

Islamic Society of Washington Area
2701 Briggs Chaney Road
Silver Spring, MD 20905
(301) 879–0390

Newspaper
New Trend
PO Box 356
Kingsville, MD 21087

Public Affairs Organization
Minaret of Freedom Institute
4323 Rosedale Avenue
Bethesda, MD 20814
(301) 907–0947
mfi@minaret.org
www.minaret.org

Pakistani American Physicians Public
    Affairs Committee
7610 Carroll Avenue Suite 310
Takoma Park, MD 20912

Religious Education Software
ISL Software Corporation
1102 Gresham Road
Silver Spring, MD 20904
(301) 622–3915
fare@islsoftware
www.islsoftware.com

Research Group
Center for the Study of Islam and
    Democracy
PO Box 864
Burtonsville, MD 20866
(202) 251–3036
feedback@islam-democracy.org
www.islam-democracy.org

Schools
Al-Rahmah School
6631 Johnnycake Road
Baltimore, MD 21244
(410) 747–4869
info@isb.org

Al-Huda School
5301 Edgewood Road
College Park, MD 20740
(301) 982–2402
obeid@alhuda.org
www.alhuda.org

Prince George's Muslim Association
    School
9150 Lanham Severn Road
Lanham, MD 20706
(301) 459–4942

Muslim Community School
7917 Montrose Road
Potomac, MD 20854
(301) 340–6713
www.muslimcommunityschool.com

Islamic Academy of Maryland
    Community College
15200 New Hampshire Avenue
Silver Spring, MD 20905
(301) 384–3454

Social Services
Fast to Feed
PO Box 10881
Baltimore, MD 21234

Islamic-American Zakat Foundation
4323 Rosedale Avenue
Bethesda, MD 20814
(301) 907–0997
zakat@iazf.org

Muslim Inter-Community Network
6911 Carlynn Court
Bethesda, MD 20817
(301) 229–6549

Turkish Children Foster Care
730 Ticonderoga Avenue
Severna Park, MD 21146
(410) 647–1315
mutlu@erols.com

Student Groups
Johns Hopkins Muslim Association
500 W University Parkway Apartment
5R
Baltimore, MD 21210
(410) 467–1154

Muslim Student Association–University
of Maryland
7604 Wells Boulevard
Hyattsville, MD 20783
(301) 699–9512

Muslim Students Association Council of
Greater Washington, D.C.
15009 Newcomb Lane
Mitchellville, MD 20716
(202) 244–5091

MASSACHUSETTS

Cemetery
United Lebanese Cemetery
250 Hampshire Street
Lawrence, MA 01841
(978) 683–5416

Coordination Councils
Islamic Association of Massachusetts
Masjid
538 Broadway
Everett, MA 02149
(617) 381–6666

Islamic Council of New England
4 Larkspur Road
Needham, MA 02492
(617) 479–8341

Education Consultant
Essential Education Services
108 Lakeside Street
Springfield, MA 01109
(413) 782–9670

Ethnic Association
Turkish American Cultural Society of
New England, Inc. (TACS–NE)
PO Box 1308
Boston, MA 02104
(617) 536–4418
tacs@world.std.com
www.world.std.com/~tacs

Iranian Association of Boston
PO Box 64
Newtonville, MA 02460
(617) 964–1498
president@kanooniran.com

Pakistan Association of Greater Boston
PO Box 412
Wayland, MA 01778
info@pagb.org
www.pagb.org/pagbweb/

Homeschoolers' Association
Muslim Home School Network and
Resource
PO Box 803
Attleboro, MA 02703
(508) 226–1638

Matrimonial Services
Soul Mates
PO Box 1104
Allston, MA 02134
(617) 787–2062

Mosques / Islamic Centers
Masjid Al Quran
35 Intervale Street
Boston, MA 02121
(617) 427–6930

Cambridge Islamic Society
204 Prospect Street
Cambridge, MA 02139
(617) 445–2345

Islamic Society of Greater Lowell
131 Steadman Street
Chelmsford, MA 01824
(978) 970–5552

Islamic Ma'sumeen Center of New
England
115 Wood Street
Hopkinton, MA 01748
(508) 497–3462

Islamic Society at Taft
PO Box 604
Medford, MA 02155
(617) 629–8820

Selimiye Camii Mosque
105 Oakland Avenue
Methuen, MA 01844
(978) 975–4593

Islamic Center of New England
470 South Street
Quincy, MA 02169
(617) 479–8341
talaleid@juno.com

Society of Islamic Brotherhood
724 Shawmut Avenue
Roxbury, MA 02119
(617) 442–2805

Mosque of New England
PO Box 222
Seekonk, MA 02771
(508) 336–9040

Islamic Center of New England
74 Chase Drive
Sharon, MA 02067
(781) 784–9897

Masjid At-Tawhid
111 Oak Street
Springfield, MA 01109
(413) 782–0929

Masjid Al-Baqie
495 Union Street
Springfield, MA 01109
(413) 732–9288

Islamic Society of Western Massachusetts
PO Box 477
West Springfield, MA 01090
(413) 788–7546

Wentworth Islamic Society
131 Coolidge Avenue Apartment 526
Watertown, MA 02472
(617) 581–3193

Islamic Center of Boston
126 Boston Post Road
Wayland, MA 01778
(508) 358–5885

Islamic Society of Greater Worcester
57 Laurel Street
Worcester, MA 01605
(508) 752–4377

Public Affairs Organization
American Muslim Political Alliance of
Massachusetts
182 Jenkins Road
Andover, MA 01810
(508) 664–1688

Schools
Al-Hamra Academy Elementary School
230 SW Cutoff Unit 4
Northborough, MA 01532
(508) 393–0171
alhamra@ultranet.com

Nur Academy
470 South Street
Quincy, MA 02169
(617) 479–8341

Islamic Academy of New England
84 Chase Drive
Sharon, MA 02067
(781) 784–0519
iane@ia-ne.org
www.ia-ne.org

Social Services
Islamic Multi Service Organization
1293 Commonwealth Avenue
Apartment 5
Allston, MA 02134
(617) 442–2805
natalia_crayton@hotmail.com

Student Groups

Muslim Students Association of Amherst
919 Campus Center
Amherst, MA 01003
(413) 546–4523

Islamic Society of Boston University
Chapter
Geroge Sherman Union
785 Commonwealth Avenue
Boston, MA 02215

Islamic Society of Northeastern
University–Muslim Students
Association
360 Huntington Avenue
Boston, MA 02115
(617) 437–2729

Al-Muslimat Student Organization
Schneider Center Wellesley College
Wellesley, MA 02181
(617) 283–7070

Muslim Students Association–Worcester
Polytech University
100 Institute Road
Worcester, MA 01609
(508) 831–5291

Sufi Group

Nimatullahi Sufi Order
84 Pembroke Street
Boston, MA 02118
(617) 536–0076

TV Program

Arabic Lebanese News Line
14 Cedarcrest Road
West Roxbury, MA 02132
(617) 469–9133

Youth Group

Muslim Youth of New England
10 Bradford Road
Framingham, MA 01701
(617) 283–7070

MICHIGAN

Charity Group

Mercy–United States of America for Aid
and Development
44450 Pinetree Drive Suite 201
Plymouth, MI 48170
(734) 454–0011
info@mercyusa.org
www.mercyusa.org

International Relief Association
17300 W 10 Mile Road
Southfield, MI 48075
(810) 772–2357
reliefusa@aol.com
www.ira-usa.org

Community Development Group

Islamic Circle of North America
Chapter
12309 McDougall Street
Detroit, MI 48212
(313) 366–6800

Ethnic Associations

Bint Jebail Cultural Center
6220 Miller Road
Dearborn, MI 48126

Iraqi Islamic Association of America
PO Box 7211
Dearborn, MI 48121
(313) 747–7433

Arab American Young Professionals
PO Box 428
Dearborn Heights, MI 48127
turklaw@yahoo.com

Arab American Cultural Society
1101 Washington Boulevard #415
Detroit, MI 48226

Nigerian Reunion Committee
PO Box 441891
Detroit, MI 48244
nrcmember@nrc-inc.org
www.nrc-inc.org

Pakistani American Congress
29482 W 10 Mile Road
Farmington Hills, MI 48336
(248) 474–3335
information@pakamrcongress.org
www.pakamrcongress.com

American Federation of Muslims from
    India
29008 W 8 Mile Road
Farmington Hills, MI 48336
(810) 442–2364

American Arab Heritage Council
PO Box 8032
Flint, MI 48501
(810) 235–2722

Lebanese American Katayeb Chapter
37209 Maas Drive
Sterling Hts, MI 48312
(810) 979–7477

Lebanese American Club of Michigan
26079 Schoenherr Road
Warren, MI 48089
(810) 758–2822

American Federation of Ramallah
    Palestine
27484 Ann Arbor Trail
Westland, MI 48185
(734) 425–1600

Turkish American Cultural Association of
    Michigan (TACAM)
28847 Beck Road
Wixom, MI 48393
(248) 348–4176
tacam@tacam.org
www.tacam.org

Guilds
National Arab American Medical
    Association
801 S Adams Road Suite 208
Birmingham, MI 48009
(248) 646–3661
naamausa@aol.com
www.naama.com

Arab American Chamber of Commerce
4917 Schaefer Road Suite 215
Dearborn, MI 48126
(313) 945–6697
nbeydoun@americanarab.com
www.americanarab.com

Turkish American Neuropsychiatric
    Association
8335 Brittany Hill Court
Grand Blanc, MI 48439
(810) 694–1808

Sharia Scholars Association of North
    America
30701 Woodward Avenue
Royal Oak, MI 48073
(248) 435–6666

Islamic Call Groups
Islamic Assembly of North America
    Chapter
3588 Plymouth Road #270
Ann Arbor, MI 48105
(313) 677–0006

United Muslim Michigan Association
22537 Fullerton Street
Detroit, MI 48223

Islamic Assembly of North America
2540 Packard Road
Ypsilanti, MI 48197
(734) 528–0006

Mosques / Islamic Centers
Islamic Center of Ann Arbor
2301 Plymouth Road
Ann Arbor, MI 48105
(734) 665–6772

Muslim Center of Bloomfield
1830 W Square Lake Road
Bloomfield, MI 48302
(248) 333–9426

Canton Mosque
40440 Palmer Road
Canton, MI 48188
(313) 729–1000

Arab Community Center for Economic
and Social Services
2651 Saulino Court
Dearborn, MI 48120
(313) 842–7010
iahmed@accesscommunity.org

Islamic Society of Dearborn
2546 Holly Street
Dearborn, MI 48120

American Moslem Bekka Center
6110 Chase Road
Dearborn, MI 48126
(313) 584–4102

Islamic House of Wisdom
7000 Barrie Street
Dearborn, MI 48126
(313) 581–7738

Karbalaa Islamic Education Center
15332 W Warren Avenue
Dearborn, MI 48126
(313) 584–2077

Islamic Institute of Knowledge
6345 Schaefer Road
Dearborn, MI 48126
(313) 584–2570
islamicinst@starmail.com

American Moslem Society
9945 Vernor Highway
Dearborn, MI 48120
(313) 849–2147

Islamic Dar-Al-Hikma
22575 Ann Arbor Trail
Dearborn Hts, MI 48127
(313) 359–1221
islamhw@linksnet.net

Masjid Al-Ikhlas
16412 E Warren Avenue
Detroit, MI 48224
(313) 881–1180

Islamic Center of Inkster
PO Box 43474
Detroit, MI 48243
(313) 961–7759

Masjid Al-Nur
318 Pilgrim Street
Detroit, MI 48203
(313) 867–9428

The Muslim Center
1605 W Davison Avenue
Detroit, MI 48238
(313) 883–3330
elamin61@hotmail.com

Masjid Muhammad
11529 Linwood Street
Detroit, MI 48206
(248) 543–6899

Masjid Al-Fatiha
2844 4th Street
Detroit, MI 48201
(313) 961–0940

Deroit Masjid of Al-Islam
17346 Plainview Avenue
Detroit, MI 48219
(313) 532–1392

Jamiyatul Nasrul Ilm
9309 Oakland Street
Detroit, MI 48211
(313) 873–7910

Masjid Haqq
4118 Joy Road
Detroit, MI 48204
(313) 897–9218

Islamic Center of Detroit
4646 Cass Avenue
Detroit, MI 48201
(313) 831–9222

Masjid al-Ikhlas
15516 E Warren Avenue
Detroit, MI 48224
(313) 881–1180

Masjid Al-Tauheed
18624 W Warren Avenue
Detroit, MI 48228
(313) 271–0731

Masjid un-Noor, Inc.
11311 Mound Road
Detroit, MI 48212
(313) 892–5450

Islamic Center of America
15571 Joy Road
Detroit, MI 48228
(313) 582–7442
tickets@icofa.com
www.icofa.com

Masjid Muath Ibn Jabal
4001 Miller Street
Detroit, MI 48211
(313) 921–7888

Islamic Center for Greater Lansing
920 S Harrison Road
East Lansing, MI 48823
(517) 337–0382

Tawheed Center
29707 W 10 Mile Road
Farmington Hills, MI 48336
(313) 893–9951

Flint Massjid of Al-Islam
402 E Gillespie Avenue
Flint, MI 48505
(810) 787–6591

Dyewood Center
5271 Dyewood Drive
Flint, MI 48532
(810) 732–9338

Masjid Mu'min
G4043 Clio Road
Flint, MI 48504
(313) 785–4001

Masjid Muhammad
2151 Division Avenue S
Grand Rapids, MI 49507
(616) 245–9175
nseifullah@aol.com

Islamic Center of Grand Rapids
1301 Burton Street SE
Grand Rapids, MI 49507
(616) 554–9980

Islamic Center of North Detroit
12502 McDougall Street
Hamtramck, MI 48212
(313) 368–5308

Bosnian American Islamic Center
3437 Caniff Street
Hamtramck, MI 48212
(313) 891–6152

Albanian Islamic Center
19775 Harper Avenue
Harper Woods, MI 48225
(313) 884–6676

Kalamazoo Islamic Center
1520 W Michigan Avenue
Kalamazoo, MI 49006
(616) 381–6611

Mosque of Imam Ali (AS)
6361 Whiteford Center Road
Lambertville, MI 48144
(313) 856–8266

Walim Mahmoud Islamic Center
235 Lahoma Street
Lansing, MI 48915
(517) 882–1883

Islamic Center of Mt. Pleasant
907 McVey Street
Mt. Pleasant, MI 48858
(517) 773–2545

Islamic Center of Greater Muskegon
2444 Park Street
Muskegon, MI 49444
(231) 739–1005

Bilal Rabah Center
1347 Pine Street
Muskegon, MI 49442
(616) 722–4673

Huron Islamic Society
2405 Gratiot Avenue
Port Huron, MI 48060

Islamic Association of Greater Detroit
865 W Auburn Road
Rochester Hls, MI 48307

Islamic Center of Saginaw
114 N 4th Avenue
Saginaw, MI 48607
(517) 752–3531

Islamic Cultural Institute
30115 Greater Mack Avenue
St. Clair Shores, MI 48082
(810) 293–5752
sensdata@aol.com

Flint Islamic Center
9447 Corunna Road
Swartz Creek, MI 48473
(810) 635–3890
www.efic.net

West Bloomfield Islamic Community
  Center
4215 Middlebelt Road
W Bloomfield, MI 48323

Ahlul Bayt Association
2230 Crumb Road
Walled Lake, MI 48390
(248) 669–5740

Islamic Association of Michigan
18171 Racho Road
Wyandotte, MI 48192

Newspaper
Arab American News
5461 Schaefer Road
Dearborn, MI 48126
(313) 582–4888

The Muslim Observer
20331 Farmington Road Suite 100
Livonia, MI 48152
(248) 426–7777
editor@muslimobserver.com
www.muslimobserver.com

Periodical
Arab American Journal
16241 W Warren Avenue
Detroit, MI 48228
(313) 846–0250
aramjo@aol.com

Public Affairs Organizations
American Muslim Political Affairs
  Committee
7040 Payne Avenue
Dearborn, MI 48126
(313) 346–8480

American Arab Anti-Discrimination
  Committee
13530 Michigan Avenue Suite 228
Dearborn, MI 48126
(313) 581–1201

Arab American Political Affairs
  Committee
PO Box 925
Dearborn, MI 48121

The Muslim Community Political Affairs
  Committee
PO Box 23936
Detroit, MI 48223
(313) 865–6770
badeel@aol.com

Islamic Health and Human Service
1249 Washington Boulevard
Detroit, MI 48226
(313) 961–0678

Council on American-Islamic
  Relations–Michigan
28820 Southfield Road
Lathrup Village, MI 48076
(248) 569–2203
www.cairmichigan.org

American Muslim Council–Michigan
3101 Northward Suite 300
Royal Oak, MI 48073
(908) 445–0312

Schools
Michigan Islamic Academy
2301 Plymouth Road
Ann Arbor, MI 48105
(313) 665–8882

Crescent Academy International
40440 Palmer Road
Canton, MI 48188
(313) 729–1000
davetauhidi@msn.com

Al Furqan School
9945 Vernor Highway
Dearborn, MI 48120

Muslim American Youth Academy
19500 Ford Road
Dearborn, MI 48128
(313) 436–3300

American Islamic Academy
6053 Chase Road
Dearborn, MI 48126
(313) 945–6504
mhazime957@aol.com
www.iiok.com

Muslim American Youth Academy
19500 Ford Road
Dearborn, MI 48128
(313) 436–3300

Islamic Dar-Al-Hikma
22575 Ann Arbor Trail
Dearborn Heights, MI 48127
(313) 359–1221
islamhw@linksnet.net

Dar al-Arqam School
4612 Lonyo Street
Detroit, MI 48210
(313) 581–3441

Greater Lansing Islamic School
920 S Harrison Road
East Lansing, MI 48823
(517) 332–3700
jonesja8@pilot.msu.edu

Flint Islamic Center School and Day
    Care
614 West Home Avenue
Flint, MI 48505
(810) 787–5525

Huda School
32220 Franklin Road
Franklin, MI 48025
(810) 626–0999

Genesee Academy
9447 Corunna Road
Swartz Creek, MI 48473
(810) 635–3890
jjones5809@aol.com
www.efic.net

Social Services
Arab American Children Center
7124 Miller Road
Dearborn, MI 48126
(313) 846–8278

Arab Community Center for Economic
    and Social Services
2651 Saulino Court
Dearborn, MI 48120
(313) 842-7010
access@accesscommunity.org
www.accesscommunity.org

Islamic Health and Human Services
15066 Fairfield Street
Detroit, MI 48238
(313) 961–0678

Student Groups
Persian Student Association at the
    University of Michigan
3909 Michigan Union
530 S State Street
Ann Arbor, MI 48109
persians@umich.edu

Muslim Students Association–University
    of Michigan at Dearborn
Student Activities
4901 Evergreen
Dearborn, MI 48128
(313) 842–3480

Muslim Student Association–University
    of Michigan at Dearborn
4901 Evergreen Road
Dearborn, MI 48128
(313) 842–3480

Muslim Students Association–Wayne
State University
4646 Cass Avenue
Detroit, MI 48201
(313) 831–9222

Muslim Student Association–University
of Michigan
4646 Cass Avenue
Detroit, MI 48201
msa-request@umich.edu

Muslim Students Association–Michigan
Tech
1500 Townsend Drive
Houghton, MI 49931
(906) 487–1887

Muslim Arab Youth Association
24525 Southfield Road Suite 206
Southfield, MI 48075
(248) 423–9020

Women's Group
League of Muslim Women
PO Box 28384
Detroit, MI 48228

Youth Groups
Qur'an for Youth
15068 Fairfield Street
Detroit, MI 48238
(313) 864–3395

Albanian Soccer Club
25484 Grand River Avenue
Redford, MI 48240
(313) 255–6810

Muslim Youth of Greater Detroit
865 W Auburn Road
Rochester, MI 48307
(313) 851–0643

MINNESOTA

Cemetery
Minnesota Islamic Cemetery Association
Inc
2336 County Road B W
Roseville, MN 55113

Ethnic Associations
Turkish American Association of
Minnesota
PO Box 14704
Minneapolis, MN 55414
(651) 631–7122
can.cinbis@ieee.org
www.taam.org

Mizna Inc.
PO Box 14294
Minneapolis, MN 55414
mizna@mizna.org
www.mizna.org

Mosques / Islamic Centers
Muslim Community Center
8910 Old Cedar Avenue S
Bloomington, MN 55425

Muslim Community Center
1916 Skyline Drive S
Burnsville, MN 55337

Islamic Center
4056 7th Street NE
Columbia Heigts, MN 55421
(612) 781–9111

Islamic Institute of Minnesota
1460 Skillman Avenue E
Maplewood, MN 55109
(651) 748–1688

Islamic Center of Minnesota
1401 Gardena Avenue NE
Minneapolis, MN 55432
(763) 571–5604

Masjid Muhammad
3759 4th Avenue S
Minneapolis, MN 55409

Islamic Center of Minneapolis
1128 6th Street SE
Minneapolis, MN 55414
(612) 571–5604

Masjid an-Nur
PO Box 11781
Minneapolis, MN 55411
(612) 521–1749
aelamia@yahoo.com

Dar Al-Farooq
983 17th Avenue SE
Minneapolis, MN 55414
(612) 502–0411
alda0001@tc.umn.edu

Masjed Abubakr Al-Seddiq
PO Box 1013
Rochester, MN 55903

Islamic Center of Winona
54 E 3rd Street
Winona, MN 55987
(507) 453–9961

Public Affairs Organization
Council on American-Islamic
    Relations–Minnesota
2525 E. Franklin Avenue
Minneapolis, MN 55406
(612) 334–9395
contact@cairminnesota.org
www.cairminnesota.org

School
Al-Amal School
1401 Gardena Avenue NE
Fridley, MN 55432
(763) 571–8886
alamalschool@hotmail.com

Social Services
Islamic Relief and Social Services
2525 E Franklin Avenue
Minneapolis, MN 55406
(612) 343–4345
irss@irss.org
www.irss.org

Student Group
Muslim Students
    Association–MacAlester College
1600 Grand Avenue
Saint Paul, MN 55105
(612) 696–6000

MISSISSIPPI

Mosques / Islamic Centers
Biloxi Islamic Center-Al Noor
205 Keller Avenue
Biloxi, MS 39530
(228) 432–7650
jmohiuddin@aol.com

Islamic Center of Hattiesburg
215 S 25th Avenue
Hattiesburg, MS 39401
(601) 544–0962
abacus2000@rocketmail.com

Muslim Association of Mississippi
2533 W McDowell Road
Jackson, MS 39204
(601) 371–2834

Muhammad Masjid
6100 Floral Drive
Jackson, MS 39206
(601) 957–2598

Mississippi Muslim Association
PO Box 7713
Jackson, MS 39284
(601) 371–2834

Masjid Bilal
John F. Kennedy Music Building
    Highway 61 N
Mound Bayou, MS 38762

Masjid Al-Haque
RR 2 Box 517A
Silver Creek, MS 39663
(601) 587–0245

Masjid Al-Halim–New Medinah
16 Al Halim Road
Sumrall, MS 39482
(601) 736–8540

Student Group
MMA
407 Winding Hill Drive
Clinton, MS 39056
(601) 924–1792

Muslim Students Association
204 Herbert Street
Starkville, MS 39759
(601) 325–5228

MISSOURI

Charity Group
Islamic African Relief Agency
PO Box 7084
Columbia, MO 65205
(573) 443–0166
iara@iara-usa.org
www.iara-usa.org

Ethnic Association
Zumunta Association United States of
American Inc.
1656 S Sonora Drive
Columbia, MO 65201
(573) 449–7206
Ibrahim@zumunta.org
www.zumunta.org

Turkish American Association of Greater
Kansas City
505 NW 41st Street
Kansas City, MO 64116
(816) 452–1968
taaofkc@aol.com
members.aol.com/taaofkc

Turkish American Cultural Alliance of
St. Louis
5614 Wieland Drive
St. Louis, MO 63128
(314) 894–1824
sadikbey@aol.com

Magazine
The American Muslim
PO Box 5670
St. Louis, MO 63121
(314) 291–3711

Mosques / Islamic Centers
Islamic Center of Central Missouri
201 S 5th Street
Columbia, MO 65201
(573) 875–4633
islam@coin.org

Islamic Society of Greater Kansas City
8501 E 99th Street
Kansas City, MO 64134
(816) 763–2267
support@isgkc.org

Al-Inshirah Islamic Center
3644 Troost Avenue
Kansas City, MO 64109
(816) 960–0475

Masjid Omar
2700 E 49th Street
Kansas City, MO 64130
(816) 924–5683

Islamic Foundation of Greater St.
Louis
517 Weidman Road
Manchester, MO 63011
(636) 394–7878
w_benjasattabuse@yahoo.com

Masjid Al-Tauheed
5010 San Francisco
St. Louis, MO 63111
(314) 381–9105

Islamic Center of Greater St. Louis
3843 W Pine Boulevard
St. Louis, MO 63108
(314) 534–9672

Almominoon Islamic Center
1434 N Grand Boulevard
St. Louis, MO 63106
(314) 771–0346

Islamic Foundation of St. Louis
2012 Westfield Court
St. Louis, MO 63143
(314) 646–7106

Public Affairs Organization
Council on American-Islamic
Relations–St. Louis
7239 Dartmouth Avenue
St. Louis, MO 63130
(314) 331–0344
cairstl@hotmail.com

Schools

Al-Salam Day School
517 Weidman Road
Ballwin, MO 63011
(636) 394–8986
alsalamday@hotmail.com
www.umsl.edu/studentlife/msa/
salam.html

Islamic School of Central Missouri
PO Box 1241
Columbia, MO 65205
(573) 875–4633
Islam@coin.org

Islamic School of Kansas City
10515 Grandview Road
Kansas City, MO 64137
(816) 767–0001
iskc89@hotmail.com
www.iskc.org

Islamic School of Greater Kansas City
10007 James A. Reed Road
Kansas City, MO 64134
(816) 763–0322
jaime@isgkc.net
www.isgkc.org

Sr. Clara Muhammad School
1434 N Grand Boulevard
St. Louis, MO 63106
(314) 531–3118
www.umsl.edu/studentlife/msa/local.html

Islamic Institute of Learning
5388 Geraldine Avenue
St. Louis, MO 63115
(314) 381–2490
amin7303@aol.com

Islamic Center Day School
3843 W Pine Boulevard
St. Louis, MO 63108
(314) 534–9672

Student Groups

Muslim Students Association–University
of Missouri
201 S 5th Street
Columbia, MO 65201
(314) 875–4633

Muslim Students Association of
University of Missouri at Kansas City
I31 University Center
5100 Rockhill Road
Kansas City, MO 64110
(913) 631–6927

Muslim Students Association–University
of Missouri
1300 N Elm Street
Rolla, MO 65401
(314) 341–7360

Muslim Students
Association–Washington
University in St. Louis
Campus Box 1128, One Brookings Drive
St. Louis, MO 63130
muslim@rescomp.wustl.edu

Muslim Student Association at CMSU
PO Box 77
Warrensburg, MO 64093
(816) 429–2552

MONTANA

Mosques / Islamic Centers

Islamic Community of Billings
PO Box 121
Billings, MT 59103
(406) 245–4551

Muslim Community of Bozeman
1145 S Pinecrest Drive
Bozeman, MT 59715
(406) 587–7162

Student Group

Muslim Students Association–University
of Montana
Foreign Student Office Lodge #1
Missoula, MT 59812
(208) 728–5731

NEBRASKA

Mosques / Islamic Centers
Islamic Foundation of Lincoln
PO Box 84133
Lincoln, NE 68501
(402) 475–0475

Islamic Foundation of Omaha
7320 Bedford Avenue
Omaha, NE 68134
(402) 572–6120
alabsy@worldnet.att.net

Islamic Center of Omaha
3511 N 73rd Street
Omaha, NE 68134
(402) 571–0720
icoahmad@ico-ne.org

Masjid Muhammad
2440 Templeton Street
Omaha, NE 68111

Islamic Center of Sioux Land
PO Box 795
South Sioux City, NE 68776
(402) 494–5152

Student Group
Muslim Students Association–Univeristy
of Nebraska, Lincoln
PO Box 84133
Lincoln, NE 68501
(402) 477–9237

NEVADA

Mosques / Islamic Centers
Masjid As Sabur
711 Morgan Avenue
Las Vegas, NV 89106
(702) 647–2757

Islamic Society of Nevada
4730 E Desert Inn Road
Las Vegas, NV 89121
(702) 433–3431

Northern Nevada Muslim Community
Center
1857 Oddie Boulevard
Sparks, NV 89431
(775) 351–1857

Student Group
Muslim Students Association–University
of Nevada, Las Vegas
4505 S Maryland Parkway
Las Vegas, NV 89154

NEW HAMPSHIRE

Mosques / Islamic Centers
Islamic Society of Seacoast Area
PO Box 52
Durham, NH 03824
(603) 868–5937
nag786@aol.com

Islamic Society of Merrimack Valley
230 Main Street
Salem, NH 03079
(630) 893–1112

NEW JERSEY

Book Publisher / Distributor
New Mind Productions
PO Box 5185
Jersey City, NJ 07305
(201) 434–1939
Marmiya@aol.com

Cemetery
Princeton Memorial Park
3 S. Main Street Floor 2
Allentown, NJ 08501

Charity Group
Bosnia and Herzegovina Relief Fund
277 W Midland Avenue
Paramus, NJ 07652
(201) 670–1765

Coordination Council
Council of Mosques and Islamic
  Organizations
20–24 Branford Place Suite 600
Newark, NJ 07102
(732) 661–0421
shura-nj@muslimsonline.com
www.muslimsonline.com/shura/nj

Ethnic Associations
Young Turks Cultural Aid Society
57 Ashley Court
Bedminster, NJ 07921
(732) 981–0099
mackinnj@aol.com

Azerbaijan Society of America
20 Skyview Terrace
Clifton, NJ 07013
(973) 471–5500
tomris@erols.com
www.azerbaijan-america.org

Turkish-American Community Center
229 State Route 33
Englishtown, NJ 07726
(732) 446–8855

Turk Ocagi
760 Pennsylvania Avenue
Lyndhurst, NJ 07071
(201) 935–7584

Hametic Arab Muslim Association
  Incorporation
80 Tillinghast Street
Newark, NJ 07108

Turkestanian American Association
266 Vail Road
Parsippany, NJ 07054
(212) 737–9703

Solidarity of Balkan Turks of America
1030 Main Street Apartment 6
Paterson, NJ 07503

Guilds
Iranian American Medical Association
397 Haledon Avenue
Haledon, NJ 07508
(973) 595–8888

Alamane Muslim Merchants
24 Branford Place
Newark, NJ 07102
(973) 565–9986

Mosques / Islamic Centers
Islamic Center of Asbury Park
209 Bond Street
Asbury Park, NJ 07712
(732) 774–2699
teacher33@aol.com

Muslim Community Organization of
  South Jersey
3536 Atlantic Avenue
Atlantic City, NJ 08401
(609) 344–1786
altaqwa786@hotmail.com

Masjid Muhammad
107 S Rev. Dr. Isaac Coles Plaza
Atlantic City, NJ 08401
(609) 347–0788
khairi3272@aol.com

Muslim Foundation Inc.
22 Tomar Court
Bloomfield, NJ 07003
(201) 338–4779

Jami Masjid of Boonton
604 Birch Street
Boonton, NJ 07005
(201) 334–9334

Islamic Center of Boonton
110 Harrison Street
Boonton, NJ 07005
(973) 334–9334

Masjid Muhammad of Al-Islam
500 Ward Avenue
Bordentown, NJ 08505

Delaware Valley Muslim Association
203 Fountain Avenue
Burlington Township, NJ 08016
(609) 386–5535

Masjidun-Nur Inc.
1231 Mechanic Street
Camden, NJ 08104
(856) 365–1551

Quba Islamic Center
1311 Haddon Avenue
Camden, NJ 08103
(856) 541–6782

Islamic Center of South Jersey
PO Box 3654
Cherry Hill, NJ 08034

Shia Association of North America
144 Jacqueline Avenue
Delran, NJ 08075
(856) 461–2221
shia-nj.org

Islamic Center of America
215 N Oraton Parkway
East Orange, NJ 07017
(201) 672–6690

Masjid Al-Hadi
PO Box 59
Elizabeth, NJ 07207
(908) 351–7238

Albanian American Islamic Center
43 Monroe Street
Garfield, NJ 07026
(973) 546–4095

Minjuaj-Ul-Quran
36 Vreeland Avenue
Hackensack, NJ 07601
(201) 641–2200

Islamic Center of Harrison
301 Jersey Street Floor 2
Harrison, NJ 07029
(201) 481–2226

Muslim Federation of New Jersey
2 Chopin Court
Jersey City, NJ 07302
(201) 433–0057

Islamic Center of Jersey
17 Park Street
Jersey City, NJ 07304
(201) 433–5000

Masjid Al-Iman
596 Communipaw Avenue
Jersey City, NJ 07304
(201) 433–0600

Masjid Al-Salaam
2824 John F. Kennedy Boulevard
Jersey City, NJ 07306
(201) 633–2990

Masjid Muhammad
295 Jackson Street
Jersey City, NJ 07205

Masjid Muhammad
297 Martin Luther King Jr. Drive
Jersey City, NJ 07305
(201) 435–6845

Masjid Free Haven
280 Ashland Avenue
Lawnside, NJ 08045
(609) 546–2995
fathee@aol.com

The Islamic Society of Monmouth
   County
PO Box 89
Middletown, NJ 07748
(732) 671–3321
webmaster@ismc.org

Islamic Society of Central Jersey
4145 Route One South
Monmouth Junction, NJ 08520
(732) 329–8126

Masjid Wadud
698 Bloomfield Avenue
Montclair, NJ 07042
(973) 744–2170
kdamin@yahoo.com

New Brunswick Islamic Center
167 Remsen Avenue
New Brunswick, NJ 08901
(732) 214–1547
his@mytalk.com

Masjid Al-Haqq
689 Springfield Avenue
Newark, NJ 07103
(973) 373–0344

Irvington Islamic Center
656 Sanford Avenue
Newark, NJ 07106
(973) 373–3141

Islamic Cultural Center
PO Box 1064
Newark, NJ 07101
(973) 623–2100

Muslim Incorporation
967 Bergen Street
Newark, NJ 07112

Islamic Center of Newark
210–216 Clinton Place
Newark, NJ 07112
(201) 824–3764

Newark Community Masjid
214 Chancellor Avenue
Newark, NJ 07112
(201) 926–8927

The Islamic Cultural Center
20–24 Branford Place Suite 703
Newark, NJ 07102
(973) 623–2100

Masjid Mohammed
257 S Orange Avenue
Newark, NJ 07103
(973) 623–3500

Oakhurst Masjid
1 Klein Street
Oakhurst, NJ 07755
(908) 531–8606

Masjid Mohammed
110 Park Street #112
Orange, NJ 07050
(202) 687–8375

United Islamic Center
23 Highland Avenue
Passaic, NJ 07055

New World Masjid
501 Getty Avenue
Paterson, NJ 07503
(973) 278–0616

Albanian Associated Fund
357 River Street #358
Paterson, NJ 07524
(973) 523–9203

United Islamic Center
408 Knickerbocker Avenue
Paterson, NJ 07503
(201) 345–6584

Masjid an-Nur
18 Fair Street
Paterson, NJ 07505
(201) 357–0122

Islamic Foundation of New Jersey Inc
61 Van Houten Street
Paterson, NJ 07505
(201) 279–6408

Paterson Islamic Mission, Inc
438 Union Avenue
Paterson, NJ 07502
(973) 389–7987

Islamic Center of Passaic and Paterson
245 Broadway
Paterson, NJ 07501
(201) 279–4151

Muslim Center of Middlesex County
PO Box 505
Piscataway, NJ 08855
(732) 463–2004

Masjid Ullah
321 Grant Avenue
Plainfield, NJ 07060
(201) 561–6796
hawm@webtv.net

Muslim Center of Somerset County
PO Box 852
Somerville, NJ 08876
(908) 526–1837
zaheerh@aol.com

Dar Ul-Islah
320 Febry Terrace
Teaneck, NJ 07666
(201) 363–0007

Islamic Center of Fairleigh Dickinson
1000 River Road
Teaneck, NJ 07666
(201) 836–6382

Muslim Society of Jersey Shore
1733 Route 9
Toms River, NJ 08755
(732) 506–0111

Masjid At-Taqwa
1001 E State Street
Trenton, NJ 08609
(609) 392–3303

Masjid As-Safaat
25 Oxford Street
Trenton, NJ 08638
(609) 392–9141

Islamic Educational Center of North
   Hudson
4605 Cottage Place #4613
Union City, NJ 07087
(201) 330–0066
miabbasi@ix.netcom.com

Islamic Education Center
585 67th Street
West New York, NJ 07093
(201) 869–7813

Muslim Community of New
   Jersey–Woodbridge
PO Box 865
Woodbridge, NJ 07095

Muslim Foundation Incorporation
104 2nd Street
Woodbridge, NJ 07095
(732) 726–1155

Pilgrim Services
Central Haj Council of North America
286 Liberty Road
Englewood, NJ 07631

Public Affairs Organizations
American Muslim Alliance–Rutgers
   University
613 George St, SAC Box 33
New Brunswick, NJ 08901
(732) 373–5915
ru_ama@hotmail.com
www.ruama.web.com

American Muslim Union
265A 3E-1 West 46
Totowa, NJ 07512
(973) 837–0604
www.americanmuslimunion.org

Religious Education Program
Ahlul Bait Foundation
PO Box 1125
Englishtown, NJ 07726
(908) 446–0554

Schools
American Islamic Academy
110 Harrison Street
Boonton, NJ 07005
(201) 333–4933

Quba School and Islamic Center
1311 Haddon Avenue
Camden, NJ 08103
(609) 541–6782

Masjid Un-Nur School
1231 Mechanic Street
Camden, NJ 08104
(856) 365–1551

Madrasatu Ahlis Sunnah
215 N Oraton Parkway
East Orange, NJ 07017
(973) 672–4124

Al-Ghazali Elementary School
17 Park Street
Jersey City, NJ 07304
(201) 433–5002
ief@juno.com
hozien@cris.com

Islamic Society of Central Jersey School
4145 U.S. Route 1
Monmouth Junction, NJ 08852
(732) 329–1988

Noor-Ul-Iman School
PO Box 3105
Princeton, NJ 08543
(908) 329–1306
bturan@sadat.com

Al-Ghazaly High School
441 North Street
Teaneck, NJ 07666
(973) 785–2300

School of Masjid As-Safaat
25 Oxford Street
Trenton, NJ 08638
(609) 392–9141

Muftah al-Uloom (Key of Knowledge)
4607–4613 Cottage Place
Union City, NJ 07087
(201) 223–9920

Social Services
Muslim Family Social Services Center
224 N 18th Street
East Orange, NJ 07017
(973) 672–1227

Islamic Community Social Assistance
  Network
20–24 Branford Place
Newark, NJ 07102
(973) 621–7311
iccnewark@aol.com

Albanian Associated Fund
456 River Street
Paterson, NJ 07524
(973) 523–9203

Student Groups
Muslim Students Association–Bergen
  Community College
75 Azalea Street
Paramus, NJ 07652

Muslim Students Association–Passaic
  Community College
95 N 16th Street
Prospect Park, NJ 07508
(201) 942–0733

Sufi Group
Sufi Way
134 Graybar Drive
Plainfield, NJ 07062
(908) 668–1991

NEW MEXICO

Mosques / Islamic Centers
Dar al Islam
PO Box 180
Abiquiu, NM 87510
(505) 685–4515

Masjid Muhammad
901 Edith Boulvard SE
Albuquerque, NM 87106

Masjid As-Sabiqun
1619 Del Monte Trail SW
Albuquerque, NM 87121

Islamic Center of New Mexico
PO Box 4582
Albuquerque, NM 87196
(505) 256–1450

Islamic Center in New Mexico
1100 Yale Boulevard SE
Albuquerque, NM 87106
(505) 256–1450

The Islamic Center of Las Cruces
1065 E Boutz Road
Las Cruces, NM 88001
(505) 522–3363

Al-Hilal Masjid and Portales Islamic
  Center
912 W 15th Lane
Portales, NM 88130
(505) 359–6874
salmanf@ziavms.enmu.edu

Islamic Society of Socorro
907 ¹/₂ Annette Avenue
Socorro, NM 87801
(505) 835–3217

Student Groups
Islamic Information Society–University of
  New Mexico
Student Center Student Union 105 #33
Albuquerque, NM 87131
(505) 821–9593

Muslim Students Association–New
  Mexico State University
1065 E Boutz Road
Las Cruces, NM 88001
(505) 522–2136

NEW YORK

Audio / Video Producer
Arabesque: The Voice of Islam Radio
764 Lincoln Boulevard
Long Beach, NY 11561

Book Publishers / Distributors
Islamic Books
305 E 166th Street #1104
Bronx, NY 10456
(718) 293–2969

Islamic Book Incorporation
554 Atlantic Avenue
Brooklyn, NY 11217
(718) 852–3602

Sufi Books
227 W Broadway
New York, NY 10013
(212) 334–5212

Masjid Al Tawheed Book Store
111 N Division Street
Peekskill, NY 10566
(914) 788–9850

Center for American Muslim Research
  and Information (CAMRI)
10343 Lefferts Boulevard
South Richmond Hill, NY 11419
(718) 848–8952
halalharam@aol.com
islambook.com

Coordination Council
Council of Islamic Organizations
676 Saint Marks Avenue
Brooklyn, NY 11216

Ethnic Associations
Nigerian-American Social and
Cultural Organization (NASCO)
PO Box 66493
Albany, NY 12206
nasco.albany@usa.net
nasco.webjump.com

The Pan-Albanian Federation of America
2437 Southern Boulevard
Bronx, NY 10458
(718) 365–6930

Turkish Cypriot Aid Society
843 Morris Park Avenue
Bronx, NY 10462
(212) 417–5304
cayonu1@cs.com

Consultive Committee on Indian
  Muslims
99 Lafayette Avenue Suite 25
Brooklyn, NY 11217
(718) 845–3810

Pakistan Community Center
925 Coney Island Avenue
Brooklyn, NY 11230
(718) 469–8458

American Association of Crimean Turks
4509 New Utrecht Avenue
Brooklyn, NY 11219
(718) 851–6621
kirimtatar@aol.com

Kurdish Heritage Foundation
345 Park Place
Brooklyn, NY 11238
(718) 783–7930
kurdishlib@aol.com

The Arab American Federation of West
    Amherst, New York
33 W Summerset Lane
Buffalo, NY 14228

United States Bangladesh Chess
    Association Inc.
4701 50th Avenue Floor 2
Flushing, NY 11377
(718) 786–3242

Afghan Peace Association
PO Box 540926
Flushing, NY 11354
(718) 461–6799
afghanpeacea@hotmail.com

Turkish American Cultural Association
222 Pearl Street
Lawrence, NY 11559

Turkistan American Association
821 United Nations Plaza
New York, NY 10017
(212) 682–7688

The Committee for Humanitarian
    Assistance to Iranian Refugees
17 Battery Place Room 605N
New York, NY 10004
(212) 425–7240
chairngo@aol.com
www.farsinet.com/chair

Albanian American Enterprise
14 E 60th Street Suite 407
New York, NY 10022
(212) 702–9102

American-Turkish Society
850 3rd Avenue Floor 18
New York, NY 10022
(212) 319–2452

Iranian Refugees' Alliance, Inc.
PO Box 316
New York, NY 10276
(212) 260–7460
irainc@irainc.org

The Albanian American Civic League
PO Box 70
Ossining, NY 10562
(914) 671–8583

United Albanian American Islamic
    Foundation
PO Box 4102
Ridgewood, NY 11386
(718) 381–3853

Turkish Society of Rochester
2841 Culver Road
Rochester, NY 14622
(716) 266–1980
www.tsor.org

Association of Eritrea Professionals and
    Academics for Development
PO Box 414
Stony Brook, NY 11790
aepad@netscape.net

Kurdish American Fraternity
PO Box 10372
Westbury, NY 11590
(631) 796–2660

Arab American Foundation
33 S Broadway
Yonkers, NY 10701

Guilds
National Association of Muslim
    Chaplains
439 ¹/₂ S Pearl Street
Albany, NY 12202
(518) 475–0437

North American Muslim Chaplains
Association
PO Box 1783
Albany, NY 12201
(518) 475–0718

Islamic Chamber of Commerce
332 E 72nd Street
New York, NY 10021

Network of Pakistani Professionals
PO Box 394
New York, NY 10274
info@dastak.org
www.dastak.org/

Turkish American Physicians Association
1350 Lexington Avenue
New York, NY 10128

Islamic Call Groups
Tahrike Tarsile Qur'an Inc.
8008 51st Avenue
Elmhurst, NY 11373
(718) 446–6472
ttq@koranusa.org
www.koranusa.org

Bilal Muslim Mission of Americas–New
York
136 Charlotte Avenue
Hicksville, NY 11801
(516) 681–8500
kabana@juno.com

Islam Propagation Center International
3951 60th Street
Woodside, NY 11377

Moon Sighting Committee
Committee for Crescent Observation
1069 Ellis Hollow Road
Ithaca, NY 14850
(607) 277–6706

Mosques / Islamic Centers
Bilal Islamic Center
596 N Manning Boulevard
Albany, NY 12210
(518) 432–0500

Albany Islamic Foundation
91 Lexington Avenue
Albany, NY 12206
(518) 433–0875

Islamic Center Astoria
2123 30th Drive
Astoria, NY 11102
(918) 699–5083

Ghousin Jamma Masjid
25–86 31st Street
Astoria, NY 11102
(718) 728–2601

Masjid Al-Bir
3605 30th Street
Astoria, NY 11106
(718) 784–0336

Majid Baitul Mukarram
2221 33rd Street
Astoria, NY 11105
(718) 278–6677

Masjid Al-Araf
135 State Street
Auburn, NY 13024

Masjid Darul Quran
1514 E 3rd Avenue
Bay Shore, NY 11706
(516) 665–9462
darulquran@juno.com

Masjid-Al-Rashid
352 Main Street
Beacon, NY 12508
(914) 838–0443

Masjid Al-Mujahideen
1719 Montauk Highway
Bellport, NY 11713
(516) 698–5794

Masjid al-Bagr
320 Central Avenue
Bethpage, NY 11714
(516) 433–4141

Islamic Association of Finger Lakes
432 Main Street
Big Flats, NY 14814
(607) 562–3869

Islamic Organization of the Southern
  Tier
37 Carroll Street #39
Binghamton, NY 13901
(607) 724–9954
bc80216@binghamton.edu

Masjid Istiqaamah
13936 87th Road
Briarwood, NY 11435
(718) 262–0329

Bronx Islamic Center
702 Rhinelander Avenue
Bronx, NY 10462
(718) 822–1922

Baitus Salaam Jame Masjid Inc.
2703 Decatur Avenue
Bronx, NY 10458
(212) 733–0991

Jihad Society
635 River Avenue
Bronx, NY 10451

Anjuman Hefazatul Islam
365 E 198th Street
Bronx, NY 10458
(718) 733–0234

Baitul Aman Islamic Center Inc.
2351 Newbold Avenue
Bronx, NY 10462
(718) 904–8828

Masjid Quba
3520 Dekalb Avenue Apartment 1F
Bronx, NY 10467

North Bronx Islamic Center
3156 Perry Avenue
Bronx, NY 10467
(718) 515–3559

Masjid Taqwa wa Jihad
901 Anderson Avenue
Bronx, NY 10452
(718) 538–2474

Parkchester Jami Masjid Inc.
1203 Virginia Avenue
Bronx, NY 10472
(718) 828–4192

Islamic Falah of America Inc.
115 E 168th Street
Bronx, NY 10452
(718) 293–5287

Masjid al-Taqwa
1266 Bedford Avenue
Brooklyn, NY 11216
(718) 622–0800

Madine Muslim Community Center
5224 3rd Avenue
Brooklyn, NY 11220
(718) 567–3334

Masjid Nur al-Islam
21 Church Avenue
Brooklyn, NY 11218
(718) 462–2674

Masjid-AL AMAN
203 Forbell Street
Brooklyn, NY 11208
(718) 277–3976

Mohammad Mosque
380 Marcus Garvey Boulevard
  Apartment 5
Brooklyn, NY 11221
(718) 919–7458

Mosque of the Crimean Turks
4509 New Utrecht Avenue
Brooklyn, NY 11219
(718) 851–6621

Masjid Arqam
651 Banner Avenue
Brooklyn, NY 11235
(718) 646–0960

Albanian American Islamic Center
1325 Albemarle Road
Brooklyn, NY 11226
(718) 282–0358

Islamic Center of Brooklyn
2015 64th Street
Brooklyn, NY 11204
(718) 331–2843
bkislamcen@aol.com

Masjid Al-Muslimeen
1928 Fulton Street
Brooklyn, NY 11233
(718) 771–1506

Islamic Foundation of America
345 Broadway
Brooklyn, NY 11211
(718) 302–0955

United American Muslim Association
5911 8th Avenue
Brooklyn, NY 11220
(718) 438–6919
merkez@fatihcami.org

Masjid An-Nur
1071 New Lots Avenue
Brooklyn, NY 11208
(718) 827–4879

Islamic Center of Brighton Beach
230 Neptune Avenue
Brooklyn, NY 11235
(718) 648–0887

Islamic Society of Bay Ridge
6807 5th Avenue
Brooklyn, NY 11220
(718) 680–0121

Masjid Ikhwa
1135 Eastern Parkway
Brooklyn, NY 11213
(718) 493–0461

Masjid Ammar Ben Yaser
4315 8th Avenue
Brooklyn, NY 11232
(718) 972–8858

Masjid Abu Bakr As-Siddiq
115 Foster Avenue
Brooklyn, NY 11230
(718) 833–0011

Masjid Abdul Muhsi Khalifah
120 Madison Street
Brooklyn, NY 11216
(718) 783–1279

Muslim Community Center
1089 Coney Island Avenue
Brooklyn, NY 11230
(718) 859–4485

African Islamic Mission
1390 Bedford Avenue
Brooklyn, NY 11216
(718) 638–4588
theimam@afrislam.com

Islamic Mission of America
143 State Street
Brooklyn, NY 11201
(718) 875–6607
yemen1@juno.com

Masjid Al-Farouq Islamic Services
552 Atlantic Avenue
Brooklyn, NY 11217
(718) 488–8711

Bangladesh Muslim Center
1013 Church Avenue
Brooklyn, NY 11218
(718) 436–1743

Lackawana Islamic Mosque
154 Wilkesbarre Street
Buffalo, NY 14218
(716) 825–9490

Darul-uloom Al Madinah
182 Sobieski Street
Buffalo, NY 14212
(716) 892–2606

Masjid Nu'Man
1373 Fillmore Avenue
Buffalo, NY 14211
(716) 892–1332

Masjd Dar Salaam
75 E Parade Avenue
Buffalo, NY 14211
(716) 896–0725

Islamic Center of the Capitol District
21 Lansing Road N
Colonie, NY 12301
(518) 370–2664

Crimean Islamic Society
24 Greene Drive
Commack, NY 11725

Masjd Nurid Deen
10501 Northern Boulevard
Corona, NY 11368
(718) 779–1060

Masjid Sulyman
459 Deer Park Road
Dix Hills, NY 11746
(631) 351–5428

Masjid At-Tawfiq
8537 Britton Avenue
Elmhurst, NY 11373
(718) 779–1519

Islamic Center of Corona
10103 43rd Avenue
Flushing, NY 11368
(718) 476–7968

Masjid Alfalah
4212 National Street
Flushing, NY 11368
(718) 476–7968

Muslim Center of New York
13763 Kalmia Avenue
Flushing, NY 11355
(718) 445–2642

Masjid Abu Bakr
14149 33rd Avenue
Flushing, NY 11354
(718) 358–6905

Muslim Community Center of New York
137–58 Geranium Avenue
Flushing, NY 11355
(718) 816–9865

Masjid-E-Noor Inc.
143–30 Sanford Avenue
Flushing, NY 11355
(718) 886–0657

Islamic Society of Niagara Frontier
745 Heim Road
Amherst, NY 14068
(716) 568–1013

Albanian American Islamic Center
    Queens
7224 Myrtle Avenue
Glendale, NY 11385

Islamic Shia Ithna-Asheri
564 Jefferson Court
Guilderland, NY 12084
(518) 433–0875

Al-Nur Islamic Center
678 Front Street Apartment E
Hempstead, NY 11550
(516) 883–6905

Al-Khoei Benevolent Foundation
8989 Van Wyck Expressway
Jamaica, NY 11435
comments@al-khoei.org

Masjid Al-Hamdulillah
121–03 Supthin Boulevard
Jamaica, NY 11436

Al-Markaz
16626 89th Avenue
Jamaica, NY 11432
(718) 658–1199

The Central Islamic Organization
13008 Rockaway Boulevard
Jamaica, NY 11420

Masjid Umar Ben Abdul Agj
8839 161st Street
Jamaica, NY 11432
(718) 262–9219

Islamic Society of Jamestown
1235 N Main Street
Jamestown, NY 14701
(716) 666–4023
samqadri@hotmail.com

Muslim Association of Ulster County
7 Downs Street
Kingston, NY 12401
(914) 339–5253

Indonesian Muslim Community
4801 31st Avenue #1
Long Island City, NY 11103
(718) 721–8881
inmucony@aol.com

Islamic Unity Cultural Center
3132 12th Street
Long Island City, NY 11106
(718) 274–6149

Jame M Alamin
3519 36th Avenue
Long Island City, NY 11106
(718) 729–6325

Masjid Tawbah
84 Genung Street
Middletown, NY 10940
(914) 346–0151

Islamic Society of Westchester in
    Rockland
22 Brookfield Road
Mount Vernon, NY 10552
(914) 668–8786

Al Marwa Center
24–30 Steinway Street
New York, NY 10004
(718) 626–6633

Masjid Al-Rohman
36 W 35th Street Apartment 5E
New York, NY 10001

As-Safa Islamic Center
172 Allen Street
New York, NY 10002
(212) 987–1600

Masjid Utmman Bin Affan
154 E 55th Street
New York, NY 10022
(212) 850–4945

Admiral Family Circle Islamic Center
475 Riverside Drive Suite 1926
New York, NY 10115
(212) 870–3597

Masjid Malcolm Shabazz
102 W 116th Street
New York, NY 10026
(212) 662–2200

Mosque of Islamic Brotherhood
55 Street Nicholas Avenue
New York, NY 10026

Madina Masjid
401 E 11th Street
New York, NY 10009
(212) 533–5060

Islamic Cultural Center of New York
1711 3rd Avenue
New York, NY 10029
(212) 722–5234

Masjid Manhattan
12 Warren Street Floor 2
New York, NY 10007
(914) 471–2978

Pan African Islamic Society
237 Park Avenue
New York, NY 10017
(212) 551–3568

Masjid Al Jihad Al Akbar
PO Box 2117
Newburgh, NY 12550
(914) 561–5610
abuu1@aol.com

Islamic Society of the Southern Tier
209 Arland Avenue
Olean, NY 14760
(716) 373–3404

Sucnnatuah Masjid
354 Hunter Street
Ossining, NY 10562

Islamic Center of Peekskill
1000 Main Street Floor 2
Peekskill, NY 10566
(914) 734–8143

Masjid Tawheed
PO Box 2561
Peekskill, NY 10566
(914) 762–3787

Islamic Center of Plattsburgh
37 Boynton Avenue
Plattsburgh, NY 12901
(518) 561–5447

Masjid ul Mutakabbir
462 Main Street
Poughkeepsie, NY 12601
(914) 471–4559

Masjd Al Hera
12505 Jamaica Avenue
Richmond Hill, NY 11418
(718) 850–3575

Islamic Center of Rochester
727 Westfall Road
Rochester, NY 14620
(716) 442–0117

Islamic Center of Rochester
PO Box 23266
Rochester, NY 14692
(716) 422–0117
icr1@worldnet.att.net

Islamic Cultural Center of Rochester
853 Culver Road
Rochester, NY 14609

Rochester Masjid of Al-Islam
370 North Street
Rochester, NY 14605
(716) 325–9200

Masjid Al-Abidin
10414 127th Street
South Richmond Hill, NY 11419
(718) 848–8759

Abdul Mahaimin Center
826 Stanley Street
Schenectady, NY 12307
(518) 377–2951

Islamic Association of Long Island
10 Park Hill Drive
Selden, NY 11784
(631) 732–1235

Staten Island Masjid
230 Benziger Avenue
Staten Island, NY 10301

Islamic Masjid of Staten Island
117 Van Duzer Street
Staten Island, NY 10301

Noor Al-Islam Center
3075 Richmond Terrace
Staten Island, NY 10303
(718) 556–9628

Masjid Alnoor
104 Rhine Avenue
Staten Island, NY 10304
(718) 442–6674

Albanian Islamic Cultural Center
307 Victory Boulevard
Staten Island, NY 10301
(718) 816–9865

Islamic Society of Staten Island
PO Box 140276
Staten Island, NY 10314
(718) 447–3914

Masjid Darul Ehsan
6 Suffern Place
Suffern, NY 10901
(914) 369–7330
darulehsan@muslimsonline.com

Turkish Islamic Cultural Center
4506 Skillman Avenue
Sunnyside, NY 11104
(718) 433–4298

Islamic Center of Central New York
925 Comstock Avenue
Syracuse, NY 13210
(315) 471–3645

Muslim Center
843 Salt Springs Road
Syracuse, NY 13224
(315) 445–0987

American Muslim Community Center
2504 S Salina Street
Syracuse, NY 13225
(315) 478–3556

Masjid Muhammad
201 Oxford Street
Syracuse, NY 13202

Muslim Community Assocation of
  Mohawk Valley
25 Irving Place
Utica, NY 13501
(315) 793–9082

Islamic Center of South Shore
202 Stuart Avenue
Valley Stream, NY 11580
(516) 285–1274

Islamic Center of Rockland
PO Box 562
Valley Cottage, NY 10989
(845) 627–0372
mziaullah@aol.com

Mid Hudson Islamic Association
125 All Angels Hill Road
Wappingers Falls, NY 12590
(914) 297–0882

Sufi Masjid
1529 Fuller Road
Waterport, NY 14571

Islamic Center of West Valley
RT 2 Fritz Road
West Valley, NY 14171
(716) 942–3474

Islamic Center of Long Island
835 Brush Hollow Road
Westbury, NY 11590
(516) 333–3495
icli.icli@verizon.net

Shia Ithna-Asheri Jamaat of New York
4867 58th Street
Woodside, NY 11377
(718) 507–7680

Masjid Al-Fatima
5716 37th Avenue
Woodside, NY 11377
(718) 476–1972

Imam Ali Center
5511 Queens Boulevard
Woodside, NY 11377

Masjid Ul Mustaqeem
138 N 22nd Street
Wyandanch, NY 11798
(516) 643–8763

Al-Jamiyat Islamic Center
221 Merritt Avenue
Wyandanch, NY 11798
(516) 491–3498

Islamic Center of Maple Hills
54 Maple Street
Yonkers, NY 10701
(914) 378–8412

Newspapers
Sada-E-Pakistan
925 Coney Island Avenue
Brooklyn, NY 11230
(718) 469–8458

Urdu Times
169–20 Hillside Avenue
Jamaica, NY 11432
(718) 297–5609
alwahid@aol.com

Muslims
695 Park Avenue #121
New York, NY 10021

Public Affairs Organization
Arab American Parade Committee
104 5th Avenue
Brooklyn, NY 11217
(718) 857–2947

Albanian American Public Affairs
  Committee
5 Old Road
Elmsford, NY 10523

Council on American-Islamic
  Relations–New York
475 Riverside Drive Suite 246
New York, NY 10115
(212) 870–2002
cair_newyork@hotmail.com

Islamic Conference
130 E 40th Street Floor 5
New York, NY 10016
(212) 883–0140
oicun@umdp.org

Religious Education Programs
Madrassah Hifzul Quran
2567 31st Street
Astoria, NY 11102
(718) 728–2601

Islamic Group
8941 Springfield Boulevard
Queens Vlg, NY 11427
(718) 740–3299

Schools
Madrasa Al-Noor
675 4th Avenue
Brooklyn, NY 11232
(718) 768–7309
www.liii.com/~hajeri/alnoor.html

Islamic Family School
552 Atlantic Avenue #4
Brooklyn, NY 11217

Masjid Musab Bin Umayer School
6807 5th Avenue
Brooklyn, NY 11220
(718) 680–0121

Muslim Center Elementary School
13758 Geranium Avenue
Flushing, NY 11355
(718) 460–2127
mces786@cs.com

Masoomeen School of Islamic Education
PO Box 525238
Flushing, NY 11352
(631) 423–5301
masoomeen@worldnet.att.net

Muslim Parochial School
RR 1 Box 28J
Hancock, NY 13783
(607) 467–2860

Al-Iman School
89–89 Van Wyck Expressway
Jamaica, NY 11435
(718) 297–6502

Muslim Model School
16626 89th Avenue
Jamaica, NY 11432
(718) 658–1199

Islamic School of Upper Westchester
19 Kisco Park Drive
Mount Kisco, NY 10549
(914) 242–0454
adiba786@hotmail.com

Sr. Clara Muhammed School
102 W 116th Street
New York, NY 10026
(212) 662–2200

School of Islamic Center of Rochester
727 Westfall Road
Rochester, NY 14620
(716) 422–0117
icr1@worldnet.att.net

Madrassah Al-Araaf
195 Nassau Road
Roosevelt, NY 11575

Al-Maida Academy
114 Frederick Avenue
Roosevelt, NY 11575
(631) 378–2104

Islamic Elementary School
13008 Rockaway Boulevard
South Ozone Park, NY 11420
(718) 322–3154

An-Nur School in Albany New York
21 Ferris Road
Schenectady, NY 12304
(518) 395–9866

Islamic Center School Building
2195 Central Avenue
Schenectady, NY 12304
(518) 395–9866

Miraj Islamic School
307 Victory Boulevard
Staten Island, NY 10301
(718) 816–9865

Al-Ihsan Islamic School
423 W Onondaga Street
Syracuse, NY 13202
(315) 472–5040
alihsan@iname.com
www.salam.muslimsonline.com/~alihsan

Crescent School
835 Brush Hollow Road
Westbury, NY 11590
(631) 333–4939

Al-Husseini Madressa Center
4867 58th Street
Woodside, NY 11377

Razi School
55–11 Queens Boulevard
Woodside, NY 11377
(718) 779–0711
Mahdi@erols.com

School of Islamic Center of Queens
5716 37th Avenue
Woodside, NY 11377
(718) 803–3747

Social Services
Islamic Group of New York
PO Box 305
Bellerose, NY 11426
(718) 740–3299
islamicgrp@aol.com

Albanian Assistance Center
746 Astor Avenue
Bronx, NY 10467
(718) 881–4732
medi3@aol.com

Arab American Family Support
88A 4th Avenue
Brooklyn, NY 11217
(718) 643–8000
aafsc@aol.com

Student Groups
Muslim Students Association–State
    University of New York–Albany
1400 Washington Avenue #116
Albany, NY 12222
(518) 437–9423

Muslim Student Association–State
    University of New York–Buffalo
316 Student
Amherst, NY 14261
(716) 825–5676

Muslim Student Association–Pratt
    Institute
200 Willoughby Avenue
Brooklyn, NY 11205
(718) 592–8126

Muslim Students Association–Polytechnic
6 Metrotech Center #657
Brooklyn, NY 11201
(718) 436–6437

Muslim Student Association–SGA
    Medgar Evers College
1650 Bedford Avenue
Brooklyn, NY 11225

Islamic Student Organization
Route 46
Budd Lake, NY 07828
(973) 426–1521

Islamic Organization of Hofstra
  University
1000 Fulton Avenue
Hempstead, NY 11550
(516) 463–2418

Muslim Students Association–St John's
  University
8000 Utopia Center #68
Jamaica, NY 11439
(718) 390–4545

Muslim Club of York College of City
  University
94–20 Guy R. Brewer Boulevard
Jamaica, NY 11451

Pakistan Student Association
142 E Market Street
Long Beach, NY 11561

Muslim Student Organization–City
  University of New York
138 Convent Avenue
New York, NY 10031
(212) 650–0406

Organization of Pakistani Students
403 Lerner Hall
2920 Broadway, MC 2601
New York, NY 10027
ops@columbia.edu
www.columbia.edu/cu/ops

Postdam Mosque–Muslim Student
  Association
110 Elm Street
Potsdam, NY 13676
(315) 265–3608

Muslim Students Association–Manhattan
  College
PO BOX 1155
Purchase, NY 10577
(914) 694–2200

Muslim Student Association–State
  University of New York
Room 153 Humanities Building
Stony Brook, NY 11794

Muslim Student Association–Syracuse
  University
Hendricks Chapel Syracuse Union
Syracuse, NY 13244
(315) 422–6325

Muslim Student Association–Renssealer
  Polytech
2339 15th Street
Troy, NY 12180
(518) 274–0137

Sufi Group
Mosque of the Jerrahi Order of America
884 Chestnut Ridge Road
Chestnut Ridge, NY 10977
(914) 352–5518
jerrahi@usa.net
www.jerrahii.org

TV Program
Arabic Channel
20 Exchange Place
New York, NY 10005
(212) 425–8822
www.ethnicnet.com

Women's Group
Al-Nissa Islamic Movement of Americas
10701 110th Street
S Richmond Hill, NY 11419
(718) 843–2183

NORTH CAROLINA

Ethnic Associations
Pakistani-American Association of North
  Carolina
PO Box 1995
Cary, NC 27512
president@ncpaa.org
www.ncpaa.org

Nigerian Community of Charlotte
926 Elizabeth Avenue Suite 403
Charlotte, NC 28204
nccweb@getechnet.com
www.nccweb.org

Iraq Action Coalition
7309 Haymarket Lane
Raleigh, NC 27615
(919) 846–7422
iac@leb.net
www.leb.net/IAC

Mosques / Islamic Centers
Islamic Center of Asheville
26 College Street
Asheville, NC 28801
(704) 258–8360
sal.ramada@worldnet.att.net

Islamic Center of Charlotte
PO Box 25612
Charlotte, NC 28229
(704) 567–0911

Masjid Ash-Shaheed
2717 Tuckaseegee Road
Charlotte, NC 28208
(704) 394–6579

Islamic Society of Greater Charrlotte
7025 The Plaza Road
Charlotte, NC 28215
(704) 536–2016

Islamic Center of Charlotte
1700 Progress Lane
Charlotte, NC 28205
(704) 537–9399

Masjid Ibad ar-Rahman
3034 Fayetteville Street
Durham, NC 27707
(919) 683–2727

Masjid-Jamaat Ibad Ar-Rahman
PO Box 1590
Durham, NC 27702
(919) 683–5593

Masjid Ar-Razzaq
1009 W Chapel Hill Street
Durham, NC 27701
(919) 493–1230

Masjid Muhammad
430 Gillespie Street
Fayetteville, NC 28301

Masjid Omar Ibn Sayyid
1831 Murchison Road
Fayetteville, NC 28301
(910) 488–7322
abeya@aol.com

Islamic Society of Gastonia
4042 Titman Road
Gastonia, NC 28056
(704) 824–7994

Wayne County Islamic Society
2807 McLain Street
Goldsboro, NC 27534
(919) 759–0737

Islamic Center of the Triad
7 Terrace Way
Greensboro, NC 27403
(336) 856–2870

Masjid Ahl al-Sunnah
E. Market Street
Greensboro, NC 274
(336) 373–1854

Islamic Society of Greensboro
2109 Martin Luther King Jr. Drive
Greensboro, NC 27406
(336) 852–3040

Islamic Center of Greensboro
2101 E Patterson
Greensboro, NC 274
(336) 851–1014

Islamic Association of East North
    Carolina
1303 S Evans Street
Greenville, NC 27834
(252) 756–6449

Masjid An-Nur
1117 W 3rd Street
Greenville, NC 27834
(252) 752–9181

Islamic Center of High Point
273 Dorothy Street
High Point, NC 27262

Islamic Society
3313 Chilham Place
Matthews, NC 28105
(704) 537–9399

Islamic Center of Morgantown
203 Bethel Street
Morganton, NC 28655
(828) 439–9487

New Bern Islamic Center
1726 Washington Street
New Bern, NC 28560

Muslim Association of the Carolinas
8290 Fayetteville Road
Raeford, NC 28376
(910) 895–3786

Salam Islamic Center
110 Lord Anson Drive
Raleigh, NC 27610
(919) 833–3358

Islamic Association of Raleigh
3020 Ligon Street
Raleigh, NC 27607
(919) 834–9572

Jama'at at-Taqwa
Islamic Studies Center Building
118 E South Street
Raleigh, NC 27601
(919) 546–8333

Masjid Al-Huada
1513 Memory Lane
Rocky Mount, NC 27804
(252) 985–1195

Masjid al-Muminin
1720 Wilson Lee Boulevard
Statesville, NC 28677
(704) 872–1428

Masjid Muhammad
719 ¹/₂ Castle Street
Wilmington, NC 28401
(901) 724–5554

Masjid Muhammad
711 S 8th Street
Wilmington, NC 28401

Community Mosque of Winston-Salem
1011 Washington Street
Winston Salem, NC 27105
(336) 748–0756

Islamic Society of Triad
4873 Bridle Creek
Winston Salem, NC 27106
(910) 922–3660

Schools
Ibad Ar-Rahman School
3034 Fayetteville Street
Durham, NC 27707
(919) 683–4311

Al-Iman School
3020 Ligon Street
Raleigh, NC 27607
(919) 821–1699

Student Groups
Muslim Student Association–University
    of North Carolina
33 Carolina Meadows
Chapel Hill, NC 27517
(919) 933–6405

Muslim Center of Charlotte
2117 Beatties Ford Road
Charlotte, NC 28216
(704) 399–0418

Muslim Student Association–Duke
PO Box 90834
Durham, NC 27708
(919) 684–5955

Muslim Student Association–A&T State
523 Homeland Avenue Apartment B
Greensboro, NC 27405
(336) 230–0100

NORTH DAKOTA

Mosques / Islamic Centers
Islamic Society of Fargo-Moorhead
PO Box 5223
Fargo, ND 58105
(701) 234–9607

Islamic Society of Minot
206 11th Avenue SE Suite A
Minot, ND 58701
(701) 838–2678

Student Groups
Muslim Student Association of North
  Dakota State University
PO Box 5223
Fargo, ND 58105
(701) 234–9607

Muslim Student Association–University
  of North Dakota
PO Box 8136
Grand Forks, ND 58202
(701) 746–1463

Muslim Student Association–Husain
  Pharmocology
501 N Columbia Road
Grand Forks, ND 58203

OHIO

Book Publisher / Distributor
African and Islamic Books Plus
3752 Lee Road
Cleveland, OH 44128
(216) 561–5000

Coordination Council
Islamic Council of Ohio
2769 Heston Court
Columbus, OH 43235
(614) 457–2518

Ethnic Associations
Arab American Community Center
10006 Lorain Avenue
Cleveland, OH 44111
(216) 631–4222

Council of Lebanese American
  Organizations
PO Box 181116
Cleveland, OH 44118

Turkish American Society of
  Northeastern Ohio
PO Box 22121
Cleveland, OH 44122
(330) 535–7478
gencer@imet.net

Bangladesh Association of Central Ohio
PO Box 20535
Columbus, OH 43220
(614) 792–3060
baco@ishika.com
www.ishika.com/baco

Greater Toledo Association of Arab
  Americans
2909 W Central Avenue
Toledo, OH 43606
(419) 537–9014

Arab American Club
PO Box 957
Youngstown, OH 44501

Mosques / Islamic Centers
Jaffery Union of Northeast Ohio
1460 Manchester Road
Akron, OH 44314
(330) 847–7280

Akron Masjid
1145 Old South Main
Akron, OH 44301
(330) 252–1622

Islamic Center of Athens
13 Stuart Street
Athens, OH 45701
(740) 594–3890
muslimst@oak.cats.ohio.edu

Bedford Mosque
297 Center Road
Bedford, OH 44146
(440) 439–4448

Islamic Society of Northeastern Ohio
4848 Higbee Avenue NW
Canton, OH 44718
(330) 455–6676

Islamic Outreach Center of Cincinnati
2147 Colerain Avenue
Cincinnati, OH 45214
(513) 651–2330

Islamic Association of Cincinnati
3668 Clifton Avenue
Cincinnati, OH 45220
(513) 221–4003

Islamic Council of Greater Cincinatti
PO Box 6835T
Cincinnati, OH 45206
(513) 281–2183

Cincinnati Islamic Center
3809 Woodford Road
Cincinnati, OH 45213
(513) 793–4508

Ugbah Mosque Foundation
2222 Stokes Boulevard
Cleveland, OH 44106
(216) 321–7906

Islamic Center of Cleveland
9400 Detroit Avenue
Cleveland, OH 44102
(440) 235–3020

Masjid Bilal
7401 Euclid Avenue
Cleveland, OH 44103
(216) 391–8899

First Cleveland Mosque
3613 E 131st Street
Cleveland, OH 44120
(216) 751–5690

Masjid Ul Sabur
936 E 128th Street
Cleveland, OH 44108
(216) 451–2709

Masjid Al-Nur
1251 E 99th Street
Cleveland, OH 44108
(216) 231–9663

Masjid Warith Deen
7301 Superior Avenue
Cleveland, OH 44103
(440) 439–5582

Masjid Uqbah Ibn Nafeh
PO Box 1973
Cleveland, OH 44106
(216) 791–8411
uqbahmf@yahoo.com

Islamic Mosque of Cleveland
12740 Lorain Avenue #42
Cleveland, OH 44111
(216) 941–0120

Masjid Al-Ansari
3520 E 116th Street
Cleveland, OH 44105
(216) 752–3323

Masjid Al-Islam
1677 Oak Street
Columbus, OH 43205
(614) 252–0338

Islamic Society of Greater Columbus
580 Riverview Drive
Columbus, OH 43202
(614) 262–1310
ifgc@muslimsonline.com

Islamic Foundation of Central Ohio
1428 E Broad Street
Columbus, OH 43205
info@ifco-columbus.org

Ahl Sunnat Wal Jammat
PO Box 151151
Columbus, OH 43215

Greater Dayton Islamic Foundation Inc.
1225 Mount Vernon Avenue
Dayton, OH 45405
(937) 429–9477

Masjid al-Taqwa
701 N Broadway Street
Dayton, OH 45407
(937) 275–5519

Dayton Islamic Center
2170 Malvern Avenue
Dayton, OH 45406
(513) 228–1503

Islamic Society of Greater Dayton
26 Josie Street
Dayton, OH 45403
(937) 228–1503
isgd@juno.com

Islamic Society of Kent
325 E Crain Avenue
Kent, OH 44240
(330) 678–4827

Lima Muslim Community Center
435 S Collett Street
Lima, OH 45805
(419) 227–6765

Masjid Al-Haqq
868 W Murphy Street
Lima, OH 45801
(419) 228–8295

Al-Muwahideen Society
PO Box 471
Lima, OH 45802
(419) 227–1327

Lorain Islamic Association
1300 Reid Avenue
Lorain, OH 44052

Islamic Center of Greater Toledo
25877 Scheider Road
Perrysburg, OH 43551
(419) 874–3509
info@icgt.org

Miami Valley Islamic Association
1800 S Burnett Road
Springfield, OH 45505
(513) 322–3266

Masjid Al-Nur Muslim Center
743 W Liberty Street
Springfield, OH 45506
(513) 322–4901

Masjid of Al-Islam
828 Ewing Street
Toledo, OH 43607
(419) 241–9522
iabdulra@glasscity.net

Muslim Community Center
724 Tecumseh Street
Toledo, OH 43602
(419) 244–4140

Masjid Saad Foundation
4346 Secor Road
Toledo, OH 43623
(419) 292–1492

Masjid Muhammad
PO Box 456
Toledo, OH 43697

Islamic Center of Greater Cincinnati
8091 Plantation Drive
West Chester, OH 45069
(513) 352–3313

Islamic Community Center of Southwest
299 E Market Street
Xenia, OH 45385
(513) 376–4111

Youngstown Islamic Center
PO Box 418
Youngstown, OH 44501
(330) 307–6162

Islamic Society of Youngstown
1670 Homewood Avenue
Youngstown, OH 44502
(330) 743–3742

Islamic Society of Greater Youngstown
535 Harmon Avenue
Youngstown, OH 44502
(330) 743–3742

Muhammad Mosque
542 Belmont Avenue
Youngstown, OH 44502
(330) 747–8833

Youngstown Islamic Center
131 W Woodland Avenue
Youngstown, OH 44502
(330) 743–1592

Prison Outreach Group
Islamic Education and Correctional
    Services
5452 Broadway Avenue
Cleveland, OH 44127
(216) 271–2121

Public Affairs Organizations
Council on American-Islamic
    Relations–Ohio
4700 Reed Avenue
Columbus, OH 43220
(614) 451–3232
ohio@cair-net.org

United Muslim Association of Toledo
1250 Flair Drive
Toledo, OH 43615
(419) 472–6613
www.toledomuslims.com

Schools
Cleveland Community Islamic School
7301 Superior Avenue
Cleveland, OH 44103
(216) 431–2088

Sunrise Academy
5657 Scioto Darby Road
Hilliard, OH 43026
(614) 527–0465
akhan@magnus.acs.ohio-state.edu

Toledo Islamic Academy
4404 Secor Road
Toledo, OH 43623

Al Noor Islamic Education
520 Madison Avenue Suite 1020
Toledo, OH 43604
(419) 472–9994

Social Services
The Muslim Women's Network and
    Community Services
PO Box 340706
Columbus, OH 43234
(614) 470–2848
mwn839@hotmail.com
mwn@yahoogroups.com

Student Groups
Muslim Student Association of Ohio
    University
13 Stewart Street
Athens, OH 45701
(740) 593–5321

Muslim Student Association
University of Cincinnati
Cincinnati, OH 45221
(513) 556–4185

Student Organization
2202 Stokes Boulevard
Cleveland, OH 44106
(216) 791–8411

Muslim Student Association–Cleveland
    State University
PO Box 665
Cleveland, OH 44107
(216) 687–6967

Muslim Student Association of Kent
    State
3 Student Life Office
Kent, OH 44242
(216) 673–4737

Women's Group
Islamic International Women's League
9406 Detroit Avenue
Cleveland, OH 44102
(216) 281–4357

Youth Group
Muslim Youth
738 Bryden Road
Columbus, OH 43205
(614) 469–4815

OKLAHOMA

Ethnic Associations
Turkish American Association of
  Oklahoma
10010 E 16th Street
Tulsa, OK 74128
(916) 665–6575
aandm@galstar.com

Nigerian Union Tulsa, Inc.
PO Box 1617
Tulsa, OK 74101
info@nigerianunion.org
www.nigerianunion.org

Mosques / Islamic Centers
Al Mahdi Foundation
5635 1/2 E 141st Street S
Bixby, OK 74008
(918) 366–6122

Islamic Society of Edmond
525 N University Drive
Edmond, OK 73034
(405) 741–1077

Islamic Society of Norman
420 E Lindsey Street
Norman, OK 73069
(405) 329–8928

Masjid Muhammad
1322 NE 23rd Street
Oklahoma City, OK 73111
(405) 424–1471

Islamic Society of Greater Oklahoma
  City
3815 N Saint Clair Avenue
Oklahoma City, OK 73112
(405) 946–2116
okcislam@yahoo.com

Masjid Wadthudeen
6035 N Stonewall Avenue
Oklahoma City, OK 73111

Muslim Community Association–Ponca
  City
2500 Wildwood Avenue
Ponca City, OK 74604
(405) 762–7732

Islamic Society of Stillwater
616 N Washington Street
Stillwater, OK 74075
(405) 377–5910

Tulsa Muslim Community
6610 S Peoria Avenue
Tulsa, OK 74136
(918) 835–1849

Islamic Society of Tulsa
4620 S Irvington Avenue
Tulsa, OK 74135
(918) 665–2023

Islamic Community Center
1436 N Cheyenne Avenue
Tulsa, OK 74106

School
Peace Academy
4620 S Irvington Avenue
Tulsa, OK 74135
(918) 627–1040
www.istulsa.org

Student Group
Muslim Student Association–University
  of Oklahoma
420 E Lindsey Street
Norman, OK 73069
(405) 364–5747

OREGON

Guild
Iranian Professional Society of Oregon
PO Box 852
Lake Oswego, OR 97034
ipso@teleport.com

Mosques / Islamic Centers
Al-Haramain
3800 Highway 99 S
Ashland, OR 97520
(541) 482–1116
q@qf.org

Masjid Bilal
4116 SW 160th Avenue
Beaverton, OR 97007
(503) 591–7233

Salman Farsi Islamic Center
610 NW Kings Boulevard
Corvallis, OR 97330
(541) 758–0329

AbuBakr Siddiq Islamic Center
PO Box 3569
Eugene, OR 97403
(503) 346–3798

Islamic Center of Portland
10200 SW Capitol Highway
Portland, OR 97219
(503) 293–6554

School
Muslim Educational Trust Islamic School
1979 SW 5th Avenue
Portland, OR 97201
(503) 228–3754
metpdx@teleport.com
www.teleport.com/~metpdx

Student Groups
Muslim Students Association–Portland
  States University
PO Box 283
Portland, OR 97207
(503) 248–0477

Muslim Students Association–Oregon
  State University
Students Activity Center
Portland, OR 97330
(503) 758–0329

Muslim Students Association of Eugene
University of Oregon
Room #202
Portland, OR 97403
(541) 346–3798

Muslim Students Association–Eastern
  Oregon State College
8th and K
Portland, OR 97850

PUERTO RICO

Mosque / Islamic Center
El Centro Islamico
212 De Diego Street
Rio Piedras, PR 00928

PENNSYLVANIA

Coordination Council
Majlis Ash-Shura of Delaware Valley
PO Box 42471
Philadelphia, PA 19101

Ethnic Associations
Turkish American Friendship Society of
  the United States
249 Saint Joseph's Way
Philadelphia, PA 19106
(215) 629–1089
tafsus@tafsus.com
www.tafsus.com

Turkish American Association of
  Pittsburg
4 Camden Drive
Pittsburgh, PA 15215
(412) 782–3393
iso9000x@aol.com

Islamic Call Groups
United Muslim Movement
800 S 15th Street
Philadelphia, PA 19146
(215) 546–6555

Islamic Propagation Group
PO Box 7525
Pittsburgh, PA 15213
(412) 734–2551

Foundation for Islamic Education
1860 Montgomery Avenue
Villanova, PA 19085
(610) 526–1955
mahmad@erols.com

Mosques / Islamic Centers
Shia Ithnusheri Jamaat
1335 W Chew Street
Allentown, PA 18102
(610) 776–5022
mkhaku786@yahoo.com
www.sijpa.org

Bensalem Masjid
3046 Knights Road
Bensalem, PA 19020

Masjid Al-Fajr
2009 W 3rd Street
Chester, PA 19013
(610) 225–2084

Islamic Center of Chester
14 E 7th Street
Chester, PA 19013
(610) 876–1270

Masjid As-Sabiqun
1105 Concord Avenue
Chester, PA 19013
(610) 490–1757

Islamic Society of Greater Valley Forge
958 N Valley Forge Road
Devon, PA 19333
(610) 688–2209

Islamic Center of Erie
9 E 12th Street
Erie, PA 16501
(814) 453–3001

Islamic Center Masjid Alsabreen
1403 S Cameron Street
Harrisburg, PA 17104
(717) 238–8313

Harrisburg Masjid
1725 Market Street
Harrisburg, PA 17103
(717) 232–4545

Islamic Center of Johnstown
PO Box 5192
Johnstown, PA 15904
(814) 266–6484
gazim01@ctcnet.net

Muslim Center
1415 Beaver Street
McKeesport, PA 15132

Muslim Community Center of Greater
  Pittsburgh
233 Seamen Lane
Monroeville, PA 15146
(412) 373–0101

Islamic Center of New Castle
1225 Finch Street
New Castle, PA 16101
(724) 658–8835

Al-Aqsa Islamic Society
1501 Germantown Avenue
Philadelphia, PA 19122
(215) 765–2743

Albanian-American Muslim Society
157 W Girard Avenue
Philadelphia, PA 19123
(215) 291–9803

Masjid Al-Qur'an
1546 N 27th Street
Philadelphia, PA 19121
(215) 763–1601
masjidaq@mail.com

Masjid Al-Mujahiddeen
413 S 60th Street
Philadelphia, PA 19143
(215) 471–7073
taalib@erols.com

Mosque Foundation of Pennsylvania
2732 N Marvine Street
Philadelphia, PA 19133

Masjid Al-Sunnah Al-Nabawiyyah
4944 Germantown Avenue
Philadelphia, PA 19144
(215) 848–2614

Masjidullah
7700 Ogontz Avenue
Philadelphia, PA 19150
(215) 424–8022

Makkah Masjid
1319 W Susquehanna Avenue
Philadelphia, PA 19122
(215) 978–9508

Islamic Community Network
2451 N 19th Street
Philadelphia, PA 19132
(215) 225–4070

Masjid al-Birr wat-Taqwa
23 S 52nd Street Floor 2
Philadelphia, PA 19139
(215) 747–3133

Masjid Al-Jamia
4228 Walnut Street
Philadelphia, PA 19104
(215) 386–3770
Sidy10@hotmail.com

The Islamic Center of Ridge Avenue
3116 Ridge Avenue
Philadelphia, PA 19121
(215) 232–9475

Masjid Muhammad
414 E Penn Street
Philadelphia, PA 19144
(215) 843–6846

The Philadelphia Masjid
4700 Wyalusing Avenue
Philadelphia, PA 19131
(215) 877–8600

Masjid Al-Islam
4309 Terrace Street
Philadelphia, PA 19128
(215) 482–9819

Masjid Madira
3130 N Broad Street
Philadelphia, PA 19132
(215) 951–9242

Masjid Taha
4665 Frankford Avenue Floor 2
Philadelphia, PA 19124
(215) 324–5076

Masjid Al-Hashr
2823 N 22nd Street
Philadelphia, PA 19132
(215) 819–5436
hashar@aol.com

Mosque M. R. Bawa Muhaiyadeen
5820 Overbrook Avenue
Philadelphia, PA 19131
(215) 879–0234

Institute of Islamic Revival
1765 N 29th Street
Philadelphia, PA 19121
(215) 232–5173

Masjid Al-Awwal
1911 Wylie Avenue
Pittsburgh, PA 15219
(412) 471–1036

Masjid Al-Alamin
7222 Kelly Street
Pittsburgh, PA 15208
(412) 241–8850

Islamic Center of Pittsburgh
4100 Bigelow Boulevard
Pittsburgh, PA 15213
(412) 682–5555
islampgh@trfn.clpgh.org

Masjid Al Mu'min
537 Paulson Avenue
Pittsburgh, PA 15206
(412) 363–1237

An-Nur Islamic Center
303 S Trenton Avenue
Pittsburgh, PA 15221
(412) 371–0447

Islamic Society of Central Pennsylvania
709 Ridge Avenue
State College, PA 16803
(814) 238–2079
badermalek@hotmail.com

Islamic Society of Greater Harrisburg
401 N Front Street
Steelton, PA 17113
(717) 939–3107
isgh@aol.com

Stroudsburg Islamic Center
113 N 2nd Street
Stroudsburg, PA 18360
(717) 421–4108

Islamic Society of Susquehanna Valley
4th and Arch Street
Sunbury, PA 17801
(570) 286–9995

Masjid al-Madina
6800 Ludlow Street
Upper Darby, PA 19082
(610) 352–7774

Islamic Center of Chester County
1001 Pottstown Pike
West Chester, PA 19380
(610) 344–9488

Islamic Center of Lehigh Valley
1798 Schadt Avenue
Whitehall, PA 18052
(610) 966–2976

Masjid Al-Noor
PO Box 5061
Wilkes Barre, PA 18710

Noor Mosque
334 S George Street
York, PA 17403
(717) 843–3162

Schools
Masjid As-Sabiqun School
1105 Concord Avenue
Chester, PA 19013
(610) 490–1757

United Muslim Movement School
810 S 15th Street
Philadelphia, PA 19146
(215) 473–6518
info@unitedmuslimmovement.org

Al-Aqsa Islamic School
1501 Germantown Avenue
Philadelphia, PA 19122
(215) 765–6660
alaqsa@msn.com

Clara Muhammad School
1900 N 54th Street
Philadelphia, PA 19131
(215) 877–9020

Sr. Clara Muhammed School
4700 Lancaster Avenue
Philadelphia, PA 19121
(215) 877–8600

Al-Shahid Islamic School
6041 Drexel Road
Philadelphia, PA 19131
(215) 473–6626

Sr. Clara Muhammad School
1900 N 54th Street
Philadelphia, PA 19131
(215) 877–9020

Habib Allah Day School
4637 Lancaster Avenue
Philadelphia, PA 19131

The Universal Academy of Pittsburgh
4100 Bigelow Boulevard
Pittsburgh, PA 15213
(412) 682–5555

Darul Uloom Al-Qasimia
818 Race Street
Shamokin, PA 17872
(717) 644–1040
alqasim@sunlink.net
www.sunlink.net/~alqasim

Social Services
Islamic Family Center
6830 Old York Road
Philadelphia, PA 19126
(215) 224–7343

Student Groups
Muslim Student Association–Drexel
  University
3017 Macalister Hall
Philadelphia, PA 19104

Muslim Student Association–Community
  College
1700 Spring Garden Street
Philadelphia, PA 19130
(215) 751–8202

Muslim Student Association
UC Box 79
UC Suite 103
5000 Forbes Avenue
Pittsburgh, PA 15213

Muslim Students Association–Penn State
  University
101 Hub
University Park, PA 16802
(814) 867–6726

Youth Group
American Congress of Muslim Youth
4807 Walnut Street
Philadelphia, PA 19139
(215) 747–7772

RHODE ISLAND

Ethnic Association
Lebanese American Community
141 Urban Avenue
North Providence, RI 02904
(401) 726–9598

Mosques / Islamic Centers
Masjid al Islam
40 Sayles Hill Road
North Smithfield, RI 02896
(401) 762–0107

Masjid Muhammad
234 Pavilion Avenue
Providence, RI 02905
(401) 467–0011

Islamic Center of Rhode Island
582 Cranston Street
Providence, RI 02907
(401) 274–3986

Southern Rhode Island Islamic Society
293 Lake Shore Drive
Warwick, RI 02889
(401) 732–6951
sharif@uri.edu

SOUTH CAROLINA

Mosques / Islamic Centers
Muslim Community Center
808 Geisberg Drive
Anderson, SC 29624
(864) 225–1061

Islamic Center of Charleston
1117 King Street
Charleston, SC 29403
(843) 958–9585

Islamic Society of Charleston Inc.
PO Box 21555
Charleston, SC 29413
(843) 723–7689

Islamic Council of Charleston
PO Box 20756
Charleston, SC 29413

Masjid As-Salaam
5119 Monticello Road
Columbia, SC 29203
(803) 252–9477

Al-Muslimeen
1929 Gervais Street
Columbia, SC 29201
(803) 254–7242

Conway Islamic Center
1370 Bucksport Road
Conway, SC 29527
(803) 397–9701

Muslim Center
1808 Racepath Avenue
Conway, SC 29527
(843) 958–9585

Florence Muslim Center
410 N Coit Street
Florence, SC 29501
(843) 629–0017

Islamic Center of Florence
1218 W Evans Street
Florence, SC 29501

Islamic Center of Greenville
2701 Wade Hampton Boulevard
Greenville, SC 29615
(864) 292–2219

Masjid Al Jami Ar-Rashid
1998 Hugo Avenue
N Charleston, SC 29405
(803) 554–1773

Masjid Taqwa
701 Russell Street NE
Orangeburg, SC 29115
(803) 534–2281

Masjid Al Fatima
742 Islamville Way
York, SC 29745
(803) 684–4986

School
Al-Muslimeen School
1929 Gervais Street
Columbia, SC 29201
(803) 254–7242

Student Group
Muslim Student Association–Clemson
  University
9817 University
Clemson, SC 29632

SOUTH DAKOTA

Mosques / Islamic Centers
Islamic Society of Brookings
803 13th Avenue
Brookings, SD 57006
(605) 697–6187

Islamic Society of Sioux Falls
1909 E 6th Street
Sioux Falls, SD 57103
(605) 333–2005

TENNESSEE

Ethnic Association
North American Bangladeshi Islamic
  Community
PO Box 6631
Oak Ridge, TN 37831
(423) 483–8189
nabic-info@globalfront.com

Mosques / Islamic Centers
Islamic Center of Chattanooga
1410 Cemetery Avenue
Chattanooga, TN 37408
(423) 698–2957

Annour Islamic Community
5311 Upshaw Drive
Chattanooga, TN 37416
(423) 490–8544

American Muslim Mission–Chattanooga
  Center TRS
504 Kilmer Street
Chattanooga, TN 37404

Muslim Community Center Incorporated
9880 Houston Levee Cove
Germantown, TN 38139

Muslim Community of Knoxville
100 13th Street
Knoxville, TN 37916
(865) 690–6826

Masjid Al-Mu'minun
4412 S 3rd Street
Memphis, TN 38109
(901) 789–1904
muslimemph@aol.com

Muslim Society of Memphis
1065 Stratford Road
Memphis, TN 38122
(901) 685–8906
mslmsocmem@aol.com

Muslim American Community
2416 Batavia Street
Nashville, TN 37208
(615) 320–5126

Masjid Al-Islam
2508 Clifton Avenue
Nashville, TN 37209
(615) 329–1646

Islamic Center of Nashville
2515 12th Avenue S
Nashville, TN 37204
(615) 385–9379
hadramut@hotmail.com

Lake County Muslim Center
RR 1 Box 330
Tiptonville, TN 38079

Schools
Islamic School
PO Box 51511
Knoxville, TN 37950

Pleasant View School
1888 Bartlett Road
Memphis, TN 38134
(901) 380–0122
webmaster@pleasantviewschool.com
www.pleasantviewschool.com

Sr. Clara Muhammed School
4412 S 3rd Street
Memphis, TN 38109
(910) 789–1904

Islamic School of Nashville
7335 Charlotte Pike
Nashville, TN 37209
(615) 352–5903
Mohsen3@ix.netcom.com

Masjid Al-Islam
2508 Clifton Avenue
Nashville, TN 37209
(615) 329–1646

Student Groups
Muslim Student Association Knoxville
Ut # 87
Knoxville, TN 37996

Masjid AnNoor–Muslim Student
    Association
3529 Mynders Avenue
Memphis, TN 38111
(901) 432–0761
Ahlussunah@aol.com

Muslim Students Association–Tennessee
    State University
2515 12th Avenue S
Nashville, TN 37204
(615) 385–9379

Youth Group
Muslim Youth Center
PO Box 101104
Nashville, TN 37224

TEXAS

Cemeteries
Islamic Janaza Service
PO Box 150003
Dallas, TX 75315
(214) 824–6462

Muslim Cemetery Inc. of North Texas
PO Box 66
Sherman, TX 75091

Community Development Group
Islamic Circle of North America–Dallas
PO Box 830152
Richardson, TX 75083
(214) 669–9625
haseeb@bnn.ca

Ethnic Associations
Iranian Cultural Community of Austin
PO Box 201913
Austin, TX 78720
icca@farsinet.com
www.farsinet.com/icca/

IAP Information Office
PO Box 741805
Dallas, TX 75374
(972) 669–9595

Nigerian Muslim Association of Dallas
PO Box 560871
Dallas, TX 75356
(214) 331–6488

Turkish American Association of
    Northern Texas
PO Box 1837
Desoto, TX 75123
(972) 223–7250
erkutay@aol.com
www.turant.com

Bangladesh Association
401 Meadow Trail Lane
Friendswood, TX 77546
(281) 996–8025

Bangladesh Association, Houston
1620 Bay Area Boulevard
Apartment 1710
Houston, TX 77058
(281) 996–8025
hasan_rahman@hotmail.com

American Turkish Association of
    Houston
PO Box 61002
Houston, TX 77208
(713) 235–4805
jccaglar@bechtel.com
www.atahouston.org

Pakistani Association of Greater Houston
9644 S. Kirkwood Suite A-3
Houston, TX 77099
(281) 933–0786
pagh@pagh.org
www.pagh.org/

Arab-American Cultural and Community
    Center
9700 Richmond Avenue Suite 111
Houston, TX 77042
(713) 783–2727
info@aaccc.com

Hyderabad Association
6314 Wagner Way
Sugar Land, TX 77479
(281) 531–6764

Matrimonial Services
Sister Zainab's Matrimonial Service
PO Box 831621
Richardson, TX 75083

Mosques / Islamic Centers
Islamic Society of Alvin
702 S Gordon Street
Alvin, TX 77511
(281) 388–2837

Islamic Center of Amarillo
601 Quail Creek Drive
Amarillo, TX 79124
(806) 358–1615
banglaguy@aol.com

Islamic Society of Arlington
100 Madinah Drive
Arlington, TX 76010
(817) 461–8415

Dar El Salam Islamic Center
747 W Lamar Boulevard
Arlington, TX 76012
(817) 265–2596

Dar Eleman Islamic Center
5511 Mansfield Road
Arlington, TX 76017
(817) 466–0505

Islamic Center of Greater Austin
1906 Nueces Street
Austin, TX 78705
(512) 258–0492
icga@muslims.net

Islamic Center of Austin
5110 Manor Road
Austin, TX 78723
(512) 476–2563

ISGH–Baytown
4506 North Main
Baytown, TX 77520

Islamic Center of Carrollton
PO Box 116406
Carrollton, TX 75011
(972) 466–1191
mhussain@gte.net

Islamic Association of Carrollton
1516 S Interstate 35E
Carrollton, TX 75006
(972) 466–1191
iac@iacnet-zzn.com

Islamic Community of Bryan/College
   Station
417 Stasney Street
College Station, TX 77840
(409) 846–4222
zxr@holditch.com

Islamic Society of South Texas
7341 McArdle Road
Corpus Christi, TX 78412
(361) 993–4690

Dallas Masjid of Al-Islam
2604 S Harwood Street
Dallas, TX 75215
(214) 421–3839

Allah's House of Islam
4752 Nome Street
Dallas, TX 75216
(214) 372–3741

The Islamic Society of Denton
1105 Greenlee Street
Denton, TX 76201
(817) 566–5927

Masjid al-Tawheed
1419 Acton Avenue
Duncanville, TX 75137

Islamic Center of El Paso
1600 N Kansas Street
El Paso, TX 79902
(919) 546–9468

Islamic Association of Terrant County
4801 Fletcher Avenue
Fort Worth, TX 76107
(817) 737–8104

Masjid Hassan
1201 E Allen Avenue
Fort Worth, TX 76104
(817) 923–5929

Islamic Association of Fort Worth
5747 Westcreek Drive
Fort Worth, TX 76133
(817) 294–1234

Galveston Islamic Society
2642 Gerol Drive
Galveston, TX 77551
(409) 744–4129

Islamic Society of Mesquite
5902 Duck Creek Drive #14
Garland, TX 75043
(214) 226–1820

Islamic Society of Texas
1817 Independence Court
Grand Prairie, TX 75052
(214) 641–7181

ISGH—Old Galveston
8830 Old Galveston Road
Houston, TX 77034
(713) 947–0394

Expo Masjid
11312 Westheimer Road
Houston, TX 77077
(281) 495–3403

Bissonnet Masjid
9651 Bissonnet Street Suite 306
Houston, TX 77036
(713) 777–5071

Bait-ul-Allah Masjid
3823 Lydia Street
Houston, TX 77021
(713) 747–4832
baitulallah@hotmail.com

ISGH–North Shore
810 Freeport Street
Houston, TX 77015
(281) 450–3070

Masjid Motors
7529 S Kirkwood Road
Houston, TX 77072
(281) 933–8550

Mecca Masjid
4010 S Dairy Ashford Street
Houston, TX 77082
(281) 496–4545
zarquani@evl.com

ISGH–South Zone
6293 Almeda Road
Houston, TX 77021

Islamic Education Center
2313 S Voss Road
Houston, TX 77057
(713) 537–1946
info@iec-houston.org

ISGH–Southeast Baytown
13818 Brownsville Street
Houston, TX 77015
(713) 455–0786

ISGH–South Zone
503 Dulles Avenue
Houston, TX 77477
(713) 261–6615

ISGH–Wilcrest
11246 South Wilcrest
Houston, TX 77099
(281) 568–6615

ISGH–North Zone
11815 Adel Road
Houston, TX 77067
(281) 537–1946

Masjid Muhammadi
11830 Corona Lane
Houston, TX 77072
(281) 498–6666

ISGH–Mission Bend
6265 Highway 6 S
Houston, TX 77083
(281) 561–8084

Al-Farooq
1209 Conrad Sauer
Houston, TX 77043
(713) 464–4720

Houston Masjid of Al-Islam
6641 Bellfort Street
Houston, TX 77087
(713) 649–7789

Madina Masjid
8015 S Kirkwood Road
Houston, TX 77072
(281) 575–1954

Al-Noor Society of Greater Houston
6443 Prestwood Drive
Houston, TX 77081
(713) 779–1304

Maxey Masjid
225 Maxey Road
Houston, TX 77013
(713) 455–8786

ISGH–South Mosque
503 Dulles Avenue
Houston, TX 77477

Islamic Society–Bear Creek
17250 Coventry Park Drive
Houston, TX 77084
(281) 859–8203

Islamic Society of Greater Houston
  (ISGH Main)
3110 Eastside Drive
Houston, TX 77098
(713) 524–6615

First Talim Masjid Muhammad
505 E 40th ½ Street
Houston, TX 77022
(713) 694–5827

Madrassah Islamiah
6665 Bintliff Drive
Houston, TX 77074
(713) 772–7000

Islamic Center of Irving
118 Village Center
Irving, TX 75061
(972) 721–9136

The Islamic Center of Momin
PO Box 142763
Irving, TX 75014
(972) 554–0200

Islamic Society of Kingsville
702 W B Avenue
Kingsville, TX 78363
(361) 592–7870

Masjid Al-Noor
PO Box 294102
Lewisville, TX 75029
(214) 415–3628
alikhan@kpmg.com

Islamic Center of the South Plains
3419 LaSalle Avenue
Lubbock, TX 79407
(806) 797–8026
y9d33@ttacs.ttu.edu

Muslim Association of West Texas
1200 S Midland Drive
Midland, TX 79703
(915) 520–4689

Islamic Association of Collin County
2109 W Parker Road Suite 220
Plano, TX 75023
(972) 758–0256

Islamic Association of North Texas
840 Abrams Road
Richardson, TX 75081
(214) 231–5698

Islamic Center of San Antonio
8638 Fairhaven Street
San Antonio, TX 78229
(210) 614–0989

Masjid Luqman
1702 Hays Street
San Antonio, TX 78202
(210) 224–5767

Islamic Mosque at Texoma
PO Box 2666
Sherman, TX 75091
(903) 786–9966

ISGH—Champion Mosque
16700 Old Louetta Road
Spring, TX 77379
(281) 528–0818

ISGH—Synott
10415 Synott Road
Sugar Land, TX 77478
(281) 495–3403

Islamic Society of Central Texas
3033 Kegley Lane
Temple, TX 76502

Tyler Masjid of Al-Islam
702 Peach Street
Tyler, TX 75702
(903) 592–2755

East Texas Islamic Society
10529 State Highway 64 E
Tyler, TX 75707
(903) 566–0606
etmasjid@flash.net

Victoria Islamic Center
201 E Airline Road
Victoria, TX 77901
(361) 575–1001
jihad45@hotmail.com

Masjid E Siddiq
2725 Benton Drive
Waco, TX 76706
(254) 662–5045

Rio Grande Valley Islamic Center
PO Box 421
Weslaco, TX 78599
(210) 969–8549

ISGH–North Zone
1370 Mill Bend Drive
Woodlands, TX 77380

Newspapers
Al-Zaitonah
PO Box 743533
Dallas, TX 75374
(214) 669–9595

Arab Times
PO Box 721438
Houston, TX 77272
(281) 799–0345
arabtimes@aol.com

Public Affairs Organizations
Council on American-Islamic
    Relations–Dallas
PO Box 393
Coppell, TX 75019
(972) 462–9630
info@cair.org
www.cairdfw.org

Dallas Muslim Council
P.O. Box 743633
Dallas, TX 75374
(972) 699–0667

Religious Education Program
Islamic Association of the Mid-Cities
PO Box 897
Hurst, TX 76053
(817) 282–2114

Schools
Dar Ul Arqam Islamic School
1600 S Center Street
Arlington, TX 76010
(817) 274–5822
darularqam@yahoo.com
www.geocities.com/athens/forum/6285

Peace Elementary School
5110 Manor Road
Austin, TX 78723
(512) 926–1737

Arabic Language School
3950 Spring Valley Road
Dallas, TX 75244
(972) 866–0266

Sr. Clara Muhammed School
1201 E Allen Avenue
Fort Worth, TX 76104
(817) 927–9871

Madrasat Al-Huda Schools
6700 Sands Point Drive
Houston, TX 77074
(713) 988–8466

Madrasah Islamiah
6665 Bintliff Drive
Houston, TX 77074
(713) 772–7000

Darul Arqam (ISGH)
3110 Eastside Street
Houston, TX 77098
(713) 524–6615

Iman Academy
PO Box 75212
Houston, TX 77234
(713) 910–3626
amjadm@swbell.net
www.786mall.com/faith

Al-Hadi School of Accelerative Learning
2313 S Voss Road
Houston, TX 77057
(713) 787–5000
alhadischool@hotmail.com
www.iec-houston.org/alhadi/index.html

Muslim Community School
11625 Adel Road
Houston, TX 77067
(281) 583–1984

Islamic School of Irving
245 E Grauwyler Road
Irving, TX 75061
(972) 579–7627

Social Services
Muslim Community Center for Human
 Services
7600 Glenview Drive
Fort Worth, TX 76180
(817) 516–8100

Student Groups
Muslim Student Association of Arlington
PO Box 19–4141
Arlington, TX 76019
(817) 277–0219

Kashmiri Students
 Association–University of Texas at
 Arlington
312 W Border Street
Arlington, TX 76010
ksa007@yahoo.com

Muslim Students Association–University
 of Texas
PO Box 7871
Austin, TX 78713
(512) 472–5222

Iranian Student Academic and Cultural
 Organization at the University of
 Texas at Austin
PO Box 7338
Austin, TX 78713
ut_isaco@farsinet.com

Muslim Student Association Texas A&M
PO Box 5688
College Station, TX 77844
(409) 846–6693

Muslim Students Association at Southern
 Methodist University
PO Box 2318
Dallas, TX 75275
(214) 706–5287

Muslim Student Association of Denton
223 Avenue G Apartment 4
Denton, TX 76201
(940) 383–8029

Muslim Student Association–University
 of Houston
Box 320 Campus Activity
Houston, TX 77004
(713) 743–8632

Muslim Students Association–Texas
 A&M University
702 W B Avenue
Kingsville, TX 78363
(361) 592–7870

Muslim Students Association at Texas
 Tech
2412 7th Street
Lubbock, TX 79401
(806) 765–5736

Trusts / Endowments
The ISGH Endowment Trust Fund
3110 Eastside Drive
Houston, TX 77098

Islamic Trust of North Texas
2912 Laramie Street
Irving, TX 75062

Women's Group
Islamic Women's Auxiliary of America
3823 Lydia Street
Houston, TX 77021
(713) 748–4114

Youth Group
Muslim Arab Youth Association Branch
6103 Larch Terrace
Austin, TX 78741
(512) 389–2141

UTAH

Ethnic Association
American Bosnian Association
1102 W 400 N
Salt Lake Cty, UT 84116
(801) 359–3378

Mosques / Islamic Centers
Logan Islamic Center
748 N 600 E
Logan, UT 84321
(435) 753–2491

Islamic Society of Salt Lake City
740 S 700 E
Salt Lake City, UT 84102
(801) 364–7822

Khadijah Masjid
PO Box 58844
Salt Lake City, UT 84158

Student Groups
Muslim Student Association–Utah
2216 Foothill Drive Apartment 215G
Salt Lake City, UT 84109
(801) 487–9551

Islamic Student Organization
403 University Village
Salt Lake City, UT 84108
(801) 582–2543

VIRGIN ISLANDS

Mosques / Islamic Centers
Masjid Ahl Us Sunnah
23 Eighth Street Kings Quarter
St. Thomas, VI 00802

School
IQRA' Academy
No. 20 & 21 Estate Mountain
St. Croix, VI 00841
(340) 772–4808
Hatimyusuf@aol.com

VIRGINIA

Charity Groups
Help the Afghan Children Inc.
4105 Fairfax Drive Suite 204
Arlington, VA 22203
(703) 524–2525
htaci@msn.com

Somali Rescue Agency
PO Box 1037
Falls Church, VA 22041
(703) 326–0895

Colleges
American Open University
3400 Payne Street Suite 200
Falls Church, VA 22041
(703) 671–2115
info@open-university.edu
www.open-university.edu

School for Islamic and Social Sciences
750–A. Miller Drive SE
Leesburg, VA 20175
(703) 779–7477
school@siss.edu
www.siss.edu

Community Development Group
Muslim American Society
3602 Forest Drive
Alexandria, VA 22302
(703) 998–6525

Ethnic Association
Somali TV and Coalition for Action
PO Box 23823
Alexandria, VA 22304
(703) 941–1815

U.S. Pakistan Alliance
4164 Elizabeth Lane
Annandale, VA 22003
(703) 978–2874

Expatriate Bangladeshi 2000
PO Box 833
Annandale, VA 22003
(877) 376–9790
info@eb2000.org

Sudan-American Foundation for
    Education
4141 N Henderson Road Apartment
    1216
Arlington, VA 22203
(703) 525–9045
lburchin@gmu.edu

Foundation of Ethiopian Muslims of
    North America
5695 Columbia Pike
Falls Church, VA 22041
(703) 933–0501

Association of Eritrean Jeberti in North
    America
PO Box 8242
Falls Church, VA 22041

The Arab-American Business and
    Professional Association
6819 Elm Street Suite 3
McLean, VA 22101
(703) 883–1994
abpa1@aol.com
www.arabamerican.com/ABPA.html

Egyptian American Cultural Association
PO Box 3725
McLean, VA 22103
(301) 808–1000

Afghan Islamic National Community
PO Box 613
Springfield, VA 22150
(703) 451–1088
arghanbab@aol.com

Association for Peace and Democracy for
    Afghanistan
6300–A Springfield Plaza
Springfield, VA 22150
webmaster@apdafghanistan.org

Ethiopian Democratic Action League
PO Box 766
Springfield, VA 22150
(703) 866–0709
tegbar@juno.com

Magazine
Al-Hewar Magazine
PO Box 2104
Vienna, VA 22183
(703) 281–6277
alhewar@alhewar.com
www.alhewar.com

Mosques / Islamic Centers
Mustafa Center
6844 Braddock Road
Annandale, VA 22003
(703) 658–3432

Islamic Society of Central Virginia
118 10 ½ Street NW
Charlottesville, VA 22903
(434) 923–8435
islam@virginia.edu

Danville Masjid
206 Barrett Street
Danville, VA 24541

Islamic Education Center
2018 Burfoot Street
Falls Church, VA 22043
(703) 442–0638

Dar al-Hijrah
PO Box 1625
Falls Church, VA 22041
(703) 536–1030

Hampton Roads Mosque and Islamic
    Center
22 Tide Mill Lane
Hampton, VA 23666
(804) 838–4726

All Dulles Area Muslim Society
12710 Fantasia Drive
Herndon, VA 20170

Afghan Islamic Gathering of Northern
  Virginia
506 Alabama Drive
Herndon, VA 20170
(703) 217–4998
saidal@ioip.com

Masjid Muhammad
2202 Garfield Avenue
Lynchburg, VA 24501

Manassas Masjid
12950 Center Entrance Court
Manassas, VA 20109
(703) 257–5537
muslims@islamic-city.com

Dar Al Salaam Mosque
15250 Dumfries Road
Manassas, VA 20112
(703) 670–0707

Muslim Community Center
1011 Fayette Street
Martinsville, VA 24112

Al-Qubu Islamic Center
1145 Hampton Avenue
Newport News, VA 23607
(757) 244–1336

Masjid William Salaam
2904 Vimy Ridge Avenue
Norfolk, VA 23509
(804) 855–5002

Norfolk Masjid
3401 Granby Street
Norfolk, VA 23504
(804) 623–2628

Petersburg Islamic Center
503 W Washington Street
Petersburg, VA 23803
(804) 861–9562

Masjid Bilal Ibn Rabah
400 Chimborazo Boulevard
Richmond, VA 23223
(804) 222–9825

Islamic Society of Greater Richmond
6325 Antler Road
Richmond, VA 23226
(804) 673–4177
info@isgr.org

Islamic Center of Virginia
1241 Buford Road
Richmond, VA 23235
(804) 320–7333

Masjid Ullah of Richmond
2211 North Avenue
Richmond, VA 23222

Masjid Bilal
400 Chimborazo Boulevard
Richmond, VA 23223
(804) 222–9825
qas98@juno.com

Kufa Center of Islamic Knowledge
PO Box 11771
Roanoke, VA 24022
(540) 563–8471
al_kufa@hotmail.com

Masjid An-Noor
8608 Pohick Road
Springfield, VA 22153
(703) 455–5604

Darul Huda
6666 Commerce Street
Springfield, VA 22150
(703) 922–0111
darulhuda.org

Islamic Foundation of America
6606 Electronic Drive
Springfield, VA 22151
(703) 914–4982
ifam@erols.com

Public Affairs Organization
Council of Pakistani American
    Organizations
933 N Kenmore Street Suite 400
Arlington, VA 22201
(703) 243–2200
metro786@aol.com

Religious Education Programs
Institute of Islamic and Arabic Sciences
    in America
8500 Hilltop Road
Fairfax, VA 22031
(703) 641–4890
info@iiasa.org
www.iiasa.org

Muslim Association of Virginia
PO Box 2551
Woodbridge, VA 22195

Research Groups
International Institute of Islamic Thought
500 Grove Street
Herndon, VA 20170
(703) 471–1133
iiit@iiit.org
www.iiit.org

Fiqh Council of North America
SISS, 750–A. Miller Drive SE
Leesburg, VA 20175
fiqh@fiqhcouncil.org
www.fiqhcouncil.org

United Association for Studies and
    Research
5524 Hempstead Way
Springfield, VA 22151
(703) 750–9011
uasr@aol.com
www.uasr4islam.com

Schools
Islamic Saudi Academy
11121 Popes Head Road
Fairfax, VA 22030
(703) 691–0000

Islamic Saudi Academy
8333 Richard Highway
Alexandria, VA 22309
(703) 780–0606

Adams School
500 Grove Street
Herndon, VA 20170
(703) 318–0529
adamscenter@erols.com

School of Islamic Center
503 Washington Street
Petersburg, VA 23803
(804) 733–1565

Islamic Academy of Virginia
1241 Buford Road
Richmond, VA 23235
(804) 320–4555

Islamic Education School
6604 Palamino Street
Springfield, VA 22150
(703) 922–4622

Social Services
AMF Health Services
3705 S George Mason Drive, Suite C65
Falls Church, VA 22041
(703) 379–2400

Student Groups
Muslim Student Association–North
    Virginia Community College
3001 N Beauregard Street #115
Alexandria, VA 22311
(703) 845–6200

Muslim Students Association–Northern
    Virginia
3917 Gallows Road
Annandale, VA 22003
(703) 642–3331

Muslim Student Federation
PO Box 11094
Arlington, VA 22210

Muslim Student Association–Virginia
Tech
PO Box 439
Blacksburg, VA 24063
(703) 552–6814

Muslim Student Association–University
of Virginia
PO Box 508
Charlottesville, VA 22902
(804) 979–8011

Muslim Student Association–George
Mason University
4400 University Drive #117
Fairfax, VA 22030
(703) 435–8824

International Islamic Federation of
Student Organizations
555 Grove Street
Herndon, VA 20170
(703) 471–6466

Muslim Students Association–Old
Dominion
822 Westmoreland Avenue Apartment 71
Norfolk, VA 23508
(804) 423–2305

Women's Group
North American Council for Muslim
Women
902 McMillen Court
Falls Church, VA 22066
(703) 759–7698

WASHINGTON

Ethnic Associations
The Association of Iranians in
Washington State (AIWS)
14042 NE 8th Street Suite B201
Bellevue, WA 98007
(425) 562–0534

Turkish American Cultural Association of
Washington
PO Box 357
Kirkland, WA 98083
sevim.d.basoglu@boeing.com

Ethiopian Community Mutual Association
2111 E Union Street
Seattle, WA 98122
(206) 325–0304
ecma@ecmaseattle.com

Islamic Call Group
Islam Presentation and Invitation Center
12733 Lake City Way NE
Seattle, WA 98125
(206) 361–8899
ipic96@hotmail.com

Mosques / Islamic Centers
Islamic Center of Eastside
14700 Main Street
Bellevue, WA 98007
(425) 746–0398

Islamic Society of Southwestern
Washington
2109 NW 47th Avenue
Camas, WA 98607

Olympia Lacey Islamic Center or Masjid
al-Nur
7945 Pacific Avenue SE
Lacey, WA 98503

Dar Al-Arqam
6210 188th Street SW
Lynnwood, WA 98037
(425) 774–8852
alaqum@wport.com

Muslim Association of Northwest
5507 238th Street SW
Mountlake Terrace, WA 98043

Masjid Al-Nor
4324 20th Lane NE #41
Olympia, WA 98516
(360) 493–2041
j1952m@aol.com

Pullman Islamic Center
1155 NE Stadium Way
Pullman, WA 99163
(509) 334–7600

Islamic Center of Tri-Cities
2900 Bombing Range Road
Richland, WA 99353
(509) 967–6695

Downtown Muslim Association
811 5th Avenue
Seattle, WA 98104

Islamic Center of Seattle
3040 S 150th Street
Seattle, WA 98188

Islamic Education Center of Seattle
1315 N 40th Street
Seattle, WA 98103
(206) 528–1990

Jama'at Al-Ikhlas
1350 E First Street
Seattle, WA 98122

Masjid Al-Tawhid
1022 SW Henderson Street
Seattle, WA 98106

Jamiul Muslimun Mosque
5945 39th Avenue S
Seattle, WA 98118
(206) 723–7677

Islamic International House
4625 22nd Avenue NE
Seattle, WA 98105
(206) 524–0566

Idriss Mosque
1420 NE Northgate Way
Seattle, WA 98125
(206) 363–3013

Spokane Islamic Center
505 E Wedgewood Avenue
Spokane, WA 99208
(509) 482–2608

Islamic Center of Tacoma
2010 Bridgeport Avenue SW
Tacoma, WA 98409
(253) 565–0314

Mas'alah Muslim Center
1218 Martin Luther King Jr. Way
Tacoma, WA 98405
(253) 305–0329
kmatcen@foxinternet.com

Islamic Society of South West
    Washington
7311 NE 43rd Avenue
Vancouver, WA 98661
(360) 694–7799

Islamic Center of Yakim
301 S 10th Avenue
Yakima, WA 98902
(509) 248–5919

Religious Education Program
Ithnasheri Muslim Association of the
    Northwest
PO Box 6544
Bellevue, WA 98008
(425) 586–6701
iman@iman-wa.org
www.iman-wa.org

School
Islamic School of Seattle
PO Box 22956
Seattle, WA 98122
(206) 329–5735
amoslim@sprynet.com

Social Services
Cham Muslim Refugee Center
5945 39th Avenue S
Seattle, WA 98118
(206) 723–7677

Student Groups
Muslim Students Association–Western
    Washington State
Vinking Union
Bellingham, WA 98225

Muslim Student Association–Washington
    State
PO Box 2216
Pullman, WA 99165
(509) 334–9424

Muslim Youth Academy
2301 S Jackson Street Suite 214
Seattle, WA 98144
(206) 329–3771

Muslim Students Association–University
of Washington
UW Box 352238
SAO Box 127
Seattle, WA 98195
(206) 543–2111

Muslim Student Association of Spokane
6101 N Addison Street
Spokane, WA 99207
(509) 482–2608

Sufi Group
The Jerrahi Order of the Northwest
7321 Glenridge Way SW
Seattle, WA 98136
(206) 938–1506

TV Program
Focus on Islam
PO Box 46881
Seattle, WA 98146
(206) 575–2740

WEST VIRGINIA

Mosques / Islamic Centers
Islamic Association of West Virginia
325 Central Avenue
Logan, WV 25601
(304) 252–8863

Islamic Center of Morgantown
441 Harding Street
Morgantown, WV 26505
(304) 598–7396

Islamic Center of Charleston
PO Box 8414
South Charleston, WV 25303
(304) 744–1031

WISCONSIN

Ethnic Association
Turkish American Association of
Milwaukee
1517 W Pierce Street
Milwaukee, WI 53204
(414) 671–1255

Magazine
Al-Jumuah
PO Box 5387
Madison, WI 53705
(608) 277–1855
aljumuah@aol.com
www.aljumuah.com

Mosques / Islamic Centers
Islamic Center and Masjid of Northern
Wisconsin
527 2nd Street W
Altoona, WI 54720
(715) 831–1560

Fox Valley Islamic Society
921 Cambridge Court
Appleton, WI 54915
(414) 722–7860

Muslim Center of Beloit
1879 Park Avenue
Beloit, WI 53511
(608) 365–7780

Islamic Society
16860 Golf Parkway
Brookfield, WI 53005

Albanian American Islamic Center
6001 88th Avenue
Kenosha, WI 53142
(262) 654–9575
emir12@execpc.com

Islamic Foundation Libertyville
3322 15th Street
Kenosha, WI 53144
(414) 552–8239

Othman Bin Afaan Mosque
1722 State Street
La Crosse, WI 54601
(608) 784–7167

Islamic Center of Madison
116 N Orchard Street
Madison, WI 53715

Masjid-us-Sunnah
PO Box 5387
Madison, WI 53705
(608) 277–1855

Masjid Muhammad
2507 N Dr. Martin Luther King Jr. Drive
Milwaukee, WI 53212

Milwaukee Dawah Center
5135 N Teutonia Avenue
Milwaukee, WI 53209
(414) 462–1998

Northside Islamic Center
513 W Meinecke Avenue
Milwaukee, WI 53212
(414) 562–2232

Islamic Society of Milwaukee
4707 S 13th Street
Milwaukee, WI 53221
(414) 282–1812
zamdan@yahoo.com

Northside Islamic Center
2401 W Vine Street
Milwaukee, WI 53205
(414) 532–2232

Masjid Sultan Muhammad Inc.
317 W Wright Street
Milwaukee, WI 53212
(414) 263–6772

Muslim Center–Racine
419 High Street #21
Racine, WI 53402
(414) 632–3751

Masjid Muhammad
1200 Dr. Martin Luther King Jr. Drive
Racine, WI 53404

Milwaukee Muslim Women's Coalition
4465 N Oakland Avenue Suite 300
Shorewood, WI 53211
(414) 964–6692
mmwc@aol.com

School
Salam School
4707 S 13th Street
Milwaukee, WI 53221
(414) 282–0504

Student Groups
Muslim Students Association
    Organization Community University
    of Wisconsin
Eau Claire, WI 54701
(715) 836–4141

Muslim Student Association–University
    of Wisconsin–Milwaukee
PO Box 413
Milwaukee, WI 53201
(414) 229–4623
msatemp@uwm.edu

WYOMING

Mosques / Islamic Centers
Islamic Center of Cheyenne
6005 Weaver Road
Cheyenne, WY 82009

Islamic Center of Larime
903 E Harney Street
Laramie, WY 82072
(307) 721–8810

Kalif Mosque
145 W Loucks Street
Sheridan, WY 82801
(307) 674–7110

Student Group
Muslim Students Association–University
    of Wyoming
903 E Harney Street
Laramie, WY 82072
(307) 721–8810

CANADA

ALBERTA

Charity Group
International Relief Association (LIFE)
9625 63 Avenue NW
Edmonton, AB T6E 0G2
(780) 430–7308

Mosques / Islamic Centers
Islamic Centre of Calgary
5615 14th Avenue SW
Calgary, AB T3H 2E8
(403) 242–1615

Hussaini Association of Calgary
3467–46 Avenue SE
PO 1418, Station T
Calgary, AB T2H 2H7
(403) 235–1212

Markaz Ul Islam
7907 36 Avenue NW
Edmonton, AB T6K 3S6
(780) 450–6170

Islamic Shia Ithna-Asheri Association of
Edmonton
4307 33 Avenue NW
Edmonton, AB T6L 4H7
(780) 463–4660

Alrashid Mosque
13070 113 Street NW
Edmonton, AB T5E 5A8
(780) 451–6694

Quba Mosque
11517 105 Avenue NW
Edmonton, AB T5H 3Y5
(780) 426–6373

Muslim Community of Edmonton
10721 86 Avenue NW
Edmonton, AB T6E 2M8
(780) 432–0208

Downtown Islamic Association
9216 105 Avenue NW
Edmonton, AB T5H 0J5
(780) 426–3632

Canadian Muslim A. of Lac La Biche
10223 94th Avenue
Lac La Biche, AB T0A 2C0
(780) 623–4578

Salah El Deen Mosque
195 Douglas Avenue
Red Deer, AB T4R 2G2
(403) 347–5812

Slave Lake Mosque
417–6th Street NE
Slave Lake, AB T0G 2A2
(780) 849–2334

Schools
Calgary Islamic School
225 28 Street SE
Calgary, AB T2A 5K4
(403) 248–2773

Almadina Charter School
411–11th Avenue SE
Calgary, AB T2G 0Y5
(403) 543–5070

Edmonton Islamic School
13070 113 Street NW
Edmonton, AB T5E 5A8
(780) 454–4573

Student Groups
Muslim Students Association–University
of Calgary
Room 209K MacEwan Hall
Calgary, AB T2N 1N4
(403) 220–7012

Muslim Students Association–University
of Alberta
PO Box 55 SUB
Edmonton, AB T6G 2J7
msa@ualberta.ca

BRITISH COLUMBIA

Ethnic Associations
Afghan Association of British Columbia
101–6955 Kingsway
Burnaby, BC V5E 1E5
(604) 9522–2340

Pakistan Canada Association
655 West 8th Avenue
Vancouver, BC V5Z 1C7
(604) 878–8899

Islamic Call Groups
Al Qur'an and Sunnah Society
PO Box 80744 Station South
Burnaby, BC V5H 3Y1

Islamic Information Centre
3127 Kingsway
Vancouver, BC V5R 5J9
(604) 434–7526
comment@al-huda.ca
www.al-huda.ca

Mosques / Islamic Centers
Kelowna Islamic Centre
1120 Highway 3
Kelowna, BC V1Y 9H2
(250) 768–9039

Nanaimo Islamic Centre
950 Hecate Street
Nanaimo, BC V9R 4K8
(250) 758–3768

Tri-City Islamic Centre
2462 Kingsway Avenue
Port Coquitlam, BC V3C 1T4
(604) 945–1885
tricityislamic@hotmail.com

Muslim Community of British Columbia
3360 Sexsmith Road
Richmond, BC V6X 2H8

British Columbia Muslim Association
12300 Blundell Road
Richmond, BC V6W 1B3
(604) 270–2522
bcmainfo@excite.com

Shia Muslim Community of B.C.
3360 Sexsmith Road
Richmond, BC V6X 2H8
(604) 270–3923

Masjid Al Huda
14136 Grosvenor Road
Surrey, BC V3R 5G8
(604) 585–4832

Surrey Masjid
12407 72 Avenue
Surrey, BC V3W 2M5
(604) 591–7601

Masjid Al Noor
13526 98A Avenue
Surrey, BC V3T 1C8
(604) 930–9742

Canadian Hussaini Association
10644 135 Street
Surrey, BC V3T 4C7
(604) 588–9294

Dar Al Madinah Islamic Society
225 West 5th Avenue
Vancouver, BC V5Y 1J3
(604) 873–8580
dar9@sprint.ca

Jamia Masjid Vancouver
655 8th Avenue W
Vancouver, BC V5Z 1C7
(604) 803–7344
abuosama@itergate.bc.ca

Masjid Al Haqq
4162 Welwyn Street
Vancouver, BC V5N 3Z2
(604) 325–0472

Victoria Masjid
2218 Quadra Street
Victoria, BC V8T 4C6
(250) 995–1422

Public Affairs Organization
Islamic Resource and Media Council
Box 7–11760 Bird Road
Richmond, BC V6X 1N9
irmc@bismillahmail.com

Schools
British Columbia Islamic School
12300 Blundell Road
Richmond, BC V6W 1B3
(604) 270–2511
tahir_ali@bctel.com

Iqra Islamic School
14590–116 A Avenue
Surrey, BC V3R 2V1
(604) 583–7530
amps@telus.net

Student Groups
Muslim Students Association–Simon
    Fraser University
8888 University Drive
Burnaby, BC V5A 1S6
msae-sfu@sfu.ca

Muslim Students Association of
    University of British Columbia
PO BOX 1, Student Union Building
Vancouver, BC V6T 1Z1
msa-exec@egroups.com

Youth Group
Muslim Youth Centre
Unit 208–7750–128th Street
Surrey, BC V3W 4E6
(604) 502–8692
muslimyouthcentre@hotmail.com

MANITOBA

Mosques / Islamic Centers
Muslim Association of New Brunswick
1100 Rothesay Road
Saint John, MB E2H 2H8
(506) 633–1675

Hussaini Association of Manitoba
59 Morningside Drive
Winnipeg, MB R3T 4A2
(204) 269–6143
masarratnaqvi@hotmail.com

Manitoba Islamic Association
247 Hazelwood Avenue
Winnipeg, MB R2M 4W1
(204) 256–1347

School
Alhijra Islamic School
155 Tembina Highway
Winnipeg, MB R3T 2E5
(204) 477–1343

Student Group
University of Manitoba Muslim Students
    Association
Box #76, University Center,
Winnipeg, MB R3T 2N2
msa-exec@cc.umanitoba.ca

NEW BRUNSWICK

Student Group
Muslim Students Association–University
    of New Brunswick
Student Union Building
PO Box 4400
Fredericton, NB E3B 5A3

NEWFOUNDLAND

Mosques / Islamic Centers
Alnoor Masjid
430 Logy Bay Road
St. John's, NF A1A 5C6
(709) 754–7526

Muslim Association of Newfoundland
PO Box 441 Station C
St. John's, NF A1C 5K4
(709) 754–7526

Student Group
Muslim Students Association of
    Memorial University of
    Newfoundland
Rm 2000, Smallworth Center
St. John's, NF A1C 5S7

NOVA SCOTIA

Islamic Call Group
Islamic Information Foundation
8 Laurel Lane
Halifax, NS B3M 2P6
(902) 445–2494
iif@muslimemail.com

Mosques / Islamic Centers
Islamic Association of the Maritime
    Provinces
42 Leaman Drive
Dartmouth, NS B3A 2K9
(902) 469–9490

Nova Scotia Islamic Community Centre
3117 Dutch Village Road
Halifax, NS B3L 4H2
(902) 453–1929

School
Maritimes Muslim Academy
6225 Chebucto Road
Halifax, NS B3L 1K7
(902) 429–9067
mma@atcon.com

ONTARIO

Charity Groups
Human Concern International
877 Shefford Road
Gloucester, ON K1J 8H9
(613) 742–5948

Human Concern International (Toronto
    Office)
206–2465 Cawthra Road
Mississauga, ON L5A 3P2
(905) 949–1098

World Humanity Fund, Inc.
1547 Merivale Road
Nepean, ON K2G 4V3

Human Concern International
PO Box 3984 Station C
Ottawa, ON K1Y 4P2
(613) 234–4585
hci@istar.ca
www.humanconcern.org

Jerusalem Fund for Human Services
PO Box 1628 Station B
Toronto, ON L4Y 4G3
(905) 897–8772

Mercy for Aid and Development
5060 Tecumseh Road E, Box 138
Windsor, ON N8T 1C1
(800) 556–3729

Community Development Groups
Islamic Society of North America
2200 South Sheridan Way
Mississauga, ON L5J 2M4
(905) 403–8406
isna@isnacanada.com
www.isnacanada.com

Al-Moltaqa Association for Social
    Activity
707–25 Agnes Street
Mississauga, ON L5B 3X7
(905) 804–1228

Muslim American Society
19 Varna Drive
North York, ON M6A 2L6
(416) 787–2146

Islamic Circle of North America
3A-100 McLevin Avenue
Scarborough, ON M1B 5K1
(416) 609–2452

Islamic Society of North America
PO Box 160 Station P
Toronto, ON M5S 2S7
(416) 977–2057

Coordination Councils
Al-Shura
99 Beverly Hills Drive
North York, ON M3L 1A2
(416) 245–5675

Islamic Schools Federation of Ontario
PO Box 2364 Station D
Ottawa, ON K1P 5W5
(613) 723–1698

Islamic Coordinating Council of Imams
2898 Ellesmere Road
Scarborough, ON M1E 4B8
(416) 282–4342

Ethnic Association
Afghan Information and Rehabilitation
Bureau
15–132 Railside Road
Don Mills, ON M3A 1A3
(416) 391–4432

Turkish Culture and Folklore Society of
Canada
50001–660 Eglinton Avenue E
East York, ON M4G 2K2
(905) 707–3044

Arab Community Centre of Toronto
324–5468 Dundas Street W
Etobicoke, ON M9B 6E3
(416) 231–7746

The Arabic Community Centre
5268 Dundas Street W, #324
Etobicoke, ON M9B 6E3
(416) 231–7746

Palestinian House
3195 Erindale Station Road
Mississauga, ON L5C 1Y5
(905) 270–3622

Islamic Association of Palestine
PO Box 45030 RPO Port Credit
Mississauga, ON L5G 4S7
(905) 278–6493

National Federation of Pakistani-
Canadians
1100–251 Laurier Avenue W
Ottawa, ON K1P 5J6
(613) 232–5346

Kawartha Muslim Association
3–880 Armour Road
Peterborough, ON K9H 2A6
(705) 748–6645

Bangladeshi-Canadian Community
Centre
24 Boyle Drive
Richmond Hill, ON L4C 6C9
mayeena@globalserve.net

Somali Bader Organization of Toronto
2376 Eglinton Avenue E
Scarborough, ON M1K 2P3
(416) 650–9808

Ogaden Somali Community Association
of Ontario
203–2355 Keele Street
Toronto, ON M6M 4A2
(416) 614–1255

Somali Islamic Society of Canada
PO Box 100 Station V
Toronto, ON M6R 3A4
(416) 533–6507

Eritrean-Canadian Society for Youth
Advancement
PO Box 19601 RPO Manulife
Toronto, ON M4W 3T9
(416) 410–8008
esya@canada.com

Canadian Arab Federation
1057 McNicoll Avenue
Toronto, ON M1W 3W6
(416) 493–8635

Canadian Turkish Islamic Heritage
Association
336 Pape Avenue
Toronto, ON M4M 2W7
(416) 469–9526

Guilds
Association of Pakistani-Canadian
Engineers and Professionals
2404 Haines Road
Mississauga, ON L4Y 4B8
(905) 279–3603

Canadian Society of Iranian Engineers
    and Architects
6021 Yonge Street
North York, ON M2M 3W2
(905) 771–7147
kanoon@mohandes.com

Islamic Call Groups
Muslim World League
1018–191 The West Mall
Etobicoke, ON M9C 5K8
(416) 622–2184

Information Da'wah Centre
616–2857 Derry Road E
Mississauga, ON L4T 1A6

Islamic Propagation Centre
6–5761 Coopers Avenue
Mississauga, ON L4Z 1R9
(905) 507–3323

Islamic Information Centre
312 Lisgar Street
Ottawa, ON K2P 0E2
(613) 232–0210
islaminf@monisys.ca

Dawa and Tabligh Association
PO Box 73088–2300 Lawrence Avenue
Scarborough, ON M1P 4Z5

Badar Dawa Centre of Canada
2183A Lawrence Avenue E
Scarborough, ON M1P 2P5
(416) 752–1200

World Assembly of Muslim Youth
3089 Dufferin Street
Toronto, ON M6A 2S7
(416) 787–7669

Islamic Information and Daw'ah Centre
    International
689 Queen Street W
Toronto, ON M6J 1E6
(416) 861–9244

Mosques / Islamic Centers
Jamiah Institute of Ajax
2944 Audley Road
Ajax, ON L1S 4S7
(905) 686–4003

Noor Ul Islam
51 Little Lake Drive RR 1
Barrie, ON L4M 4Y8

Islamic Centre of Brampton
98–900 Central Park Drive
Brampton, ON L6S 3J6
(905) 458–7142

Jami Masjid Brampton
8450 Torbram Road
Brampton, ON L6T 4M9
(905) 458–8778

Islamic Society of Peel
PO Box 51034 RPO City Centre
Brampton, ON L6T 5M2
(905) 458–8778
agsheikh@netcom.ca

Halton Islamic Association
4310 Fairview Street
Burlington, ON L7L 4Y8
(905) 333–9856

Islamic Centre of Cambridge
16 International Village Drive
Cambridge, ON N1R 8G1
(519) 740–6855

Cambridge Muslim Society
315 Elgin Street N
PO Box 22
Cambridge, ON N1R 8C9
(519) 623–0568

Alansar Masjid
1 5–132 Railside Road
Don Mills, ON M3A 1A3
(416) 391–4432

Islamic Society of Toronto
4 Thorncliffe Park Drive
East York, ON M4H 1H1
(416) 467–0786

Rexdale Mosque
8–1694 Albion Road
Etobicoke, ON M9V 1B8
(416) 747–0646

Canadian Islamic Association
80 Avenuening Drive
Etobicoke, ON M9V 1Y1
(416) 748–4902

Ummah Nabawiah Mosque
2074 Kipling Avenue
Etobicoke, ON M9W 4J9
(416) 748–8033

Bosnian Community Mosque
4146 Dundas Street W
Etobicoke, ON M8X 1X3
(416) 233–5967

Bosnian Islamic Centre
75 Birmingham Street
Etobicoke, ON M8V 2C3
(416) 255–8338

International Muslims Organization of
    Toronto
65 Rexdale Boulevard
Etobicoke, ON M9W 1P1
(416) 742–6776

Islamic Community Center of Ontario
30 Waulron Street
Etobicoke, ON M9C 1B5
(416) 621–4411

Etobicoke Muslim Community
    Organization
130 Westmore Drive
Etobicoke, ON M9V 5E2
(416) 745–3626

Khalid Bin Al Walid Mosque (SISCA)
16 Bethridge Road
Etobicoke, ON M9W 1N1
(416) 745–2888

AlHuda
3–6 Dixon Road
Etobicoke, ON M9P 2L1
(416) 245–3733

Hamilton Mosque
1545 Stone Church Road E
Hamilton, ON L8W 3P8
(905) 383–1526

Hamilton Islamic Centre
712 Mohawk Road E
Hamilton, ON L8T 2P8
(905) 387–4956

Islamic Society of Hamilton Wentworth
734 Rennie Street
Hamilton, ON L8H 3R2
(905) 544–9016

Islamic Center of Kingston
1477 Sydenham Road
Kingston, ON K7L 5J8
(613) 542–9000

Masjid Hussein
65 Fifth Avenue
Kitchener, ON N2C 1P5
(519) 748–0194

Ahlul-Bayt Islamic Center of London
134–4096 Meadowbrook Drive
London, ON N6L 1G4
(519) 681–7829
datoo@sprint.ca

London Muslim Mosque
151 Oxford Street W
London, ON N6H 1S3
(519) 439–9451

Islamic Center of Southwest Ontario
951 Pond Mills Road
London, ON N6N 1C3
(519) 668–2269

Islamic Society of York Region
24–415 Hood Road
Markham, ON L3R 3W2
(905) 474–9292

Wali-Asr Islamic Center
14&16–7725 Birchmount Road
Markham, ON L3R 9X3
(905) 479–2345

Canadian Islamic Organization
29 Burr Crescent
Markham, ON L3R 9B8
(416) 745–1211

Istiqamah Islamic Centre of Ontario
3410 Semenyk Court Unit #3
Mississauga, ON L5C 4P9
(905) 270–6999
unity@istiqamah.com
www.istiqamah.com

Islamic Society Milli Gorus
5280 Maingate Drive
Mississauga, ON L4W 1G5
(905) 629–0477

Darul Arkam
285 Matheson Boulevard E
Mississauga, ON L4Z 1X8
(905) 670–3860

Alfarooq Masjid
935 Eglinton Avenue W
Mississauga, ON L5M 2B5
(905) 858–7586

Ummat Al Islam
5116 Fallingbrook Drive
Mississauga, ON L5V 2C6
(905) 821–0107

Muslim Community Centre of Canada
335 The Collegeway Suite 19–20
Mississauga, ON L5L 5T3
(905) 569–6222

Islahul-Muslimeen
370 Huntington Ridge Drive
Mississauga, ON L5R 1P1
(905) 890–2047

Al Jamia Al Islamia Canada Ltd.
3153 Hurontario Street
Mississauga, ON L5A 2G9
(905) 279–3040

Jamia Islamia
10–780 Burnhamthorpe Road W
Mississauga, ON L5C 3X3
(905) 279–3040

Islamic Society
4627 Full Moon Circle
Mississauga, ON L4Z 2N7

Malton Islamic Centre
6836 Professional Court
Mississauga, ON L4V 1X6
(905) 677–8175

Bani Hashem Society
52–5359 Timberlea Boulevard
Mississauga, ON L4W 4N5
(905) 212–1472

The Islamic Centre of Canada
2200 South Sheridan Way
Mississauga, ON L5J 2M4
(905) 403–8406

Shalimar Complex Mosque
80–3024 Cedarglen Gate
Mississauga, ON L5C 4S3
(905) 897–8605

Islamic Centre of Toronto
45–2445 Homelands Drive
Mississauga, ON L5K 2C6
(905) 823–6255

Omar Masjid
572 Moodie Drive
Nepean, ON K2H 6P6
(613) 828–4495

Islamic Ithna-Asheri Association of
     Ottawa
3856 Richmond Road
Nepean, ON K2H 5C4
(613) 829–6931

Islamic Society of Niagara Peninsula
6768 Lyons Creek Road
Niagara Falls, ON L2E 6S5
(416) 295–4845

Niagara Muslim Society
RR 1, Niagara-on-the-Lake
Niagara Falls, ON L2

Zafar Mosque
153 Bentworth Avenue
North York, ON M6A 1P6
(416) 789–3445

Imdadul Islam Centre
26 LePage Court
North York, ON M3J 1Z9
(416) 636–0044

Ontario Muslim Association
73 Patricia Avenue
North York, ON M2M 1J1

Omer Al Faruk Islamic Centre
65 Wingold Avenue
North York, ON M6B 1P8
(416) 784–2013

Revival of Islamic Da'wah Centre
1888 Wilson Avenue
North York, ON M9M 1A7
(416) 744–1479

Talim Ul Islam Centre
86 Rivalda Road
North York, ON M9M 2M8
(416) 745–5606

Noor Ul Haram Masjid
2478 Ninth Line
Oakville, ON L6J 4Z2
(905) 257–1342

Alfalah Masjid
391 Burnhamthorpe Road E
Oakville, ON L6J 4Z2
(905) 257–9997
icnacanada@aol.com

Bilal Masjid
4509 Innes Road
Orleans, ON K4A 3J7
(613) 841–0786

Oshawa Islamic Centre
26 McGrigor Street
Oshawa, ON L1H 1X7
(905) 436–9310

Islamic Center of Oshawa
PO Box 1062
Oshawa, ON L1H 7H8

Altaqwa Mosque
117 Mann Avenue
Ottawa, ON K1N 5A4
(613) 233–2845

Dar Assunah
2&3–2401 Bank Street
Ottawa, ON K1V 8R9
(613) 247–0674

Abu Thar Al-Gofary Mosque
273 Donald Street
Ottawa, ON K1K 1N1
(613) 747–6252
della1@sprint.ca

The Ottawa Muslim Association
257–Northwestern Avenue
Ottawa, ON K1Y 5W9
(613) 722–8763
mukhtarmalik@hotmail.com

Ahlul-Bayt Center
2285 Saint Laurent Boulevard
Unit 10, Row B
Ottawa, ON K1G 5A2
(613) 526–1259

Othman Masjid
2065 Brock Road
Pickering, ON L1V 2P8
(905) 426–7887

Council of Islamic Guidance (Al-Mahdi
     Center)
510 Concession 3 Road
Pickering, ON L1X 2R4
(905) 294–9402

Ihsan Muslim Heritage Society
173–138 Yorkland Street
Richmond Hill, ON L4S 1J1
(905) 770–5696

Sarnia Muslim Association
281 Cobden Street
Sarnia, ON N7T 4A2
(519) 336–9022

Malvern Muslim Association
28 Nahanni Terrace
Scarborough, ON M1B 1B8
(416) 472–1082

Scarborough Muslim Association
2665 Lawrence Avenue E
Scarborough, ON M1P 2S2
(416) 750–2253

Bilal Islamic Association of Toronto
87 Gennela Source
Scarborough, ON M1B 5B7
(416) 287–3259

Islamic Foundation of Toronto
441 Nugget Avenue
Scarborough, ON M1S 5E1
(416) 621–0909

Islamic Society of Willowdale
3530 Pharmacy Avenue
Scarborough, ON M1W 2S7
(416) 495–9021

Ahlul-Bayt Assembly of Canada
1166 Warden Avenue
Scarborough, ON M1R 2R1
(416) 750–1707
sajan@pathcom.com

Iranian Islamic Centre
55 Estate Drive
Scarborough, ON M1H 2Z2
(416) 438–2221

Islamic Museum Toronto–Husainiyyah
328 Passmore Avenue
Scarborough, ON M1V 5J5
(416) 754–7906

Shahid Al-Sader Islamic Center
120/122–2220 Midland Avenue
Scarborough, ON M1P 3E6
(416) 984–5216

Islamic Institute of Toronto
101B-1825 Markham Road
Scarborough, ON M1B 4Z9
(416) 335–9173

Alnoor Masjid
117 Geneva Street
St. Catharines, ON L2R 4N3
(905) 641–8007

Islamic Association of Sudbury
755 Churchill Avenue
Sudbury, ON P3A 4A1
(705) 525–7729
ias@cybertech.net

Ja'ffari Islamic Centre (Islamic Shia Ithna
   Asheri Jamaat of Toronto)
7340 Bayview Avenue
Thornhill, ON L3T 2R7
media@jafari.org
www.jafari.org

Thunder Bay Muslim Association
PO Box 24026, 70 Court Street
Thunder Bay, ON P7A 4T0
(807) 767–7380

Hamza Mosque
1285 Queen Street W
Toronto, ON M6K 1L6
(416) 534–3669

Jami Mosque
56 Boustead Avenue
Toronto, ON M6R 1Y9
(416) 769–1192

Afghan Islamic Community Centre
508–600 Bay Street
Toronto, ON M5G 1M6
(416) 599–0123

Masjid Al-Rasoul Al-Azam
120 Bermondsey Road
Toronto, ON M4A 1X5
(416) 750–8725

Bader Islamic Association of Toronto
474 Roncesvalles Avenue
Toronto, ON M6R 2N5
(416) 536–8343

Albanian Muslim Society of Toronto
564 Annette Street
Toronto, ON M6S 2C2
(416) 763–0612

Altaqwa Masjid
14 Ladysmith Avenue
Toronto, ON M4J 4H7
(416) 406–6282
76125x@interlog.com

Omar bin Al Khattab Masjid (MCDT)
240 Parliament Street
Toronto, ON M5A 3A4
(416) 861–9288

Sunnatul Jamaat of Ontario
347 Danforth Road
Toronto, ON M1L 3X8
(416) 690–2298

Afghani Islamic Center
22 Hobson Avenue
Toronto, ON M4A 1Y2
(416) 757–2553

Masjid Muhammad
PO Box 2022
Downsview, ON M2H 2LI

Taric Mosque
99 Beverly Hills Drive
Toronto, ON M3L 1A2
(416) 245–5675

Alnoor Masjid
277 Scott Road
Toronto, ON M6M 3V3
(416) 658–6667

Fatih Mosque
182 Rhodes Avenue
Toronto, ON M4L 3A1
(416) 462–1401

Canadian Society of Muslims
PO Box 143 Station P
Toronto, ON M5S 2S7
(905) 272–5959

Madina Masjid
1015 Danforth Avenue
Toronto, ON M4J 1M1
(416) 465–7833

Kichener-Waterloo Islamic Association
PO Box 33028 RPO Beechwood Plaza
Waterloo, ON N2T 2M9
(519) 885–2225

Muslim Society of Waterloo
213 Erb Street W
Waterloo, ON N2L 1V6
(519) 886–8470

Islamic Society of Welland (Masjid
AlHouda)
1–649 King Street
Welland, ON L3B 3L5
(905) 732–7575

Windsor Islamic Association
1320 Northwood Street
Windsor, ON N9E 1A4
(519) 966–2355
imamwiao@yahoo.com
www.wiao.org

Alhijra Mosque
5100 Howard Avenue
Windsor, ON N9A 6Z6
(519) 966–8276

Prison Outreach Group
Islamic Chaplaincy Services
PO Box 1829
Bancroft, ON K0L 1C0
(416) 712–7861

Public Affairs Organizations
Toronto Muslim Education Assembly
911–7 Richgrove Drive
Etobicoke, ON M9R 2L1
(416) 744–8372

Council on American-Islamic Relations
  CAN
PO Box 67058, Westboro R.P.O.
Ottawa, ON K2A 0E8
(866) 524–0004
canada@cair-net.org
www.caircan.ca

Canadian Muslim Civil Liberties
   Association
14–885 Progress Avenue
Scarborough, ON M1H 3G3
(416) 289–9666
cmcla@cmcla.org
www.cmcla.org

Canadian Islamic Congress
420 Erb Street W Suite 424
Waterloo, ON N2L 6K6
(519) 746–1242
cic@cicnow.com
www.canadianislamiccongress.com

Religious Education Groups
Muslim Arab Youth Association
Huntington Ridge Drive
Mississauga, ON L5R 1P1
(905) 890–2047

Muslim Arab Youth Association
PO Box 741 Station B
Ottawa, ON K1P 5P8
(613) 745–0837

Religious Education Programs
Islamic Forum of Canada
22–200 Advance Boulevard
Brampton, ON L6T 4V4
(905) 790–8859
info@islamicforum.net
www.islamicforum.net

Malton Islamic Association
7344 Custer Crescent
Malton, ON L4T 3K7
(905) 671–0891
shabirh@msn.com

Ottawa Muslim Community Circle
PO Box 29105 RPO Barrhaven
Nepean, ON K2J 4A9
(613) 825–7059
omcc@pccs.ca

North American Shia Ithna-Asheri
   Muslim Community
300 John Street Box 87629
Thornhill, ON L3T 7R3
(905) 763–7512

Research Group
Kashmiri-Canadian Council
44516–2376 Eglinton Avenue E
Scarborough, ON M1K 2P3
(416) 282–6933
kcc@kashmiri-cc.ca
www.kashmiri-cc.ca

Schools
Aliman School
253 Summerlea Road
Brampton, ON L6T 5A8
(905) 799–9231

Al Madrasah Tul Islamia
7 Colchester Avenue
Brampton, ON L6Z 3R1
(905) 840–7126

Cambridge Islamic School
16 International Village Drive
Cambridge, ON N1R 8G1
(519) 624–5333

Alazhar Academy of Canada
2074 Kipling Avenue
Etobicoke, ON M9W 4J4
(416) 741–3420

Muslim Girls High School
10 Vulcan Street
Etobicoke, ON M9W 1L2
(416) 244–8600

Alashraf Islamic School
23 Brydon Drive
Etobicoke, ON M9W 4M7
(416) 744–8141

London Islamic School
157 Oxford Street W
London, ON N6H 1S3
(519) 679–9920

Muslim Education Istitute of Ontario
36 Calderbridge Crescent
Markham, ON L3R 9M4
(905) 470–9912

Iqra Islamic School
5753 Coopers Avenue
Mississauga, ON L4Z 1R9
(905) 507–6688

Alsafa Islamic School
90 Dundas Street W
Mississauga, ON L5B 2T5
(905) 566–8533

Safa & Marwa Islamic School
5560 McAdam Road
Mississauga, ON L4Z 1P1
(905) 822–6542

Islamic Community School (ISNA
   School)
1525 Sherway Drive
Mississauga, ON L4X 1C5
(905) 272–4303

Ottawa Islamic School
10 Coral Avenue
Nepean, ON K2E 5Z6
(613) 727–5066

Niagara Islamic School
6768 Lyons Creek Road
Niagara Falls, ON L2E 6S6
(905) 295–4845

Almanara Academy
86 Rivalda Road
North York, ON M9M 2M8
(416) 744–3636

Al-Falah Islamic School
391 Burnhamthorpe Road E
Oakville, ON L6J 4Z2
(905) 257–5782

AlHuda Academy
200–170 Metcalfe Street
Ottawa, ON K2P 1P3
(613) 231–1090

Madinatul Uloom Islamic School
11–55 Nugget Avenue
Scarborough, ON M1S 3L1
(416) 332–1810

Alazhar Islamic School
205–100 McLevin Avenue
Scarborough, ON M1B 5K1
(416) 321–9636

Salahuddeen Islamic School
741 Kennedy Road
Scarborough, ON M1K 2C6
(416) 264–0906

Islamic Foundation School
441 Nugget Avenue
Scarborough, ON M1S 5E1
4163213776

Islamic Academy
7 Ambercroft Boulevard
Scarborough, ON M1W 2Z6
(416) 499–7785

Assadiq Islamic School
9000 Bathurst Street
Thornhill, ON L4J 8A7
(905) 771–9917

Alnoor Islamic School
1320 Northwood Street
Windsor, ON N9E 1A4
(519) 966–4422

Alhijra Islamic School
5100 Howard Avenue
Windsor, ON N9A 6Z6
(519) 966–8276

Social Services
Muslim Community Services
304–150 Central Park Drive
Brampton, ON L6T 2T9
(905) 790–8484
muslim_community@hotmail.com

Islamic Humanitarian Service
153 Frederick Street #101
Kitchener, ON N2H 2M2
(519) 576–7111

Hidayet Muslim Family and Child
   Centre
26 LePage Court
North York, ON M3J 1Z9
(416) 638–1866

Rehma Foundation (Muslim Elders)
59 Larabee Crescent
North York, ON M3A 3E6
(416) 391–5507

Muslim Welfare Centre
4A-100 McLevin Avenue
Scarborough, ON M1B 5K1
(416) 754–8116

Muslim Immigrants Aid
1795 Markham Road
Scarborough, ON M1B 2Z7
(416) 321–3523

Islamic Social Services (ISSRA)
2375 St. Clair Avenue W
Toronto, ON M6N 1K9
(416) 767–1531

Muslim Marriage Mediation and
  Arbitration Services
PO Box 143 Station P
Toronto, ON M5S 2S7
(905) 272–5959

Muslim House
2–219 Beverley Street
Toronto, ON M5T 1Z4
(416) 971–6058

Afghan Women's Counselling
205–2333 Dundas Street W
Toronto, ON M6R 3A6
(416) 588–3585
Aniazi@afghanwomen.org

Muslim Welfare Home
425 Dundas Street E
Whitby, ON L1N 2J2
(905) 665–0424

Student Groups
Muslim Students Association at
  University of Guelph
University Centre, Room 222
Guelph, ON N1G 2W1
msa@uoguelph.ca

Muslim Students Association–University
  of Toronto at Mississauga
Room 242
3359 Mississauga Road
Mississauga, ON L5L 1C6
fattah@uoftmsa.com

Pakistani Students
  Association–University of Ottawa
85 University Private, Suite 07
Ottawa, ON K1N 6N5
psa_ottawa@hotmail.com

Muslim Students Association–University
  of Ottawa
85 University Private, Suite 07
Ottawa, ON K1N 6N5
msa_mail@yahoo.com

Arab Student Association–University of
  Ottawa
85 University Private, Suite 07
Ottawa, ON K1N 6N5
uottawaasa@yahoo.ca

Solidarity for Palestinian Human
  Rights–University of Ottawa
85 University Private, Suite 07
Ottawa, ON K1N 6N5

Trent Muslim Students Association
Trent University, 1600 West Bank Drive
Peterborough, ON K9J 7B8
tmsa@faisiz.net

Muslim Students Association–University
  of Toronto at Scarborough
1265 Military Trail
Scarborough, ON M1C 1A4

Muslim Students Association at York
210 Scott Religious Center, 4700 Keele
  Street
Toronto, ON M3J 1P3

Bangladeshi Students' Association at
  Ryerson University
350 Victoria Street, Rye Student
  Administration Council
Toronto, ON M5B 2K3
bdsa@ryerson.ca

Muslim Students Association–University
of Toronto at St. George
21 Sussex Avenue, Suite 405
Toronto, ON M5S 1J6
msa_uoft@yahoogroups.com

Ryerson University Muslim Students
Association
Office A459
350 Victoria Street, Rye Student
Administration Council
Toronto, ON M5B 2K3
rmsa@acs.ryerson.ca

Pakistani Students' Association
350 Victoria Street, Rye Student
Administration Council
Toronto, ON M5B 2K3

Muslim Students Association–University
of Waterloo
200 University Avenue West
Waterloo, ON N2L 3G1
msaexecs@yahoogroups.com

Sufi Groups
I.S.I.J. of Hamilton
95 Mead Avenue
Hamilton, ON L8H 3T6
(905) 312–0508
saira.manek@sympatico.com

Sufi Study Circle of the University of
Toronto
PO Box 143 Station P
Toronto, ON M5S 2S7
(905) 272–5959

Women's Groups
Canadian Council of Muslim Women
513–2400 Dundas Street W
Mississauga, ON L5K 2R8
(905) 823–3804
jaff1@telusplanet.net
www.ccmw.org

United Muslim Women of Canada
708–9 Roanoke Road
North York, ON M3A 1E3
(416) 449–0836
anisaali@idirect.ca

The Federation of Muslim Women
424 Freeman Crescent
Oakville, ON L6H 4R3
(905) 849–8083
info@fmw.org
www.fmw.org

Youth Groups
Muslim Youth Association of London
PO Box 24051 RPO Westown
London, ON N6H 5C4
(519) 642–7184

Ashbal Scout Troop
1525 Sherway Drive
Mississauga, ON L4X 1C5
(905) 272–4303

Somali Youth Association of Toronto
2007 Lawrence Avenue W #25
York, ON M9N 1H4
(416) 247–6333

PRINCE EDWARD ISLAND

Mosques / Islamic Centers
Muslim Society of Prince Edward Island
12 Poplar Avenue
Charlottetown, PE C1A 6S7
(902) 566–3865
mali@upei.ca

QUEBEC

Charity Group
Azzahra International Foundation, Inc.
241 rue Anselme-Lavigne
Dollard-des-Ormeaux, QC H9A 3H6
(514) 486–1259

Community Development Group
Islamic Circle of North America
1155 boul Rome
Brossard, QC J4W 3J1
(514) 637–2755

Coordination Council
Islamic Council of Quebec
PO Box 1614 LaCite
Montreal, QC H2W 2K6
(514) 482–2498

Ethnic Associations
Arabic Heritage Revival Centre
4–1668 boul de Maisonneuve O
Montreal, QC H3H 1J7
(514) 591–4438

Estrial Islamic Cultural Association
CP 36012 Csp du Carrefour
Sherbrooke, QC J1L 2L3
(819) 820–1566

Islamic Call Group
Information Centre of Islam
2–2054 rue Saint-Denis
Montreal, QC H2X 3K7
(514) 844–2029

Mosques / Islamic Centers
Khalid Bin Al Walid
1330 rue Antonio
Chomedey, QC H7V 3N4
(450) 680–1612

Islamic Centre (West Island)
3943 boul Saint-Jean
Dollard-des-Ormeaux, QC H9G 1X2
(514) 624–5748

Canadian Islamic Centre
416 boul Neptune
Dorval, QC H9S 2L8
(514) 633–5353

Islamic Association of Longueuil
2144 St. Helene
Longueuil, QC J4K 4B7
(450) 674–9018

Jamia Islamia Mosque
2144 rue Sainte-Helene
Longueuil, QC J4K 3T6
(514) 674–4433

Abu Bakr Al Siddik Mosque
Montreal, QC H2R 1W7
(514) 279–6251

Masjid As Salam
16 rue Ontario O
Montreal, QC H2X 1Y5

Al Ummah Mosque
20–70 Clark
Montreal, QC H2X 2R7
(514) 843–7866

Al-Sunnah Al-Nabawiah Association
7220 rue Hutchison
Montreal, QC H3N 1Z1
(514) 844–2029

Al Oumma Al Islamaya Mosque
1590 boul St. Laurent
Montreal, QC H2X 2S9
(514) 843–7866

Alrahman Mosque
3630 Jean Talon E.
Montreal, QC H2N 1X6
(514) 593–9523

Dar Al Arqam
3661 rue Jean-Talon E
Montreal, QC H2A 1X7
(514) 374–9572

Muslim Community Centre
1670 boul de Maisonneuve O
Montreal, QC H3H 1J7
(514) 939–6288

Noor El Islam Mosque
4675 rue Amiens
Montreal, QC H1H 2H6
(514) 325–5557

Alumma Al Islamia Mosque
1245 rue Saint-Dominique
Montreal, QC H2X 2W4
(514) 879–9677

Fatima Mosque
2012 boul Saint-Laurent
Montreal, QC H2X 2T2
(514) 684–4865

Islamic Society of Concordia
2090 rue MacKay
Montreal, QC H3G 2J1

Muslim Community of Quebec (MCQ)
7445 av Chester
Montreal, QC H4V 1M4
(514) 484–2967
mcq@muslim.com

Younes Mosque
6378 Street Laurent Boulevard
Montreal, QC H2S 3C4
(514) 279–1836

Mountain Sights Mosque
83–7835 av Mountain Sights
Montreal, QC H4P 2B1
(514) 737–7586

Madani Mosque
12080 boul Laurentien
Montreal, QC H4K 1M9
(514) 331–0733

Aliman Masjid
5405 av du parc
Montreal, QC H2V 4G9
(514) 270–9437

Al Qods Mosque
PO Box #203, Succ. St. Michel
Montreal, QC H2A 3L9
(514) 376–9678

Fatih Sultan Mehmet Mosque
7387 boul Saint-Laurent
Montreal, QC H2R 1W7
(514) 272–0009

Bar Islamic Centre
6955 boul Lacordaire
Montreal, QC H1T 2K5
(514) 255–6460

El Kairouane Mosque
3726 rue Jean-Talon E
Montreal, QC H2A 1X9
(514) 728–2922

Dar Al Quran Al Karim
2–7387 boul Saint-Laurent
Montreal, QC H2R 1W7
(514) 273–2653

Makkah Mosque
11900 boul Gouin
Pierrefonds, QC H8Z 1V6
(514) 421–1455

Islamic Cultural Centre of Quebec City
796 av Myrand
Sainte-Foy, QC G1V 2V2
(418) 832–9710

Islamic Centre of South Montreal
1885 rue Nielsen
Saint-Hubert, QC J4T 1P1
(514) 443–3482

Islamic Centre of Quebec
2520 ch Laval
Saint-Laurent, QC H4L 3A1
(514) 331–1770

Association Culturelle Islamique de
   L'Estrie
1200 rue Masse
Sherbrooke, QC J1H 5X2
(819) 820–1566

Trois Riviers Mosque
3009 boul des Forges
Trois-Rivieres, QC G8Z 1V3
(819) 371–7938

Religious Education Program
Alrisalah Association
7482 rue Berri
Montreal, QC H2R 2G5
(514) 276–9900

Schools
Montreal Islamic Primary School
7435 av Chester
Montreal, QC H4V 1M4
(514) 484–8845

Montreal Islamic High School
2255 boul Cavendish
Montreal, QC H4B 2L7
(514) 484–5084

Ibn Sina Academy School
5121 av Earnscliffe
Montreal, QC H3X 2P7
(514) 722–0925

Canadian Muslim Youth School
5919 boul Henri-Bourassa O
Saint-Laurent, QC H4R 1B7
(514) 956–9559

Dar Aliman School
4505 boul Henri-Bourassa O
Saint-Laurent, QC H4L 1A5
(514) 274–5268

Social Services
Therapie Familiale Canadienne Islamique
5304 av Westmore
Montreal, QC H4V 1Z7
(514) 487–5693

Student Groups
Islamic Society of McGill
3480 rue McTavish
Montreal, QC H3A 1X9
(514) 284–5107

Muslim Student Association at
    Concordia University
Room H-637
1455 de Maisonneuve Boulevard W
Montreal, QC H3G 1M8
(514) 848–7442
msaconcordia@vif.com
www.concordiamsa.com

Sufi Group
Center of Soufism
5978 av de l'Esplanade
Montreal, QC H2T 3A3
(514) 277–9868

Youth Group
Association of Muslim Youth
6–3881 av Linton
Montreal, QC H3S 1T3
(514) 7370325

SASKATCHEWAN

Mosques / Islamic Centers
Islamic Association of Saskatchewan
    (Regina)
3273 Montague Street
Regina, SK S4S 1Z8
(306) 585–0090

Islamic Association of Sasketchewan
222 Copland Crescent
Saskatoon, SK S7H 2Z5
(306) 665–6424

Islamic Centre of Swift Current
25 Central Avenue S
Swift Current, SK S9H 3E7
(306) 778–3311

Student Group
Muslim Students Association at
    University of Saskatchewan
RPO University Box #285
Saskatoon, SK S7N-4J8
(306) 477–0962

INDEX